Baksheesh and Brahman

Baksheesh and Brahman

Indian Journal 1954–1955

Joseph Campbell

Edited by Robin and Stephen Larsen
& Antony Van Couvering

Collected Works of Joseph Campbell
Robert Walter, Executive Editor

HarperSanFrancisco
An Imprint of HarperCollins*Publishers*

Grateful acknowledgment is made for permission to reprint:

From *The Art of Indian Asia: Its Mythology and Transformations* by Heinrich Zimmer, edited and completed by Joseph Campbell. Copyright ©1955, 1960 by Princeton University Press. Used by permission of Princeton University Press.

HarperCollins books may be purchased for educational, business, or sales promotional use. For information, please write to: Special Markets Department, HarperCollins Publishers, Inc., 10 East 53rd Street, New York, NY 10022.

HarperCollins Web Site: http://www.harpercollins.com

FIRST EDITION

Antony Van Couvering, Managing Editor, Collected Works of Joseph Campbell

Illustrations and Maps by Carol Pentleton

Library of Congress Cataloging-in-Publication Data

ISBN 0-06-016889-7 (cloth)

ISBN 0-06-092477-2 (pbk.)

97 98 99 ❖/RR RRD 10 9 8 7 6 5 4 3 2 1

Contents

Editors' Foreword

The journal from which this book was fashioned comprised over a thousand pages in its original handwritten form. It was kept from 1954 to 1955, as Joseph Campbell traveled throughout India, Southeast Asia and Japan. Later he would flirt with the idea of publishing it, though he never attempted it. Now, eight years after his death, this work will hold a central place in the *Collected Works of Joseph Campbell,* helping us to form a more complete evaluation of both the man and his work.

The journal appears at times to be a personal diary—as close as Campbell ever came to autobiography. In other places he seems to be keeping an intellectual notebook, grappling with the scholarly details of an Indian cave temple, or getting indigestion over the rampant anti-Americanism in the Indian tabloids. At times he wrestles with the difficulties of arranging a dance tour for his wife, Jean Erdman, throughout India; at others he notes his ambivalent reactions to meeting with a guru. In general, he records entries several times a week, with characteristic thoroughness, perhaps in part for documentation of the details of his trip for the Bollingen Foundation, from whom he was continuing to receive grant support during this time; sometimes, obviously, as formulations related to future writing projects.

As editors we faced many choices; for example, of retaining or omitting what to some might seem obsessive rumination, and to others a fascinating scholarly detail. Our objective throughout has been to keep the reader moving right along with Campbell's own explorations, encounters and revelations. Wherever possible we have tried to add reference material to help identify people, places, events and ideas that are significant elsewhere in Campbell's life and work.

As a single volume the "Asian Journal" would have been unwieldy, and so we decided to divide the material into two volumes. The present volume records Joseph Campbell's encounter with India alone as he travels through the subcontinent; its sequel, beginning in early 1955 in Sri Lanka, follows his onward journey through Southeast Asia and Japan, and will be published separately under the title *Journey to the Sun's Door.* These volumes should be readily accessible to the general reader and require no prior reading of Campbell. Readers familiar with Campbell's work will find these books especially fascinating for the glimpse they offer into the central period of his life and his intellectual development.

In the first half of his life, Joseph Campbell had not yet identified himself as a comparative mythologist. In 1954 he had just turned fifty: time, perhaps, for a re-evaluation of his life-purpose, or a mid-life crisis. In fact, it was to be a little of each. Often it is apparent from the outside that Campbell was the last one to see how own experience was at work upon him. Some of the most painful conflicts he experienced led to the very insights and personal breakthroughs he sought. Today, with his biography completed and much of his work in print, we can see how Joseph Campbell's approach to mythology emerged from this one seminal geographical and psychological journey.

In order to understand the significance of this expedition more fully, we need to consider the evolution of Joseph Campbell's romance with the East, which certainly constitutes one of the major foci of his scholarship. At the time of his trip to India, he was best known in many circles as the editor of Heinrich Zimmer's works on Indian art and civilization. But much earlier biographical and intellectual events paved the way to Campbell's mid-life encounter with the Orient which is the subject of this book.

In 1924 the twenty year-old Joseph Campbell, a student at Columbia College, traveled to Europe. On the ocean liner were some young people with whom he felt a ready affiliation: an aristocratic-looking Indian man with a philosophical penchant, whom Campbell, in his diary of the time, and without a clue as to his real identity, called "Krishna." There were a couple of other Indian men, and two American women spending time with them.[1] The Indian was Jiddu Krishnamurti, the Messiah-elect of the world Theosophical movement. An electrical atmosphere of spiritual and intellectual excitement seemed to crackle around the conversations of this little group, and when one of the two women gave Campbell *The Light of Asia*, Edwin Arnold's moving life of the Buddha, his own life, as he later declared, was changed forever.[2]

In 1927 Campbell went to Europe again, this time on a Proudfit Fellowship to study Arthurian romance and Provençal literature at the Sorbonne. Campbell encountered Krishnamurti again. (They had corresponded in the intervening years, and Campbell now knew his identity.) At one of Krishnamurti's public lectures, Campbell had, by his own report, an important personal realization. It was right after this time that he ceased to practice Catholicism, the religion of his upbringing, in any formal way, though he continued an intense kind of metaphysical self-questioning that persisted the rest of his life. Perhaps the transformation was triggered by Krishnamurti's ideas on spiritual self-determination.[3]

After a year in Paris, during which time he also discovered the writings of James Joyce, Campbell's enthusiasm for Old French and Provençal waned, and Oriental and German philosophy began to beckon. When the Proudfit committee agreed to extend Campbell's fellowship for another year, he horrified his Francophile friends by deciding to study German, and to attend the University of Munich. Soon he was reading Freud and Jung, and taking courses in Sanskrit at the University. Simultaneously, then, Campbell discovered German Romantic Philosophy, Depth Psychology and the Sanskrit spiritual literature. His fascination with India had been deepened by many of the Theosophists he met at Krishnamurti's estate at Eerde, Holland, and he began to plan his own trip to India at the end of the year. But news of the onset of the Depression, and his family's precarious financial situation, brought Campbell back to the U.S.A. in 1929. The plan would not be fulfilled until twenty-five years later, as the trip which is the subject of this journal.

Campbell now tried to weather the Great Depression through a career in writing fiction, but his personal journals of this time abound with metaphysical speculations and insights triggered by his association with Krishnamurti. In 1934 Campbell was hired to the faculty of Comparative Literature at Sarah Lawrence College in Bronxville, N.Y. His preferred sources, kindled by his readings in Germany, were Kant and Schopenhauer, Thomas Mann, historical visionary Oswald Spengler, whose writings he had encountered in Carmel, California,[4] ethnologist Leo Frobenius, Sir James Frazer of The Golden Bough, Freud and Jung, and James Joyce. His Oriental interests seem to have became more or less dormant through his early years of teaching—except of course for the references to the Sanskrit literature he kept finding throughout Schopenhauer and Joyce.

That interest was abruptly reawakened, however, in 1940. Through the family of one of his Sarah Lawrence students, Peggy Davidson, Campbell had met their spiritual teacher, Swami Nikhilananda. (Both Elizabeth Davidson, Peggy's mother, and the Swami appear prominently in this book.) The Swami was very impressed by Campbell's knowledge of Sanskrit literature as well as his literary abilities. Nikhilananda asked Campbell to help him complete the book on which he was working—the life of the nineteenth-century Hindu saint, Ramakrishna. Ramakrishna had had an overwhelming experience of divine bliss—*nirvikalpa samādhi*—and thereafter was "God-intoxicated." Ramakrishna said, speaking of his own illumination, "Like a madman I began to shower flowers in every direction. Whatever I saw, I worshipped!"

Having rejected formal religion, Campbell was nonetheless impressed by the profundity revealed in the thought and life of Ramakrishna and the idea that neither a religious organization nor elaborate rituals were necessary to encounter the sacred—a humble, uneducated man of relatively modern times could enter the realm of divine intoxication at will. References to Ramakrishna are found throughout Campbell's later lectures and writings.

Through Nikhilananda and the Davidsons, Campbell met in 1941 the man whom he later named as the most important intellectual influence of his life, Heinrich Zimmer, the German professor of Oriental studies. Older than Campbell by fourteen years, a man of immense erudition and great personal charm, Zimmer arrived penniless in New York with his wife and three boys, as refugees from the Nazis. As a well-known university professor, he had spoken out publicly against Nazism; and his wife Christiane von Hofmannsthal, daughter of the famous poet Hugo, was half-Jewish. They fled, first to England, then to America.

Zimmer had been invited to lecture at Columbia University. Zimmer's lectures soon required a larger room—then one still larger. Joseph Campbell became numbered among the most loyal students of the Orientalist.

In 1943, however, a shocking event occured that drastically altered the course of Campbell's life and work. The seemingly robust Zimmer caught walking pneumonia, but kept working and teaching. The illness finally brought him down and on March 20, Heinrich Zimmer suddenly died.

Zimmer's widow, Christiane, asked Campbell to take on the job of editing Zimmer's papers, which existed in the form of copious and somewhat disordered notes, jottings and marginalia. The Bollingen Foundation, publisher of Jung's writings and other classics in the creative arts, religion and mythology, agreed to support the project. Campbell put aside his other work and began an intellectual labor that saw into print *Myths and Symbols in Indian Art and Civilization* (1946), *The King and the Corpse* (1948), and *Philosophies of India* (1951), published under Zimmer's name, but with himself as editor. The work culminated in the year of the Indian journey which is the subject of this book, with the publication of the illustrated two-volume *The Art of Indian Asia* (1954). Campbell was still correcting the proofs as he traveled through India, and the published work would reach him the following year, in Japan.

These experiences set the stage, then, for Campbell's journey to India. If it seems a journal of disillusionment, we must remember that neither Campbell nor his esteemed mentor, Zimmer, had ever encountered the realities of India. The learning that had so inspired them was from the sacred texts, mostly from ancient times. The social, political and economic actualities of India would provide a rude awakening for Campbell.

If Swami Nikhilananda had been less of an enthusiast, perhaps Campbell would have encountered India differently. "In a queer way," Campbell wrote in his journal a few weeks after arrival, "I am beginning to be afraid that Swami Nikhilananda and Mrs. D. are ruining my experience of India. Everything that we see evokes some unpleasant comparison with its American counterpart and a patriotic waving of the new Indian flag."

Campbell, had, up to this point in his life (and later as well) tried to identify himself as 'apolitical'. He would rather talk philosophy or literature, feeling, probably correctly, that politics was not one of his strengths. But here, somehow, spirituality and politics were getting all mixed up, and it triggered something in him. "I came to India to hear of Brahman," (transcendent wisdom), Campbell wrote, "and all I have heard so far is politics and patriotism."

Moreover the spirituality he was encountering in India seemed not to be transcendent *(Brahman),* but devotional *(bhakti).* As Swami Nikhilananda and his devoted ladies marked their foreheads with *tilaka*, prostrating themselves before every temple and shrine, Campbell recoiled somewhat from the odor of sanctity. After all, he had always identified himself with *jñāna*, gnosis, the intellectual path.

Nationalistic or religious chauvinism with a spiritual rationale, whether Indian or American, Hindu or Christian or Jewish, often provoked an angry response from Campbell. "Zimmer's formula appears to be correct," he wrote in his journal a few weeks later in India, "Devotion to the Mother has become a devotion to Mother India. We are witnessing the birth of a new, patriotically oriented religiosity; or perhaps, only religiously flavored patriotism, somewhat comparable to the American Protestant idea that Christianity and American Democracy are the same thing."

When he stayed for any length of time in India's major cities, Campbell moved in rarefied circles. During his half-year stay he met many of India's more prominent citizens, including President Nehru and his sisters; the Vice President and scholar Sarvepalli Radhakrishnan; the wealthy Sarabhai family of Ahmedabad; the Yuvaraj Karan Singh of Kashmir; Pupul Jayakar, the biographer of Krishnamurti, and many others. But in these circles and in the daily papers the atmosphere was the same. America was generally disparaged, and the Soviet Union and Communist China glorified.

"I am definitely on the other side of the Iron Curtain," he lamented to his journal. "I have a strong feeling that the U.S.A. has lost the world, will be used by everybody as a 'fall guy,' and is the Dragon to be tricked and plundered: old Fafnir with his gold-horde and grandfatherly willingness to be of help to his own destroyer. My sympathy, this time, is with the Dragon."

Two decades earlier Campbell had idealistically espoused the cause of Communism, but after the horrors of Stalinism he did an about-face and considered it a mind-enslaving and authoritarian system. His reaction to Communism was exacerbated by encounters with leftward-leaning faculty at Sarah Lawrence who emphasized the social and political dimensions of most issues, while Campbell preferred to dwell on the philosophical and transcendental aspects. Now here it was again, only mixed with spiritual chauvinism—which he had himself engaged in, often vaunting the deep and luminous insights of Eastern spirituality over Western religion's Biblical literalism and sense of historical mission. Now it was being turned around on him and he didn't like it very much.

His resolutions began to betray an acknowledgment of his earlier romanticism about India: "I, personally, shall do nothing more to advertise, blurb, and explicate India, for India and Asia are obviously at the beginning of a prodigious boom and can be counted on to take care of themselves."

Campbell's greatest annoyance during this trip was what he came to call "The Baksheesh Complex." Other Westerners traveling in India have experienced its more public manifestation: insouciant beggars in the streets, plucking the heartstrings of pity and guilt. Campbell learned to his disgust that many were professionals, some even maimed by their families to suit them for their unhappy role. At another level Campbell found the unsolicited, unctuous con-men, selling something, anything—including psychic and spiritual advice. Campbell found himself susceptible to one of them, and then, falling into shame and anger at his own vulnerability, began to compare his experience to being drafted to working on the Ramakrishna project —without compensation—by Nikhilananda.

Probably the event that upset Campbell the most was an instance of public plagiarism. He found his own prose, from one of the Zimmer books, in the daily paper—without any attribution whatsoever. In a fury, he wrote: "Mr. Pyarelal Nayar steals my paragraphs; an urchin tries to rob my pocket; an Indian movie firm steals an American film; Mr. Nehru accepts American aid and abuses America in every public pronouncement." Campbell did not like ingratitude. Perhaps in an unconscious way, he felt identified with the image of the generous, ugly American with which he kept being presented; it rankled him that the fiercest critics were, at the same time, asking for a handout. Everyone, he swore, was trying to get something from him—and putting down his culture. Again and again he heard the Americans described as inept do-gooders—their programs and initiatives as self-serving. He rankled, half agreeing, half offended.

Culture shock was evident in Campbell throughout this journey, but it seemed to work in two directions. Hearing the ugly American so described, Campbell began to notice that Westerners in India knew nothing of its languages and cultures, and seemed to care less. He often found himself identifying with his hosts' caustic assessment of individual visitors from America, and beholding, with a certain horror, their cultural gaucherie. "Americans who are not vulgar always hear the remark (which is regarded as a compliment), 'But you aren't like an American!'" which Campbell resented for its patronizing tone. A resolve began to crystallize in Campbell to do something about this situation. It would mature on his return—through the sixties and into the seventies—as years of service with very little compensation for the Foreign Service Institute, a branch of the U.S. State Department. His unremitting goal was to help to prepare American diplomats more adequately for service abroad.[5]

It took months for Campbell to realize that he himself was the victim of archetypal factors: his socialization as a Westerner, and his own self-inflicted idealization of the Orient. Oriental cultures, he wrote, were ruled by archetypes, individuality drowning in the collective patterns. He began to see his own (archetypal) romanticization: "For a Westerner, Oriental literature, which is a rendition of archetypes, has the quality of fairy tale."

At his most insightful, Campbell seemed to realize his own defensiveness, and became determined to let the trip open his mind and his feelings. On encountering the Dīpāvalī, the festival of lights, he wrote,

> It is a festival of the New Moon, representing re-creation and rebirth—and I have actually a feeling that I can make it a rebirth festival of my own, if I go at it correctly. This morning, in that horrible train compartment, I was sitting up at the hour of sunrise, looking out the window. And there appeared in the sky, about an hour before the sun, a lovely object, the dark moon, lightly revealed by the coming sun, and with its lower surface brightly illuminated—like a silver platter holding the darker disk.... And I had a pleasant feeling about my India journey....

On another occasion, watching a film, we see him setting his own subjective confusions aside. The sublimity of his own journey breaks upon him:

> Seeing again in the movies what I had already seen with my own eyes, I had a very pleasant sense of the magnitude of the experience that I have been having this year. In the course of my tour I have been seeing India only piece by piece, little by little. Seeing it all again—as it were all at once—I felt how big this whole thing is. The Orient is a vast natural phenomenon, like a continent of trees, mountains, animals and peoples.

At times he seemed to grow by virtue of the very contradictions—little enlightenments triggered by a succession of irresolvable koans: "When you look at India from the outside it is a squalid mess and a haven of fakers; but when you look at it from the inside...it is an epiphany of the spirit...the eye sees a river of mud and the inner eye sees a river of grace."

Campbell had admitted to himself in one of his earlier journals that the reason that he taught at a women's college (Sarah Lawrence) was that he loved to be surrounded by beautiful and intelligent women. To the best of posterity's knowledge, Campbell never engaged in improprieties of any kind—he just seemed to admire and enjoy the company of women. He began to admit to himself in the Indian portion of his journal just how much he missed the mingling, the little flirtations that one experienced in Western high society.

"India is without romance," he wrote, "the sun dries the juices out of the body." At the social clubs the men sat on one side, the women on the other. "Indian wives cannot talk of anything except the three K's: Kirche, Küche, Kinder," he complained. And again, "Women in the Orient represent archetypes and do not have to depend upon the radiance of their individual personalities. Furthermore, since marriages are arranged by families, they do not have to pull themselves together to 'win' someone. As a result, they seem comparatively secure and uninteresting."

It takes some discernment to locate the emotional heart of this journal, his relationship to his wife, the dancer Jean Erdman. While Joseph traveled throughout India, Jean was teaching at Bard College in New York State. She only joined him for a month in India, at midwinter.

Campbell's vexation and emotionality may have been fueled by an enforced monasticism. He didn't acknowledge his loneliness much, but his entries became almost breathless as Jean was about to arrive, and after she left, he immediately got quite sick.

Jean Erdman was the first modern dancer from America to do a solo tour of India. (Martha Graham's more publicized tour would take place several years later.) But all of the Campbells' efforts ahead of time to seek government and institutional support for the project were futile. It was only Joseph's individual efforts that brought the tour into being. In each major city he had to identify key people and arrange venues and advance publicity. Not infrequently much more was promised than fulfilled, and often and again he found he had to persevere in the arrangements.

With Jean's arrival, not unexpectedly, the journal, companion of his solitude, was neglected—the entries almost disappear. Thus we are deprived of much detail about the love affair that was probably the central event of Joseph Campbell's emotional life. He never wavered in the care and concern that he showed toward his partner as she moved around the globe toward him. What was more important for him was obviously what was more important for her—her artistic fulfillment. Though they moved in different orbits, it was characteristic of these two highly creative people to be totally devoted to each other. Joseph's perseverance as advance agent paid off. With several successful concerts and demonstrations in the three major cities of New Delhi, Bombay and Madras, and highly favorable reviews, the U.S.I.S. and embassy cultural services—too late to be of any use, as Campbell lamented to his journal—began to take notice of the presence of a major American artist in India.

Not infrequently Westerners go to India to find a guru. Campbell acknowledged himself to be in search of *Brahman*—but, as he wrote, "I doubt that I shall find a guru here." When he had an actual encounter with a living God-intoxicated saint, Ānanda Mayī Ma, Campbell retreated to his *jñāna* position and asked her a doctrinal question based on the Vedas. Though he liked her answer, it is clear that he was not thrown into *samādhi*, or rapture, by the *darśana*. But he appreciated the feisty individuality of a 116-year-old guru, whom he heard about but missed seeing: "'Anxiety doesn't eat me,' says the old chap, I eat anxiety.' Heavens and hells, past and future, are all figments of the mind. 'God is not the creator of man; man is the creator of God.' This sounds to me like the type of holy man I came to India to see," he wrote.

The spiritual high point of Campbell's trip, nonetheless, was to be his meeting with a guru: Sri Krishna Menon of Trivandrum, a living saint who had earlier had a career as a postal employee. The guru was surrounded by Westerners, who generally filled Campbell with disdain—"mostly psychological cases!" he thought. Campbell found two things remarkable in his meeting with the guru. First that Krishna Menon was able to encounter him lucidly on his own intellectual level, and in fact gave a discourse on states of consciousness from the *Māṇḍūkya Upaniṣad* that was one of Campbell's favorite summations of spiritual wisdom. Second, the guru told him that the question Campbell first asked him was the very one that Menon had first asked his own guru many years before.

"And I feel (I think properly) that my India journey has been perfectly fulfilled," Campbell wrote of this meeting. Though he was invited by the guru to stay for an additional five days of instruction—in part because he himself was, as the guru put it, "so close to realization"—he declined, being unwilling to impose upon the elderly teacher who had been advised by his doctor not to tax himself. "I think what he (already) gave me today will be enough for me," Campbell decided. "The chief value of my conversation with Krishna Menon is that it assures me that my own reading of the teaching coincides with the authority of at least one Indian sage. I know, furthermore, that the conversation and image of the teacher in his room of teaching will remain very clearly in my mind." Thus Campbell felt he had been given the signal to go on to the next stage of his journey, toward Japan, just six months after he had first landed in India.

A kind of core realization can be found in Campbell's confession of the paradoxical nature of his thought—matching the contradictions he found in India—"In the Orient I am for the West; in the West for the Orient. In

Honolulu I am for the 'liberals,' in New York for big business. In the temple I am for the university, in the university for the temple. The blood, apparently, is Irish."

[1]One of the other youths was Rajagopal, Krishnamurti's lifelong manager and companion, whom Rosalind Williams, one of the American women, would later marry. On the voyage also was Helen Knothe, the violin prodigy and international explorer, also in her early twenties, who would later become Helen Nearing. Nearing, with her husband Scott, became an internationally known authority on natural living. Together they wrote *Living the Good Life!* and many other books.
[2]See *A Fire in the Mind,* p. 41–43.
[3]See *A Fire in the Mind,* pp. 41 and 87–94. See also Pupul Jayakar, *Krishnamurti: A Biography,* and Jiddu Krisnamurti, *You are the World,* and *The First and Last Freedom.*
[4]See *A Fire in the Mind,* Chapters 8 and 9.
[5]See *A Fire in the Mind,* pp. 426–429

Notes on the Text

The journal entries were made not daily, although Campbell organized them so. Often they were composed at the end of a trip, and sometimes he would spend an entire day catching up on the last week. There is a sense that he wrote some of it, at least, with an eye to eventual publication, although certainly not in the form here presented. The book is therefore at some points closely written, at others wide-ranging and informal. There is much philosophical meat in these pages, and each reader will chew and digest it according to his or her own constitution. The extensive endnotes should help; they offer pointers also to Campbell's later work, where ideas that appear here only in germ bear full fruit.

The text has been edited to preserve the flow and interest of Campbell's narrative. Cut from the text are tentative itineraries, times of missed appointments, names of people met in passing and never seen again, long quotes from contemporary newspapers, and other details. Also removed are several political meditations that are later repeated in more cogent form. Punctuation has been altered where necessary for ease of reading, and the occasionally awkward sentence has been recast. Many of Campbell's frequent lists are now run on in narrative text. Nowhere has the meaning been altered.

Sanskrit words have been transliterated with full diacritical marks. Place names, where usage dictates, are spelled without diacriticals.

Campbell from time to time included rough drawings to illustrate his text. These have been redrawn and placed without captions in the text where they occurred. The photographs included were all taken with Campbell's camera, either by his own hand or by a traveling companion. The maps were commissioned by the editors to help the reader follow the geography of Campbell's travels.

Acknowledgments

None of the work on *Baksheesh and Brahman* would have been possible without the generous and unswerving aid of Jean Erdman, who as muse to Joseph Campbell begot these diaries, and as President of the Joseph Campbell Foundation is midwife to their production. Jean was also available to help our search for detail, by reminiscing about a time, now over forty years ago, when these events unfolded.

This book would have nowhere near its present resonance and depth without the extremely valuable work of John David Ebert. His great knowledge of Campbell's work and sources and his steady flow of constructive suggestions for improvement, especially for further reading in Campbell's works, make him an important editorial contributor to this book. Arthur Moore, as well, out of interest in Campbell, and with a passion for research and detail, volunteered his time, and supplied many footnotes.

Sue Davidson Lowe, Joseph Campbell's 1945–46 research and editorial assistant, daughter of Elizabeth Davidson (a prominent figure in these pages), was extremely helpful with biographical and historical details.

Dr. Walter Spink of the University of Michigan was most helpful in updating the chronological chart of Indian art (Appendix B).

Andrew McCord supervised and rationalized the transliteration of Sanskrit, Hindi, and Urdu words. He also marked, edited and checked the manuscript for errors and assisted with the glossary. Erik Rieselbach assisted with the page layout and with digitizing the photographs.

Carol Pentleton drew the illustrations and maps. Scott Taylor made fonts with Sanskrit diacriticals, relieving us of our greatest production nightmare. We'd also like to thank all the people who answered the queries posted by Antony Van Couvering on the Internet Usenet newsgroups, and most especially the generous and helpful members of the Desktop Publishing and Quark Users forums on Compuserve.

Baksheesh and Brahman

Prelude

Thursday, August 25, 1954 ***New York–Beirut***

Pan American Airlines tourist class to Beirut via Shannon; Paris, with a four-hour delay for repairs and two breakfasts; Rome and an Italian lunch; and finally the Bristol Hotel in Beirut, two days plus four hours from New York. Air-conditioned room with shower, and nice Arabs—great, but dog-tired. Nikhilananda[1] is supposed to arrive tonight.

Saturday, August 27 ***Beirut–Jerusalem***

Up at nine or so. Breakfast in the hotel dining room and a walk to town. Gradual recognition of the Orient: *Arabian Nights* associations at every hand.[2] But what a city! New buildings going up everywhere: concrete, modern style, and good. The first part of my walk was through a residential section. A young woman, approaching alone, pulled her black veil down over her face like a hangman's hood, and I had my first experience of *purdah.* Lots of it, here and there, in the town thereafter. An old man with a long stick, in the long white gown and red-fez white-turban headgear of the *Arabian Nights* went by. Craftsmen in their shops, various characters on various asses, porters, girls with loads on their heads: the whole picture built up gradually, and when I came, finally, to the heavy traffic of the city and the vivid markets, then the wharfs and various busy squares, the whole thing was around me and I was in it.

I finally realized that I did not know how to find a taxi. Then I saw a man who looked like a doorman, before a theater. *"Parlez-vous français?"* I asked. He took me in to the verandah where there was a girl at a table. She asked whether I wanted to ride alone (that would be expensive: five *livres),* or with others (one *livre).* I said with others and she pointed down the street. I went off and knew that I still did not know how to find a taxi; but more of the shops attracted me and I moved on, vaguely, until a man called "Taxi?" and I got in. Price: two *livres;* about sixty-five cents.

After lunch I went up to my room, and I was sitting pleasantly on the toilet when there was a knock at my door; another; and another. I was finally able to open it, and there was Swami Nikhilananda, looking healthy and happy, with his camera over his shoulder. Two ladies, Mrs. Davidson[3] and "the Countess,"[4] were down the hall. "Come! Come!" said Swami. "Come to lunch!" "I've already had my lunch. I was just going to lie down." So they went to lunch, and I lay down. Then we packed off to the airport; in another hour and a half, we would be in Jerusalem.

The hostess on the plane was a very handsome Armenian girl, and when she returned to take my empty ice cream plate, I asked where she had learned her English, which was very good. She looked a little embarrassed and said, "Beirut." I thought I had offended her, but shortly later, she returned and asked if I would like to go up forward, into the captain's cabin. She took me through the door, forward, and introduced me to the captain and co-pilot. The Dead Sea could be seen to the left; Jericho, other places, and then Jerusalem. The captain let me stay up there for the landing; then my pretty girl called me and we disembarked.

A Franciscan, Father Eugene, was at the little airport in Jersusalem to meet us. Irish, he was very strong in his feeling of what the Jews had done: three-quarters of Jerusalem had been taken by Israel; only the Old City remained to "us"; "they" had the cenacle of the Last Supper, but everything else (except decent lodging) was on "our side." To cut the city in two, a great wall had been built, with holes in it here and there, through which to shoot. And there was a barrier across the road through which the car had to wind. "We're at war," said Father Eugene. "Six years of it."

We were driven to a little hotel, the Orient House, where we left our things. Then Father Eugene's secretary, a refugee from the other Jerusalem and a very competent guide, took us to the gate of the Old City. The Jewish wall was just to the right, and there were sandbags and stacks of tar-barrels, behind which the citizens could duck when the Jews began to shoot. We entered the gate—and suddenly we were back several centuries: the covered alleys, lined with little shops; the women, many of them veiled; the donkeys, amazing old men, running kids; smells of fries and spices; lots of stepped streets, climbing up and down, criss-crossing. And then suddenly our guide said: "This is the Via Dolorosa, and this is the place of the seventh station." I was struck pretty hard. And from there on the visit was a weird experience.

We saw the Church of the Holy Sepulchre, within which are Calvary, the so-called tombs of Joseph of Arimathea and Nicodemus, and the Mosque of Omar. After dinner, I sat in the garden, listening to the dance music, under a lovely sky, and wrote cards and letters home.

Sunday, August 28 ***Jerusalem–Bethlehem–Beirut***

Visit to the great Mosque of Suleiman, then to a convent (Sisters of Zion, French) built over the court of Peter's denial of Christ. Plenary indulgence for an Our Father, Hail Mary, and Gloria. After visiting the Mount of Olives, spot of the Ascension, and so on, we drove to Bethlehem.

After lunch, plane back to Beirut and dinner with the Pan American agent, Mr. Cornwall, and his wife. Finale with Cornwall and wife in the Bristol Bar after the retirement of the angels.[5]

Monday, August 29 ***Baalbek–Damascus***

A long, twelve-hour, fatiguing, but very interesting drive: camel herds, camel caravans, wild driving, Bedouins, gypsies, refugees from the Jews. Damascus is a wonderful city—a vast oasis in a western-type desert, a boom town like Beirut: buildings going up everywhere in a strong, modern, Los Angeles style; wonderful market streets; and a charming, *Arabian Nights* garden.

Joseph Campbell's passport photo

Travels with Swami

New Delhi

Tuesday, August 30 ***Basra–Karachi–New Delhi***

After stops at Basra (amazing scenery: desert and date palm gardens—incredible from the air) and Karachi (dreary desert set-up), we arrive in New Delhi at 8:30 P.M.

Wednesday, August 31 ***New Delhi***

Upon arrival last night at the Palam Airport on the Pan American Clipper Ponce de León, we were met at the gangplank by a sadhu in a saffron robe,[6] holding a lei for Nikhilananda. Assorted press photographers (gentle, soft-spoken) stopped photographing Senator So-and-so, who had arrived on the same Clipper, to make the four of us line up: Nikhilananda with his lei, handbag and several cameras; Mrs. Davidson, mild and hardly touching the world, holding satchels; the Countess, whining tentative complaints through

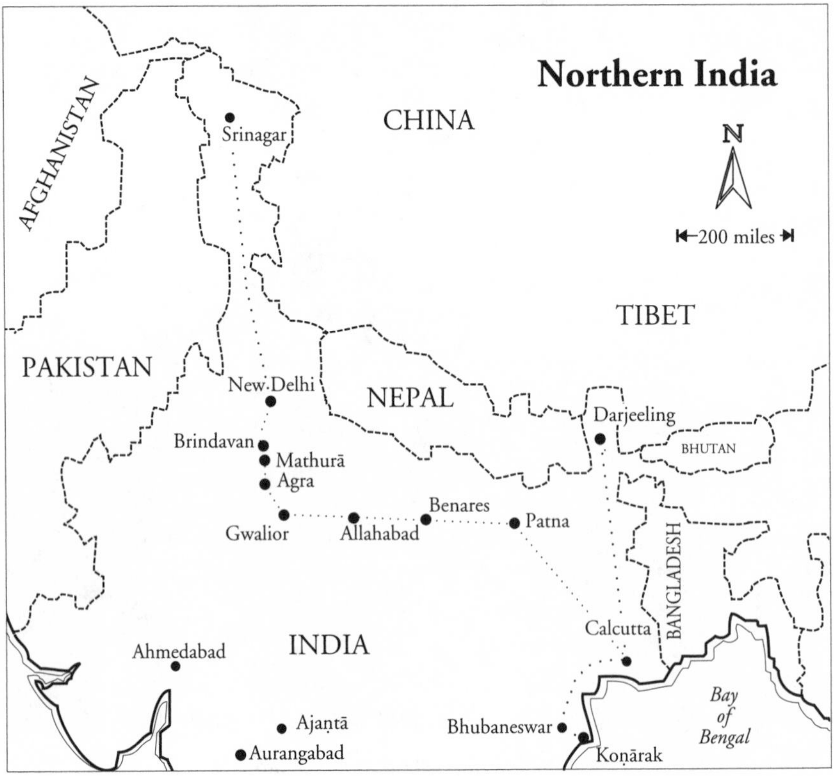

her long nose; and myself, pouring beads of perspiration from every pore, my blue Dacron suit as heavy as an Eskimo parka, my second-hand Leica slipping from my shoulder, my thirty-year-old English raincoat over my sweating arm, my equally old Zeiss field glasses in that hand, and in my other hand a leather bag that Jean and I had bought in a Madison Avenue luggage shop seven days before. More sadhus appeared, all standing, quietly smiling with luminous eyes, regarding principally their returned brother, Nikhilananda. Then a great deal of "this way please," "passports please," luggage examination, filling out of forms, forgetting of this and going back to get it, misplacing of that, and general search.

I was pleased to see, at every hand, examples of the modern Indian masculine types: one tall, good looking, young officer of some kind with a black beard and well-set turban was particularly conspicuous in the last stage of the processing of our company, and as we left bade us "a sweet night and a sweet trip." One helpful official in civilian gear loaned me a pen at one point, and then disappeared; no one then knew who was the owner, and a young assistant, with a smile, after holding it up to ask whose it was, tucked it into his own pocket. Sadhus were everywhere, helping, two carrying in their fists their closed umbrellas. Nikhilananda was losing and then finding everything, searching his pockets, and receiving help. Some kind of government person appeared and said a few words to the customs man who was to examine my bags; the customs official told me not to open them, asked me a couple of questions, and then gave his rubber stamp.

In the waiting room of the airport a thousand people were attending to our bags: sadhus, porters, and a number of other gentlemen. Clinging to all my things and sweating like a cheese, I was beginning to become a spectacle. Smiling cameramen and newspaper reporters were still looking for something to do. Leis had by now gotten around the necks of us all, and the fellow with the beard asked if he could take our picture again. He said he had done something wrong and had not gotten us right before. And so it took another fifteen minutes or so before Nikhilananda, Mrs. Davidson, the Countess, and I were again lined up properly and shot. Then we entered automobiles and started for the Hotel Cecil in Old Delhi.

The drive, through the dark, revealed brief glimpses of practically everything I had expected to see in India: wandering cows, multitudes of wildly assorted people, people sleeping in beds out along the sidewalks, a holy man with a little circle of people around him, bullock carts, water buffaloes, turban varieties, saris, etc. The same general Oriental effect of Beirut, but definitely of another racial cast: a different swing, a different set of details or motifs. We turned in first to the mission—and there was a live *nandi* reclining, by chance, near the gate. The Ramakrishna mission was adorned with the East 94th Street motifs.[7] Then we drove to the hotel. Nice room suites with ceiling fans (salvation). I showered, and then went down to the Honolulu-style porch for two sodas and salt, and listened to the middle-class British talk of cricket.

This morning (Wednesday), to the Ramakrishna Mission. *Pūjā* in the chapel, Swami now in his yellow robe. Plans for our visit to New Delhi, Swami Ranganathananda presiding (a fine, clean cut, intelligent, efficient man: the one who first met us at the plane). Visits to the Jama Masjid and the site of Gandhi's cremation, which is now a great park of well-kept lawns, with a sort of cenotaph in the center. We placed leis on the cenotaph.

In the evening we drove to the university, where the swamis began talking with a gentleman about some lectures that were to be given. I gathered that they were speaking of me—and became a little peeved. I got the idea that Swami was trying to use me as an advertisement of the sort of American he is winning to his work in the U.S.A. This has made me a little sore. I managed to kick the thing off—but I'm in for a lecture at the Ramakrishna Mission itself.

Thursday, September 1

Visit to the Red Fort:[8] a wonderful suggestion of the harem world of the Mughals: "The Land of Paradise." An inscription on one of the walls, from some Persian poem: "If there is a paradise, it is here, it is here," an echo of a Tantric theme.[9] Various baths and dressing rooms of queens and concubines: The Mughal had four legitimate wives and 175 concubines. As we moved about the green lawns, I saw a woman speak to one of the guards; he pointed to a water faucet on a standing pipe, and without ceremony she opened her sari and crouched under it for a bath.

We next went to the Indian Tourist Office, and I to the American Express to collect my mail: a lovely letter from Jean and a few lost bits of proof from Pantheon with a couple of notes from Bill McGuire.[10] I decided not to go with my party tomorrow to Kurukshatra, but to stay home and do a bit of work. It took us from ten till about one to finish our plan-making at the Tourist Office and to get our permits for Kashmir. Then I cashed a fifty-dollar travelers check at the American Express office and returned to the hotel for lunch.

After lunch: a nap, tea, then a lively bit of sight-seeing. First to the Tomb of Humayun[11]; then the Qutb Minār Enclosure, Guwwat ul Islam Mosque, and Iron Pillar—elements of earlier Hindu and Jain temples, with stone handled as wood, and the most interesting affair so far. After that, now nearly dark, a visit to the new Birla temple, Hinduism modern style, and visits to all the shrines: Viṣṇu and Lakṣmī, Śiva, Durgā. Finally on to the Buddha temple, and then the Durgā temple, where we had a taste of holy water and sweets; and then home.

Friday, September 2

Up at seven to the knock of the man with the tea. After breakfast, I attended to my proofs, and then I took a taxi to the National Museum to see what items had been brought there from the other Indian museums.

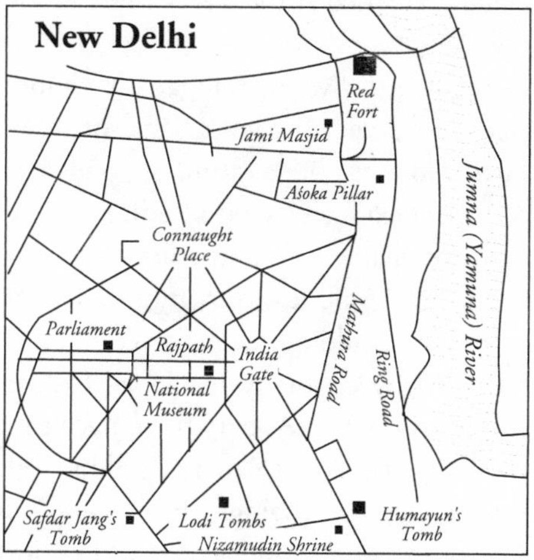

Filled with priceless pieces, the National Museum is an old, domed, government building lit by a vast, old-fashioned chandelier hanging from the ceiling. So I had the experience of viewing sculpture in semi-darkness—an absolutely crazy situation. As I was looking closely at a case of Indus Valley seals, I was addressed by a Sikh police officer: "Who are you? Where do you come from? How long will you be in Delhi?" I told him that I was on a tour of India, "Well," he said, "I am a free man. I will go with you. Where are you staying? What is your room number?" He wanted to visit me at the hotel. I was having a hard time shaking him off, so I asked him to help me get to see the director of the museum, and he turned me over to one of the guards. We shook hands, and then I shook hands with his sidekick, and finally I was led into a room, where one man sat at a desk and several others stood around. "My name," I said, "is Joseph Campbell." "Joseph Campbell?" said a young man dressed in white, who was standing at the director's left hand. "The editor of Heinrich Zimmer's books?"[12] I nodded, and I was "in": a delegation was assembled to help me get the measurements that I needed, and the young man, Pramod Chandra—whose father, now the curator of the museum in Bombay, was formerly at the National Museum, but quit because of government red tape—invited me to have lunch with him tomorrow.

After lunch at the hotel, we had a series of contrasting visits to make: first, Swami Ranganathananda showed us the new tuberculosis hospital being erected by the Ramakrishna Mission; then, we proceeded to a new, low rental, housing development (quite vast), where a devotee of Swami Nikhilananda's writings entertained us in a very touching—and utterly embarrassing—style; for the tenement was without plumbing yet, and none of us dared to take more than a token nibble of the bounteous fare that was set, almost as an offering, before us: drinking water (from a well or pipe line of some kind) with a lemon infusion, and then trays of sliced apples, pears, curds with grapes, grapes, and so on and so forth. It was a heartbreaking event: We sat on the floor and gingerly sipped, while the denizens of the tenement, crowded at the doors and windows, watched. They were people from the Punjab and Kashmir; refugees. One young woman, a teacher, talking strongly with Swami Ranganathananda, told him of her work: a school of eight hundred. One got a sense of serious and important social work being carried forward bravely and in good style.

Our next tea was with Radhakrishnan, Vice President of India. He greeted us cordially and talked for an hour and ten minutes in his living room about how America, hurt by the defection of China after the years of help and so on, could not be expected to know how to take it and was going to be hurt next by Germany and Japan (Adenauer had told him that the Germans would let the U.S.A. help them back to their feet and would then know how to handle us); about America's aid to Pakistan being the real thorn in India's side,[13] but there being a basic good will toward India on the part of the American people, and so on and so forth; and about how India, in seven years, had gained the respect of the world for integrity, was acceptable to both the U.S.A. and Russia as a "middle man," was mastering its economic problems, and was looking forward to peaceful co-existence, as a "block," with China and Southeast Asia.

Saturday, September 3

A morning visit to Parliament: Upper House, Lower House, and then a talk with Mr. Mavlankar, Speaker of the House. Swami asks why congress doesn't open with a prayer and is brushed off with smiles. Then I had them leave me at the door of Gaylord's restaurant, where I was to meet my young friend Chandra. I had an hour and a half to spare. After wandering in the hot streets for a while, I went into a movie house and took a seat in a box. The film—*Chālīs Bābā Ek Chor* (my Hindi dictionary is in New York, so I don't know what this means: forty somethings and one something)[14] was horrible: a young woman taxi driver and a horde of kids—corn *à l'indienne*; but the newsreel was interesting: Indian water and river projects on the grand scale;

an Indian cultural delegation (dancers, musicians, and such) to Russia.

Then my lunch with Pramod Chandra. A graceful lad of twenty-four, he studied at Harvard for goverment service, but then met the Coomaraswamys and learned of art.[15] Now, disappointed in government work, he wants to return to Harvard to study museology. I told him that would be an important work for India. We ordered cocktails: they didn't know what a daiquiri was, so we settled, he for a martini, and I for a gin and tonic. (Later, the poor kid spilled most of his cocktail over his pretty dhoti). Then we had a light curry and rice, ice cream, and a fine chat in that air-conditioned restaurant.

Tea this afternoon was *chez* Madam Pandit.[16] She talked of her recent visit to Indonesia: how India should be sending cultural delegations there and not only to China and Russia. (I thought of the film I had just seen.) Swami asked, "Would Americans be ill-treated in Indonesia?" Answer: America was not liked there, but Americans individually were welcome and should go to help good will. Swami asked, "How did India know that China would not continue to try to expand into Indo-China?" Answer: India didn't know, but believed that China had enough to do now at home to keep busy.

My own feeling, now, about Asia, world anti-Americanism, and so on, is that our do-goodism should now be definitely and absolutely stopped, since it is succeeding only in fostering a malevolence that may be our ruin, and any giving or helping should be precisely and firmly of the sort that it is everywhere said and thought to be—namely, carefully selfish; and also that I, personally, shall do nothing more to advertise, blurb, and explicate India, for India and Asia are obviously at the beginning of a prodigious boom and can be counted on to take care of themselves. Moreover, why should it be Americans who are always trying to create an understanding of others, when no one seems to feel the least impulse to seek to understand America? In fact, to hell with this whole "service-to-this-or-that-section-of-the-world" idea.

Which returns me to the basic and original purpose of my visit to the Orient: to study, not India primarily, but mythology in operation.

In this context, my most interesting observations so far are: the modern, self-sufficient, progressive Orient, secular style; then, the Birla Temple: a typical bourgeois transformation of an ancient religion, comparable to American church-life. Also, the relationship of the Ramakrishna Mission to, first of all, the Birla Temple devotees, who everywhere get down on their knees to take the dust from the Swami's feet; then to the ministers of the state—who all know and accept them familiarly into their homes and confidences; and finally to the TB clinic: comparable to St. Vincent's Hospital, but, of course, as yet much smaller. The Mission, with ten hospitals and seventy open-air clinics, treated two million patients last year.

There has been a bit of religious agitation of an amusing sort since our arrival: anti–cow-slaughter demonstrations by old-style sadhus are being quelled by the police. Yesterday morning I saw a group of them parading toward parliament with yellow pennants on their staffs. They were a wild-looking lot: one was practically naked, with only a minute black apron before his second *cakra.*[17] Their stratagem was described in *The Statesman*[18] with pictures as follows:

> Small groups organized by the Ram Rajya Parishad have been demonstrating outside Parliament almost every day this session demanding a ban on cow slaughter. The sadhus carry a saffron flag incribed with a swastika.[19] On arrival they meet in an orderly manner behind the fencing and try to convince the Sub-Inspector of Police on duty of the rightness of their cause. Then suddenly they rush and try to break the police cordon outside Parliament House and are brought back to the original enclosure when one of the oldest among them gives a religious discourse.

Swami Ranganathananda declares that such oldsters represent a rapidly dwindling and unimportant religious force.

Sunday, September 4

Saturday, after breakfast, a reading of the papers, and a bit of brooding. I came to India to hear of *Brahman,*[20] and all I have heard so far is politics and patriotism. Zimmer's formula appears to be correct: devotion to the Mother has become a devotion to Mother India. We are witnessing the birth of a new, patriotically oriented religiosity; or, perhaps, only religiously flavored patriotism, somewhat comparable to the American Protestant idea of Christianity and American Democracy being the same thing.

I am now definitely on the other side of the Iron Curtain. The main links of sympathy are with China, Southeast Asia, Russia, and, perhaps, even East Germany—this morning's paper features pictures of an East German trade delegation. Britain, moreover, is flirting with China; and France, with Russia. I have a strong feeling that the U.S.A. has lost the world, will be used by everybody as a "fall guy," and is the Dragon to be tricked and plundered: old Fafnir with his gold-horde and grandfatherly willingness to be of help to his own destroyer.[21] My sympathy, this time, is with the Dragon.

What I thus far have witnessed and heard of the sadhus is not particularly impressive. They appear to be associated with the misery of the "old India" that is being sloughed off, and—like all clergymen everywhere—they manifest themselves in the role of reaction: for example, their anti-cow slaughter demonstrations.

The Ramakrishna Mission, Birla Temple kind of Hinduism is comparable to the Christianity of the bourgeois church and Catholic hospital—and the people representing this movement, moreover, have their precise counterparts in the church circles of the United States.

The present leaders of the Government are of a distinctly secular mentality: witness, particularly, Speaker of the House Mavlankar, who parried all of Swami's requests that religious forms of some kind—opening prayers and so on—should be introduced into the conduct of the Indian parliament. Again I see a parallel to the two traditional strains in the U.S.A.: that of the Puritan tradition ("In God we Trust") and that of the 18th-century Enlightenment ("Novus Ordo Seclorum").[22] Said Mavlankar, with a knowing smile, "But are we really following, or has anyone really followed, Gandhiji?"

Today with one of the swamis' little lady patronesses to help, and under instructions from Swami, I bought two dhotis, two Indian shirts, and a shoulder cloth. Then I went for a stroll and was accosted by a sly fortune-teller swami who managed to seduce me out of thirty rupees by telling me nothing. I felt—and am still feeling—greatly the fool. As soon as I left him, another approached me with the same voice and line; and when I reached the hotel, there was a phone call from a young man who has been pestering me for an interview—and again the same voice and line. By chain-reaction, I have now associated the principle of my fortune teller with Swami, who seduced me into editing his books for him—always keeping me, in a very subtle way, pitched forward toward a vacuum, where, finally, I would discover that I had been used. And again by association, I now think of India-Russia-China and the U.S.A. I am going to keep, as a sign of my shame, the little token that the guy left with me.

Kashmir

Monday, September 6 ***Kashmir: Pathankot to Srinagar***

Two swamis saw us off on the night train to Pathankot—and the night and subsequent day are not to be forgotten. We had a second class compartment, designed for "six persons sitting, four sleeping." The two seats were converted into four bleak bunks, onto which we opened our four bed-rolls: I above, Swami below me; Mrs. D. above, the Countess below her. Two electric fans did not suffice to keep the heat down. It was actually a furnace of a night. I fell asleep slightly, well after midnight, though we turned our light out about 8:30.

At 7 A.M. we were in Pathankot, where a gentle couple met us and supplied us with breakfast in the waiting room. Swami took a shower and was looking spry. The rest of us were a bit shaken. What impressed me most here was the vitality and virtuosity of the porters. They piled the luggage on their heads, hooked more to their arms, and, when they had delivered their burdens, trotted back to the train for more.

The Kashmir problem is at present rather hot, and so there was a conspicuously military character to the event of getting us across the border. The kind gentleman who had met us supervised the packing of our luggage into a large Chevrolet station-wagon; he then preceded us in a military jeep to the checking post, where two extremely polite officers made notations from our passes, after which we returned to the station wagon for the wildest mountain drive that I can remember.

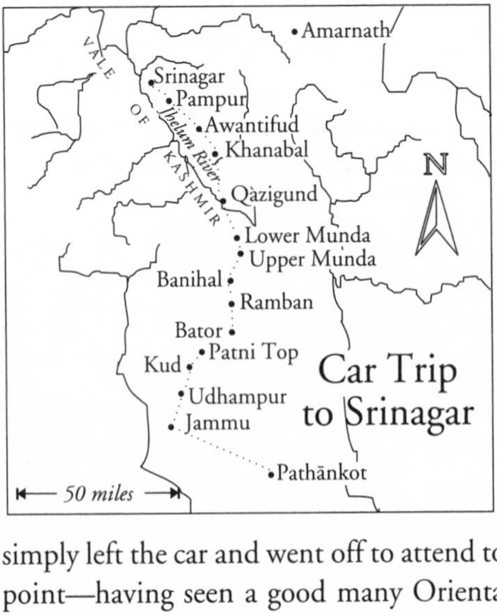

The driver was a Sikh. The road went from Lakhanpur, the place of the Customs barrier, 56 miles to Jammu (1000 ft.), then 41 miles to Udhampur (2,248 ft.), where the ladies paused for refreshment at a Dak bungalow, and I sat in the car watching our stuff. The driver drove me to a spot in the market, where he simply left the car and went off to attend to some business of his own. At this point—having seen a good many Oriental markets—I began to feel that I had gotten the idea and that it was no longer very interesting. The driver returned, we drove back to the bungalow, all the others got in, and we were off. After another 24 miles, we were in Kud (5,700 ft.), where again we descended before a Dak bungalow—this time for lunch. It was already about 2 P.M., and there was some question as to whether we would make Srinagar that night. Ants had somehow gotten into the best part of our provisions, so we had to content ourselves with tea, hard-boiled eggs, and bananas. From Kud, we drove four miles to Patni Top (6,447 ft.), and from there, eight miles to Bator (5,170 ft.).

By now it was evident that our driver was a phenomenon: over a pretty rugged and occasionally heavily populated road, he kept a pace of 35 to 40 miles per hour, negotiating the turns with an apparently reckless precision and with unwavering alertness: people, chickens, water buffaloes, trucks, goat herds, cows—nothing stopped him.

From Bator, we careened seventeen miles to Ramban (2,250 ft.) and then began the climb to Banihal (5,650 ft.). All along the way, we passed trucks—perhaps over a hundred—coming in a steady stream in the opposite direction, and since we were on the outside ("keep to the left") of a precipitous mountain highway, some of the moments were pretty spectacular. Swami became distinctly nervous and, at one moment, actually scared: that was when we backed up a little—without any wall between us and the precipitous drop—to let a van wriggle by. At about 6 P.M. we arrived before the Dak bungalow at Banihal, where the driver stopped. He very much wanted us to spend the night there, but the ladies and Swami, after examining the premises, decided to press on.

During this pause I had another remarkable glimpse into the character of our driver. Before him, propped against the windshield, he had a little picture of the Sikh prophet Nānak. At Banihal, while the bungalow was being examined by his passengers, he got out of his seat, went to a hedge of flowers, and plucked a big red blossom of some kind, which he then tucked above the picture. When Swami returned, the driver argued strongly for going no further, but acquiesced without any intentional display of impatience—though I noted that, while preparing for the hard run ahead, he was a bit more grim and firm in his manner than he had been before.

To quote from the tourist pamphlet:

> From Banihal the road ascends at an easy grade in a wonderful series of zig-zags on which one can look down from above. As the automobile climbs, the spectacle of the thin white road winding around the hills at various levels and disappearing into the hazy valley below presents a magnificent view. Banihal pass road is the highest highway in the world and is at a height of 8,985 ft. above sea level. [They apparently don't know about Pikes Peak, Independence Pass and

> Monarch Pass, Mt. Wilson, Long's Peak, and so on.] From the summit one gets a most thrilling view of the Banihal Valley, stretching in pensive quietness below. White clouds float around you. There is a sudden change in the landscape as the automobile passes through a tunnel and crosses straight through to the other side of the mountain. From the tunnel, the road descends in sweeping hair-pin bends for twenty-nine miles.

During the course of the descent, night came upon us, and we entered the Vale of Kashmir in darkness. Upper Munda, the first village after Banihal, is at a height of 7,227 ft. Lower Munda is five miles further on; Qazigund, four miles further, is at a height of 5,667 ft. Then come Khanabal, after eleven miles; Avantipur (where the ruins of the temples of King Avanti Varman[23] have been excavated), Pampur, and finally Srinagar (5,214 ft.). We pulled in at about 9 P.M. and were soon settled into Nedon's Hotel, which reminds me a good deal of Mokuleia[24]. The lights are the dimmest, however, that I have ever encountered in a public building. The bar was teeming with Englishmen. The atmosphere is that of a wealthy family resort. Dead tired, we ate, and, as soon as possible, went to bed.

During the night and morning, rain, even thunder—the first since my departure from New York. And then I realized that my raincoat, which I had bought in London in 1928 and had brought with me to be left in India, had indeed been left—I had left it hanging in the waiting room at Pathankot, where we'd had our breakfast.

After breakfast at Nedon's, Swami and the ladies joined a Swami who had arrived from the Ramakrishna Mission—lately established here, it's interpreted by the Pakistanis as an effort to convert to Hinduism the 90-percent–Muslim population—while I, on the pretext of preparing my talk for Sunday night, strolled off alone. I viewed a series of bad watercolors by some Hindu lady, which included a piece labeled "McCarthyism" that depicted a sort of green-eyed, wild-haired monster. Then, as I moved out for a stroll to town, I was approached by taxi men, guides, merchants: "Please let me alone; I don't need you," was my formula, and it finally worked. But the rain began again, and, trotting, I took refuge in a couple of shops that shared a verandah. The proprietors, of course, tried to sell me something. I was shown bolts of fine Kashmir tweeds and rich furs: a pair of slacks would cost about seventy rupees, a fur coat about five hundred rupees (one hundred dollars)! But I was firm—perhaps, too firm—being somewhat desperate about my money, which is rolling out these days at about three times the rate anticipated.

Returning to the hotel when the rain cleared, I settled to the present piece of writing. With respect to my general impression of the Orient and India, a couple of matters are to be recorded:

The gentleness and politeness of everyone is most remarkable. This struck me first, and immediately, when I stepped from the plane at Beirut; and it has remained the rule (without exception), from the approaches of the beggars, to the reception by Radhakrishnan and the attitude toward Swami of our remarkable Sikh driver.

The religious atmosphere and attitude are ubiquitous and strong. I was hit by it myself in Jerusalem. In New Delhi, wherever Swami goes he is greeted by men and women who stoop to touch his feet. Our taxi driver had his picture of Nānak on the windshield. Our tourist questionnaires for Kashmir, India, and Nepal had the query "Religion," and it is expected to be answered. Swami Ranganathananda tells me that more than 95 percent of the Indians practice, outwardly at least, the forms of some religion. Some of the western-educated intellectuals have rejected religion, but they are rare exceptions to the general rule.

The principal lack that I feel in India—and, I dare say, should have felt in the Near East also, had I remained there—is the lack of beauty, and of any feeling for beauty, in the contemporary life. In Beirut I saw, at least, some beautiful women; but in India, I have not yet seen even a beautiful young girl. The city of New Delhi is, from an aesthetic point of view, simply an unthing. The circumstances of the masses are simply squalid. The housing projects and the new buildings are, from a practical point of view, good and sound, but hardly beautiful. The bourgeois homes that we have visited are decorated in a trite, sort of Grand Rapids, manner. The British contribution to the city is a horror. And the Muslim remains—apparently the last creations of taste (and a rather flamboyant, though elegant, taste it was) in all of India—are mostly ruins. I am curious to know at what point in my travels an experience of aesthetic form will occur.

In a queer way, I am beginning to believe that I have already experienced, in New York, the best of what India is going to offer me. In my visit to the National Museum, I actually saw some of the objects that I had learned to know through my photographs; but the Museum's lighting was so bad that the effects of the actual objects were slighter, in every case, than those of the photos.

But in a queer way, also, I am beginning to be afraid that Swami Nikhilananda and Mrs. D are ruining my experience of India. Everything that we see evokes some unpleasant comparison with its American counterpart and a patriotic waving of the new Indian flag. I cannot permit myself to admire anything any more; for even a word will call forth the question: "Is it not better than your American so-and-so?" This situation, coupled with Swami's anti-

Americanism in the matter of the U.S.-Pakistan *vs.* U.S.S.R.-China tie-up, makes for a very unpleasant atmosphere.

Swami himself has begun to sense my disappointment, and he has suggested that, given my interest in museums, I should perhaps plan for a slightly looser relationship to his tour. This I am going to do. For the most part, Swami is dashing about a little more than I like, and the money is pouring out like water. I've got to find my own feet now, and pinpoint my searches according to my own set of problems. Today, for instance, I am letting them worship the Mother, while I sit here writing. I believe I shall stay in New Delhi for a few days after their departure and perhaps meet them again in Benares; go on with them to Calcutta, and decide then whether I want to join them in their visit to the south.

The two ladies returned from their worship of the Mother with red dots on their foreheads, which they wore until bedtime—like Catholics, on Ash Wednesday, bearing on their foreheads the dust of time's ruin. I find it a little difficult to walk with composure beside all this.

Swami has learned, to his considerable discomposure, that the Muslims of Kashmir (56 per cent of the population), who, he had thought, were solidly for India, actually are inclining to Pakistan. Furthermore, Kashmiri rice, which here sells for seven rupees per mound, in India sells for twenty; hence, there is a lively smuggling commerce going on. As we saw on our drive, Kashmir is occupied by the Indian army, which is a delicate situation for Nehru, who has been crowing about alien armies supporting puppet governments in Korea and Indo-China.

At the time of Partition, in 1948, there was a great raid of Muslim "tribesmen" (as they are called here) into Kashmir. And the story goes that Kashmir was saved by its women. The raiders were so busy raping them that the Indian army had time to arrive and drive them off.

Tuesday, September 7 ***Srinagar***

Worked on the outline for the talk I'm to give until 10:15, when I had my interview with Mr. Pandit. Upon returning, I changed into my blue Dacron suit and went with Swami and the ladies to lunch with Yuvaraj Karan Singh, the 24-year-old son of the former Maharaja of Kashmir, who is now the first president of the province. A very handsome and gracious young man with a game right leg (from tuberculosis—it was operated on in a New York hospital), he received us in the most gentle fashion, with his two bodyguards always in the room, conducted us to an elegant lunch, and then sat with us on his lawn, overlooking the two vales of Kashmir. The conversation ranged considerably over a variety of subjects—the Ramakrishna Mission, education in India and America, the scenery of Kashmir, and so on—with certain points of importance being:

The U.S.A.'s support to Pakistan has definitely queered us with India, and our support to the French in Indo-China has queered us with Asia. This young man confessed that his sympathies and those of all of India had been with the Viet Minh.[25]

Communism is not the least bit frightening to Asia. The people see what it has done for Russia in forty years, and the benefits seem to warrant whatever sufferings, injustices, and so on may have been entailed. "What good is freedom, if it is only freedom to starve?" This attitude—the true sign, by the way, of the Fellaheen—is something very different from Spengler's "Better dead than a slave."[26] Perhaps we can say that to the Asiatic world—which, for centuries at least, has not known the taste and feel of freedom—our American experience and consequent ideals can have no meaning whatsoever. The Sikh Sub-Inspector of Police at the National Museum told me that he was dissatisfied because there was no higher position for him to achieve. He had killed a man and been cited for bravery; the job was a dangerous one, and he wanted out: however, there was no out. Such a chap, I should think, might have an idea that freedom of opportunity would be a good thing, but he certainly could never have *experienced*—that is, actually known the feel of—freedom.

In the late afternoon, we took a boat ride through the canals to Dal Lake: a lovely, lotus-bordered, mountain-girded lake with many large houseboats, many cruising boats like our own, and many work boats. Indeed, everybody lives in boats, and kids hardly big enough to walk can paddle. The people look vigorous, courageous, and filthy dirty. Hundreds live in a squalid series of houseboats along the willow banks. Floating gardens abound, and the water—near the houseboats, at any rate—is quite foul. We had four paddlers: one, probably the father; the others, young boys, one of them blind—and they chugged away at a sharp clip, without letup, for three-and-a-half hours.

At the dinner table I had a conversation with Swami: Indian scholars and historians are now taking an anti-European position, which is the counterpart of the earlier European neglectfulness of Asia. It's a kind of revenge situation, ill-becoming the scholar. Resolution: no patriotism, no partisanship, in my further writings and, again, no more blurbs for India. They're doing it, and let them do it, themselves. In fact, this whole patriotic atmosphere is extremely disappointing. Yet, I should have expected it. It is certainly timely; but it is far, indeed, from the sort of equipoise that is supposed to be the particular gift and lesson of India to the world.

Early to bed tonight. A big day tomorrow: some kind of great trip through the valley, and then, in the evening, the Yuvaraj's movies of his trip to Amarnāth. As we left, he gave us copies of his account of his trip and, when he learned that I was the editor of Heinrich Zimmer, said that he had just read *Myths and Symbols* with great delight—a pleasant bit of news—and that he also owned and knew *Philosophies of India*.[27]

Wednesday, September 8 ***Amarnāth***

At 8:10 A.M. we got into a car for a drive to neighboring towns, and particularly to pause at Pahalgam, which is the traditional starting point for the annual pilgrimage, about the middle of August, to the Śiva Sanctuary, a natural cave with an ice-covered stalagmite, at Amarnāth. There we had a picnic lunch in a setting very like a Rocky Mountain valley; and we returned to the hotel about 5 P.M.

The drive gave me a rather solid impression of the people of this valley, as well as of the valley itself: a great flat plain, about seventy miles long by twenty wide, surrounded by Himalayan foothills about ten thousand feet high. The valley is fertile, planted with rice (of which we saw a great deal), saffron (of which we saw several fields), and wheat. The people: in the fields, peasants with short hand-adzes and sickles; handsome, very dark, dark-eyed, sturdy people, bearing burdens on their backs or tending flocks of cows, goats, or sheep; mostly Muslim, with little skull caps or caps of fur; the women, the handsomest I have seen so far, but almost all in dirty rags. More people: in the towns, the shopkeepers, cobblers, fruitsellers, and so on; the river-people in their houseboats and long skiffs; a wild tribe of nomads, who came trudging with their cute kids and stocky pack-ponies to a bit of grassland beside a stream and pitched their tents—the women, somewhat like Navaho, only not so big and handsome; the priests at the little folk temples.

We visited two temple compounds, each with several such temples. In the temple ponds were multitudes of fish. At one of the ponds, a few bas-relief fragments (showing deities that I could not identify from my distance) were set up against a wall, and people would stoop to splash a few handfuls of water at them, then sip a bit of water from their cupped hands. In this compound, a holy man, smeared with ashes and quite black, was squatting among brass vessels filled with water and, a few, with flowers. At another of the temples was a great crowd of Hindu visitors, who had arrived in a van; the priests of the temple had great long visitors' books, in which all were asked to sign. The chief guardian of the place recognized Swami as a

Ramakrishna monk and even knew his name. Swami and the ladies visited the Sūrya Temple that was there, and we all signed the book.

We also found and photographed two Hindu Temple ruins from about A.D. 1050: one, a neat little *garbhagṛha* set in a square pond; the other, a large compound with a high shrine (destroyed) in the center and a run of four shrines behind it. I took photos of the *yonī* (at A); of the shrine with the *yonī* (from B); of the central shrine (from C); of a damaged panel of Śiva, Devī, and an attendant (at D); and of another damaged panel of a *maithuna* (at E).

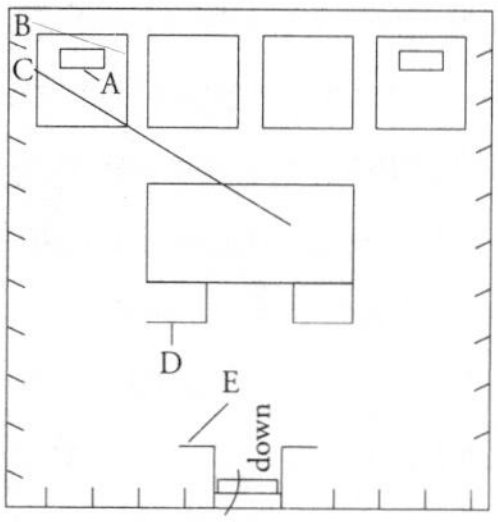

During the drive I had time to brood a bit more on the Indian problem. It was interesting to be in a landscape so close to that of the Rockies and certain parts of Switzerland, and yet in a world of such different feeling. In contrast with Switzerland: there were no flowers, there was no charm, there was no *intentional* decoration or beautification of anything except of the temples, and the beautification there, of course, was simply vulgar and gaudy. A comparison with America might be possible if one thought of the America of the Indians. That tribe of gypsy-like campers made me think of the Navahos a bit. They were the same kind of rugged race. But the tilling of the soil belonged to the 6000 B.C. category—and the work of the peasants, some of the images that I saw, rang echoes for me from Europe as well as from Japan.

Here, then, is a great base of the agricultural stratum—with its religiosity; which has jumped the Atlantic to shape the Bible Belt. The world of religion that I entered at Jerusalem, was there represented to me by the French nun who showed us through the Convent of the Sisters of Zion and reminded me of Aunt Clara, and the Irish Franciscan, Father Eugene (recall that Grandma belonged to the lay order of St. Francis). Let it be the Bible Belt or the Koran Belt, a temple of Kālī or of Notre Dame, the fundamental context, today, is the same: that of a folk piety rooted ultimately in the sphere of agriculture and the petty shop. Ancillary to this sphere is that of the nomads and their flocks: many of the men that I saw today could well have been Abraham, Isaac, or Jacob. The most vivid symbol of this religious sphere is the solitary Muslim, on a rug somewhere (in a grove, in a field, beside a pond), bowing in prayer. Last evening, during our boat ride, I saw a woman standing alone, in one of those canal-vistas, and she seemed to me to be linked to nature in the way of these people, that is to say, linked to nature by being linked to a principle beyond nature, through a ritual attitude: something very different from the romantic return to nature and intuition of God through nature.

Against the ground base of this primary population and religious attitude (as capable of fanatical fury as of gentleness), the bourgeois Hindu girls in their saris or pajamas look distinctly like something else. For these, the religion of the Birla Temple.

And then, one remembers, above these, the well-westernized Nehrus and Mavlankars: of a secular cast of mind, for whom religion, surely, is either a pose or a slight problem.

But the source of ideology of this directive group is Europe and America, and it is they who are building, through the vehicle of education, the contemporary sari and pajama girls. And so we arrive at a formula:

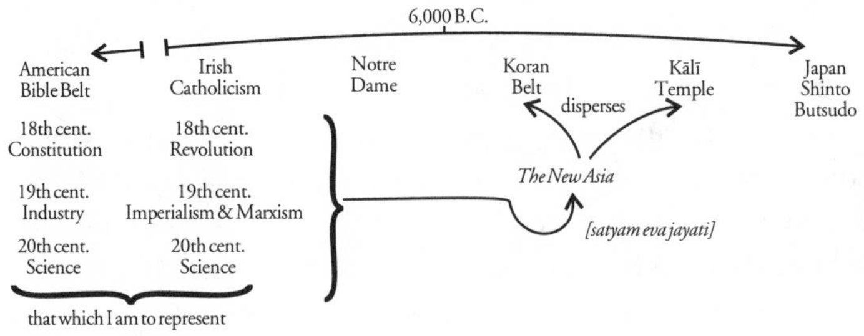

The lead is definitely with the West. The new world that I thought might be found in the Orient is certainly not here yet—and will not be here in my lifetime. They are learning from *us*. Europe is the *present* home of *my* mind—and of Asia's too.

But, on the other hand, what I am to study is definitely here: folk religion, with its roots in the deep past; aristocratic religion, represented in the ruins of the temple art of India; the phenomenon of the sadhu—past, present, future; the bourgeois religion of the Birla Temple (and compare that with St. Patrick's Cathedral) and Swami's idea that the priests of India (as distinguished from the sadhus) should have degrees in Hindu theology; then, finally, the operation of science in this context. Moreover, it is just possible that there may be someone in all of this from whom I may wish to learn something fundamental.

After dinner, we drove up to the palace of Yuvaraj Karan Singh to view his color movies of his pilgrimage to Amarnāth and his visit to Ladakh. In his little booklet on "The Glory of Amarnāth," he has stated the principle of pilgrimage in the following way:

> A pilgrimage symbolizes, as it were, the long pilgrimage of the soul towards its ultimate, sublime goal. Almost all the most important pilgrimages in India take the devotee along dangerous and hazardous paths, testing his devotion at every step. It is seldom possible for the pilgrim, if he is deterred, to reach the goal. If

> he pushes on bravely with courage and confidence, and with faith in God, he is bound to triumph.[28]

> The goal of pilgrimage at Amarnāth is a cave of truly colossal dimensions. Its outer mouth must measure almost forty yards across, and it is about seventy-five feet high and at least eighty feet deep along its downward slope into the heart of the mountain. Inside, an imposing ice formation rises about five feet and ends in a glistening cone, the famed representation of the Lord Śiva. To the right is a block of pure white ice, about six feet high and three feet broad, which represents Ganeśa, while to the left is a smaller ice formation regarded as the symbol of Śiva's consort, Pārvatī. These ice formations are believed to wax and wane along with the moon, reaching their climax on the full-moon day and vanishing completely on moonless days. The cave is one of the most sacred places in all India.

"As I entered it," Yuvaraj Karan Singh continues, "I suddenly had the curious feeling that I had been there before, and, certainly, the unusual atmosphere of the cave affects many people powerfully. I was overawed as I entered its hallowed precincts."[29]

Swami Vivekananda visited this cave in 1898, after his return from America. Sister Nivedita records in her "Notes on Some Wanderings with the Swami Vivekananda," that the Swami was so overwhelmed when he entered the cave that his whole frame shook and he almost swooned with emotion. "I thought the ice-*liṅga* was Śiva himself," the Swami said later. "And there were no thievish brahmins, no trade, nothing wrong. It was all worship. I never enjoyed any religious place so much." Vivekananda imagined at this time that Śiva himself appeared before him and granted him the Boon of Amarnāth, the Lord of Immortality—not to die until he himself should choose to throw off his mortal bonds.[30]

This illustrates very well the radical difference between the modern Orient and modern Occident, which I am feeling, one way or another, all the time. I think again of Tenzing Norgay and Hillary on Mt. Everest:[31] the expedition as pilgrimage, and the expedition as conquest.[32] On the pilgrimage to Amarnāth the pilgrims sing *kīrtanas*, meditate on Śiva, etc.—as we used to meditate on Jesus at Canterbury School retreats.[33] The conquest idea, on the other hand, belongs to the romanticism of Rousseau, and before him, of Petrarch. The impact of the cave and *liṅga* ("I suddenly had the curious feeling," as the Yuvaraj wrote, "that I had been there before") is probably adequately explained by the rather obvious psychoanalytic interpretation: that is to say, the legendary interpretations of the force of the experience as being a revelation of the god are merely rationalizations—as are also the western explanations given by our mountain conquerors for the fascination of the peak that is to be climbed. What is the lure of Mt. Everest? What is the lure of Śiva? Coomarawamy has written respectfully of *le symbolisme qui sait* and disrespectfully of *le symbolisme qui cherche*, identifying the first with traditional and the second with modern art and thinking. Let us now say, rather, *le symbolisme qui pense qu'il sait,* and we are in better perspective.[34]

Following the film of Amarnāth came that of Ladakh—and here was something great. The Yellow Cap Lamas—"Devil" dancers—great horns—people greeting their Yuvaraj. On the wall of Karan Singh's thoroughly Occidental living room there hangs a lovely *tanka* of the Buddha in the *bhūmi-sparśa-mudrā,* framed handsomely and simply, as a picture, with a sort of tan silk matting and not a gilt but a golden-toned simple wooden frame, lightly decorated at the four corners.

A final film was a glimpse of the Indian folk-dance festival that is held in Delhi every January 25. (A *must* for Jean.) Among the glimpses there were three greats: the Santāls of Bengal, the Nāgas of Assam, and another group from Hyderabad—the latter pure Africa-Haiti: shoulder dances and precisely the rhythms.

Thursday, September 9

The sky is a bit overcast and Swami seems disinclined to adventure, so we are not doing anything until this afternoon. At breakfast he sounded off about how horrible he thought Indian girls looked in Western dress. There was such passion in his tone that it actually spoiled my breakfast. I find him an extraordinarily mixed-up person: he really hates the West but thinks he has some love for it. The whole Ramakrishna-Vivekananda movement has been heavily supported by Americans—India is being helped more than it will admit by America—and these fake non-dualists, who have transcended the sphere of the senses, so hate to think of their debt, that everything flashes and cracks. The disciple is supposed to take the dust from the feet of his guru voluntarily. America is the guru, India the disciple in all that matters today. But in order to stand erect, the Indian saintly one brings the great message of India (non-dualism and the harmony of religions) as a gift superior to that which he is receiving, and those mildly mixed-up souls who find consolation in the words become the symbols of America's discipleship. Meanwhile, the actual religiosity of India is dualistic *bhakti*—the *iṣṭadevatā* of this particular Swami being, not God, but India—as that of the Jews is not God, but Jewry. This, I think, is perhaps the inevitable formula for the tribal-local as contrasted with the world religious.[35] That little glimpse of Ladakh, last evening, in the Yuvaraj's film gave me a feeling of participation that I am unable to bring to these Hindu forms—though, God knows, if I actually visited Ladakh (which I can't, apparently, for political reasons: too close to Pakistan) I might well find that it too is not quite what it seems.

As for Hinduism and its future: I am convinced that in India it is secure. The Yuvaraj was at his evening *pūjā* when we arrived. He is a thoroughly religious young man—and Swami, by the way, has made a conquest. (My guess: when Nikhilananda leaves 94th St. he comes into the palaces of Yuvaraj Karan Singh of Kashmir, if the Yuvaraj is still in a fortunate position.) The closeness of these Swamis to everybody in the government is amazing. The pandits, for patriotic reasons, are going to line our modern learning up with Indian, rather than European, history and philosophy—which should actually be even easier than the alignment of Christianity with science which our theologians think they have achieved.

In the main, I should say, popular Hinduism is much like popular Catholicism: a little dirtier and less well-organized, but with much that I find woefully familiar. The two additional features that I see are the ash-smeared sadhus, and the doctrine of non-dualism and the harmony of religions, which has no visible effect. Even the swamis are really dualistic patriots and worshippers.

Swami let drop a good observation, on the difference between the American and the Indian social attitude: the American cherishes and expresses fellowship and equality, but the Hindu, reverence. That is the explanation, I believe, of the impact that I felt of the gentleness of the Orient.

Friday, September 10

Yesterday afternoon we drove out to see some of the nearby sights: the reservoir—with no water in it; the trout hatchery—with almost no trout in it; the Mughal gardens—with a lot of big chinar trees that in the past two or three hundred years have grown to such a height that the proportions of the garden design are completely lost—and again the water, which must have been the jewel in the setting of the garden, was completely lacking; and finally, another garden—a great affair in raised stages, which, if the central flow of water and fountains had been there, would have been a considerable spectacle. As we walked about the garden grounds we heard two or three guys hooting and shouting up at the trees, and then we saw that they were trying to kill the pretty green parrots with an old fashioned slingshot—the David and Goliath kind.

Following this event we proceeded to the Srinagar Ramakrishna Mission where Swami delivered an excellent talk to a little outdoor gathering. Here he did what could be done to stress the contribution of America and Americans to the work of the Mission and to India. Only two questions were put to him; the first, by a somewhat aggressive youth of a type that I remembered having seen before: "You have said that Americans are idealistic; but we know also that they are pragmatists: how do you reconcile these two positions?" Reply: "The Americans are idealists; they are generous; they love freedom, they believe in equality, and they *help* people to these. And they are

Mrs. D. and the Countess

pragmatists because they believe that ideals that do not show themselves in life are worthless." The second question had to do simply with the actual work of Swami's mission in New York. What did he do there? He answered and the meeting closed.

A number of young students came up to talk with us. One of them said that the Ramakrishna Mission was the one institution that could bridge the way between America and India. He had formerly been impressed by communist writings and despised America; but then he had read Vivekananda and had seen that Americans were good people.

The Indian press and government seems actually to be suppressing all news of America's contributions to India's fight for a decent level of life. Russia has not yet contributed a thing—and is India's hero. In yesterday's *Statesman* I read an article on the problem of the Outcastes in India. The case is much like that of the Negros in the south: legally there is no recognition of caste, but actually there is discrimination—job discrimination and educational discrimination, with no practical means of redress.

It is now time for me to pack and prepare myself for our return (by air, thank God) to Delhi.

From New Delhi to Calcutta

Saturday, September 11 ***New Delhi***

The flight back was very pleasant. We saw, from the sky, the Golden Temple in Amritsar. The plane paused at Jummu, and Amritsar, and arrived in New Delhi last night at 7:10. Sadhus. The Mission. The Hotel Cecil, same room. After dinner I had a soda and salt with the young man who is manager, and talked with him of Kashmir, of poverty in a rich land, because the people were drained by the father and grandfather, he said, of the gentle young man Yuvaraj, who, with his wife, was performing *pūjā* when we arrived. My host showed me the swimming pool in this place, and I thought, a nice place to be with Jean when we come for the Dance Festival, January 26.

With Swami, at the Mission, I met a nice young man named Jnanendra Jain—who turned out to be the editor and publisher of *Seva Gram*, the little paper in Hindi with which I learned to read. His wife, apparently, knows one of the celebrated Indian dancers—and so, another lead for Jean. Today we are to meet Rajendra Prasad, the President of the Republic.

I went this morning to see Mr. William B. King, Isadora Bennett's friend, at the American Embassy. We talked of Jean's plans for a concert, and I was invited to luncheon tomorrow at the King's home. My thoughts are, now, that I should return to New Delhi in January to get things moving for Jean's concert. Jean could arrive here, give her concert, see the Dance Festival, proceed to Bombay, dance there, and then go on to the south.

Swami delivered his lecture tonight at the mission before an audience of about 1500, introduced by Madam Pandit. A young Mr. and Mrs. Anderson were present—here on the American Technical Aid to India program.

Monday, September 13

Yesterday morning I worked on the talk that I was to deliver in the evening at the Ramakrishna Mission.

At noon I went for lunch with the Kings, who are now dwelling in the stately, air-conditioned mansion of Mr. George Allen, the U.S. Ambassador to India. Also present were a Mr. and Mrs. Flanagan, Roman Catholics, just back from Holy Mass, who are in charge of U.S. Information and Cultural Accord (or something such) in India. It was evident after the first two minutes that neither the Flanagans nor the Kings knew anything whatsoever about Hinduism, though they had had a great number of glimpses of its operation; e.g. the sacrificial beheading of a water-buffalo in Jaipur; the reaction of an Indian crowd to the death of a cow in an automobile collision, the obscurity of Radhakrishnan's book on Indian philosophy.[36]

Mrs. King had been to a Hindu concert the evening before, where she had discussed the possibility of a concert by Jean with various people, and the prospects seem favorable. A certain Mrs. Menon said, "Jean Erdman? Well, indeed!" Mrs. King wants information about Jean's recent work, and this should come from Isadora Bennett.

Following lunch I went with Mrs. King to an exhibition of Indian Home Industries, and saw a lot of pretty cloths and bowls, some Jagannātha Purī pictures, etc. Then I returned to the Cecil, to prepare myself for my talk.

The crowd was about the size of Swami's last evening and the talk went off rather well. The chairman introducing me was a Mr. Kamarkar, President of the New Delhi mission and a former cabinet officer, who, by chance had visited Sarah Lawrence in 1949. Following the talk a horde of young students flocked up to hear further words. I have the impression that the young crowd is considerably less anti-American than the Nehru contingent; that is to say, when they are not young communists.

At luncheon this afternoon it was claimed that the Hindus who lose Hinduism become Marxists. This may be so. But if it is, then America's best bet here are the Hindus: not, perhaps, the old-guard sadhus, but certainly the Ramakrishna following.

After the talk I was both greatly relieved and greatly fatigued. I came back to the hotel for dinner, and went early to bed.

This morning, before I was up, Mrs. Davidson and the Countess took off with Swami for Haridvār. My day began with a conversation here at the hotel with a young man named K. Narasimhan, who has been pestering me for a meeting. The young man, rather nervous but charming, talked for an hour. He wants me to do something for him but can't bring himself to tell me what it is. The history: age twenty; five years ago evacuated from Pakistan to India, when he lost his father, mother, brother, and sister; taken in by the Ramakrishna Mission. Works as stenographer at Parliament for 250 rupees a month; is studying the *vīnā* with a master who charges forty rupees a month for lessons. There is no future in the Parliament job: enormous competition here for even the most menial posts (same story, approximately, as that of the Sikh Police Inspector who picked me up in the museum). The boy hopes that some day he may be playing the *vīnā* for cash of some kind—though, as he said, "I hate to sell my art."

He talked of the dance here. Bala Saraswati is the great one: rather old now. Kamala is the young hope: about 18 or 20. Rukmani Devi is a next: also rather old. Many Indian artists are going to Russia on cultural missions—and the U.S. refuses visas to those who have done so; so, it seems, the Indian boys and girls have to decide which state they would prefer to visit. (Situation comparable to that of the Arabs and Israel.) After an hour the youth departed, hoping to see me again when I return to New Delhi from my Indian tour.

September 14 ***Mathurā***

Got off to a good start, and was sitting in the train, in my second-class (no first class in India now) compartment, when two Americans came—Mr. and Mrs. Cummings, a husband and wife of the Bible Belt variety—with nine pieces of luggage, including a violin. The man spoke Hindi to the coolies, very easily, and the lady too. They were definitely missionaries. The man was John Cage,[37] at the age of about sixty. A young Indian joined us, and for the better part of the trip he and the lady conversed; but she had her prayer book in her hand and presently went to that, whereupon the youth fell asleep. Meanwhile, Mr. Cummings told me of his visions (literally) of Christ, with a charming, boyish, forthright confidence that he was now fit to be a witness unto..., etc. His exposition of his experience was liberally ornamented with Biblical quotations and there was no question in his mind but that his way was *it.* He was a Pentecostalist. He had been a missionary largely among the Muslims, who had argued back hard, asking how he could bear witness, etc., if he hadn't witnessed. And so he had called upon Christ, arguing with his deity that if he was to bear witness to Christ among these people, Christ should allow him at least as much of an experience as that which the twelve—who had already witnessed him in the flesh—received on Pentecost, when the Spirit descended in tongues of flame and they spoke in tongues. Well, the long and the short of it is, that Christ came through, and he had a wonderful experience, and spoke in an unknown tongue, and then later his wife had a wonderful experience too (she was now reading her prayer book) and they were very happy missionaries (obviously they were).

When, later, he began on Hinduism, and the importance of the Christian concept of personality, I said that I thought their experience was of the transcendent aspect of divinity, the unutterable. "Yes," he said, "They always retreat to that position." "It isn't a retreat," I said, "it is the positive content of their experience: it is affirmed in all of their writings. Moreover," I went on, "for me, who have had no experience, it is not to judge between such an experience as yours and such an experience as that of the Indian tradition. I simply compare them—and if I have a faith in such things, it is that what the Indians have experienced *this way*, Christians experience *your way:* the two are glimpses of a mystery of the spirit." But the dear man had nothing in his head but his Christ and his Christian work. He asked if the college in which I taught comparative religion was sectarian. Mathurā came, and I got out with their good wishes. They would be seeing the Taj Mahal tonight by moonlight and I should probably meet them there.

The Mathurā adventure was something!

My porter brought my things to the second-class waiting room, and I gave the Sikh attendant one rupee to keep them under his surveillance. Then I took a tonga to the Museum. Arrival at 10:00; museum not yet open. An attendant pointed around to the side, so my driver conducted me around there and a gate was open. Simultaneously, an English lady who had arrived in a car was hoping to get in and she followed. I had the experience of going through the Curzon Museum of Archaeology, Mathurā, attended, and sometimes closely followed, by my tonga driver, half a dozen kids, and three museum guards.

My impression of the sculpture was less strong than I had expected it to be. I think the exhibition of these important pieces is simply no exhibition at all. Too many things in too little space. Also, the actual carving on the early *yakṣas* was, from some of the less photographed angles, rather sketchy. Perhaps the light was not quite right. In any case, I went through the museum carefully, pleased to see a number of fine things that I recognized from the Coomaraswamy photos. Even the celebrated Gupta Buddha[38] was hard to experience, however, and I concluded with a distinct sense of disappointment. If the better pieces had been isolated and the others either stored or placed as they are, but in a separate room, the effect would have been much better.

The curator, Mr. K. B. Bajpai, was not in; but I had a look into his office, and could see that he knew very well how to arrange things for himself. It was a very nice, spacious office, with the desk in the center, on a rug that left a handsome margin around the edges: bookcases around the walls, and well placed pictures—including, high on the right, that photo of Coomaraswamy that appears on the dust jacket of *Time and Eternity.* The office and photograph made me feel at home in this spot, in a way, somehow, that the art did not!

Following my somewhat disappointing visit to the Museum, I said to my driver, "Hotel," hoping that I might find someone who could speak English and from whom I might procure a bit of help—for my Hindi was a complete blank: I was unable even to formulate the simplest problem (I have not had time even to look into my Hindi books since my last lesson, a week before my departure from New York.) I was driven through a pretty cluttered series of streets to a hotel; but I entered a shop across from it—a kind of accounting office—and found a very gracious gentleman who told me that Brindavan (which I wanted to see) was only five miles away, and that it would be quite possible to go in a tonga. The fee was arranged for 10 rupees, and I started away.

Five plus five miles in a tonga on a hot day, from 10:45 A.M. until about 3:00 P.M.—too much.

The country is perfectly flat—whatever forest may once have been here is completely gone. After about a mile we paused at a large new temple of precisely the Birla Temple type—same stone, same art and architecture. The main image was of Kṛṣṇa holding a *cakra*, like a saucer, on the tip of his right forefinger: black image dressed in red cloth, with a garland. There was a stone sign, inlaid in both Hindi and English, that appeared at several points around the outside and at the doors of the temple, welcoming all Indians of all sects, but warning: "Spitting, deciphering and disfiguring strictly forbidden."

Here we picked up a chap who offered to be my guide to the temples of Brindavan, and spoke an almost intelligible English. He followed my tonga on a bicycle, occasionally shouting out the names of the places we were passing. I felt quite romantic about Kṛṣṇa's boyhood. The peasants were in the fields and along the roads. We passed a couple of camels and a little baboon sat by the roadside like a very small man.

Then we came to Brindavan and a wildly rushing visit to the temples began. I thought of Jerusalem: same idea only a little shoddier. A great number of hideous temples. We climbed around the outside of one that had a number of southern-style *gopuras*, the Rangji Temple, biggest in the city, built between 1845–1851, and had a good view of the whole city from one of its towers. The Govind Dev Temple ruin, *c.* A.D. 1590, I saw from the road: a considerably better style. Next, I was conducted through a run of narrow streets, and entered a place with votive stones all over the floor. Leaving my shoes, I was conducted into a small room with a number of priests sitting around before a shrine, which was lighted for me. Within were five images—father and mother in the rear and rather large, three children before—Kṛṣṇa, Bālarāma, Subhadrā—all crude and tawdry, dressed and completely unalive. I was told that this was one of the oldest temples in Brindavan and these very old images, and I was to make a donation of three-quarters of a rupee. When I offered three-quarters I was told that that was the minimum. Having seen a good deal of misery on the streets and believing for a moment what I had been told, namely, that the money was for the poor, I gave six rupees and annas (about two dollars) and was given *prasāda*, asked to write my name and that of my father in the big book, and pleasantly dismissed.

At the place of departure, there was a scattering of annas on a tablet. I was told that four annas had to be given here. And then there was the shoe boy: two annas. "No more temples," I said to my guide. "Back to the tonga." He conducted me around a few corners and before I knew it I was in a second "very old" temple, where I was given almost exactly the same story—and I was now sore. "I told you," I said to my guide who was sitting beside me, "no more. I will not give six rupees or three rupees". But to save the situation I gave two: refused however to sign my name in the book—took the *prasāda* angrily, and left. We returned to the tonga. I was shown the place (tree and pond) "where Kṛṣṇa dove from the tree to kill Kāliya"![39] The guide demanded ten rupees (like a fool, I had failed to ask his fee at the start), and I sat in the tonga while my driver finished eating.

The drive back to Mathurā was distinguished, pleasantly, by two events. When we passed the little baboon the driver tossed him some food, and a whole tribe of his kind came down from all the trees; little mothers with their babies hanging to their necks, underneath; and they were still coming the last we saw them. Then, suddenly, I heard in loud duet: "Baksheesh Sahib!..." on and on, and turning to look back found two youngsters, a boy and a girl, hanging on to my tonga, running magnificently, and shouting into my face. When they had run about one hundred and fifty yards, I handed each two annas and they let me go.

Passing the museum again, I thought for a moment that it might be worth stopping to see if the curator had come in, but decided against it. I was dead tired, disgruntled, and had a bit of a headache. So I returned to the station. My train to Agra was to leave at 7:00 P.M., which meant that I had four hours to spend. But when I entered the waiting room the Sikh attendant drew a large easy chair up to a table for me, and a little boy brought me tea and cake. I drank all the ice water out of my thermos, I had a little doze, and I woke up about four, feeling fine. Then—chastened by the adventures of the day—I got out my Berlitz Hindi book and reviewed the first forty pages before it began to get dark.

Life in the waiting room and on the station platform was something wonderful. People sleeping, changing their clothes, monks, soldiers, whatnots. When the trains arrive, they get in and out from both sides—the platform side and the other. They hop down onto the tracks and run across. Guys are urinating everywhere. Vendors are shouting everywhere, with stoves smoking on their heads, trays of cakes etc.—and wicker stands in their hands upon which they set their trays, taking them down from their heads. Two earlier trains for Agra passed, but they were only third-class and I let them go. I was having a fine time at the station. Then at seven my train came and I was off for Agra.

Another good hotel, Laurie's: same management as the Cecil in Delhi. The taxi driver who took me from the train offered to drive me to the Taj for seven rupees, after dinner. I got cleaned up, had dinner, and went to the Taj. Full moon. Really lovely. Like a fool I had left my camera at the Hotel—could easily have taken a picture. At the gate, I met the Cunninghams, who helped me get past a little guide named Jimmy, so that I might see the Taj alone. And I remained about an hour. Went down into the crypt. Heard all the stories, paid all the little tolls, and returned to the hotel for a good night's sleep.

September 15 ***Agra***

Mother's birthday: last year Jean and I were in Paris.

Agra, definitely, is for tourists, and the hotel reveals, even at this early, pre-tourist season, a number of the standard American types: the fat ladies with their husbands, from Ohio or New York, the drinks before dinner crowd, etc. At the entrance to the hotel sits a man with a snake—once it was two men, one with a cobra in a basket, the other with a mongoose on a string. For a sum, one could see the mongoose and cobra fight.

My driver took me to the Fort, where I had an excellent guide, then to the Taj—where Jimmy got hold of me, and finally to the tomb of I'timad-ud-daula across the river. In the afternoon I decided to go to Fatehpur Sikri by bus. I received my information from the Tourist Bureau, and took a bicycle-rickshaw to the bus terminal. I was about an hour ahead of time, and so, went for a walk through town.

Quite a town! Camels here and there. One naked old man blandly walking around. One young woman with a rather stupid look and her head shaved, wearing a dirty sari without bodice, and the end of the sari simply flung over one shoulder. Cows and water buffalo, everywhere, of course. Streets and streets of shops. A great emphasis on shoe shops and shoe manufacture. Horrible food displays. Kids, half or totally naked, everywhere. I took another rickshaw back to the stinking bus terminal. Men's urinals and women's urinals: the air was thick.

The bus was full of noisy and pleasant males on their way back to their villages. Beside me, however, in the "upper class" seat was a surly Indian gentleman, who was totally out of the picture. It took an hour and a quarter, with very long stops at two or three villages, for us to reach Fatehpur Sikri, so that I had very little time in which to see the buildings. A tall youth showed me the old walled city of Akbar in excellent style, and I returned to the road just in time to catch the bus home.

These two days have given me a rather close look at the village life of this part of India. The level of dirt and well-being is about that of the Pueblos of New Mexico, I should say. This, apparently, is the basic level of India. The peasant life, in fact, might be said to have determined the character, also, of the cities: cows, water buffalo herds, goat, donkey, and sheep droves even on the main streets. But in the cities one finds a heavily populated level even lower than this: that of the beggars and the utterly destitute. These two levels are met by that of the tiny shopkeeps in the towns and cities. Millions of people—millions of little jobs well done—and the total is a curiously unsystematized cultural vitality. The people in their misery and absolutely gentle and strong. And yet the whole thing has something crazy about it, which is epitomized in this nutty business of the cows. India will never become a modern nation as long as these cows are here—even the trains have to watch out for them. It is the cows that slow down the whole pace and make for a kind of general Bohemia. With them, naked old men and everything else is possible. Without them, India will be out of her troubles!

My train left at ten-something, and at Gwalior, 12:20 A.M., I took a tonga to the Hotel—an Indian-run hotel this time. The porter was sound asleep at the entrance. The door was open for me. I was conducted to my suite of rooms (glorious, but with practically all of the mechanical elements somewhat out of order), and went right off to sleep.

Thursday, September 16 *Gwalior*

I woke up to rain—a strong pouring. The man who brought my bed tea said it was going to rain all day, and for several days. I thought of giving up my Khajurāho plans; but decided to wait before making my decision. I wrote all morning in my diary. But by lunchtime it was clear and I went with a guide to the fine tomb of Muhammad Guus—with a squad of soldiers sleeping in its verandah; then up to the Fort. On the way up to the Fort, the gigantic Jain statues of Gwalior. On the plateau of the Fort, a perfectly charming series of Hindu palaces and little temples including a frightening subterranean chamber where prince Murad was hung from what formerly had been the rings of a swing, by his younger brother Aurangzeb. Yesterday I saw where this same Aurangzeb imprisoned and then blinded his father Akbar.[40]

Also the tomb of the musician Tansen. (The tree that is supposed to give one a singer's voice is no longer there.) By far the most interesting adventure so far.

The Archaeological Museum has a fine lot of Śuṅga, Gupta, and later pieces—not too well displayed, however, in the rooms of what was once a palace. Many pieces of sculpture with which I was familiar turned up. The bronzes are exceptionally interesting: many Hindu and Buddhist Tantric pieces—crudely labeled, and exhibited in glass cases (some with rippled glass) that make it very difficult to see.

The Gwalior palaces give a somewhat richer and more charming effect than the Muslim palaces that I have seen. It is clear, also, that the basic architectural principles of the Muslim works in India are not very different—if different at all—from the Hindu. The Muslims had a much more grandiose eye than the Hindus for geometrical spatial arrangements of buildings over and against each other; also, apparently, for all their abhorrence of sensuous pictures and images, a much stronger emphasis on actual erotic enjoyment: checker boards with girls for pieces—hide-and-seek buildings—ponds where girls would sit playing lutes while Akbar bathed, etc. etc. The Hindu princes may have had all this too—but it doesn't show in the buildings: or rather, perhaps yes; for what went on in these curious little swing rooms?

The palace was a new experience for me; and the little temples that I saw were charming. The day gave me a pleasant feeling of having broken through the Muslim crust, at last, into the Hindu world.

Friday, September 17 ***Gwalior–Allahabad***

A railroad record: Gwalior to Allahabad in fifteen hours and forty minutes—a distance of about 250 miles—average rate of travel, about fifteen miles an hour. But I saw the countryside and the villages.

I got up at 5:30 A.M., had tea and toast, walked to the station beside a man who was carrying my luggage on his head, and boarded my train. Two sleepers in the lower berths. I opened my bed roll on an upper, and lay down. At 6:00 A.M. change trains at Jhansi, in the pouring rain. We arrived at Harpalpur, the place from which I was supposed to take a bus to Khajurāho at about 9:00 A.M. But the station master refused to take charge of my baggage (it was a minute and dirty county station, about as big as Mast Hope,[41] in which there would not be any place for me to sleep—and, besides, it was raining a little), so I decided to pass up Khajurāho and go on to Allahabad. At Manikpur I had tea and a cake of chocolate (my only bite since 3:45 A.M.) and a little chat with a gent at the station. He said that the richest part of India agriculturally was that between the Ganges and the Jumna. The area that I was in, however, was rocky and poor. The people looked poor, all right, but they have looked poor everywhere I have been.

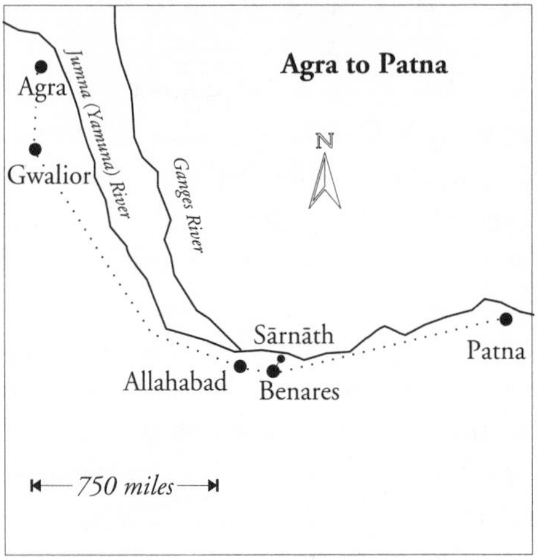

The rain now was coming down hard, and the rivers that the train crossed were flowing, full of muddy water, between sprawling banks. Made me think of the Kansas-Nebraska area. And the people looked like figures from eighteenth-century travelers' engravings of India—the men with moustaches and shaved heads, save for the orthodox hair tuft at the place of the cowlick; wearing dhotis, either with or without a shirt; and the women, of course, simply bundled in their usually rather drab and dirty saris. (I find that though the sari may look fine as a sort of surprise in a New York drawing room, as a regular thing it is a dismal flop.) Particularly notable following the rains was the vivid bird life all along the way: the most beautiful herons and cranes in every field and puddle.

At one of the stations before Manikpur, a young couple with their baby got into the compartment and conversed a bit in English together. The baby slept soundly; the girl paid close attention to her needlework; the husband looked out the window. At Manikpur they waited, not far from me, in the "Refreshments" building—the girl again strictly devoted to her needlework. I have the impression that men and women do not have much in common in this country, except their children, whom they treat very sweetly. I notice few couples. Usually it's men together and bunches of women together. (At the Mission talks, the men and women sat separately.)

When I finally boarded my train I was placed in a compartment with three large gents—a Sikh and two others. One of the others invited me to sit on the bench with him, and recognized me as American (in fact everyone does). We conversed in a strong yet friendly fashion, and I got the whole Indian picture, I think, of the U.S.A:

(1) Not Russia and China, but the U.S.A., is the power itching for a fight. The concept of Asia for the Asians is simply an *a priori* in this part of the world, so that China's claim to Formosa is simply unquestioned. Chiang Kai Shek is despised, and the U.S. support of him is regarded as a belligerent act. (2) The U.N. is not really a union of all nations, but a clique, representing a limited set of interests. (3) American aid to India is a device to create military allies, and also to get rid of American goods, so that the wheels of our industry can keep turning. (4) The war criminal trials were a farce: Roosevelt and Churchill should have been tried. (5) The two atom bombs on two cities in Japan were dropped *after* peace negotiations had been opened, as a military test of the force of this weapon. (6) War is on the way right now, and will probably break in two or three years. (7) This war will finish both Russia and the U.S.A. (8) The hot spots are Formosa and Pakistan.

This gentleman, Mr. Ghosh of Calcutta, is an engineer, and has no love for the British. He has a cousin who was in a British jail during the troubles, and is now an invalid—from what they did to him: they made him sleep naked between two cakes of ice, one above, one below; and they hung him from the ceiling by the wrists, with weights on his ankles, so that now all his joints are ruptured. Mr. Ghosh, also, was born in Dacca, and tells the old tale of what Warren Hastings did to the weavers of Dacca.[42] He invited me to visit him in Calcutta, and we exchanged addresses.

Saturday, September 18 ***Allahabad***

After breakfast I took a cycle rickshaw to the museum, which is full of both good and bad: the bad is modern—and includes the Roerich Collection that used to hang in New York. The good is a fine lot of sculpture, from Bhārhut to Khajurāho; and a wonderful collection of Mughal and Rajput paintings. Practically everything is displayed against the light or in glass cabinets, so that it is impossible to see.

Following my visit to the museum, I asked my boy to peddle me to the Fort, where there is an Aśoka pillar: but we found that the Fort was now Restricted Military Property—and so I asked to go to the junction of the Ganges and the Jumna. Presently and suddenly four shouting men were hooked to my rickshaw, running beside me. They wanted me to ride in their boat. Finally I gave in and was whisked up an embankment and into one of the large skiffs that lined the shore.

Four men rowed, one steered, and we soon were out in the vast stretch of muddy water where the two rivers (waters of different colors) joined—just off a little island formed of the silt, where a colony of little hut-shrines, with staffs and banners, could be seen, filled with people attending to various religious tasks. I was told to take a sip of the water and place a paper rupee on the water as an offering. I obeyed, and one of the boatmen, with a laugh, took up the rupee.

We went around behind the island and put to shore, at a point below the wall of the fort, where there was an entrance. A childish figure of Kālī, with her tongue out, was on the shore—a kind of doll, which an old woman had set up and was guarding—before which money might be dropped. Also there was a man there with a cow that had a curious loose growth coming out of its neck with an extra set of horns at the end. The man was exhibiting his animal and collecting coins. And there were the usual saintly beggars—as at Brindavan and Jerusalem.

I followed a guide who took me through the portal along a narrow walk between high walls, to an open area, where a lot of voices could be heard coming up through air vents, out of the ground. "Underground Temple," I was told; and so it was. I removed my shoes and went down with a swarm of pilgrims. I was conducted through the underground vestibules, where there were dozens of assorted images: a few old pieces in a style of *c.* A.D. 1000-1200 (dancing Ganeśa, Śiva, Pārvatī, Viṣṇu, etc.) but also many curious folk-pieces of gods whose names I had never heard. The full list of gods: Dharmrājā, Annapūrṇā, Viṣṇu, Lakṣmī, Ganeśa, Bālamukunda, Durvāsa, Prayāgrājā, Satyanarāyaṇa, Kāla Bhairava, Dattatreya, Narasiṁha, Śaṅkarajī, Surya Narāyaṇa, Hanumān, Yamunā, Siddha Nātha (a *liṅga*), Gaṅgā, Kubera, Veda Vyāsa, Pārvatī (with the child Ganeśa), Gorakha Nātha, Agni Deva, Venimādhava, Sarasvatī, Ram and Sītā with Lakṣmana, Śeṣanāga, Yamarājā, Jagannātha and two or three more *liṅgas.*

I returned to my boat, purchasing on the way, a picture of the temple with its gods, and was rowed ashore. A quibble over the fees, and then a rickshaw ride back to my hotel.

The name of the underground temple is Akṣaya Vṛkṣa, and it is the temple (I now read in *Murray's Guide*) of the "Undying Banyan."[43] The tree was described by Hiuen Tsang (A.D. 629–645): "In the midst of the city," he states, "stood a Brahmanical temple to which the presentation of a single piece of money procured as much merit as that of a thousand pieces elsewhere. Before the principal room of the temple was a tree surrounded by the bones of pilgrims who had sacrificed their lives there." All seems to be associated with some sacred banyan Akṣaya Vṛkṣa. The pilgrims, like myself, went from image to image as their guide, like mine, rapidly named the deities. Many placed little coins at the feet of the figures, touched the feet and then touched their heads.

The Ganges at this place is one-and-a-half miles broad, and the Jumna half a mile broad. "The shallower and more rapid Ganges [on which my trip commenced] is of a muddy color, the Jumna is bluer with a deeper bed. The Māgha Melā, a religious fair of great antiquity, is held at Triveṇī every year, between 15th January and 15th February...and every twelfth year the festival is known as the Kumbha Melā." Here, then, was that great calamity of this year when hundreds were killed in a great crush. Off these shores, also, is the place where Gandhi's ashes were consigned to the waters. Well, it was a considerable spot to which I was conducted by my lunatic boatmen: and now I do not begrudge them their fee of—twenty rupees! Very tired, I simply remained in my room, sleeping and writing, all afternoon.

Allahabad, I find, is a comparatively clean and orderly city—quite modern, really (at least, what I have seen of it), except, of course, for the ubiquitous cows. I have a feeling that there must have been an American military post here during the war, because everything has a rather American tone. My hotel is an Indian hotel—with the radio playing American jazz and the girl at the desk (daughter of the manager) wearing a western dress.

And I should record that when my train pulled, last night, into the big station, I felt—after my week of little whistle stops, quaint villages, and rural scenery—definitely at home and greatly relieved. The city, I guess, is the normal place for man, because shaped by man to the needs of man; whereas the country is simply a transitional zone, which man inhabits between his state as animal and his full estate as man. (A bit of heresy, to contradict the Romantic "back to Nature.")

Sunday, September 19 ***Allahabad–Benares***

I begin to think that the main division between the past and the future of civilization is that of *literacy*—made possible by the machine (the press), and representing the viewpoint of the scientific method.[44] In India, Jerusalem, and Lourdes, we see the survival of the past. The dark side of literacy is Yellow Journalism and Demagoguery. Meeting the minds of the not-yet-quite literate. I do not know how far the crude protelariat atheism of the Russians and the late nineteenth century counts in all this, but perhaps it should be reckoned to the dark side of literacy.

The chief spiritual problem of literacy is to retain the positive values of the ancient mythological mode of pedagogy without falling back into superstition. This problem is being faced by the Zimmer-Jung-Eranos team.[45]

The educated preachers of religion today are the protectors of the Western soul, for which an effective new pedagogy has not yet been devised. In the past, the creative, vitalizing principle in religion was the intelligent thinking and self-discipline of the élite. Today this élite is not religious. The religious, consequently, have declined to the level of popular superstition, and on two levels: that of bourgeois religiosity, and that of folk or peasant religiosity.[46]

And so now to Benares.

No second-class car on the train, so I rode third class: not uncomfortable, though a hard seat; and not as smelly as second class, because the toilet was down the other end of the car instead of immediately next door. Nice people, as always; mostly of the farmer type, with a couple of something else: fine old gentlemen (one spoke English very well) with Śiva marks on their foreheads. One had his white beard knotted curiously underneath.

Arrival in Mughal Sarai about 3:20. Another case of very slow travel: three hours for about seventy-five miles. Then a tonga, some eight miles, to Clark's Hotel, Benares. Tired, I showered, had dinner, and went early to bed.

A few thoughts on the road and in the hotel. I am now realizing that much of what I at first thought was great poverty is only the norm of peasant life in a pre-industrial society—that, let us say, is the norm of India. Below that, however, there is real poverty in abundance. There is no bottom here to the distance one can drop.

Everywhere, one meets with the same gentleness and general good humor, also an easy friendliness with life's dirt, reminding me, I think, more of Italy than of any place else I've ever seen. Again a fundamental peasant quality? On the other hand, a certain very hard attitude toward each other in the matter of money. The tipping of porters, etc., is on a cruel level. I watched a tea-vendor wait for the last *paisa* from a blind beggar boy before he would hand out his cup of tea.

At the hotel a radio was playing American jazz music, with advertisements, etc., in an English accent, broadcast from somewhere in India. A curious shock: but not unwelcome either. Someone sang *Mammy* (can you believe it?)—and I thought, not a bad song at all in Annapūrṇa's city! "I'd go a million miles for one of your smiles, my Ma...ammy." And the town is full of pilgrims; full also of Indian holy pictures no less awful, as art, than Jolson's *Mammy.*

At the hotel, also, a number of American guests: one male with an appallingly coarse-looking, leather-tanned, heavily developed face. A very different type than the noble Indian faces I had been seeing on the peasants. But then, also, a few non-peasant Indians are in the hotel also—and they are nothing better than the Americans. On the other hand, when I think of Vermont farmers, etc., it seems to me that we may have a touch of the peasant type also: just a touch, however, since our peasantry is not of the primary stock, for the most part, but rather a deterioration from originally bourgeois immigrants.

Monday, September 20 ***Benares***

I went in the morning, by cycle-rickshaw, to the Ramakrishna Mission, where I found Swami and the ladies. Mrs. D. was laid up with a broken toe, fractured in a slip at that temple-dock at Allahabad. I was conducted through the premises. Impressive: a considerable hospital and old-folks home with an ashram attached; many monks, doing hospital work: about a thousand patients treated a day—I went through some of the wards. The Ramakrishna Mission is definitely a strong and respectable organization; and it now is enjoying the support of the Indian government. It seems likely that this kind of work will continue to grow, and will represent a valid and effective adjustment of Hinduism to the modern world. Compare the work of the Franciscans, Little Sisters of the Poor, St. Vincent's Hospital, etc.

Stayed for lunch at the ashram (sattvic food and edible); then had my cycle-rickshaw take me to the river, where I visited a couple of the ghats. And here again, I was properly impressed—by the faces and quietness of the people at the Ganges. Strange little streets leading right to the water; little shrines close to the river; a young cow standing on a platform; people sitting; a few dipping into the water; many with forehead markings. Boatmen approached me, but my reply was "not today," and they didn't overdo their pressing (for a pleasant change).

I returned to the hotel and rested. Worked a little on proofs and Hindi and went to bed. The weather is fearfully humid and hot, and I seem to get tired very fast.

Benares along the Ganges

Tonight I feel that in Benares I have found something closer to the India I came to see than anything I saw in New Delhi. A great inconvenience, however, is the distance of the hotel from everything. One can understand it, though—one can also understand the British dinner-jacket formula. The whole pattern of Indian life is so alien—and dirty—and so many of the people are sick—that, unless one is bent on "losing oneself" it is not possible to move right into the native cities. These English "cantonments," furthermore, show what India would be if the Indians would pay a bit of attention to space: and I note that they are supplying the model for much of the building of the new India.

A few little notes: I perceive that my table cloth is slightly dirty, from the people who were at the table before me. In no hotel that I have visited have the fixtures been in perfect repair—except, perhaps, the Hotel Cecil in New Delhi, where the only trouble was the archaic character of the fixtures. The meals, in general, are to be graded "poor to fair." Too bad it was the English kitchen (the worst in the Occident) that was introduced to India. I am sure that there is not a really decent place to eat in the whole subcontinent—and that the Indians don't even know it. My formula for touring in India now is: *the most interesting and least enjoyable country in the world.*

Tuesday, September 21

This afternoon immediately after lunch, I set off for Benares Hindu University with my same cycle-rickshaw to meet a Professor Das Gupta[47] who was going to show me around. It took over an hour to complete the trip, however, and the campus was huge, so I failed to find him.

I paused first at the Museum, and asked my way; then went to the Arts Building and goofed around. Went finally into a room marked "Philosophy," where I had seen a huge, light-colored monk (plump and about 6 ft. 9 in. tall), and this man met me at the door.

"Guten tag," he said. "Sind Sie Deutscher?"

"Nein," I answered, "Ich bin Amerikaner."

"Aber Sie sprechen sehr gutes Deutsch," he said.

He was Viennese—now a Śaṅkara monk—and knew Swami Nikhilananda; his name: Swami Agehananda.[48]

And so my first encounter with India's pandits was in German.

On the wall of the office were photos of Jung, Freud, Charles Moore of the University of Hawaii, Radhakrishnan, and some others. The Viennese Swami is teaching philosophy at the college and attended to a few students while I sat and recovered a bit from my rickshaw ride. He failed to help me find Das Gupta, and presently, after cruising a bit more around the campus I returned home.

My sins must be dropping from me, because I begin to feel that I am recovering something of a repose that I remember from long, long ago: I don't know when. Part of it, of course, is that I am taking things very easily. Part of it is that no more jobs-to-do are piling in on me. But there is something more than that to it, and I think it's very nice.

Wednesday, September 22

I spent the morning preparing the talk for this afternoon, then took my rickshaw to Vasant College at Raj Ghat, at the northern terminus of Benares, where the Varuna River enters the Ganges. A Miss Telang met me and introduced me to her brother and another gentleman—all teachers at the college. Then we had a nice Indian lunch—on the mild side as to heat. I was shown about the establishment: the little ones were at lunch; sitting in a large circle on the floor of their kindergartens—very cute. I saw the art class, a dance class, a music class, and glimpsed several lecture rooms at work. The whole effect, quite idyllic and pleasant. The youngsters learn history and geography of India, mathematics, music, Hindi, a bit of Sanskrit, science, and a few other items. I noticed some emphasis on crafts (leatherwork).

I had been told that my lecture would be for faculty and a few upper classmen. Actually, a large auditorium was full of students sitting on the floor: three quarters girls, in front; one quarter boys. My first lecture without shoes. The questions were cute: What is done in America about the health and recreation of the students? What about military training? Have you been to Red China? What do American students think of Indian students? What about sport? Do you teach gardening? Are students interested in music? What do you think of Indian students? I had tea with some members of the faculty and took my rickshaw home.

Thursday, September 23 ***Sārnāth***

Took my rickshaw at 9 A.M. to Sārnāth, about five miles: a beautiful museum, and a beautiful visit, with my scrawny rickshaw man as guide. Returned to the hotel by 1 p.m, and at 5 P.M. I took my rickshaw to the Durgā (Monkey) Temple. The priests sort of fastened on to me, and I was sitting with one of them in the rickshaw, when a car stopped: Swami and his party! Pleasant greetings, and our separate cruises continued.

The whole political level of the visit, has, I hope, been passed. My last observation on the subject: Nehru told Swami, when Swami visited him, that it might well be that China and India would grow geographically. "Strong nations always grow." And so what has this to do with the Peaceful Coexistence formula? Answer: Peaceful Coexistence is the *Artha Śāstra's* *saman*—singing a soothing song, till strength is available for *daṇḍa*, hitting.

As I look at this country and think of America, I see two very different worlds. The two cultures have stemmed from the conditions of two very different sets of historical circumstances. As I stated in my Delhi lecture—Indian philosophy, inasmuch as it has influenced the American mind, has done so only to the extent of giving fresh stimulus to ideas that were present in the American philosophy in the first place, e.g. a metaphysical tone to the "all men are equal" idea. Comparably, the American machines, democratic principles, etc. are going to be taken by India in her own way.

At Sārnāth, the lovely spirituality of the Buddhist images was immensely impressive. I visited the museum, whereI was addressed by a Hindu gentleman who was there with his wife and family. When he learned I was from New York his wife couldn't drag him away. And I soon was wishing that she would succeed. He was full of advice for me, as to how to see India. Really a charming gent, but enough was enough. He was tall, lean, with shining eyes, a prodigious voice, and a heroic flourish. A kind of Bengali Don Quixote. When his wife finally walked out and later sent the guard in to get him, he left, but soon was back; then at last left for keeps. "If I were alone," he said, "we could talk; but, you see: I am with my wife!"and then a Jain temple: quite modern: the guard showed me the main image: obviously Ṛṣabhanātha (with the bull symbol on the pedestal) but the guard declared it was Pārśvanātha.

Then on to a modern Buddhist temple built with money from Ceylon, Japan, and Honolulu: pictures of the Buddha life by a Japanese artist. The Chinese Buddhist temple I saw next was somewhat different in spirit: the pictures around the walls, however, were trite English prints of the Buddha's life in a semi-Indian style.

Finally I came to the Monkey Temple mentioned above. The same impression overcame me here as in Brindavan: the main interest of the priest was that I should put some money down on the altars. He had a couple of worn heads, from perhaps the Gupta period, and a coarse statue of Hanumān. He wanted rupees for each. I gave him one rupee for all—and seeing that I knew what he was doing, he finally had to smile.

I noticed that the place where a goat is sacrificed every morning (and a buffalo on feast days) is situated about where the *nandi* is placed in a Śiva temple compound. So: *nandi*, the sacrifice, has become the vehicle of the god (a general law here for *vāhana*?). Is the buffalo sacrifice (beheaded with one stroke of the priest's sword) related to the theme of Durgā, slayer of the buffalo demon? Here is a great sacrifice, as in voodoo. Mediterranean goddess associated with goats (see Ras Shamra bas relief); goat sacrifice belongs to same culture context as pig-sacrifice, in the Melanesian context, cf. Sebseb of Malekula. It is said that earlier than the goat sacrifice in this temple was a human sacrifice (Polynesian context).[49]

Next to the Monkey Temple, across the pond, is a white marble tomb, to Swami Bhāskarānanda—the only object of beauty that I have seen in Benares.

Friday, September 24

Submitted this morning, before breakfast, to the quiet barber who has been pestering me every day: and he gave me a very good haircut. I felt like an eighteenth-century gentleman with the barber visiting me in my own rooms.

After breakfast my rickshaw man carried me off toward the river. Near the Dasāśvamedha Ghat he stopped, got off his cycle, and fetched me a man with yellow and white lines on his forehead, who was to be my guide for the trip. This gentleman saw me into a skiff, climbed in beside me, and named the buildings and ghats as we passed them: first, upstream close to shore, then downstream, out in the river, then back upstream again (with great difficulty) to the Dasāśvamedha Ghat, or rather something close to it, where we disembarked. I paid the boatman and followed my guide through a labyrinth of narrow alleys, populated as heavily with cows as with Hindus. We saw the Nepalese temple of Paśupati Nātha (the so-called Temple of Love) with its mildly obscene little carvings, the Golden Temple, the Jñāna Vāpī (Well of Knowledge), Temple of Annapūrṇa and Temple of Sākhī Vināyaka—all crowded among narrow cow-filled alleys. Cows were in the temples. Beggars lined the walls of the alleys. There was one spectacular row of some thirty widows, sitting in silence with their empty rice bowls. A fantastic place. I was again pursued by priests for baksheesh, and was finally glad to get out. We then passed through alleys of shops and finally sat down for a nice warm Coca-Cola.

My rickshaw next brought me to the Ramakrishna Mission, where I found Swami down with a slight fever and sore throat, Mrs. D. with her foot still in a cast, and the Countess with some kind of stomach ailment. I had lunch with the ladies—a slightly palatable monk's meal (no wonder they all feel ill!)—and decided that I had just about finished my visit to Benares. So I told them I'd see them all in Calcutta and pushed off.

I spent the afternoon asleep and writing to Jean. They had a letter from her over at the Mission. Nice news about Bard.[50]

Benares traffic: cows, goats, a few dogs, stray chickens, occasional camels, millions of bicycles and cycle-rickshaws; occasional cars, bullock carts, donkeys, guys everywhere taking leaks, kids shitting in the gutter, hundreds of little shops full of people, other shops, larger, nicely rugged, with gentleman-shopkeepers peacefully lounging, often reading books.

The temple traffic: a great business of tossing flowers at gods, touching their feet, sipping water, and passing along. I now want to see Lourdes.

Saturday, September 25 ***Benares–Patna***

I think what strikes me most about Benares is the combination of ancient Indian religiousity with the new institutions of learning. The city is full of schools and colleges: Vasant College, Hindu University, Anglo-Bengali College, and others; also, Theosophical Society, and the Ramakrishna Mission. It is definitely a focus of a typically Indian spiritual ferment.

One month ago today, my departure from New York. I have come to some thoughts on Sārnāth-Benares.

The spirituality of the Gupta Buddhas and bodhisattvas was dramatically evident in contrast to the coarse quality of the contemporary Hindu cults. The Hindu gods represent those very powers of *māyā* from the grip of which the bodhisattvas bring release.[51] Consider the Monkey Temple, the coarse images of Ganeśa, Hanumān, etc., and the religious traffic of the ghats and temples. Durgā leads us back to Melanesia.

The Buddhas and bodhisattvas have absorbed many elements from Hinduism, but an essentially psychological orientation remains fundamental to their character.

The Jain attempt to break free from the clutches of the gods is less sophisticated than the Buddhist; Śaṅkara's way seems to carry more of the Jain world-negation than of the Buddhist world-assimilation via psychology.[52]

Zimmer's suggestion was that Hinduism spiritualized through the influence of Buddhism, and with the disappearance of Buddhism, the Hindu image returned to the level of the folk fetish. The problem here is: Buddhism is a continuation of the Upanishadic direction. What is the relationship of the Upanishadic tradition to folk-Hinduism?

Here is a project for a second visit to Benares: to study, one by one, the several cults of the several ghats—their histories and disciplines—also, to study the functioning and influence of the modern institutions: the colleges, Ramakrishna Mission, Theosophical Society, philanthropic institutions, etc.

Finally, a question for Ceylon, Burma, Siam, and Japan: what is the degree of Buddhism's decline in the realms of the folk.

At noon I leave for my train to Patna, which is due to arrive about 8 P.M. Another of these Indian locals. The guide, Mr. Alley, accompanied me to the station, bought my ticket, and, while waiting for the train talked about religion. He is a Mohammedan. Most of the boys and men I saw this morning were Mohammedans. He said that the Hindus in Benares are trying to pass a ruling forbidding Mohammedans to serve as guides in that city. (One sees how the Hindus can make it difficult, here and there.)

Then he gave me his statement on religion. All religions teach love, peace, and the road to heaven. Also, it is like a circle with a central point: some stress the central point, some the radii to the center, others, with many gods, the circumference; but all recognize the central point. And so all religions agree. But the priests of the religions teach prejudice and the supremacy of their own religion—and this is to their personal interest. Religion is all right, it is only what we make of it that is wrong.

Not bad, from a tourist guide: it can be used as a basic formula.

Sunday, September 26 ***Patna–Gaya–Patna***

I'm at the Grand Hotel in Patna. Very conspicuous plumbing: no water, except in a bucket.

My day in Patna began with the discovery that to get to Nālandā, I should have gotten up for a 6:25 train. I would have to save that for tomorrow. Gaya, however, could be reached by a 10:50 train. I had a cycle-rickshaw take me for a look at the nearer parts of the town and a pause at the museum. Along with several Satī stones, lots of terracottas from Maurya and later times, and the Chowry-bearer from Didarganj; all rather cluttered but not too badly arranged.

On the train to Gaya I shared the compartment with two Mohammedan gentlemen, one, a supervisor of schools in the Bihar area, about to retire; the other a district government supervisor of some kind. The latter, particularly, was eager to talk. I should visit Pakistan he said; they were very grateful there for American aid. "That is surprising," I said: "that anyone should be grateful there for American aid." "No," said my friend; "in Pakistan they are really grateful. They are different from the Hindus. Give to Hindu, they say, and he will insult you." I got the feeling that the Mohammedans in India do not share the Hindu resentment for American aid to Pakistan. They said that what America has given India in the way of aid is actually more than what is being given to Pakistan.

In Gaya I had a Sikh driver take me by taxi to Bodhgayā, where I viewed the temple and adjacent lotus tank, with bathers, for about an hour. My Bengali friend from Sārnāth came shouting up the stairs to greet me. And I took a lot of photos. There was not time enough to visit the Viṣṇupada

Temple, where there is an imprint of Viṣṇu's foot; but did visit an Akṣaya Vṛkṣa (another "deathless banyan"—cf. Allahabad[53]), where I found a rather nice ancient temple (perhaps A.D. 1100) beside the affair now in use. Two of the priests approached me, smiling, and, now as tired of priests as of beggars, I made my escape by pleading train time.

On the return train, which left Gaya at 4 P.M., I shared the compartment with a doctor, supervisor of the work being done in these districts. I asked whether his work had been helped at all by the World Health Organization. "Yes," he said, "but." And the buts were that the WHO does not employ enough Hindu doctors—they could make more use of the good men already in India; and that the people they send out are not particularly great: they sent one Dane who was no good, and a woman from somewhere else, who was better. He spoke also of the American technical aid to the farmers as though it meant something positive.

And then, of course, we droned off onto the problems of India's reconstruction and the differences between India and America. As for the slowness of the trains: India had had two terrible accidents some years ago, and now the trains (those, that is to say, that are not the great Mail trains) have to keep below 30 miles per hour—the tracks, for the most part, won't stand anything faster. And he advised me, furthermore, to go to Nālandā and Rajgir by a 6:00 A.M. bus.

When our train pulled into the station at 7 P.M. (again a three-hour ride) a multitude of students swarmed out of it, shouting, and gaily hopped all the barriers past the guard.

Monday, September 27 ***Patna–Nālandā–Patna***

Up at 4:45 A.M. for breakfast and a get-away to the bus station. My hotel proprietor had his two men-of-all-work give me a package of sandwiches for the day, and I took also a thermos of cold water. The bus actually left at 6:30 A.M., and at 11 A.M. it set me down at a crossroad marked Nālandā, sixty-three miles from Patna. A boy with a cart and a poor, miserable horse offered to drive me to the University ruins[54] for two rupees, so I boarded his contraption. He kept striking his nag on the tip of its prominent spine, which was such a torture for the poor animal that it continually kicked; I was dead tired, besides, and the sun was like fire. When I was set down at the path to the University, I walked slowly and was gradually revived by the sight of the red brick walls. One could already feel the campus atmosphere! The size of the compound is impressive, and the orderliness very pleasant. The guard had me sign in his book, and I was so shaken I spilt the bottle of ink over the page. In silence we blotted it up. I toured the grounds and took a few photos, then went to visit the museum; Moitessier's Buddha, Naga King, and the rest.

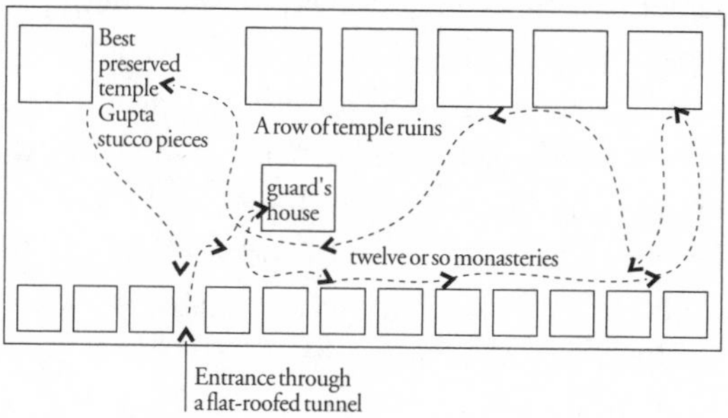

On the drive back the horse was made to kick more than ever, and I was really irritated, but my Hindi was not up to telling the kid to quit, since I was in no hurry. Getting back to the crossroad about noon, I managed, however, to learn that the next bus to Patna would not come until 3:00 P.M. I would have time to drive the four miles to Rajgir, but I would have to go with that kid and horse, and besides, the sun was getting worse; I decided instead to go and lie down under a tree and eat my lunch. At the crossroad there were a few little huts with people consuming food, and so I moved down the road a few yards. At the huts were a number of students who had been to visit the ruins, and a few of the peasants of the neighborhood with their kids.

I am getting quite a view of the peasant life of India on these trips, so the hours spent are not a total loss. This time, as I opened my package, a tall man approached and quietly stood watching me. I found that I had a bunch of little bananas in my bag. Taking one of them I gave him the rest and he went away. When I had finished eating I lay down for a rest, and another nice man came and stood by smiling. I had left about two bread-and-butter sandwiches in the bag. So I gave him these and he went away. A chipmunk halfway up the tree presently discovered me and made a lot of amusing noise.

At about 1:15 P.M. there was a lot of noise over toward the crossroad and along came a little narrow-gauge train, heading Patna way. I got up, ran for it, and caught it. The students caught it also. They boarded the first car, I the other. The inhabitants were peasants, and one young fellow in the usual white started a conversation; he proved to be an inspector of the villages in connection with the government's rehabilitation project. The conductor of the train, who could hardly catch our English, sat and listened. I was told of the work being done and of some of the problems. One problem was that of arousing in the villagers a desire to help themselves; another, of course, that of money: very little could be done, but a few selected villages were being assisted—and these might serve as examples for others. The main plan was to furnish implements, seeds, etc. on long- and short-term payments, the villagers were to repay the government from the proceeds of their produce; the repaid money would then be invested for other villages. One of India's great problems of the past was the absentee landlord *(zamindar)*, who did nothing to improve the farm's condition but simply received his money (contrast the American big-farmer and rancher, e.g. Ronald von Holt[55]). India now has to breed its stock, crops, and everything else. (I have noticed that the native plows and method of plowing is precisely that shown on Egyptian reliefs!)

Presently the conversation shifted toward America and I was back in my act. The kibitzer-conductor asked the standard communist line question—"Why does America want war?"—but walked away before I could reply.

The night ended at 6:00 A.M. with a great banging at my door. I opened, and an Indian gentleman got in; but his wife called that she had found an absolutely empty compartment, so with a brief apology he got out again. I ordered tea and started the day. At 7:00 A.M. we stopped again. A sweeper came in and dusted out the sooty compartment, and two gentlemen entered. The one who sat on my side of the car was an engineer, and his conversation was another of those fine things that make one realize how much of old India is living still in these unlikely circumstances. We rehearsed what are by now the trite themes of India's improvement, the contrast with America, Nehru's importance ("we don't know what will happen when he goes"—my own guess: "peaceful coexistence" boys will move in from points north), and so on. Then we began talking about India's philosophy, and this engineer had the whole thing: he was a Hindu, and looked forward to the spread of education and elimination of superstition among the masses. He saw yoga as "achieving while alive what is achieved in death," and named an important sage, somewhere, whose name I have mislaid.

Calcutta

Tuesday, September 28

Calcutta is a great and very welcome change. I like the feel of a big city after all the rural life. One feels England here, more than any place so far. A considerable port. A sort of Chinatown with a great new city growing all around it. Cows are fewer than elsewhere. The rickshaws are hand-drawn. The traffic is heavy.

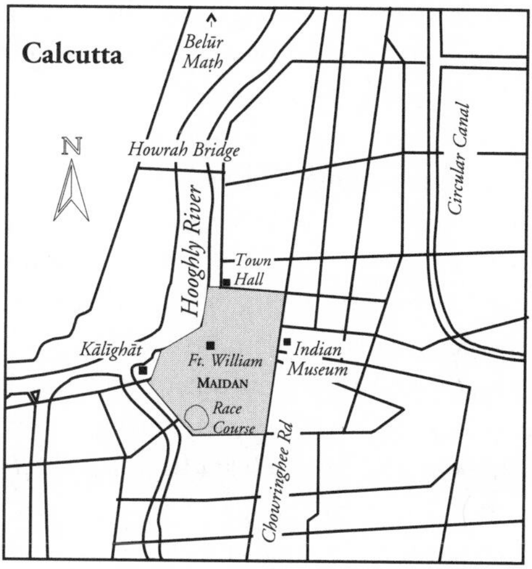

When I had rested and cleaned up, shaved and bathed in cold water at the Grand Eastern (vast hotel, cold water: India!), and felt a bit refreshed (the amount of soot that came off was incredible), I found my way to the American Express, collected my mail, and then began arranging for a visit to Darjeeling by air. The rest of the day was sleep. Good god I was tired. After dinner I went out for a stroll and was approached by about eight pimps advertising whore houses: "beautiful French girls." Even if they *had* been beautiful I would have been too sleepy even to look! I went back to my room and again hit the sheets.

Wednesday, September 29

I woke up, greatly refreshed, at about 6:00 A.M. and began writing. At 7:00 A.M. my morning tea arrived with the newspaper. Headline: *Seventy-three killed in rail crash near Hyderabad* (later news: more than 126). Train plunges into flooded river as bridge collapses. It gave me a chill. Every river in India is in flood. Srinagar, since our departure, has been nearly lost: villages are being dumped into rivers everywhere.

A meditation: this has been going on here for 8,000 years. Only the Occidental contribution of dams and river control, which the Indians are now installing, will relieve the situation—and create simultaneously the electric power and adequate irrigation.

After breakfast I went to the Indian Museum and viewed the rich but horribly exhibited collection. The Bhārhut railing and *toraṇa*[56] in the pitch dark! Then I went upstairs to a highly advertised exhibit, visited by thousands, of

"World History in Pictures"—a puerile series of Communist-type posters illustrating the epochs of world history. The point: Imperialism, Capitalism, Fascism *vs.* Democracy, Socialism, Communism. Where have I heard that one before? But what hit me, seeing it all so simply set forth at this late date, was the curious spottiness of the whole historical panorama of these people, as well as the curious suggestion that, although everything has somehow been progressing, it has somehow been all wrong. Two or three amusing curiosities: Mesopotamia was placed in Turkey; A.D. was consistently written A.C.; Russia's absorption of Lithuania, Latvia, and Estonia was represented as a recovery of lands rightfully Russian. The last word on the Machine was that it had made the rich richer but had done nothing for the poor—a view that *may* have been correct in 1890, but certainly has no application to the only land where the Machine has really been made to work: capitalistic U.S.A., where every worker drives to work in his own car.

After lunch I went out to Belūr Maṭh, in time to greet Swami and his two angels. It was a lovely change: suburban quiet, on the Ganges shore. One can see Dakṣineśvara from the *maṭha.* Many many monks. Tea among them. Visits to the principals. A frightful Church-Temple designed by Vivekananda (reminds me of the Mahayana Buddhist Cathedral in Honolulu), where an incredible image of Durgā was being fashioned by a couple of artist craftsmen. During the evening worship of the Ramakrishna image I sat forward among the monks, and let me say that the gestures and posture of the young monk offering the fire, water, flowers, etc., and swinging the chowry were the first evidences of real elegance that I have seen, to date, in India. At this service I got the feel of India's monastic life—and talking with the monks in their yellow robes, I required only a slight jog to find myself at Elūrā and Ajaṇṭā. Hurray for the monks.

The drive home, with two of the order, was wonderful: at the Howrah Bridge, a two-hour traffic jam, the like of which I have never seen and would never have thought possible. Rickshaws, hand trucks, busses, herds of cows and goats, porters with loads on their heads, beggars, yogis, trolley cars, pedestrians infiltrating everywhere, shouting, honking, taxis, motorcycles, bikes, more cows, a peasant girl with a filled basket on her head shouting "Mama," trying to cross through ten lanes of traffic; five plus five lanes of traffic trying to converge into two; every tenth truck unable to start again after stopping; one truck with a flat tire trying to cut across the side; guys jumping out every two minutes to crank their cars; more cows; policemen here and there; people sleeping along the sidewalks of the great bridge; boat traffic below; a crescent moon in the dark by the time we arrived. It was simply great, that's all.

Thursday, September 30

One month in India, and beginning to feel that I know how to handle a few of the problems. Perhaps time, too, for a few more reflections.

As to who broke India: Islam. The humanistic glow given by Akbar and Shah Jahan, at the last minute, to a period of some nine hundred almost unrecorded years of war and iconoclasm, should not be allowed to distort the picture. Moreover, these good men were followed by Aurangzeb.[57]

Or blame the Caste System: for it is said that India was betrayed from within, the chief converts to Islam being members of the *śūdra* and scheduled classes. It is also said, on the other hand, that the caste system became petrified only *after* the coming of Islam, which cannot be true if the other theory is true. And a reading of the pre-Mohammedan Laws of Manu and Institutes of Viṣṇu makes the first theory seem the more likely.

As to what I have found of real power and value in India: certainly, the character and quality of the peasants and the poor (something, however, perhaps not peculiar to the peasants and poor of India—compare Italy, France, perhaps even Mexico); also, a comparable graciousness and hospitality right up to the top (for instance, *chez* Radhakrishnan, and the people we met in Delhi—again, perhaps, to be matched elsewhere, but I still think there is something special about the quality or tone); then the work of the Ramakrishna monks, their social work, their *pūjā*. Also of value: the Five Year Plan; the spiritual span, in Benares, between the Durgā Temple and the Hindu University; and the conversations I have had in the trains.

But, heavily on the debit side: the poverty, which has conduced to a certain miserliness on the part of the wealthy (or perhaps it was vice-versa). They do not let their well-being shine out into the city, but close it away behind walls. Corollary: instead of turning for investment money to its own rich, India turns to the World Bank. Exceptional men have endowed and built temples—for which they gain heavy credits in heaven. There is also among all literate Indians a fantastic spiritual pride which gives rise to a pose of spiritual superiority; and there is also a class of grossly westernized persons, quite conspicuous in a way, which I cannot yet judge, since I have not conversed: they are rude in trains and seem to represent the antithesis of my "good Indians."

As to Islam: I find the Mohammedans that I have met entirely praiseworthy—forthright and intelligent; also, I should say, somewhat more Occidental in character than the Hindus.

I note also a couple of themes for research: the cults of the temples of Benares; and the symbolism of the Satī stones.[58]

I spent most of this day in my room, writing, and dealing with New York problems: Zimmer proofs and the Irma Brandeis-Bollingen project.[59]

At 6:30 P.M. I went to the Calcutta Club to meet the pleasant man whom I encountered on the train: and here was a view indeed of another of India's million faces. The club is Calcutta's second, the top club is The Bengal Club, where Indians are excluded. But in The Calcutta Club the organization is such that the Board of Directors is half Indian, half European, and the presidency alternates. At present the membership is mostly Indian, but they are holding to the 50-50 organizational principles.

I entered, in my blue Dacron suit, and my friend met me at the door, in open shirt. I noted both types of dress in the Club, and so felt at home. He ordered drinks (he later told me he did not drink ordinarily, and I noticed that he dallied long showed me around and introduced me to friends) but every friend to whom he introduced me ordered drinks immediately—apparently they've taken on drinks as the primary symbol of British good fellowship. Anyhow, before the evening was over I had had a lot of whiskey and soda.

The atmosphere was entirely that of a club in London or New York, and I was filled all evening with a kind of admiration for the power of certain British ideas to make a world statement. We sat for a while in the pool room and watched a number of the members put on a standard American or British pool-room performance. I recalled every sound, every phrase, every gesture from those old pool games, long ago, at the Forest Lake Club.[60] We watched the poker and bridge games, and talked of stud poker. After about seven whiskey-and-sodas and a good deal of wandering around we sat down to an excellent chicken dinner—and I had to revise some of my thoughts about the Indian handling of Western food.

The members of the Club are, of course, business, industrial, and professional gentlemen; mostly Indians, but I also met a couple of second-class Europeans—or rather, Britishers. One of the members, putting on a fairly good performance at the pool table, was said to be India's most successful industrialist—owner of all kinds of things. Another, with whom I had a pleasant chat about Darjeeling, had the name of Birla. He was more interested in his racing fillies than in Hinduism, and was, apparently, the black sheep of the pious Birla family (donor of the big New Delhi temple). A sane gentleman, a Mr. Sen Gupta, claimed to be an atheist, but his wife was a pious devotee of everything.

Certain meditations, following my conversations of last evening, have absorbed me and I sent part of them off in a letter to Jean. They have to do with my feelings about India and India's women.

Ever since my arrival I have felt an obscure sense of disappointment in my perambulation of India. I have been trying to put my finger on it: blaming the railroad service, poverty, drabness of the buildings, lack of civic pride, etc. I now realize that there are practically no women visible—and that, consequently, what the hell? The streets and buildings, coffee houses, and so on are swarming with men—but the only women (save for an occasional exception) are the poor drab beggar women with their naked kids and almost equally drab vendors. It is to be noted that these miserables often wear their dirty saris without bodices, and that frequently the right breast is either almost or completely uncovered—and that it doesn't matter. The worst I ever saw was this afternoon: a blind beggar woman with a naked, scrofulous kid on her arm, the other hand holding out a begging bowl. The kid had pus of some kind dripping from its nose, and the woman, like all of these poor things, simply walked ahead slowly, in her darkness, calling "Babu," rather softly. At this point my beggar resistance broke.

The very few women above the beggar-vendor level that one does see (in the cities, that is to say; for in the villages and fields the women—drab, however, as beggars—were much more in evidence) fall into two classes: matrons—with the look, very often, of Durgā; and childlike, nice-looking, little girls and young wives. I have noted also, for example in the case of the couple who entered my railway carriage on the way from Gwalior to Allahabad, that the wives are absolutely of the domestic sort—and I have heard that Indian wives cannot talk of anything but the orthodox three K's (*Kirche, Küche, Kinder*). The concept of a spiritual companionship of the sexes seems not to exist. And this whole thing about India was impressed upon me dramatically at lunch today, when I saw an elegant modern Japanese wife with her husband and two youngsters at a nearby table. She had a real style—decent, wifely, but interestingly sophisticated. I thought, "My god, these Indians have a long way to go!"

I would say that in India the French *jeune fille de famille* idea prevails, without, however, the French correction of the marital triangle. As a result of all this the cities have the air of a men's club: the step to The Calcutta Club is not a great one: nor is the step to the Monastery. *Purdah* and the Mohammedan *burqa'* (covering veil) represent, therefore, only a vivid presentation of a formula that is ubiquitous in the Orient that I have seen.

What is the relationship of all this to the lovely *maithunas* (the tender and gentle ones) of Bādāmi and others? What is the relationship of all this to the heroic spirit of the epics? Can it be that we here have something that came into India with the Mohammedans? I think not. I think it was here before, but that there was some kind of shift of emphasis at that time, which screened the other out.

At this point, another series of meditations not unrelated to the above:

India has turned its poverty into a kind of *sādhanā;* Gandhi stressed this. There is consequently a quality of spirituality about this Indian poverty, which is impressive. Other *sādhanās,* however, were possible in the past: the kingly *sādhanā* of Arjuna, for example.[61]

Involuntary poverty is not the same thing as the voluntary poverty of the monk; it may lead to and represent a quite different spiritual state. Outwardly, however, the two poverties tend to complement each other, and the monk easily becomes the elder brother of the poor man—himself, perhaps, even tending to identify wealth with sin.

Involuntary poverty—unless spiritually transcended—keeps its victim in a subject, servile, dependent position: this position is that of the dependent child to its mother. Entirely appropriate to India's poverty, therefore, is the Mother-*bhakti* recommended by Ramakrishna to his devotees and represented in the Durgā Pūjā (which is to be celebrated in Calcutta next week).

The way of *bhakti,* the *kīrtana,* the Mother, etc. became stressed in India following the Mohammedan conquest and the liquidation of the medieval aristocratic tradition, (Caitanya, Tul Sidas, Ramakrishna).

Here, then, is a possible formula:

Hinduism, post A.D. 1200	Medieval India
sādhana of Poverty	Aristocratic *sādhana*
Śakti as Mother *(paśu)*	*maithuna (vīra)*

As for the formula of the city as a men's club and the *purdah* of the *jeune fille* and matron—I ran into the inevitable corollary in the course of my after-dinner stroll. I went along Chowrunghee Road, slowly, looking for a possible movie theater—accosted, of course, by pimps (another touch of France), rickshaw boys, taxi drivers, and vendors of all kinds; then turned to the left following the lights, and was amazed at the vitality of the business life at this hour: all the shops open, as ever—though I never see anyone buying—and the streets simply crowded. At one point I passed a huge, covered, fruit and vegetable market. At this point a rickshaw boy started following me, jangling his bell, to my great annoyance, and I determined to walk him off. I don't know how long he followed, but in the course of my stroll, and while he was still with me, I suddenly realized that I was deep in a red-light district.

I haven't seen anything on this level outside of Panama City:[62] on either side of the street, little stalls, each with its filthy girl, and occasional larger doorways in which a number of women would be standing and where a team of pimps, like Indian shopkeepers, would be loudly calling and beckoning you. The doors of these larger establishments were open and one had vistas of very dirty rooms and patios, with a few dreary whores in their saris, sitting quietly on chairs. The girls, for the most part, looked just like any other Indian women you might see—childlike, as unsexy as any women I've ever seen; but a few of them were dolled up with slightly colorful saris (nothing gaudy) and powdered faces (the sort of purple powder used by the girls in Harlem). Four or five were dressed in short skirts and brazen sweaters, like western picture-book whores. But on the whole, it was an amazingly subdued bunch of sirens—extremely easy to pass. And my rickshaw boy kept right at my heels.

I knew that I was past the whorehouses when I got the reek of a brace of urinals. After that, the business was hardware, vegetables, candy, magazines, and the general whatnots of India. The rickshaw boy dropped me and I hailed a taxi (taxis have meters, so you know what to pay: the rickshaw boys always ask for more—and having watched them run for a couple of miles at their amazing dog-trot, I always feel like paying them more than the ride was worth). At the door of my taxi a pimp kept telling me to come with him and see the beautiful girls. "Just look," he said, like every storekeeper, "I have one very nice girl for you. Just look. Sahib, Sahib. No?" I let my Sikh taxi-driver drive me home to the Great Eastern Hotel.

Saturday, October 2

Something very interesting in the morning paper (*The Statesman*, p. 8, continued on p. 6!): an article by a certain Pyarelal Nayar on Gandhi. A statement is given here on Gandhi's two fundamental propositions:

> I recognize no other God except the God that is to be found in the heart of the dumb millions...and I worship the God that is Truth or Truth which is God, through the service of these millions. [i.e. Vivekananda's formula after his visit to America.]
>
> I believe in the absolute oneness of God and therefore of humanity. What though we have many bodies? We have but one soul. The rays of the sun are many through refraction. But they have the same source. I cannot, therefore, detach myself from the wickedest soul, nor may I identify myself with the most virtuous. [This is not so clear: but it rings a bit like Ramakrishna.]

Further on in this article we come to a discussion of *satyagrāha*—and what do you think?—lifted (without credit) from Zimmer-Campbell, *Philosophies of India.* As follows:

> There is an ancient philosophical belief in India that one who has been true to the law of his essential being without a single fault throughout his life, can cause anything to happen by the simple act of calling that fact to witness. He becomes a "living conduit" of cosmic power, the power of Truth (*satya*) "the highest expression of the soul." This is known as making "an act of Truth." The truth must be firmly rooted in the heart so that it manifests itself in human relations as infinite compassion or identification with everything that feels....[63]

After lunch I went to the racetrack, hoping to see a crowd, but the fields and stands were empty (actually, I learned later, I was three-quarters of an hour early), and so I took another walk. I went to the great market that I had seen last night: it was a lovely spot. I was amused to see a number of precisely such porters with their baskets, as they appear in "The Porter and the Three Ladies of Baghdad" in the *Arabian Nights.* I also sought and found again the street of whores: four or five blocks of them, just off Surendranath Banerji Road, on a street called Mistree Lane (!) which intersects with Umā Dās Road—and at the intersection, standing with a bored look at her stall, was an actually beautiful, tall, dark, girl. The whole area was almost as busy as the night before—in fact, perhaps more so; for, to my surprise, there were a number of shops and craft workshops scattered among the whores, kids were flying kites in the streets, and the whole thing was just like any other shopping neighborhood. The time was about 3 P.M.

At 6:30 P.M. I was joined by my Hindu friend Dhar, who took me, this time, to the Calcutta Punjab Club—a smaller, more intimate club than the other, and one where the husbands are allowed to bring their wives. The idea was to let me see a bit of Calcutta's mixed society. When we arrived, two poker games were in progress on the lawn—and a few of Dhar's friends were at the bar. Everything was male. The game of drinks began. Presently four couples arrived. I was introduced and sat among them in a corner on a couple of wall-benches; the women were all on one with the men on the other. Result: the women talked together; the men talked together. More couples arrived and divided. Presently the men were all standing at the bar and only the women were seated. And finally the women were somewhere else (I don't know where), and I was having dinner with three men. A mixed party in the Orient. Dhar said: "Well, you see, the women don't drink whiskey, and they like to talk of their own affairs."

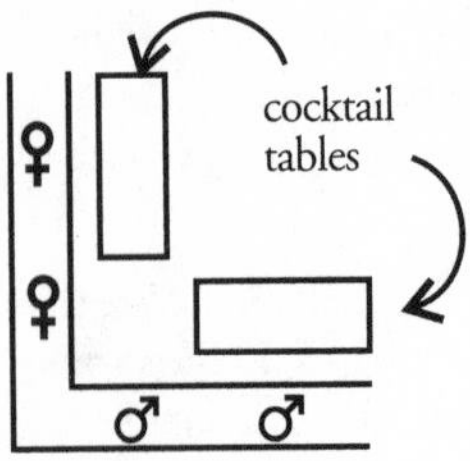

Sunday, October 3

This morning I decided to go the Kālīghāt Temple, took a taxi, and was met, as I descended, by a brahmin priest who showed me the whole job. Obviously a very busy resort: beggars, pilgrims, vendors, priests, in multitudes. Had some of the air of the Benares temple labyrinth—only here it was all a great open area with lots of buildings: the temple itself (from A.D. 1601) a hostel for pilgrims, and many other buildings. It had been my hope that I might see the sacrifice of a goat or buffalo, but I lost interest when I saw the two stocks: big, for the buffalo; little, for the goat, the latter fresh with brilliant blood, with the severed bodies and heads of four little animals laid out in state at one side. Presently, a pilgrim and priest began preparing a cute little black fellow for his immolation, and I was glad to follow my priest-guide as he bore me along to other sights: the riverside, where the pilgrims were descending to bathe; the areas where the brahmins of the temple sat in great number, reading the *Gītā;* the numerous booths where the little packets of offerings were for sale; the puddle of water from the goddess's feet, which the pilgrims stooped to take up in their hands and even to sip; a great line of pilgrims going into the temple. The priest then took me to the burning ghat, and I could see and smell (and found myself in the smoke of) three cremations.

My brahmin had the usual priestly talent of extracting money, but I didn't mind this time: it was quite a show; and as he showed me around he gave explanations that were clear and concise. The allegorical reading of the goat and buffalo sacrifices was interesting: the goat is the symbol of lust, the buffalo of anger; these passions are sacrificed with the sacrifice of the animals.[64] They are placed in the stock, and are slain with a single stroke: not at any regular time of day, but whenever a pilgrim makes the offering.

Following this event I returned to my street of whores to see whether it was at work also in the morning—and it was, though I didn't see any male actually go into any of the stalls or reception halls. As in all of the Oriental shopping areas I've seen, the noise and circumstance were all out of proportion to the business done. (The stall at the corner of Umā Dās and Mistree, however, was closed and locked from the outside.) Oh yes, and by the way, when I mentioned this street to Dhar last night, he was amazed: prostitution, he said, is against the law!

I spent the afternoon sleeping and writing in my room, and after dinner went for a long walk through all kinds of streets, finding Durgā Pūjā shrines set up everywhere in little sheds, often of sheet metal, decorated with colorful paper and brightly lit. These shrines have as the central figure a representation of the Goddess slaying the Buffalo Demon. The demon has emerged from the buffalo completely and is receiving the blow of the Goddess' lance full in the chest. He is moustached and the goddess, in some of the shrines, has lassooed his neck with a cobra. The rendition of this formula varies slightly from shrine to shrine. The scene is flanked by four standing figures: two represent the goddesses Lakṣmī and Sarasvatī; two are Ganeśa (pink!—origin here of the pink elephant idea?) and Kārttikeya—Ganeśa may be accompanied by his rat, and Kārttikeya rides the peacock. The shrines had just been completed, and many of the neighborhood's old ladies and their families—often nicely and freshly dressed—were coming out to view the local version.

Before one of the shrines a large crowd of men and boys was gathered, and there was the beating of a drum and clank of cymbals. I went to see what was going on and found two fellows, one with a moustache, engaged in the sort of stick-duel that I had witnessed in Benares. The fellow with the moustache put one adversary out and another got up to engage him. The new contestant was a lively chap in a green dhoti and blue shirt. The contestants moved about quickly, keeping time with the music, and most of the time at some distance from each other; then they would come in for a couple of cracks and slashes and quickly duck out.

When I had seen enough I took a rickshaw home—and again, the boy didn't know where he was going and dragged me about three miles.

Monday, October 4

I was roused this morning at about 5:30 by a sound of quick drums and cymbals going past the hotel. Then again, some ten minutes later, this motif was repeated. Finally getting up, I saw the procession: a chap with a plant of some kind held aloft, followed by a man with a drum and a boy with a metal clank-instrument, who were followed in turn by a man bearing an offering on his head. This little procession simply passed along the street, and a beggar woman made a gesture of reverence. Other processions were a little larger. In one, there were two men in bright red robes and another holding a bright red umbrella over the head of a man with a small image on his head. Still other processions were smaller: a man bearing something and a kid following beating a gong.

I learned from the morning paper that the little shrines are called *paṇḍals;* also, that last evening at about 10:30 (just after my return home) ceremonials invoking the Goddess into her image were performed throughout the city.

This morning right after breakfast I went to Belūr Maṭh for their morning *pūjā,* which lasted from 9 until 12. It was conducted before their temporary image (same type as those of the *paṇḍals* in town), which is placed halfway down the aisle of their temple, on the Ganges side. Before it, on the floor, there is a large lotus mandala in the paving: above, in the temporary cloth decorations of the ceiling, there was another mandala. Since the ceremonial of the Durgā Pūjā is one for laymen and not properly for monks, the celebrant was a young *brahmacārin* (but of brahmin caste), who has learned this whole four-day series of ceremonials by heart and must fast each day until evening.

According to Swami, there are several layers of allegorical reference implicated in the Durgā Pūjā:[65]

The Vegetational: this is the period of the harvest. The plant that I saw this morning was a plantain bough and leaf, with a few sprigs of paddy.[66] This *is* the goddess: it is also the first fruits. (We are here on the trail of Demeter and Kore: but definitely!)[67]

The Domestic: at the time of her marriage, the Bengali girl, shortly after the wedding ceremonies, returns to her family for three days: Umā returned to King Himālaya for three days after her marriage to Śiva: the three days of the Durgā Pūjā are comparable to those three days[68]—at the end, the immersion of the image is the departure of the bride from her family: the Bengali mothers cry at this time. (Here again we must keep Demeter and Kore in mind.)

The Moral: the goddess's slaying of the Demon Buffalo is the conquest of evil by good.

The Spiritual: during the hot and rainy seasons one's spiritual life is sluggish, but with the clearing of the skies the spirit is to be cleared and renewed. (Consider the Anthesteria.)[69]

A still deeper mystery is indicated, however, in the ceremonial enacted this morning; for not only the Goddess and her entourage, but also the Buffalo is invoked and garlanded as a god. (Here is Zimmer's great theme.)[70]

At the ceremonial this morning I was impressed very strongly by a number of elements in the liturgy suggesting the Roman Catholic Mass; and when I tried to think of the possible background of these correspondences, I could not get Ephesus out of my mind. The great cult and temple of Artemis, source of so much in the Catholic cult and worship of the Virgin,[71] is *certainly* a Near Eastern counterpart of this Bengali Durgā. Theme for research: the history and sources of the Christian Liturgy: the history and sources of the Tantric Liturgy.

When I entered the Temple the sound was precisely that of a Catholic service: someone was reading in a liturgical monotone, and the Sanskrit, for a moment, sounded like Latin, and the ornamental inflections were like those of certain parts of a Gregorian Mass. This continuous reading went on throughout two of the three hours of the service: part of the text was from the *Devī Mahātmya*, where the account is given of Durgā's slaying of the Buffalo Demon. Over the ground bass of this chant the rite was performed.[72]

The *brahmacārin* celebrant, seated before the panel of images, among the vessels and offerings of the service, chanted for three hours the prayers of offering. A monk sat at his right with the text of the liturgy before him—as prompter; and another monk, very tall, stood behind the celebrant and supervised the actions of the piece. A youth in a fine white dhoti and shawl served as altar boy, lighting the incense sticks, placing the blessed flowers on the images, and so on. The celebrant *brahmacārin* was in white, and his head, save for the brāhman tuft, had been freshly shaved.

The area of the ceremonial action was marked off from the rest of the temple floor by a low barrier of wood, and within this area sat the monks of the *maṭha* (Nikhilananda, of course, among them). To the left of the celebrant (right of the image) were the women (on the side of Ganeśa and Lakṣmī) and the men were opposite (side of Sarasvatī and Kārttikeya). The service consisted in blessing flower and food offerings, the latter brought in on lovely trays (somewhat like those carried on the heads of the Balinese in all the movies!), and the former, after each blessing, placed in the hands or around the neck of the intended image. The blessing rite involved sprinkling water and tossing flowers over the fruits etc., then waving a stick of incense, while ringing the service bell with the left hand. At one great moment, about one hour after the commencement of the service, drums, gongs, and other machines of noise began going outside, and everyone who was standing (myself included) went down in a long salaam: as though the Goddess, at this moment, were accepting the sacrifice.

(Before I forget: the Goddess slays the Buffalo, and so Mithra slays the World Bull.[73] In Africa, the Goddess is shown standing between the horns of the bull[74]—compare the Pallava image of Durgā in the Boston Museum,[75] and see also Frobenius's account of the founding of a Syrian city (clay houses—of India!).[76] Also to be seen here: the bullfight,[77] the Assamese bull ring, the Cretan bull ring, the Kālīghāt buffalo sacrifice.)[78]

After this great moment in the service there was nothing new in the way of motifs. Presently the chant of the *Devī Mahātmya* ceased and the service went on, in comparative silence for another hour or so. The old monk who is the President of the *maṭha* came in, sat a special mat for a while, performed his *pūjā*, and went out. The youngsters in the temple began to be a bit restless, and there was a good deal of incidental noise. The length of the service was determined by the number of offerings that had to be blessed and presented. A team of boys was busy throughout, bringing in sets of trays and then taking them away (this food was distributed after the service to the poor). Food and garlands went first to the Goddess herself, then to Ganeśa, Lakṣmī, Sarasvatī, Kārttikeya, and the Snake and Buffalo.

The celebrant then tossed a great handful of flowers at the whole affair. Flowers next were distributed to the monks: they all tossed, salaamed, and withdrew. A lively, sturdy monk then sprinkled holy water over the women and men. Flowers were passed to the women. They were led in a brief prayer by the monk, and all tossed their flowers. Same for the men. Finis.

I had lunch with Swami and the two ladies and returned to the hotel.

Elements immediately suggestive of the Catholic liturgy: the chant, the choir area for the monks, separation of the sexes (Russian Orthodox—the mixing in Europe has something to do with my major discovery about the Orient-Occident sexual crisis!), holy water, flowers before images (all, however, here blessed), ringing of the bell at the moment of the offering, concept of the divine presence, motif of the sacrifice (here the buffalo; there the Savior himself), prayers for the faithful after the main service, celebrant and assistants, some of the *mudrās* of the celebrant, all the demonstrations of piety on the part of the faithful (ladies bowing, making the prayer sign with their hands), and finally, the look of the whole congregation coming out of the church.

This afternoon I started work, seriously, on the Sarah Lawrence chapter that I have to write, and this evening went for another walk along Surendranath Banerji Road. There was an immense crowd, a great noise of *pūjā* gongs and drums, flashing neon lights and illuminated archways—mostly concentrated, however, in the neighborhood of wonderful Mistree Lane. The population of the streets tonight had a larger proportion of women than usual—all (or rather, many) prettily dressed and on their way to do *pūjā*.

The little side streets leading to the shrines have illuminated archways before them (there were five or six, not very far from each other, just beyond the "Elite" movie theater), and there comes out, from far down a little street, a great din of gongs and drums. A dividing rope runs down the middle of the street: ladies right; men left; and this division goes right up to the shrine. The men's side is jammed; there are very few women. The crowd moves slowly down the little street, its storekeepers and inhabitants lining the way, and then comes to the bedlam of the shrine, where a priest sits waving a lamp before the panel of images and a cluster of boys bang drums and gongs. There is a policeman in a white suit and tall red hat to keep order. People stand a while, press up to the shrine, receive some smear on their forehead, make the usual pious gestures, and move away, going back the way they came—the two crowds in the crowded men's aisle, slowly passing each other.

The fun, of course, was the shrine that carries its crowd directly down one of the streets of The Quarter. Here the girls, like the other shopkeepers, stood at their doors, lining the way, and plucked off their customers. There was no lack of business in this little system of streets tonight! There was no shouting of pimps: it was unnecessary. Some of the girls quietly tossed little *pūjā* firecrackers, to call attention to themselves; but in general they were busy enough. I noticed that in many cases, men simply walked past the girl door guardian into her stall and she remained: these were simply doors, apparently, to larger establishments in the rear. I noticed also, tonight, one rather cute little room, open to the street, as though perhaps prepared for an exhibition of some kind; so when the procuress sitting before it beckoned to me I went over. She was fat and middle aged. "Young girl," she said. "Very nice, very good." I looked toward what she was showing me. A kid about thirteen years old in a kid's red-figured wash dress. "That?" I said. "No thanks." "Very nice," she said. "Very good." "No thanks," I repeated; and moved away. Many of the stalls that were open were simply that: stalls—dirty and small, with a bed (also small—one, amazingly small, about three feet square) in a corner. No sanitary facilities anywhere to be seen. One of the houses had a batch of lively Chinese girls before it.

On Surendranath Banerji Road I came across a great crowd gathered around a bundle of noise, and when I approached saw a group of five musicians—one with a musette, two with drums hung from their necks, two with cymbals—capering a little while they played. I paused a while to watch. Rupees were being handed to them occasionally. But they were not much good, and I moved along. Another batch of chaps was trying to get a bull to mount a cow. Everywhere, scattered along the sidewalks, were the usual sleepers, beggars, and vendors. At every other step I would be set upon by kids, rickshaw boys, vendors, and pimps. I must say, walking in Calcutta is an aggravation, particularly for a "Sahib" with a high degree of social visibility. The worst tonight was a kid who followed me for six blocks, saying, continuously, "I very poor, no matha, no fatha, no seesta, no bratha, no khana, you rich, you Sahib, I very poor, no matha..." etc. *de cape, ad nauseam.* He finally dropped me, but when I was returning to my hotel hooked on again, soon to be followed by another, then one with a still smaller kid in his arms: a rickshaw boy, meanwhile, had begun to follow me along the gutter, clanking his bell to attract my attention. I told him no, but he continued. The kids began touching my hands, then I felt the hand of the original fellow try to slip into my pocket and I wheeled with a slap. "Say!" I said: and before you could say Henry Morton Robinson[79] all the kids had vanished.

I must say, the whole thing gives me a sick feeling at this moment: Sri Pyarelal Nayar, in yesterday's paper, lifts two paragraphs, without credit, from my book; a youngster, tonight, tries to lift from my pocket; Dhar told me of an Indian movie company that had copied an American film *in toto*—and when the Americans sent a group to investigate, they found such an incredibly squalid studio that they knew there was no point in suing; the papers are full of articles by Indian pandits on Indian philosophy, religion, etc. all quoting—and simultaneously abusing—the Western scholars: India has a so-much-higher spiritual threshold.

Well, in a way, India has: in its rituals and in its mythological and philosophical traditions there is a more successful rendition of the non-dualistic principle than in the liturgies and traditions (orthodox, that is to say) of the West. This comes down, like a thin thread of gold, from ages past: but what the ages present have added to the inheritance is largely pretentiousness and poor taste. I am, today, in a strongly negative mood.

Tuesday, October 5

I have now seen everything. Actually, an ash-smeared yogi lying in a bed, not of nails, but of tangled barbed wire—on one of the walks of the Howrah Bridge. He was a big fellow, of handsome physique, perfectly smeared, and with the proper hair and whisker do.

I drove out to Belūr Maṭh to see a charming *kumārī pūjā* (worship of a little girl), which Swami had told me was to commence at 11 A.M. I arrived at 10:30—and there was a prodigious crowd of people at the grounds and swarming into and out of the temple. Swami saw me. "Have you just come?" he said. "Yes," I answered. "Well," he said, "you have missed everything." I was a bit sore, but, I think, concealed it. He introduced me to some gentlemen on the monastery porch, and I sat down, to make the best of it. He himself went into the temple, in a little while, for whatever was going on in there; and I conversed about India with a couple of the gentlemen on the porch, while watching the lovely crowd move about the grounds and temple. India's middle class: professional men and their families, small business people, clerks. All were very nicely dressed; the women—at last—looked charming, and the atmosphere was that of a gentle, sort of Easter Sunday, social-religious event. People, men and women, were everywhere touching the various swamis' feet. This group, or stratum, constituted, I was told, about forty per cent of Calcutta.

Piety, *bhakti,* was evident everywhere, and can be said—certainly—to be a distinguishing trait of India. One of my gentlemen discoursed to me on the permeation of the Indian spirit by the principles of Indian philosophy and religion: in the Vedic age the principles were the possession of a few; in the Puranic age they were allowed to suffuse and revitalize the popular cults and became the possession of all; and in the period of the *bhakti* poets ("*Bhakti* originated in the south, came north with Rāmānanda, and was disseminated by Kabīr and Nānak"), the folk languages were infused with the quality of piety that has distinguished Indian thought ever since. It is this spirit, this piety, which is the sustaining force of Indian life.

The transcendental emphasis of Indian metaphysics makes all cults acceptable as approaches. The masses (this gentleman admitted) know nothing of the experience of *Brahman;* those that I had seen swarming to the *paṇḍals* and these now at Belūr Maṭh represent, for the most part, simply an experience of *bhakti,* not of transcendent realization—but they are on the path. The important thing about Indian religion is that from this step of simple *bhakti* to the ultimate realization there is an open way, without barrier.

As far as I can see, this is the great point about India: and (I am sorry to say) as far as I have seen, this is the only point about India today.[80]

I spoke to the gentlemen about the yogi in the barbed wire bed. "Such fellows," he said, "know nothing but how to lie on nails."

One of the Swamis spoke of his attempts to get in touch with and learn the *sādhanā* of a group in the south, called *siddhas,* said to be the followers of old Agastya. He himself was from the south; he heard a good deal about these men and their wonders, but he never came close enough to any of them (if any actually existed) to find out what it was all about.

Another of the Swamis spoke of a group called *nāgas* (L. *nag,* naked), who are an extremely aggressive lot and seem to have as their philosophy "We come first." When they come to bathing places, in force, they make all stand aside, etc. They flourish in Uttar Pradesh and put on demonstrations. They are the descendants of a military group that was formed, originally, to protect sadhus. They have evolved, however, into a sort of sadhu-sport themselves: militant sadhus!

After the temple service, literally thousands of people were served *prasāda* on the temple grounds. I went around to the guest house where Mrs. D. and the Countess are staying, and found there a handsome Hindu girl from Trinidad: an M.D. here working in a hospital. Swami arrived, and we had lunch. In the conversation after lunch I rose to the defense of the modern world against Swami and the Hindu girl who were talking the usual line about the deterioration of the spirit in the modern age. This conversation has led me to another formula. It came to me when I forced Swami back to his second line of defenses. "Well," he said, "there is no progress, only change." "I used to think that too, Swamiji," I said, "but since coming to India I have changed my mind. I think there is progress, and I think India will begin to experience progress too, pretty soon." Swami was shocked. He ended with the grandiose declaration that he would rather see India remain as it is than become what America is: there would be no Buddhas, no Ramakrishnas, any more.

And so *there* is a problem.

But my formula touches something else: Swami's "change" theory, and the often heard Indian line of "no progress," which has been my own line too, is based, I now think, on India's unquenchable *pride.* It is obvious (I should think) to anyone who has actually beheld the two culture worlds, that not only mechanically, but also in the matters of physical health, social well being, intellectual vitality and originality, philanthropic sympathy, general knowledge, science, scholarship, ability to help others, etc., there has been an actual and even measurable advance. But since Indians cannot admit inferiority, they counter all this with a spiritual claim, which is supposed to settle everything.

My review of the spiritual claim is set forth [*supra,* p. 64]. I not only admit it; I celebrate it. But in its actual effect on Indian life, I wonder how far it goes beyond the rendition of a spectacle of piety. Besides this spectacle of piety, I can record also—and have recorded—my delight at the manner in which Indian philosophy pours forth from the mouths of the people whom I meet in trains. There is no question: it is functioning here and now. One hears from contemporary mouths ideas announced in the texts of the eighth century B.C. Moreover, with Gandhi these ideas were given social expression (we shall come back to this in a minute).

But: a learned Mr. Pyarelal Nayar steals my paragraphs; an urchin tries to rob my pocket; an Indian movie firm steals an American film; Mr. Nehru accepts American aid and abuses America in every public pronouncement; everyone I meet is trying to get something from me, plans to come to America some day, wants a hand out right now, or something; the rich in India hang onto their cash and let the whole place starve. I don't know; it is an odd thing: when you look at India from the outside it is a squalid mess and a haven of fakers; but when you look at it from the inside (perspective Belūr Maṭh), it is an epiphany of the spirit: Buddhas and Ramakrishnas and pious men and ladies.

The eye sees a river of mud and the inner eye sees a river of grace.

Gandhi, sitting on the ghat at Belūr Maṭh, was heard to say that his whole life was an effort to bring into action the ideas of Vivekananda. Vivekananda learned a lot about social service in the U.S.A. A lot of the money for Belūr Maṭh came from the U.S.A.—and more is coming, if I may judge from words let drop today by Mrs. D. and the Countess. Talk about spiritual influence! I think that a good deal of what today looks like an application to life of the Indian spirit is actually an Indianization of the American spirit.

I drove back from Belūr Maṭh with the Indian M.D. girl and some other people, in a large Packard, to have a bit of a nap and to write these pages. Tonight I am going out there again for the *great* service of the Durgā Pūjā: that of the *sandhi*, the juncture—marriage—of the second and third days of the festival, at midnight.

When coming to India one is told: "Don't see the dirt only; see the spirit." I think it is proper to reply: "When looking at America, don't see the chromium only, see the spirit." The spirit is everywhere—as far as my own experience of people goes; and I must say, I don't think the actual Indian inflection is anymore impressive than what I know of the French, German, or American. People are nice everywhere. People are pious, sympathetic, and intelligent everywhere. But people aren't everywhere quite as poor as they are in India—and if one has a particular reverence for poverty, one may be fooled into thinking that the poverty itself is a sign of the spirit—whereas it is a sign only of a sociological or technological failure.

The spiritual principles that India expresses with a metaphysical inflection (all is *Brahman*), the Christian expresses theologically (love thy neighbor as thyself for the love of God), and the secular democrat rationally (all are equal before the law). India's destiny may be to keep the metaphysical drone bass sounding while the rest of the world works out the actualization of man's equality on a level somewhat higher than that of the dust bin and the village cottage. The great traditions of India's past have been channeled now into the piety represented by *bhakti*. But the new age is also approaching India.

My present personal problem is that of assimilating a large-scale disappointment in India. The problem is not the dirt and poverty—those I expected. Nor is it finally that of the armed camp or lumbercamp atmosphere, which I did not expect. It is not the nature of the religion—that is even more interesting and easy to study than I expected. So then what is it?

The arrogant anti-Americanism, when they are doing everything they can to take over American ideas, is point one. This I did not expect; I do not like; and I cannot feel sweet about it. It is coupled with a frequently expressed disdain for American "rush," "materialism," and "money," expressed to your face while you are looking at a mess of beggars sleeping in an open drain. And these feats of the spirit are not rare, but normal. This, I believe, is what has gotten my goat. And I am trying, meanwhile, "not to see the dirt only, but the spirit." When I sit talking with the representatives of the spirit, they talk like sociological idiots. I think perhaps Swami's foolishness has aggravated the situation for me; but he is only an acute case of something that is chronic. Mr. Nehru is the keynoter of this refrain.

The anti-Americanism is the negative side of an Asia-for-the-Asians' patriotism, which is actually anti–white-man. This has resulted in a sentimental line-up with China that has thrown India into the communist camp as a fellow-traveler. Nehru's great talk of Neutralism—which was an attempt to play, on a world scale, Britain's balance of power game, with the metaphysical air, however, of being beyond the pairs of opposites—has ended simply in the sort of thing that distinguishes the Sarah Lawrence Social Science Department. This is a fine lesson to have come all the way to India to learn.

The economic plight of India is of disaster proportions, and although much is being done to help the situation, there is so much to be done that India will certainly not be out of trouble (that is to say, will not have overcome its inferiority complex) before the end of this century.

The economic plight is matched by a cultural plight. The pandits are a shoddy lot, showing all the traits of the mind of small learning. They seem to be more interested in glorifying and whitewashing India than in objective scholarship, and their principal sources seem to be the Occidental scholars. I see little possibility of profit from a large scale study of their works at this time. In contemporary literature and art also, there is going to be little to devour. Perhaps two or three individuals will be met, but are not likely to be of the stature of, say, Tagore—not to mention Joyce, Mann, Proust, or even Gide or Sartre.

In other words:

A. *India as a modern nation does not interest me at all.* It would be of great interest, however, to a sociologist, engineer, or industrialist.

But, on the other hand:

B. *As an archaeological museum, India is even more interesting than I had expected it to be.* Most valuable, I think, is the survival here (as in the Orient in general) of a religious atmosphere that has simply vanished from the West. This is a prodigious force—and I doubt very much whether science and technology are going to do much to dispel it within the next hundred years. I can no longer think of this as something of the past. Valuable also is my experience here of the character of the Fellaheen (in Spengler's sense).[81]

Finally:

C. *As to whether anyone whom I am likely to encounter here would be one to serve, in any sense, as a guru—I very much doubt.* So far, the people I have spoken to keep repeating things I already know—what may be called the clichés of India's opinion of herself.

Countering the negatives of points one and three, on the other hand, are my numerous and continuous experiences of the personal charm of Indian individuals. This positive personal factor (call it D) and the archaeological (B), are henceforth to hold my eye. The various disappointments and irritations of the A category can be disregarded—or at least endured. And, of course, there is always the possibility of an interesting vista into the realm suggested by C.

The visit this evening to Belūr Maṭh was very interesting. The crowd in the temple was not large and it was easy to see what was going on. The service was conducted with great dignity by the same functionaries as yesterday's. Commencing at about 11 P.M., it lasted about an hour.

I was particularly interested in watching the opening phase, when the chief celebrant performed the rite of dedicating his body. This was followed by a blessing of the food and garland offerings. Then three pans of lights were lighted and the main part of the service began. It consisted of a waving of lights, etc., like the service I had observed on my first visit to the *maṭha.* First is waved a great stand of lights, then a smaller, then a conch containing water, then a cloth, then a flower, and finally a chowry—the celebrant ringing, all the time, a bell with his left hand. When this was finished there came an event of even higher tension. The assisting monk arose and picked up a small sickle-like knife, touched the buffalo of the image, and then, with a sharp little cry, came down on—what should have been a goat, but was in this case a substitute: a banana! Meanwhile, from the beginning of the light-waving, a noise of drums, gongs, and cymbals. This event was followed by the *pūjā* of the President of the Order, the monks, and the congregation. I returned home by taxi.

Wednesday, October 6

Having admitted to myself that India is a large disappointment, I today had a very pleasant day. In the morning I went to a very nice dance concert, a "Manipur Dance Festival," presented by The Manipur Sangeet Natak Sammelan. The event had received a very unfavorable review in *The Statesman* by "Our Art Critic," but was, on the contrary, very good indeed. An excellent company presented twelve numbers to an audience of about two hundred, who seemed not to know how to applaud. I found that after sixteen or twenty claps I was going it alone. If it hadn't been for myself and an American couple down in the orchestra, there wouldn't even have been a second bow after the final number. It was a nice theater and I tried to see the General Manager, but his office was closed for the holiday.

This afternoon I took a bus out to Dakṣineśvara to see the temple in which Ramakrishna served as priest. There was a great crowd of visitors, very much like the crowd yesterday at Belūr Maṭh. I strolled around for about three quarters of an hour, saw the banyan, the Kālī image, and the secondary shrines. It was a pretty evening. Then I took a bus home, sat up front with the driver, and had a really wild and amazing drive. The city, the suburbs, in fact every inch of the way from Dakṣineśvara, was swarming with people in holiday gear. The bus—every bus—was jammed. The noise was incredible. *Paṇḍal* gongs the whole length of the way, shouting people, horns, rickshaw bells, and our driver with a voice like a tiger. I had a headache when I got to the hotel—but the drive had been well worth it. India seemed, for a moment, a different place: the crowd was gay and lovely and full of pretty women! I don't understand this place at all.

Thursday, October 7

Let me, this morning, try to start a summary of the positive values that I can discover in India for the modern world. I am taking for granted India's value as an ethnological museum. At present I can think of the following points:

1. *Brahman-ātman:* stress on the transcendent—this breaks the claim of every orthodoxy to exclusive validity, supplies a metaphysical background to the tolerance of the secular state, supports a democratic world affirmation, and points up the secondary character of all moral (mores) systems.
2. *Śakti:* mythology and psychology of the experience of the world as energy.
3. *Yoga:* techniques and pyschology of the transformation of the personality.

These, briefly (*ātman–śakti–yoga*), are the sum total of what I can draw from the main line of Indian thought as pertinent to the modern West (that is to say, the future world); and I can add one or two more:

4. *Rasa:* Indian aesthetic theory, Oriental aesthetic theory.
5. *Purāṇa:* Indian mythology, an elucidated mythos.

Perhaps I should also add:

6. *Pūjā:* the principles of effective rite.

Most valuable for an understanding of these is the history of Indian philosophy and art from the Vedic period to circa A.D. 1250 (Koṇārak).

The patterns of *bhakti* belong essentially, I now think, to folk religion. It may be that in the West this will grow in force with the coming of Spengler's "Second Religiousness";[82] however, it is also possible that with the critical transformation of the personality, which literacy, science, and technology are effecting, *bhakti* is to disappear. My present decision is to regard it as a phenomenon of the past, belonging to what may be called the medieval structure of consciousness. I do not see how it can be brought into accord with modern spirit, since wherever it prevails (in the West, for example, in the Catholic Church), there is an actual resentment of modernity (Nikhilananda shows this conspicuously).

Archaism number one, then, is *bhakti.* It is to be studied as an ethnological phenomenon. On the other hand, as general reverence for life, it is to be fostered. I would not know where precisely to draw the line between *bhakti* and reverence—particularly if one adds to reverence the concept of "all is *Brahman.*" Perhaps the line is between worship and reverence.

There have been rains during Durgā Pūjā, and these have left the air cooler and lighter. It is pleasanter than it was to move around. Also, the memory of yesterday's crowds (*la vie en fleuve*) has given me a better feeling than I'd had about India. One thinks of Disney's *The Living Desert:* at certain moments it shows its hidden life, and after one has seen it, one looks at the desert in a somewhat different way. And finally, my thoughts this morning about *ātman–śakti–yoga–rasa–purāṇa–pūjā* have given me a positive attitude toward the tradition. The little concert yesterday helped a lot too.

Spent the morning at the American Express making arrangements for my Bhubaneshwar-Puri-Koṇārak and Bhubaneshwar to Madras stages. In the middle afternoon took a taxi up to Belūr Maṭh, to see the last event of the Durgā Pūjā, the Immersion, which would take place after dark. There was a moderate crowd. I sat around among them, here and there, took a couple of pictures, and then had tea with the ladies and Swami.

At tea, Swami noted my improved mood about India, and this loosened his tongue pleasantly; but then, as always in his conversation, a good feeling about India implied, and gave an occasion for his communicating a disdain for the West, and particularly for America. This pattern, which is not peculiar to Swami (see, for example, A. K. Coomaraswamy, Danielou, Guénon[83]), I shall have to accept as normal before I can begin to look at India properly. Swami told of conversations he has had here with swamis and pandits, all of whom have a positive hatred for America. One had said, "A nation of upstarts, they will have their day and disappear." You get this every day in the papers too. I felt the attitude most strongly, and almost fiercely, in New Delhi, in Mme. Pandit, particularly in a look that she gave me as she introduced

Swami and told her audience that the Westerners whom they saw in India were examples of the confusion and emptiness of the foreigners, who had to come to India to find something of value.[84] After tea I wandered around some more, watched a bit of the *pūjā* before the Ramakrishna image from outside the temple, and noticed that the women were watching it from outside too (apparently, in certain monk rites, woman's place is *not* in the temple). The crowd was gathering along the river wall and at the ghat, so I moved in that direction.

Then a young man in white, a Ramakrishna *brahmacārin*, approached me and very cautiously opened conversation. I was from America? Came with Swami? A devotee? (No.) What religion? (None.) What was my interest in religion? What religion flourished in the U.S.A? What did Americans think of Ramakrishna? (When I told him that not many more than one in a hundred thousand had ever heard of Ramakrishna, he was a little shocked and saddened.) What did they think of Vivekananda? Gandhi? (I gave him a nice blurb for Gandhi.) Nehru? (They are not so sure, I told him, about Nehru.) Did Americans drink? Why? Did it not destroy character? What about divorce? What about purity? (I gave him some real surprises here.) Did Americans believe in God? Why did I not let the monks initiate me into Hinduism? What did I think happened after death? What about spirit? Then I was a materialist? ("Yes," I said, "in this context I am a materialist.") Were there beggars in America? What are the buildings like? What salaries do professors get? How much did my shoes cost? Did I have a car? Did all Americans have cars? What was the situation about the Negroes?

Presently the image was brought out of the temple. Empty brass jars were carried before it down to the Ganges. The image was set on the top step of the ghat with its back to the river. The drums and gongs were going great guns and a little hopping dance of boys and swamis took place before the figure. "It is only an image now," my *brahmacārin* told me. "Everything has been withdrawn." After the dance (simply hopping and clapping the hands above the head) the image was carried down to the river, set on the lowest step, and one by one the Goddess's weapons then were taken from her: trident, sickle, sword, etc. Then, to a cry, she was tipped back and into the water. Four or five men pushed her out into the Ganges, and she sank. The brass jars then were filled with Ganges water and carried into the temple to be splashed about onto people's heads. Some people went into the temple, the rest dispersed.

I returned to Howrah by bus, walked across the bridge, and saw a number of the *paṇḍal* images going into the river. The images are made of clay, painted and dressed. The different neighborhoods, I have learned, take up collections and build their *paṇḍals;* but this is a relatively new custom. Formerly, the images were in private homes, where, however, caste rules made for a kind of exclusiveness that is no longer favored. All castes can participate in the ceremonies of the neighborhood *paṇḍals.* The first night the goddess is invoked, then, in the morning of the first full day (October 4), is the ceremony that I observed at length, *saptamī pūjā.* On the second day, *mahāṣṭamī,* the biggest day of the *pūjā,* comes the *kumārī* ceremony, and that evening, toward midnight, the *sandhi.* Day number three, *mahānavamī,* was a day of throngs, and was for me the brightest day, so far, in India. Then, at the conclusion of the fourth day (today), we had the Immersions. The Goddess had come and gone—and was rather cute.

Friday, October 8

The general social atmosphere of India is that of a co-ed boarding school with segregated sexes and depleted finances.

Surprise: I went at four to pay a small sum at the American Express, and sitting on the sidewalk, flat against the office-building, was an absolutely naked little black woman with buck teeth and a grimace of disgust, right leg out straight before her and left knee up against her left shoulder, leaving her *yonī* exposed and blazing red at the world. Over her left shoulder was a filthy piece of cloth, about the size of a face towel. Otherwise, as far as I could see, there wasn't another woman in the city. The streets were full of men, as usual, pissing in the gutters, etc., and nobody but myself even turned to look at this incarnation of Kālī. Well: in India it's either too little or too much. And both leave you cold. In this case, however, I think the woman's vagina was perhaps inflamed and that she was exhibiting her disability intentionally, just as the leper, some thirty yards further along the wall, was exhibiting his disabled hands. The first time I saw the woman—when I went into the American Express Office—she was sitting with her right side to the wall and her left knee up against her chin; as though, having taken off her shred of cloth, she were now waiting to get up the nerve to proceed to the next stage of her exposure. When I came out of the office, some fifteen minutes later, the exposure was complete.

Inside the office were, by chance, Swami Nikhilananda, the Countess, and two other swamis. One, who is leaving next week to take charge of the New York Center until Nikhilananda returns, asked how I had liked the Durgā Pūjā; he said that most of the images in the town *paṇḍals* were sort of new-fangled: neither traditional nor graced by any significant innovation—"like a modern Indian girl." And so there it was again: the monks representing a resentment of the modern movement. He next asked me if I knew

Professor Spiegelberg in California. I said I had met him. "He was in India to see if Indian religion was still functioning, or something," said the Swami, "and I believe he wrote a little book about it; but I don't think he met the right people." "The right people," I said, "are hard to meet in India. The Indians hide their jewels." But what I had in mind, was that in India, one authority's "right person," is every other authority's "wrong person."

Saturday, October 9 ***Darjeeling***

Things have begun to happen so fast that I shall just note events for the next few days, and perhaps develop my thoughts when I get to Madras. Up this morning at 5 A.M. to catch 6:15 airplane-bus. A boorish Indian family had copped all the window-seats in the plane. I sat beside one of the sons, who was a fidgit. Plane landed at Baghdagra airport at about 10 A.M. Controversy about seats in the automobile. Mountain drive to Darjeeling: two Californian ladies in the car on a world tour, Miss Ronni Leitner and Miss Pam Tylor, about forty and fifty-eight respectively, gave me a lot of dope on travel in Japan, and became my pals for the Darjeeling day.

On the first part of the drive I noticed a lot of interesting black people wearing colorful reds and greens: Santāls? They inhabited very neat palm-thatch huts, quite un-Hindu in appearance. As we got up into the mountains Nepalese and Tibetan types began to appear, and by the time we reached Darjeeling we were practically in Tibet. Beautiful view of Mt. Kanchenjunga (28,156 feet) from the Mt. Everest Hotel. Good lunch, with a superb treacle tart, the best pastry since New York.

After lunch we took a car to see a nearby pair of lakes and a Red-cap Lamasery, which was almost (if not actually) abandoned. When we descended from the car an obliging little monk met us at the entrance and conducted us into the temple; we were not required to remove our shoes. There was a great, ceiling-high image of the Buddha wearing the crown and teaching (golden face and hands), and at either side, in cases, two shelves of smaller figures: Mañjuśrī, Avalokiteśvara, the founder of the order, the local abbot, and others. A number of votive lights, two slowly revolving prayer wheels turned by the hot air rising from burning wicks, and several images filled the little room. The walls were lined with pigeon holes containing prayer-book packets, and there were also Buddha murals, in a style suggesting that of twelfth-century Nepalese palm-leaf manuscripts. We left our offerings, were shown a palm leaf manuscript, and went out, only to be beckoned into another building by another little man, who had a sort of machine shop of prayer wheels: one was turned by pulling a rope, others were turned by hot air. The little man showed us his beads, Buddha images, prayer book, and paraphernalia—and when we left our offerings presented his son, who was to receive something too. Our chauffeur told us that the first man was a monk and could not marry, but that the second was a priest and married.

We returned to town in time to watch the breaking up of the Saturday market—and what an assortment of faces! Tibetans, Nepalese, Bengalis, Lepchas, and whatnots! Simply wonderful!

We then returned to the hotel, had a couple of drinks, chatted with some of the tourist gentry, and afterwards retired early, since we are to be called at 3:30 A.M. to see the sunrise from Tiger Hill. There is some question as to whether there may be too many clouds: but if it will be impossible to see anything, we shall not be called.

The rather general and carefree talk about travel and touring with these nice, simple people gave me a strong feeling of the wonderful privilege that my year of sheer sightseeing really is, and I began to feel silly about my heavy-headed East-West agony. Darjeeling, I believe, is somewhat clearing my mind.

Sunday, October 10

Up at 3:30 A.M.; morning tea; and a drive with my two friends to Tiger Hill to see the sunrise strike Mt. Kanchenjunga. Tiger Hill itself is 8,514 feet high and has a little observatory on its summit, which was thronged with Hindus from Calcutta when we arrived. There were heavy clouds in the valleys below us, and the eastern horizon, as well as much of the vast mountain panorama was obscured; but Kanchenjunga was there and when the clouds shifted we caught views of the other peaks. At the moment of the sunrise Kanchenjunga became wonderfully luminous; one could only imagine what the whole mountain scene would have been had the clouds not been there. On the way down, our driver paused to show us the peak of Mt. Everest peeping over a mountain ridge far away.

After breakfast we strolled slowly down to the town, where I arranged to leave on the afternoon plane from Baghdagra. A telegram arrived last night from the American Express to tell me that it would be impossible to visit Koṇārak on the twelfth, since the pilot of the plane would then be in Calcutta, so I am trying to advance my schedule by one day. We next paid a visit to the new home of Tenzing Norgay, conqueror of Mt. Everest, where we found a huge crowd of visitors, but no Tenzing Norgay. He was away for the day. His wife, however, played hostess, while the swarm of Bengalis and ourselves examined all the trophies, wrote in the guest book, and took pictures.

The ride back to Baghdagra seemed very long. We hit a dog on the way and had to pause in the town while the driver talked it off with a man whose hand the dog then bit. I felt very strongly the transition from the mountain world, with its atmosphere of Tibet, to the land of the plains—Santāls and Bengalis.

An easy flight to Calcutta; beside me, a very nice young Hindu, Ram Sharma, who had spent a year at some college in America. We talked of the American-Indian contrast, and, when we arrived at the air field, had a drink. In Calcutta, I got a pleasant reception from all the waiters, doormen, etc. at the Hotel Great Eastern. Found Pam and Ronni at a table in one of the lounges penning an irate letter of some kind to the American Express office, had dinner with a little couple I'd met in Darjeeling, and, leaving an order for tea at 4 A.M., went to bed.

Orissa

Monday, October 11 ***Bhubaneshwar***

Woke with a threatening throat-cold, caught, I dare say, on Tiger Hill. Got the 5:15 A.M.busto the airport. Early morning in Calcutta: all the people who sleep on the sidewalks in various stages of getting up, cleaning their teeth at muddy hydrants, and so on. At one point the bus had to go around a young man doing his sitting-up exercises in the middle of the road—stark naked.

At the airport: Nikhilananda, two or three Ramakrishna monks, and the two ladies. Greetings! I took breakfast in the airport restaurant, and our plane took off at about seven. At 8:45 A.M. we began coming down, and I could see to the left the great Liṅgarāja Temple compound, and to the right the new city, laid out in blocks, with its new, California-type buildings—in one case facing a block of palm thatch homes.

Orissa I find really fine: the best thing so far in India: lovely air, beautiful skies, fertile flatland by the sea, and, after Calcutta, clean and orderly looking people. Orissa, I am told, has a population that is between twenty and fifty percent tribal. I notice many very black people, and garb has a lot of color in it, like that of the Baghdagra area.

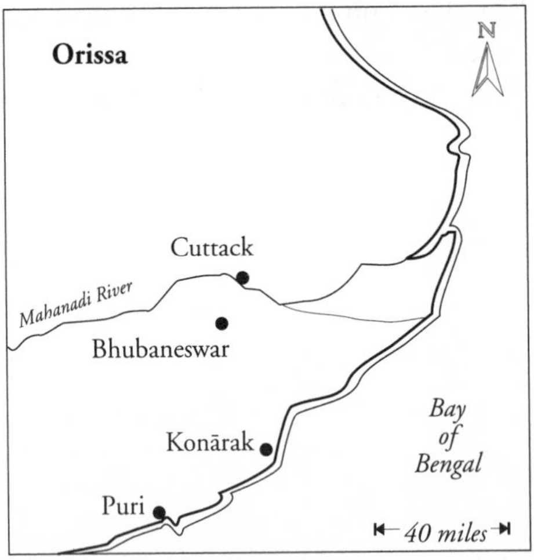

Our comical party are the State Guests of Orissa, and so we were met at the plane by a pleasant delegation of young men and their superiors, packed into cars, and driven to the State Guest House—a nice, clean, well-serviced sort of small hotel—one-storied, with the rooms along a long verandah, and patriotically Indian-type toilets. After a brief wash-up, we were ready to go visit temples, but Swami said that if I wished to go *into* the temples I would have to wear Indian dress. One of the young men helped me into the yards of khaki I had bought, on Swami's suggestion, in New Delhi; then Swami took my picture, and we were off.

The temples that we visited—the Rājarāṇī, Paraśurāmeśvara, Mukteśvara, and Vaitāl Deul—were all old and abandoned and required no such rigging at all; I was surprised at the charming smallness of them all:

some of the figures were no larger than my little finger. I also began to realize what a job of photographing Eliot Elisofon[85] had done. I took a few pitiful photos myself, and then was driven to the railroad station to cancel my ticket to Madras (since I must now go at a later date). The station master took one hour and a half to fill out half a sheet of form. I sat in the station feeling like a perfect fool: the only white man in the place, and the only man in the place wearing full Indian regalia.

When I got back to the Guest House I changed back into slacks and a shirt and joined my friends for lunch. We all then had our naps and at about 4:00 P.M. began to get ready for our visit to the great Liṅgarāja compound. I remained in my western gear and Swami said it would be all right, that I could take photos from the outside while they went in. We drove up to the small space before the temple, and two of our young men were there. They had arranged everything for us and had a priest who would be our guide. So we took off our shoes and socks, left our leather camera-cases and wristwatches with leather straps, and went in.

I stuck close to B. B. Nath, the Museum Curator, and he showed me the details of the sculptural decor. I made appreciative sounds and remarks. Priests, meanwhile, were shouting at us from every direction to come visit *their* shrines—just like the shopkeepers of Calcutta. Nath took me up to a Ganeśa shrine. The priest was at hand. Semi-reverently I laid a rupee at the deity's feet, and we went off. Next we visited Kārttikeya—another priest and another rupee. I bowed before the image and we went away. Pārvatī was next: one more rupee. I bowed, took the dust off the goddess's feet, was given a garland, and gave another rupee. Next came a shrine of Viṣṇu (surprise!). A rupee—but by now a swarm of priests, shouting like fishwives for rupees. I had no more one rupee notes. "Five rupees for all!" they shouted. "Yes! Yes!" I dallied a while, and finally produced the five-rupee note. Twenty hands were before me. Everybody was shouting.

I looked quizzically about, and then they all got together on it and pointed to one young hand that was held out with a dramatic readiness. "That one?" I said. "Yes! Yes!" the priest-swarm shouted. "O.K." and I placed the five rupee note in the hand. They all ran off like urchins: all except one. "One rupee, one rupee!" he said, with his hand held out, and he followed me until, on the point of leaving the temple, I gave him ten annas; whereupon he turned away in glee. But at the other side of the gate I was met by a swarm of beggars; and then Swami came, followed by the whole horde of priests. The car, pulling away, had to begin very slowly, or we should have been held for mass homicide.

Tuesday, October 12 ***Puri***

Up early and off to Puri, for a complicated day. First we paused at the Liṅgarāja Temple again, so that Swami and the ladies could go into the main sanctuary, which, last night, was closed. I was glad to remain outside and take a few photos—one from the platform erected outside the wall for *mlecchas* like myself. But when the holy ones came out again (followed, of course, by the brahmins, every one of whom I recognized) I was told that they had asked where the man was who had accompanied them the day before: namely, the man with all the rupees.

Next we paused at a little town of thatched huts around a temple called Sakhī Gopāl, where I drank some coconut milk while the others went inside.

After that, we headed straight for Puri and arrived about 10:15 A.M. I and one of the young men went in for a swim. The sand of the broad beach was so hot I could hardly bear it, and I ran for the water. Then two lifeguards came trotting up the beach to help us (they had already been sent for), and each of us went in then, like girls, to breast the waves. There was great talk of a heavy undertow, but I didn't feel it. Still, I didn't feel like making a scene either, so I submitted to this silly affair. The little lifeguards wore curious, tall white cones on their heads, each with a number. After our swim, we tipped them one rupee each.

After lunch, Swami wanted to sleep, and his two ladies, who had already been sent up to sleep for the morning, were overtly annoyed. B. B. Nath and I drove with them to town so that they might buy some cards and writing paper and cigarettes, after which they returned willingly to the seraglio. Nath took me to visit a few craft shops and when we returned, Nath went to sleep while I sat and looked out the door at the sea.

At 3:30 P.M. all were again astir and our viewing of Puri commenced. First, the great square before the temple with its three wagons (Jagannātha's with sixteen wheels, Subhadrā's with twelve, and Balabhadra's with fourteen). They were in the (slow) process of being dismantled. We went up into the Ramakrishna library for a magnificent view of the temple and city. Three elephants were in the square, mildly entertaining people; beggars, sadhus, pilgrims, were everywhere; the shops were full, and the commerce of the god was great. We next drove around the city a bit, visiting places of interest to Swami, where he and the ladies could bow before various deceased people's shoes, cots, and photographs. Traveling along the main Jagannātha road I had the real feeling of being in India: it was rich and delightful. We came at one point to a ghat by a pond inhabited by great tortoises, and a priest made a calling sound that brought one blinking to the surface. The people tossed food of some kind, at which he snapped.

Before a monastery said to have been founded by Śaṅkara, one of our two cars ran its back left spring up onto an iron spike, and it took us some time, in the gathering twilight, to get it down. Meanwhile, the other car went off to deliver Swami to the temple, and from this point onward the mix-up was great. Following his visit to the temple (which lasted two hours), Swami wanted to visit some old Ramakrishna monk; and so it was about 9:00 P.M. before we started the long drive home. The Countess, meanwhile, lost a purse containing a thousand rupees; and for a moment I thought I had lost my camera.

But the main thing was that in Puri—a city devoted to a celebration that takes place once a year, and to its temple—I felt for the first time the real throb of India. A fully medieval combination of religion and life, with people doing crazy things (way better than the Surrealist effort) because of the God—a great clatter everywhere, and all with a transcendental reference.

At one moment a little cluster of late middle-aged and oldish men went past, clanking cymbals, beating a drum, bearing staffs, and with religious markings on their foreheads, singing a *kīrtana* of Caitanya; I thought their physiques looked very much like those with which I was familiar from the New York Athletic Club baths. Then I asked myself what the counterparts of these oldsters would be in New York: the members, perhaps, of some poetry society with an aesthetic-rational orientation; humanists perhaps. And then it came over me that:

The great difference between our two civilizations is the humanist versus transcendental orientation; the humanist now having broken through to a subliminal and even transcendental level, but the reference-emphasis remaining, even so, phenomenal man.

The second great difference (which is perhaps a function of the other) is a consequence of the partition of the sexes. The chance of a personal adventure, determined by the personality of a representative of the opposite world and energized by an unpredicted interplay of the two fundamental human attitudes, is simply not permitted to occur. The results are numerous, among them being a sort of proto-homosexuality, a lack of life-inventiveness, and a satisfaction with clichés.

A third difference (perhaps a function of the second) is the caste principle: no one is an individual—everyone is but a fraction—which accounts, I believe, for the absence of anything resembling civic consciousness.

In my chats with one of the young men who are watching over us in Orissa, I have gotten a bit of the feeling of the young Indian marriage. He is a handsome, very gentle and affectionate young brahmin—about twenty-eight, I should say. He is married and has two children, never saw his wife until the day of their marriage, and now lives in the same house with his elder brother, who is also married. These two days have been his holidays—and instead of having planned some sort of holiday with his wife and kids, he has been free (and glad) to spend them with us. Puri, anyplace but in India, I should think, would be a booming beach resort, but here four meager little hotels and the big house of some maharaja constitute the beach front. The young man and I went swimming this morning, and there was no one else in sight. This evening, while waiting for Swami, we walked on the beach in the light of the full moon. It was lovely. There were perhaps two hundred people sitting along the high-wave mark—all in their saris and dhotis and shirts, all in absolute silence: a very mild affair indeed. I remarked on this, and my young man said that Indians don't have any idea of what to do on holidays. To go to the beach would be an enormous operation: children, servants, problems of cooking, procuring food; and then who would be there? Etc., etc. My god! What a joyless lot!

Dryad beneath a palm, Bhubaneshwar

After dinner, I sat out on the lawn of the Bhubaneshwar State Guest House, chatting with a character with a pipe, about fifty-four, who has been pestering me for a talk ever since I arrived. South Indian brahmin family; proud of his service with the British Navy, now writing a book on contemporary Orissa. He wished to talk to me about Koṇārak, which I am to visit tomorrow, and had two ideas about the erotica, and then a third which he simply rejected as unlikely:

1. They had something to do with the idea of heat, the sun's heat, and generation.
2. They were to be transcended by the one seeking *mokṣa.*
3. They were there to protect the temple from lightning.

I suggested that 1 and 2 might be readily combined, since the sun (sun-door) was both the generator and sustainer of this world and the symbol of the way to the transcendent.

The solar symbolism of the temple, the gentleman said, was an intricate representation of the diurnal, planetary, annual, etc. rhythms and cycles; and there was some sort of order to the sequence of symbols on the twenty-four wheels that had not yet been deciphered. I was to look out for it tomorrow.

He spoke also of the great gurus and sages, who are the life of India, though hardly to be seen; told how it is in the blood of all Hindus to begin hankering for a guru at the age of about forty-five: spoke of Sri Shivananda Saraswati, and Aurobindo (whom I brought up). He spoke also of the two contemporary Vaiṣṇava attitudes: that of the baby monkey (⋃ on forehead) and that of the kitten (with a V)—see Ramakrishna's discussions of these two attitudes—clinging to the mother, and crying for the mother.[86]

Wednesday, October 13 ***Koṇārak***

Woke at 5:30, got up and shaved. At about 5:50 my morning tea arrived, and by six I was ready for the car that was to take me to the Flying Club, my date with the airplane being for 6:30. By 6:10 I began to be impatient and started walking down the road. No car. I saw a squad of about sixteen lusties in khaki trunks and white shirts trotting in unison, on some kind of early morning drill. They were followed by a man who was trotting also, but with a bicycle by the handlebars. I asked the latter which way to the airdrome, and he pointed ahead, then mounted his bicycle and caught up with his crowd. Chaps were beginning to drop out and walk back to what I now saw was their fire-house. I began to trot myself, holding my camera with my left hand and field glasses with my right. At the next crossroad I asked a kid: "airplane?" He pointed and I trotted some more. I began to get tired after fifteen minutes, but could see the airdrome just ahead, and so pressed on. At 6:35 I arrived. A young man with a beard was up in the tower. Dog tired, I got up to him, only to be told that the Flying Club was down the other end of the runway—about half a mile more. It was the longest half mile I ever ran in my life—longest and slowest.[87] I came wobbling toward my little biplane two-seater at about 6:50. The flyer, Mr. K. S. Krishnan, piled me into his plane and flew me to my goal.

A great thrill! Eighty-one miles per hour, 1100 feet in the air, in an open cockpit—over the Liṅgarāja Temple compound and then, twenty minutes later, over Koṇārak. We landed in an open field between the temple and the sea. Mr. Krishnan asked a boy to get me a coconut for refreshment and I drank the milk while we walked to the temple. I spent a lovely hour and a half there, and the return home was even more delightful, somehow, than the trip out.

Mr. Krishnan then invited me to his house, right by the airport, for a cup of tea. I met his wife and saw the photos from a trip that he had taken with her and his children: got the feeling that life here was a bit more modern than the Indian norm. Then my State Car drove me to the airport, where I found Swami and the girls, as well as the Director General of Archaeology and his friends, who were to be flown to Koṇārak next. In fact it was their date with

Mr. Krishnan that had thrown my plans, as well as Swami's, into a cocked hat. Swami and the ladies, finally, couldn't get to Koṇārak at all.

We visited the caves of Udayagiri, but were too fatigued to climb; then the Khandagiri hill to the Ananta cave.

I got home, at last, took a shower, and went to sleep, while the others went back to Cuttack where Swami was to deliver a lecture. I woke at about 6:00 and took another shower; but this time felt a chill and knew that I had a fever. After dressing, I had tea with the man with the pipe, who talked now about his drinking adventures in the navy. Swami & Co. arrived: we dined and went to bed. I first, however, took two full doses of aspirin.

I feel at this point that I know a great deal more about India than I did five days ago. At Darjeeling I acquired a fresh taste for my year of travel, and in Orissa I got a sense, at last, of touching the India I had come to find. A few meditations:

1. India's enormous tolerance of apparently irreconcilable elements.
2. India's strength: her transcendental orientation; the guru idea.
3. India's homosexual atmosphere: sex separation, momism (Durgā), phallic interest (*liṅga*), woman for reproduction (Platonism); no individual experience of unpredicted relationships with individuals of opposite sex—lack of life invention, satisfaction with clichés; no real life verve.
4. Caste system—failure of civic interest and adventure.
5. India's contemporary problem:
    a. Spiritual aspect: Can an Oriental state be a secular state? Can a non-secular state be a democratic state?
    b. Political aspect: A common border of several thousand miles with communist powers; a great need for U.S. aid and advice; a greater need for time (perhaps a hundred years).
    c. Emotional aspect: A feeling of common cause with Asia; a feeling of common cause with British democracy; a feeling that India should somehow be the world axis.
    d. Mechanical aspect: Can India make the machine serve Indian ends? The machines that she is buying and copying were invented by Westerners to serve Western ends: they tend to bring their entelechies with them[88] and so create in the Orient a pathological anxiety about machines and what they are doing to the world. For machines to serve Indian ends Indian inventors must arise. What is the likelihood of such an event?
6. The line of contrast between Oriental and Occidental ideals:[89]
    a. Western humanism: The total man, not the caste man. This ideal may be Greek, but in Greece the sex partition was probably as strong as it is here. This ideal belongs, I think, to a much later Europe: the Europe of the Germanic north. It is an aristocratic idea, I think, and *may* have played a brief role in the Orient of the Epic period. But Koṇārak represents a more idyllic eroticism, less personal than that here involved.
    b. Western eroticism: The sense of life's adventure and play, and of personal growth through these.

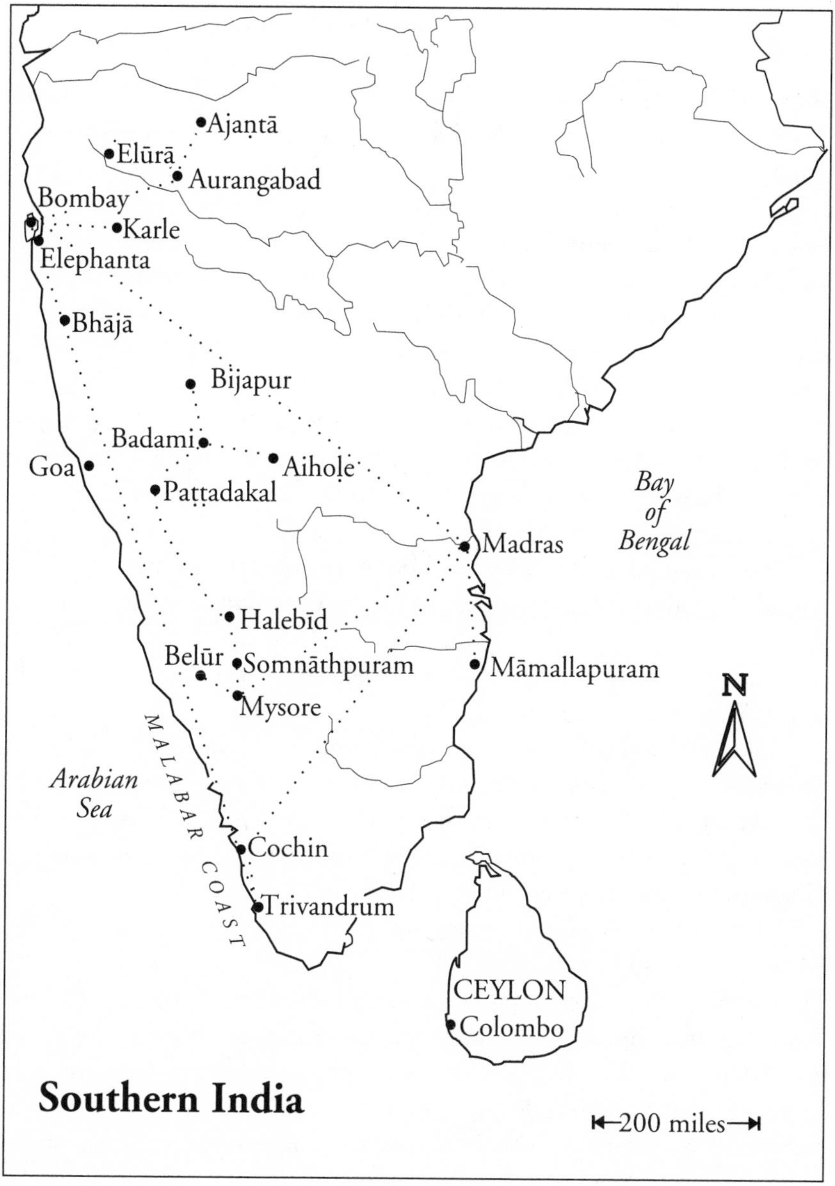

Southern India

Madras

Thursday, October 14 ***Madras***

Flight from Bhubaneshwar to Madras, 9 A.M. to 1:30 P.M. A huge delegation of monks showed up to meet the plane. Lunch at the Connemara Hotel, and a nap. My temperature has gone and the cold is about gone too. I simply took it easy all afternoon, bathed, and enjoyed my very nice room. Still a bit stiff (Achilles tendons) from yesterday's three- or four-mile jaunt.

After dinner I went out for a little stroll and was finding Madras very clean and pleasant when the begging began: first, a dirty woman with a child on her arm, then a couple of kids. I came with this following to a crowded square with a lot of stalls and with people sitting all around: "Ha! Sahib!" from every vendor's stall; "OOO Babu!" from every beggar in the world. When I saw a man with bandaged legs see me, then get up and walk in my direction, I was through, turned, and started home.

Two kids hung on for about six blocks. Several rickshaw boys had to be walked off, and then a neat little black chap, in white Indian clothes, came up to me. "Girls?" he said. "Nice girls?" "No thanks." "Boys? Young boys? My young boys very nice; very nice." "No," I said, "not boys. I don't even like the idea." "You want nice English girl?" he asked. "No thanks." "Mohammedan girl? I got Mohammedan girl." "No thank you." "Hindu girl?" "No." "You want nice hospital nurse? I got hospital nurse. Nice Indian girl." "Well," I said, "you got everything!" "Yes sir," he said, "Everything. Very nice. You want nice young boys?" When I turned into the hotel, he called after me, "Tomorrow night? Yes! Very nice!"

Friday, October 15

The morning newspapers carry the story of India's new Cardinal, His Eminence Cardinal Gracias, who is to be accorded a civic reception on his arrival in Madras. The long article is very favorable to the Catholic spirit. The Roman Catholic Cathedral (A.D. 1504) in Madras is reputed to cover the remains of St. Thomas, who is supposed to have been martyred on St. Thomas's Mount (mentioned by Marco Polo) while praying.

After breakfast I took a taxi to the American Express office and found a letter from the Hindu kid in New Delhi who came to visit me at the hotel after my talk. After lunch I rented a car and toured the town.

Madras is by far the cleanest and pleasantest Indian city so far, with many modern buildings and more going up; a large, wealthy looking section of new American estates, and another of new Indian estates (copying the American exactly in design): also new office buildings. The city is growing rapidly.

There is something neater about palm thatch than about mud for the poor. Madras, consequently, though apparently as full of the very poor as New Delhi, seems very much tidier. More women are visible in the streets here than elsewhere, and many look very nice. And the hand-cart men, nearly naked, have strong, handsome physiques. (The more I live here, the better I understand Monroe Wheeler's joy in the place!)

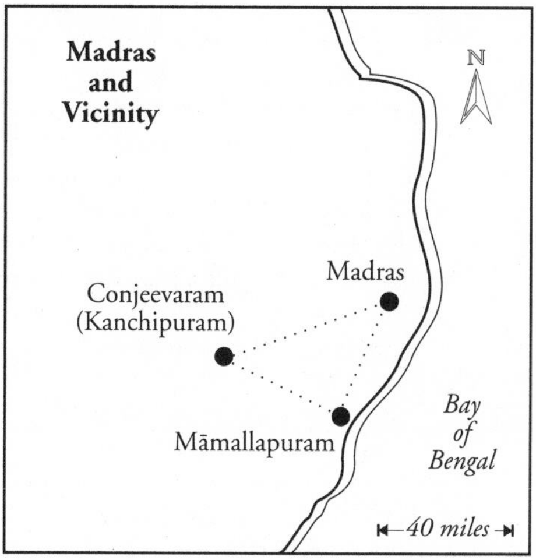

The main language, after Tamil, is not Hindi but English. In contrast to the North, all signs are in English. Most people speak it. Many Europeans and Americans are visible. The Catholic Church is very strong. One sees also YMCA and YWCA set-ups.

And, I must say, after what I have seen of Hindu *bhakti*, Roman Catholicism doesn't look too bad for the Indians. Mrs. D. tells me that it is very strong in the South because here the very conservative brahminism was extremely hard on the *śūdras*, Untouchables and Tribes. Well, O.K. It has all worked out very nicely.

During my tour I visited St. Mary's Church (built 1678–1680), the first English church in India (rebuilt 1759), and paused a while to read the epitaphs on the grave slabs in the churchyard: mostly young and young middle-aged men, *c.* 1652–1759. Made me think of the Honolulu Christians a century later. Strange, bold, and fateful old days! I visited also the great Śiva Temple: my first view of one of these gaudy southern things: freshly painted: my oh my!

And so now, the gem for today: my letter from New Delhi.

My dear Professor,

Received your kind letter of today. Extremely glad to go thro' the contents. when. I was completely disappointed, for, I never received a reply for a long time. [He wrote to me in Calcutta and I sent him an answer after some delay.] But I understand the situation for the delay. I have seen [?] your acquising [sic] me in your letter "your expression of feelings...indeed is bad..." [He must have misread something.] How can you say that. It is not a brief one or for the time being till I forget you. It has come naturally in my heart when I saw you on the very first day. So whether I am in your company or not that will be the same. Since it became so deep, even your photo, why so much as even your letter is enough to satisfy that hunger. When the love is too intense physical meeting is nothing to do with that. That is only till we are together. One can enjoy ever if it is from the heart. If you say it is bad I won't agree. and that will not disappoint me. Always I look forward and I will sacrifice myself for that when I feel it is normal and correct. Still I am ready to take your advice. Do then do you mean to say I should suppress that love and affection towards you because we cannot meet each other often. At least in our mythology there are several instances, where two met only once in this lifetime, they were friends through out their life. But if you say this is modern age I want to know that. Can we not be united, even without seeing each other? Don't you think it is true [sic], it will be so sincere also.

Then you have written "when one travels this kind of thing happens." Here also I do not agree with you. How can you judge and compare me with others? At least why don't you test my sincerity after coming across though several such instances (?) Have some patience to find out whether I am sincere or not. Why you see me like a passerby. Test my sincerity. I can repeat only this.

Only so much I can say whether you show your affection towards me or not. I do not mind. Still I love you. Hereafter also it will be the same and I sacrifice myself for that.

From your letter I understand you are extremely happy in my place of India. Why don't you write in details where—[?] you had been to show you enjoyed, so that I too will share the happiness. At least when you go to Madras and when you see temples in south and those beautiful Belūr, Halebīd, and Somnāthpuram in Mysore you please write a detailed letter about how you have enjoyed and how you are interested. As you are a professor in literature I have no doubt that you will give me a fine description about what you have seen.

Expecting eagerly the month of December I hope we will meet in Delhi.

All are doing well here.

with love from K. Narasimhan

N. B. Nobody can go against God's will. He created this in you in my mind. At the same time if he wish that we should not meet each other and we should be far, I can't help. I have to suffer for that.

K. N.

Excuse me for writing in pencil.

Saturday, October 16

Started the day with an answer to young K.N.

My dear Narasimhan:

I am sorry that my last letter disappointed you and am afraid that the present one is going to disappoint you too. For it appears that you are expecting much more from me than I am going to give. Please remember when you write to me that I am a rather busy person, of late middle age, happily married, with many many friends to whom I am writing; I simply cannot begin writing long letters to you descriptive of my travels, feelings, thoughts, or anything else. Moreover, the whole prospect of a love union is to me, at my age, utterly uninteresting. A quarter of a century ago I had a number of such eternal unions—all, however, with members of the female sex. And my present eternal union is with my wife. I am not going to test your sincerity, ask you to sacrifice yourself, or engage in any of the great gestures of love. You asked me to be your friend and to reply to your letters; I shall be pleased to do so. But I must tell you now—simply and coldly—that I am extremely busy; already well taken care of, as far as love is concerned; disinclined to love affairs with males; and too old for romance of an idealizing nature.

If you wish to write to me again, please do not do so right away. Read this letter of mine several times. Let ten days pass and read it again. Realize in your ardent heart that you are writing to a person who has not fallen in love with you, of whose life you know absolutely nothing, whom you have no right to command, and who does not want to hear any more about sincerity, sacrifice, or eternity. You may regard me as a friend, if you wish, but not as a lover.

What you are in love with is a projection of your own imagination. You cannot be in love with me because you do not know me. Break up this figment of māyā that has caught you and please do not begin to write to me again until you begin to feel (sincerely) that your attitude has changed. This is the only sacrifice that I shall ask of you.

And so, with sincere good wishes, and the suggestion that you begin this difficult work of spiritual discipline right away, I am,

Yours very sincerely, &c.

After breakfast, walked to the Madras Government Museum, which is, by far, the best museum I have visited in India. The bronze collection is elegant; also, of course, the Amarāvatī panels and fragments. Among the bronzes are a number of Buddhas with the flame rising from the *uṣṇiṣa.* There are a couple of Rāma and Sītā pairs, a handsome sitting Mahiṣāsuramardinī, three fine Śiva Naṭarājas, and an interesting collection of carved wooden beams and jambs. Also rooms of tribal and folk exhibits, including a couple of figures of the village deity Aiyanār, with his wives Puranai and Pudkalai; some wooden, painted deities of the fishermen of Orissa; a cute set of the avatars of Viṣṇu; and some photos of the dancing dress of Indian shamans that suggested, on the one hand, the Kathakali costumes and, on the other, some of the dancing gear of Melanesia. There was a carved figure from Malabar used in sorcery which suggested Africa. I noticed also that an exhibited zither was called a *swara maṇḍala* and wondered whether the word mandolin might be related. Certainly sitar, zither, and guitar go together.

At 3:30 this afternoon I joined Mrs. D. and the Countess for a visit to the Ramakrishna Maṭh. A particularly fine set of buildings. We then went with Nikhilananda and another swami to the home of a Dr. Ramakrishnan (M.D.), where we had a delightful "tea": tasty Indian sweets, prepared and served by the gentleman's daughter and granddaughter, and then a wonderful café au lait (tasting like a mocha). The people showed us through their house, which was one of the new buildings that I saw from outside while on my sightseeing tour: two stories, upstairs verandah, lots of air, handsome Burma-teak woodwork (doors, windows, stairs), and dull-red, shinily waxed, tile-like, composition floors; living and bedrooms in Western style; kitchen and pantry store-room, however, rather Indian. The first room that they showed us was a little family chapel, with a figure of Ramakrishna and about ten of those holy pictures of the Hindu gods. Dr. Ramakrishnan himself had his sleeping quarters in a little pseudo-simple, neatly housekept "hut" in a slightly removed corner of the lot.

From this pleasant household we drove to the Vivekananda College, where Swami lectured on the Upanishads to a large gathering sponsored by the Philosophical Society of Madras. The lecture was a pell-mell of all those themes introduced to me during that year in New York when I was editing *The Gospel of Sri Ramakrishna.* I don't know what the "philosophers" really thought of it, but the words of praise that I heard seemed sincere enough. There were as many as three introductory speeches and two envois. The Indians certainly like to sit and listen!

We next toured the building and then went to a Ramakrishna orphanage, where Swami was asked to say a few words to a very well-behaved and attentive lot of nice-looking young boys. He told them to enshrine Mother India in their hearts. I then was asked to speak, and I told them that everybody in the world was telling Americans that their American patriotism was out of date, that we were trying hard to put it behind us and become true citizens of the world, and that I hoped that they too would try to make their patriotism harmonize with a feeling of world brotherhood and love. (I think I won the day.)

From the orphanage we were driven to a large mansion inhabited by a charming family from Calcutta: father, mother, two sisters, and a boy who wants to go into the navy (but his father is for Oxford). Western style with Indian effects. We were greeted with leis (jasmine) and treated to the supreme dinner of the Indian tour. The younger daughter was really worth looking at, and the elder (Indian chubby type) sang two *kīrtanas* very simply and well to the accompaniment of her harmonium. I was impressed to see—again—a family chapel (in this case rather elaborate) with figures and pictures of Ramakrishna, Vivekananda, and the Holy Mother. The family had two photo volumes, which they showed us: one full of Vivekananda photos and the other with pictures of the other early members of the Order. Swami allowed himself to be praised considerably and at 10:45 we left for home.

Today I have the feeling that I have caught a glimpse of the point of view of the well-off group in India: I can see, how, for them, the spectacle of the poverty of the poorer classes would be comparable to that of the Pittsburgh slums for the well-off people of Pittsburgh. In America, being of the well-off class oneself, one sees the poverty as an evil that is counter-balanced by the happiness of the majority. In India, when one comes as a visitor, all that one sees are the poor. Dr. Ramakrishnan spoke of the rising demands and pay of workers in precisely the terms that I have heard in Honolulu and Mount Kisco; yet here a bricklayer gets five rupees (one dollar) a day, whereas in America (last I heard) the pay was twenty-seven times that sum. The people on top, whether in India or the U.S.A., regard the life needs of the worker as greatly less than their own.

Let me develop a theme that came to my mind while Swami was lecturing. There are two blocks of people in India: the "Folk" and the "Leaders."

The Folk, whom I would identify with the "working class" of Priestley's remarks can be divided into the Non-literate (India's majority), and the Literate (not numerous in India). The Folk *receive* ideas, are filled with *bhakti,* and desire simply to look *(darśana).* In a non-literate state they are moved by the traditional ideas of a steady, slowly changed, ancient inheritance, which is religious in tone. In a modern, literate society, they are moved also by the press, radio, and political parties.

The Leaders are, in all modern societies, literate; and it is they who render the ideas to which the Folk respond. The Leaders may be divided into two main groups: the Traditional *(le symbolisme qui pense qu'il sait),* and the Creative *(le symbolisme qui cherche).*[90]

The Traditional, whether proper to the culture (in India, Jainism, Hinduism, etc.), or Intrusive (in India, Zoroastrianism, Islam, Christianity), tends everywhere to be religious in style. In India the Traditional—represented by monks, priests, and Catholic clergy—is predominant.

The Creative, which predominates in the West, is secular and of two types: the Ephemeral (journalistic, sensationalist) and the Epochal (scientific-scholarly, fundamental). In the popular view of America, the Ephemeral type is conspicuous; actually, however, the Epochal type is perhaps even more effective in America today than in Europe.

Representatives of the Creative in India are my friends the Well-Offs, but they are only *secondarily* creative. Their function is to apply to India the findings of the West; and in this function they face a sensitive problem: to let the principles of Indian civilization transform the intrusive heritage, rather than allow the reception of the Western forms to Westernize the Indian mind.

The machines, for example, have been shaped by Western minds to serve the ends of a Western—that is to say, a fundamentally humanistic—life orientation. If it is true, as Gandhi has said, that "India has a greater destiny than merely to copy the West," then some sort of Indian mind has to begin thinking about creating machines to facilitate the rendition of Indian life-aims, which, I believe, are trans-humanistic. If Western humanism is accepted, there is no problem—we shall have, simply, a Western province with Oriental effects. But if Western humanism is rejected, then the machines will have to be creatively transformed. A machine tends to impose upon its master the teleology of its own form—and this explains, I think, some of the impulsive anti-westernism in the westernized Indian of the Nehru type. The machine and aid that you know you require, yet haven't yourself created, tends to press you toward the alien life-style that brought it forth, and you react by biting the hand that's feeding you.

In terms of my division above, what strikes the eye of the voyager in India is the poverty and *bhakti* of the Non-literate Folk. What seems to strike the eye of everyone looking at America is the hurly-burly of the Literate Folk/Creative Leaders combination. To judge either community by this surface flash is to be superficial. The substance of India is in the Traditional Leaders, but also of the Intrusive types; and that of the West is in the Creative Leaders of the Ephemeral type, with an icing of the Epochal.

The Well-Offs of India are of two types: the Tradition-oriented and the Creative-oriented. The Tradition-oriented have altars in their homes; the Creative-oriented drink.

Sunday, October 17

Decided this morning that it would be interesting to see a group of Indian Catholics at mass, and so, asked a taxi driver to take me to San Thome's Cathedral. He took me, instead, to St. Thomas's Mount, where a guide immediately took me to the summit—up the 135 steps to the little chapel. There was sound of singing in the chapel. My guide made a sign to someone inside, and out came a nice little Irish nun who invited me inside for Benediction. I found a little company of about five nuns (mostly Indian) who sang the hymns (which I remembered from Canterbury School), and some twenty very tiny Indian girls in white veils, who said their prayers aloud and in unison. The celebrant was a young Indian priest whose Latin was clear and nicely pronounced. The children, I had been told, were "unwanted children": and this little rescue party seemed to me to epitomize the whole pattern of the Christian mission in India: "the stones rejected by the builders"; "the excluded factor." Islam had built from the same root in India.

Moreover, while listening to the Catholic hymns and prayers, after having heard for some weeks only the Hindu, I found myself not caring much which system prevailed. *Bhakti* is *bhakti.*

After Benediction the nice little nun showed me the so-called Bleeding Cross, a stone with engraved cross, supposedly carved and revered by St. Thomas himself, and said to have sweated water on December 18 very frequently between the years 1551 and 1704; and the "Picture of Our Lady," supposedly painted by St. Luke and brought to India by Thomas, but looking rather like a 14th-century Siennese job. Then I went down the hill again, boarded a bus, and returned, hot and tired, to the Connemara Hotel.

At 6 P.M. I went to the inauguration of the new Madras Roman Catholic Cultural Center, where a crowd of about three thousand saw a dance concert given in honor of India's first cardinal, Cardinal Gracias—a tall, good looking Indian with grace and elegance in his language and presence. After the surprise of this morning and my afternoon of reading about St. Thomas in India, this evening's event gave me a considerable sense of the force of Catholicism in India.

Cardinal Gracias spoke with sympathy of the new nationalist interests of India. Formerly, he said, parents used to tell him that their daughters were studying French and the piano; now they told him they were studying Hindi and Indian dance. One of the numbers this evening, performed by the students of Stella Maris College, was a semi-Indian dance interpretation of St. Francis' "The Canticle of the Sun." I was reminded of much that is going on in New York, and particularly of Haddasah's performances. Apparently the whole female world has become dance conscious. In India, however, the dance is now on a strictly amateur level—when the girls marry, I am told, it is finished.

Monday, October 18

Up early in the morning for an expedition to Māmallapuram[91] and Conjeevaram.[92] By taxi with Mrs. D. and the Countess to the Ramakrishna Maṭh, where we learned that Swami had a fever and would not be able to come; in fact, he would probably not be able to leave for our tour of the south tomorrow. Besides, it was raining cats and dogs. Nevertheless, the party would proceed—and indeed it did, after a delay of about an hour.

The party consisted of myself and the two ladies, two swamis, a young Indian lady, and seven gentlemen in white, with various types of tonsure and beard. All very gay and pleased to be starting off on a semi-religious bāt.

We started at about 8:15 and arrived about an hour later at a crossroad where we were met by four additional gentlemen and a car. Their car soon had a flat, however, so they sifted into ours and left someone to fix their flat. We drove to the Dak bungalow at Māmallapuram, where we were met by a young man in khaki, a "sub-inspector," who would be our guide to the monuments—and here we made the first pause of the day. All drank coconut milk and chatted pleasantly, while an old black man silently pulled rhythmically on a rope that set in motion a large fan-contraption hanging from the ceiling.

After the coconut milk we stepped into the cars and drove to the five *rathas*,[93] next walked to the Descent of the Ganges complex,[94] and to the Shore Temple,[95] then returned to the cars, which had come to meet us. I was impressed particularly by the cave containing the Viṣṇu Anantaśāyī[96] and Mahiṣāsura-mardinī[97] panels. In the central shrine (A) was a panel of Śiva-Pārvatī with a male figure at the lower left sacrificing his head. I couldn't photograph the panel because the light was very bad. I realized when we were in Conjeevaram that we had missed the Ādi Varāha Cave,[98] but we had been shown everything else that I wanted to see, and I was delighted with the place. The visit was marred a bit by a couple of beggars who concentrated on me, but otherwise was fine.

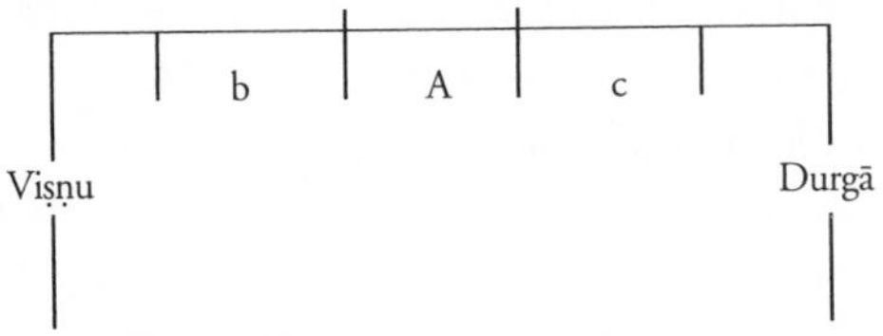

We drove next to Chingleput to visit the Ramakrishna Mission and school, which involved standing reverently before a number of Ramakrishna-Vivekananda-Holy Mother shrines and inspecting, first, the boys' school, then the girls'. In the latter, a darling moment when, in the auditorium, which contained the shrine and was chock full of standing students, the whole group sang in unison a rather complex hymn. I was particularly fascinated by a cluster of sixteen little eight- or nine-year-olds who sang with their big eyes and funny little faces covertly inspecting every inch of the clothing of Mrs. D. and the Countess. After the hymn these little things spun around two or three times quickly patting their own cheeks. I don't know what this means; but I saw it again, later in the day, in one of the temples of Conjeevaram.

On our visit to the schools we were joined by a couple of gentlemen with odd tonsures and were driven to somebody's home for the most fantastic lunch that I've ever shared. Later we learned that these people had never entertained Westerners in their home before. The lunch, presently, was served on the living room floor. Sixteen or twenty cushions were placed around the walls, and before each was half of a banana leaf, which was to serve as plate and table for the occupant of the cushion. All took their places. Rice, dhal, various thick liquids, odds and ends and whatnot were dumped in various quantities directly onto the banana leaves; grace was sung; and the company, including the ladies, set to work with their right hands. Water was drunk from brass cups, but poured into the mouth, so that the cup should not touch the lips. For this feat of acrobatics the left hand was used. It was a wild half-hour: all I could think of was a Hawaiian luau. To see them perform the miracle of getting liquids into their mouths from the banana leaves by way of a saturated mess of rice was something of a marvel. Thank God they gave me a fork and spoon.

Following the meal, we sat around for about an hour and a half and then began our drive to Conjeevaram—but again we stopped at the Ramakrishna Maṭh and again we found ourselves doing reverence to one of those shrines. I was pretty tired of *bhakti* by now; and since Conjeevaram is full of important temples I was becoming a bit impatient. This particular shrine was up on the roof, under a corrugated iron canopy; and since there were a number of cameras present a great many pictures had to be taken of various groupings. We then descended to the main room, where there was a big round table and lots

Descent of the Ganges

of floor space: many sat on the floor, a few joined the ladies and me at the table, whereupon tea was served: that is to say, a considerable meal. I thought we'd never move. However, we presently did—about an hour before dusk.

We drove first to the Kailāśanātha Temple, which for me was a disappointment.[99] The seventh-century sculpture had been covered, at some date, with a plaster coating, into which eyes, noses, mouths, etc. had been incised. The effect was crude and worthless. But here and there the plaster was gone, and a lovely seventh-century face or two peeked through.

We next went to the great Viṣṇu Temple and when we came out it was dark. But I had seen enough of the carved *maṇḍapas*, colonnades, and so on, to get the feel of it. In the dark we visited the temple of Śiva (the great temple of the *bhūmi liṅga*)[100] and the temple of the Goddess Kāmākṣī. At both, our numerous friends led us around gaily through the magical labyrinths of the corridors and shrines. We circumambulated a great mango tree; stood before Śiva's *liṅga* while the priest recited *mantras* and finally gave us each a handful of ashes to rub on our foreheads; and again stood before the *yonī* of the Goddess while the priest recited her 108 names—at each name tossing a pinch of vermillion into the *yonī;* we then received some of the vermillion back from the *yonī,* carried it to a little side shrine, deposited it there and then took a fingertip amount for our foreheads. The whole thing was wild and great. And, of course, at the exit of each temple the beggars were terrific. The priests though—I must say—were decently behaved.

The drive home was interrupted by a pause for lemon pop at the town where Rāmānuja was born.[101] We arrived in Madras about 9:15. I went up to see Swami, who was in bed still, and said he would not be leaving tomorrow and for me to decide what I wanted to do. I got home by rickshaw, and, after a bit of tea and bread and butter, went to bed.

Tuesday, October 19

Decided to postpone my tour of the deeper south until Jean arrives, and to go tomorrow to Bangalore. Went to the American Express to make arrangements, and finally returned to the hotel for lunch with the two ladies, who had been to see Swami. Apparently he is feeling better, but is going to remain another week in Madras. He thought my plan a good one, and so tomorrow I start the second stage of my India visit—definitely alone.

After lunch I went to the Museum (second trip) to measure a few of the Amarāvatī pieces, and the remainder of the day was spent writing in this book and writing letters.

Three nice letters arrived two days ago from Jean and one from Helen McMaster: all giving a wonderful account of Jean at Bard and of her great lecture demonstration at Cooper Union. It sounds as though everything was going really beautifully.

There was an article in yesterday's newspaper about Vinoba Bhave[102] which I liked. He spoke out against Nehru's "welfare state," and declared that what was required was local initiative and spirit on the part of the villagers. He also spoke out a bit against *bhakti* and caste: *pūjā* before images and then caste avoidances before men he found untimely. Reading his words, I thought it would be men like Vinoba who would rescue Hinduism from its own past. Ram Mohan Roy, Ramakrishna, Vivekananda, Gandhi, Vinoba: that would seem to be the line.

Meanwhile, something can also be said for the images, the pilgrimage centers, the *bhakti* and all. They are focal points of communal concentration, representing syndromes of ideas and ideals. The problem is to release the ideas and ideals into contemporary life: the Redemption to the Redeemer theme. That is the problem of my course and study.

An amusing set of exchanges while driving to and from Māmallapuram: through an idyllic rural countryside of paddy fields, thatched villages, coconut palms, goats and cattle. On the way out, a gentleman sitting beside me spoke of the landowners to whom all the property belonged, told of how these people starved when the rains failed, as they had recently for a run of some five to seven years, and lamented their ignorant misery, which, he thought, better agricultural methods were already beginning to improve. On the way back, one of the monks was beside me, and he spoke of the wonderful timelessness of it all, and of how happy these people were in their simple lives.

India seems right now to be in a state, as it were, of nonentity: drawing its future from Europe while at the same time searching into its own past to try to find out what it once was. The question is: Will the past (India's proper dynamism) have the power to convert the Western gift into a vehicle for *Indian* life? Or will India become simply a sort of Western nation with Oriental effects (saris in their movies instead of low-cut gowns)? In other words: will Vinoba win or will Nehru?

Temples and Monuments

Bangalore and Mysore

Wednesday, October 20 ***Bangalore***

Packing finished, I joined the ladies for a brief visit and farewell to Swami, then returned to the hotel for lunch, after which I caught my plane.

Arrived about 3:30 in Bangalore, found the West End hotel, where they gave me a whole cottage (too bad Jean isn't here!), and I went then to arrange for my visits, tomorrow and the next day, to Mysore, Somnāthpuram, Belūr, Halebīd and the great Gommaṭa statue.

Bangalore is cool, high, and pleasant. A clean, attractive city—but hardly Indian. The atmosphere is that of a pleasant Anglo-Saxon resort. I even put on my blue suit for dinner. Then I repacked for the great expedition and went to bed.

I think that my earlier edginess has worn off. It was partly Swami and the ladies; they could never see anything in India without running down its counterpart in the U.S.A. Yet I'm glad for our time together; it helped me to see the absurdity in this India *über alles* attitude: it also helped me to appreciate the U.S.A. Anyhow, that one's over—and I seem to be enjoying India very much.

Thursday to Saturday, October 21-23 ***Mysore***

The great Mysore adventure! Rain, rain, rain—but no rain check. I went through with it nobly: visited the charming little temple of Somnāthpuram on Thursday afternoon, toured the larger and even more marvelous temples of Belūr and Halebīd Friday morning and early afternoon, and on the way back to Mysore ascended barefoot the six hundred and fifty rock-cut steps to the great Gommaṭa statue at Śravana Beḷgoḷā—only to find the image completely covered with bamboo scaffolding for the workmen who are trying to do something about some cracks that have begun to appear. Furthermore, with roads comparable to those of the Navaho reservation (we actually got stuck once fording a stream) and the car hire eight annas per mile, I lost all desire to go on with this rough game of visiting the great Hindu monuments. I abandoned the Hyderabad-Aurangabad idea and came back to Bangalore by bus (eighty-eight miles in five hours), and will leave tomorrow by train to reach Bombay at noon on Monday. And, by God, if Bombay doesn't register you can have Mother India anyway you like her, for all of me.

It is strange but important that all of the temples of the great pre-Mohammedan days are in spots that once were great capitals, but now are practically abandoned, and can be reached only by private or hired car, or by airplane (too expensive), or by train or bus, which is more than the body can stand—practically all day going and coming, with a brief moment at the monument. Perhaps I shall find some other way to manage when I get to Bombay, but if I don't, I think I'll settle for Elephanta, Ajaṇṭā, and Elūrā, which I can reach from Bombay.

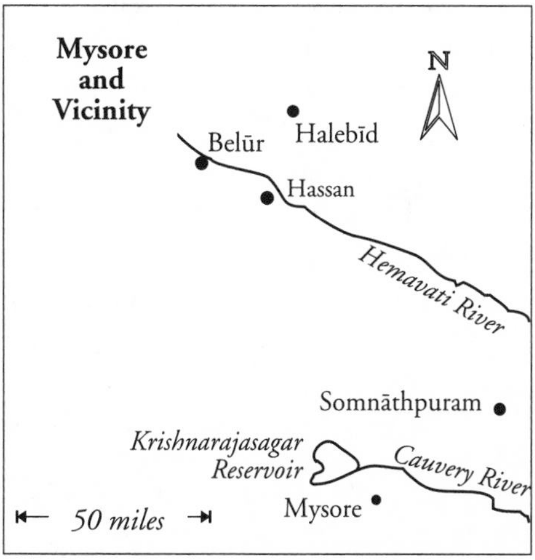

In other words, there is a geographical as well as a temporal and a spiritual break between the classic periods of Hindu art and the modern so-called Indian (actually Islamic-Hindu-Occidental) world. The influence of the ancient art has simply withdrawn from the modern field; or rather, the capitals of modern India have grown in new sites (mostly ports: Calcutta, Madras, Bombay), with Dẹlhi on a site where all the Hindu monuments have been razed, except that ruined and re-used temple by the iron column. Modern India, reaching back to make contact with the earlier styles, isn't going to manage it.

A fantastic example of the contemporary effort is the new palace of the Maharaja of Mysore, which I saw this morning, before leaving for Bangalore. The palace stands in a great, grandly landscaped enclosure. In fact, the landscape situation in Mysore is by far the best that I have seen in India: the Maharajas have actually designed their city: they have also provided a handsome holiday resort with gardens and lovely fountains at the great reservoir of Krishnarājasāgar. But—my Lord!—when you enter the palace! (My guide said that I should take my time in the palace, because in the whole world there was no palace so beautiful: a combination of Madison Square Garden and Coney Island would be elegant in contrast. Green, yellow, and maroon are the predominant colors: bulbous columns with maroon base, green and yellow shafts and capitals support (with a curiously chunky effect) huge domes of green-, yellow-, and maroon-stained glass.

There is a great ballroom or audience hall, then another, then something that looked like a magnification of the old Hippodrome. The door frames are carved of ivory (cracking) and silver, elaborately figured with imitations of ancient motifs; there are rooms with carved sandalwood panels, and one with a waxwork image of the present Maharaja's father, with a life-sized, cut-out color photograph of a palace officer standing beside him. And along the walls! In one room, ten or twelve large paintings, English-Indian olios, of gods and goddesses; in another room, wall after wall of an absolutely naturalistic portrait-panorama of the Mysore state processions (painted 1938 or 1939), showing every soldier of the band, horse guards-man, the Maharaja on his elephant, and so on; and finally in another room, a lot of bric-à-brac connected with images of the gods, including (believe it or not) Ganeśa flanked by two mirrors—one concave, the other convex—so that when you stood before the god you see yourself transformed to right and to left.

In the nearby *citraśāla* (painting gallery), I saw rooms of recent Indian art labeled "Gujarati School," "Āndhra School," "Malabar School," "Santineketan School," etc. And what were they? Maxfield Parrish, Aubrey Beardsley, pre-Raphaelite, and (more commonly) fairy-tale illustrations—*à l'indienne*—nearly all, of course, of *Mahābhārata* and *Rāmāyaṇa* themes. (They'll wear these out some day.) There were a couple of attempts at more modern watercolor styles, and a room or two with works imitating the standard British Academy brand of naturalism.

Slightly more interesting than those upper-caste efforts were the lower-caste achievements: cabinets of sandalwood, ivory, or ivory-inlay, intricate carving, and such impossible stunts as images of the basic Hindu pantheon carved from rice-grains. So what! Whereas in the Hoyśala temples of Somnāthpuram, Belūr, and Halebīd one marvels at the art as well as the craftsman's patience, now one marvels only at the patience and the craft. The vision has withdrawn.

Amen to the past.

The Maharaja has sixteen Rolls Royces; but he has done so well by his people that Mysore is far and away the comeliest, least squalid province of India that I have seen. The villages have comparatively sturdy houses, most of them with tile roofs (there is a tile factory in Mysore). Most of the villages have electricity: the only electric power lines I've seen in India crossed the rich paddy fields of Mysore. Both Mysore and Bangalore are very pleasant, clean, and well-off cities. Besides, the climate is nice, and the little mountains add a touch of scenic interest. So Mysore illustrates for me what the new India may be, if it's lucky: a great rural area rendered prosperous by a well-calculated application of modern—i.e., Western—improvement (dams, electricity, fertilizer, etc.), with pleasant provincial cities full of bicycles, and with a few great metropolises of a completely Western character, but with Indian effects: movies in Hindi, Bengali, and Kannada; photos of Indian babies; little shops with people sitting on the floor.

On the other hand, a little episode that I spied in the train may point to something further. In Bangalore, a gentleman in European clothes, a professional man of some sort in his middle or late fifties, entered the compartment, sat at one end of the seat across from me, took a booklet from his satchel, and began quietly reading. He was hardly seated when some coolies brought in a great number of pieces of luggage and began stowing them under the seats and on various shelves. Then three people entered, two young men and a young woman who wore an ugly dark greenish sari and spoke Indian English. She and one of the men sat on my side of the car, the other sat across from me. They ordered three breakfasts and talked a good deal, somewhat cryptically, among themselves. One of the young men had a small book, V. Gordon Childe's *History,* from which he occasionally read excerpts to the young woman: their rather effortful, unseasoned intellectualism made me think of New School of Social Research people.

The breakfast I had ordered was brought to me, and when the bells and whistles of departure sounded, I had already finished it. The breakfasts of the trio, however, had not yet appeared. They looked from the window; one of them got up and went to the door. The train moved, and then a couple of waiters came running down the platform, one of them with a heavily loaded tray, which he passed to the man at the door. There was a questionable moment—but the tray was safe. We all laughed, and one of the waiters climbed aboard.

He was a very dark little man, with fine features, dressed in the dirty white of the station waiters and wearing the turban. He helped the trio with their plates and then sat inconspicuously on the floor near the entrance while they ate. I sat watching the scenery go past beneath a heavily clouded and rainy sky. The gentleman who had entered alone continued to read his book; the trio, eating, carried on their unconvincing conversation. When they had finished, the waiter got up and began collecting the plates. He took my tray first and set it on the floor. Then, coming up to take the trio's tray, he briefly, quickly, and very lightly touched the shoes of the gentleman who was still quietly reading and then brushed his hands swiftly over his own forehead and chest. I don't think the gentleman himself knew that anything had happened, and certainly the chattering trio saw nothing. The waiter caught my eye and saw that I had seen but made no sign and went on with his work. When the dishes and two trays were stowed on the floor, he resumed his self-effacing position, silently squatting on the floor by the door, and when the train reached its next stop, about an hour later, he picked up his trays and left.

Having seen the act of reverence to the gentleman's feet—precisely the kind of reverence that is brought to the feet of the swamis—I tried to think what might have been the cause. Was there any sign on the man to indicate what he was? I could discover nothing. But then I saw that the book that he was reading was the Ramakrishna Maṭh edition of the *Taittirīya Upaniṣad*—and I was amazed: the waiter must have seen the word "*Upaniṣad*." If he did, and if his reverence was to the spiritual moment of a man reading the Upanishads—then I think there is something here that can hardly be matched by anything known to me in the West. No effort was made to touch the feet of the chap reading V. Gordon Childe.

In the Hotel Metropole in Mysore, where there were bats in my bathroom, a number of Americans of a sort of "expert" type were talking seriously about something with a company of Indians, which included—lo!—my trio of the train. My guide told me that this was a conference on tax collection; and later, when I climbed the 650 steps to the scaffolded image at Śravana Beḷgoḷā, I learned that American experts had been called to analyze the stone and make suggestions about how best to fix the cracks. Furthermore, I read in the newspapers that a review of the Indian educational system has been undertaken by a committee of experts, on a grant from the Ford Foundation.

American aid, American advice, American money and brains: but in the newspapers and out of Nehru's mouth, no good word for America, but only for the "peace-loving" Communists and Russia's offer to install one steel mill. India's collision with America is based partly on the fact that, for us, the China issue is a problem of Democracy *vs.* Communism, whereas Nehru (the great liberal!) sees only Occident (Colonialism) *vs.* Orient. Such willy-nilly identification with the Orient is related to the present Indian effort to recover its own Asian roots. It may also be related, however, to England's anti-American operations, rendered in this case by way of Lady Mountbatten.

Modern India's disconnection from its own past is vividly symbolized, it seems to me, by the geographical remoteness of *all* of the great Indian monuments of the classical periods, by the almost impassable roads that lead to them, and by the lack of accomodations in the neighboring towns. In the modern northern cities there are only modern buildings and Mohammedan monuments, while in the south, the large Hindu temples that rise in the cities are of the late southern style—which even in the twelfth century represented a decline in India's religious art.

Since the classical art of India is so geographically and spiritually remote from the modern Hindu world, the modern Hindu, not really appreciative of its beauty, says, "How beautiful!" with equal rapture before a modern Durgā Pūjā shrine. Nor can he interpret one of its most conspicuous elements—namely, the erotica.

In the decor of the temples of Somnāthpuram, Belūr, and Halebīd, I found erotic scenes quite as obscene as anything at Koṇārak, only not quite so conspicuous. The temples are of precisely the same period. One motif, repeated at Belūr and Halebīd, was that of a woman taking one man's penis in her mouth and another's in her tail. Figures of this sort cannot be explained in terms of Coomaraswamy's "each is both" idea;[103] neither can some of those complicated arrangements at Khajurāho. The problem of India's temple erotica, therefore, would seem to require discussion under two headings:

I don't know when the earliest examples of the Loving Couple theme occurs: perhaps the royal donor couples on the Bhārhut pillars can be regarded as announcements of the motif; the *gandharva* couples at Aihoḷe and Māmallapuram perhaps come next; and then the overtly loving couples on the balcony railings in the Laṅkeśvara Cave[104] at Elūrā, where "each is both".

I think there may be some connection between the Multiple Lover motifs at Khajurāho, Koṇārak,[105] Belūr and Halebīd, and the Black Mass which appeared in Europe at about this time.[106] The Khajurāho fragments suggest some sort of erotic yoga. At Koṇārak there is another effect to be noted, a type of visage that suggests the Greek satyr—this whole thing has to be worked out, somehow, for my *Basic Mythologies*[107] book.

Indian religious history falls into three main periods: the Vedic Upanishadic—Early Buddhistic; the Puranic Tantric (Mahāyāna and Hindu)—Vedantic; and the Popular (*bhakti* cults, *kīrtanas*, etc.)—Monastic. Indian art of the classic periods illustrates the Puranic Tantric. Its tone is aristocratic, and though many of the religious motifs survive (e.g. *pūjā;* Durgā; Mahiṣāsura-mardinī), the spirit has changed, so it is very difficult to connect it with the Popular period.

And now we may add a fourth period: the Modern, which at present I interpret as being almost completely a translation of Western, humanistic, progressive, spiritual ideals into Indian, metaphysically toned terms. The primary Moden sequence: Ram Mohan Roy, Vivekananda, Gandhi, Vinoba. Ramakrishna comes in as a focal center of Popular period ideals, rendering them as a foil to the Occidental side of Vivekananda.

It is important to note in this connection that both Vinoba and

Aurobindo[108] have found ways of transforming the Indian idea of declining history (the four *yugas)* into a kind of apocalyptic progressive view. According to Vinoba, the Kālī Yuga is almost at its end and will be followed immediately by the Kṛta Yuga (no period of dissolution between).[109] Aurobindo's idea is a bit more complicated.

As far as western ideals of social improvement and optimism for the future are concerned, I think India will be able to integrate these without too great a case of indigestion—though I should not like to try to predict what will happen to the current sort of *bhakti* when literacy, science, and scholarship become general (if they ever do). A great, almost immediate problem, will be the total psychological transformation that may supervene when Indian boys and girls begin to become interested in each other as individual personalities, not merely as functionaries in a bio-mytho-logical mystery. When that happens, the present almost absolute segregation of the sexes outside of the home will begin to break down, people will begin to make their own decisions about whom they shall marry, the sexes will begin to act upon each other psychologically and pedagogically, and the present pattern of willed infantilism will dissolve. What precedent in Indian life will the young people then be able to find? My suggestion would be to search the annals and art of the Tantric Puranic period.

There is a subtle problem here, however. I have a feeling that in the Orient there *never* was the kind of humanistic intellectual intercourse between the sexes that is characteristic of the modern West. (It did not exist in ancient Greece either.) The *sahaja* ideal is still bio-mytho-logical—and so, our spontaneously humanistic reading of the *maithunas* is probably a misinterpretation. Certainly, here there is a pattern suggesting the corybantic orgy and the yogic crisis rather than the humanistically toned heterosexual relationship.

All of this makes me see much more clearly the point of Jung's warning that Westerners cannot safely take over the symbolism of the East.[110] The reference of the symbols is to a psychological structure very different from ours. It is a structure such as was the West's, perhaps, in the Middle Ages; but for the modern man, who has had too much of the rational and humanistic and is searching for a fruitful contact with *his own* unconscious, these symbols from a world that has not yet developed an effective humanistic view can serve only as hints of what is to be found. In the conscious life of the Indian there are all these Divine Mother images to which the actual women are held subordinate, in the conscious life of the modern Westerner are a number of actual women, each quite different from the other, whom he hardly associates with the Great Mother archetype—though in his unconscious he is certainly doing so.

Sunday, October 24 ***En route to Bombay***

Off on the 9:45 A.M. for Bombay. At about 5:45 P.M. arrived at a junction where I had to change trains. I had gone all day without food, but had a rather good dinner at the junction railroad station. My train for Bombay pulled in a little over an hour late, and I was assigned to a compartment with two utterly horrible Indian gents. One, a dark-visaged, sturdy, middle-class thug, shouted at the waiter who brought him his three-rupee dinner because salt and butter had been omitted from the tray, raised his hand as if to strike him, and then shouted some more at the obsequious restaurant manager who came rushing to see what was the matter. I thought, My God, to have to cater to men like this! Then I had a new illumination about the gentleness of servants in India: gentleness to those above, brutality to those below.

The other gent in the car was a paunchy, somewhat older man, who wheezed, coughed, cleared his throat hideously and spat out the window, and kept going into the stinking Indian-style toilet room, all night. Every time he would come out of the toilet room, he would fail to lock the door, so that it soon would swing open, letting the reek fill our compartment. Neither of the Indians seemed to mind; so it was I who got up every time, walked the length of the compartment, and fixed the latch.

Bombay and Aurangabad

Monday, October 25 ***Bombay***

at 6 A.M. I got tea and toast at a station, while my gentlemen companions cleared their throats, got up, spit out the window, and prepared to face the day. At another station, at 9 A.M., I ate another breakfast with an omelette. We arrived in Bombay at about 1:30 P.M. (775 miles in 28 hrs, or about 28 miles an hour).The weather in Bombay was clear and cool: very nice for a change.

The Grand Hotel is pleasant and reasonable: eighteen rupees a day, with good meals. I bathed, shaved, had lunch, and took a taxi to American Express, to find no mail. After tea I took a long walk past Victoria Station and along Mohammed Ali Road, viewing the markets and the wonderfully busy and crowded streets, to Sandhurst Road, where I took a taxi home. After a good dinner I returned to my room and wrote to Jean.

I have arrived at a festival moment, namely that of the Divālī or Dīpāvalī, the Festival of Lights, a festival of the New Moon, representing re-creation and rebirth—and I have a feeling that I can make it a rebirth festival of my own, if I go at it correctly. This morning, about an hour before sunrise, I was sitting up in that horrible train compartment, looking out the window, when a lovely object, lightly revealed by the coming sun, appeared in the sky: the *dark* moon, and with its lower surface brightly illuminated—like a silver platter holding the darker disk. We were passing through pleasant country when from a little farmhouse, decorated with the colorful lanterns and strings of paper pennants characteristic of the festival, there came the sound of firecrackers greeting the festival, and I had a pleasant feeling that with Bombay my India journey commences. I have been voyaging for two months, have circumambulated the country in the sunwise direction, have assimilated the unpleasant aspect of the Indian picture, and now I can begin to take things at my own pace and in my own way.

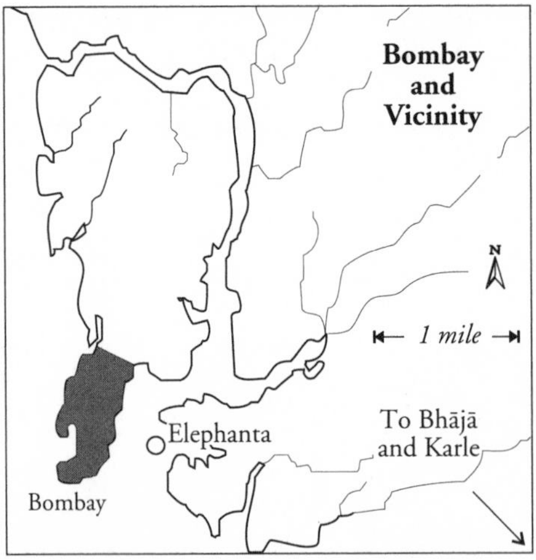

Tuesday, October 26

In this morning's *Times of India* there were a couple of feature articles about the Divālī festival, from which I glean the following:

The name *dīpāvalī* is derived from the Sanskrit *dīpa* (lamp) and *valī* (line): a line of lamps. Another name is *dīpa-mālikā* or *dīpa-mālā*; a string or garland of lamps. It is a festival of lights.

It is compared, in one of the articles, to the fire festivals of the Celts: the Halloween Fires (with a quote from Frazer[111]), which come at about the same time of year. On the primitive level, such a feast is regarded as a dispeller of baneful influences; among the cultured of India it is celebrated as symbolizing the triumph of light over darkness (the same interpretation was given to the Durgā Pūjā in Bengal).

"In many parts of India the night of the Divālī is known as the Kāla-Rātrī, the most dreaded of all nights, when the goddess Mahā-Kālī with her attendant deities and Devils, known respectively as *bhairavas* and *pisācas*, is to be propitiated by the performance of secret rites and orgies at dead of night [a clue here to the multiple-partner class of erotica?]. On this night, it is believed that evil spirits, both disembodied and natural [sic], hover about, and that they must be kept away from the homes of the living by the lighting of lamps and fires, the performance of ceremonies for the propitiation of the deity whose will they obey. These illuminations came to form an integral part of the Divālī festival."

Gambling is permitted during the Divālī. The feast is associated with the myths of Kṛṣṇa's slaying of Narakāsura, Rāma's return from exile to be King of Ayodhya, and Viṣṇu's marriage to Lakṣmī.

After breakfast I went for a long walk, all the way from my hotel, which is in the Ballard Road area, to Malabar Hill, where I took a bus all the way back again and around to Colaba, where I had another walk. I returned again by bus, in time for a little nap and then lunch.

It was a lovely walk and put me in a good mood for Bombay. A few people were fishing along the sea-wall by the gymkhanas,[112] and others quietly praying, a touch that one would hardly encounter in the West. On the bus-ride I saw a Jain monk and then a couple of nuns, with their mouths covered—but no brooms! All afternoon I worked to bring this diary up to date, and after supper I went again to Malabar Hill, by bus, and returned.

The city was full of lights and gaiety and noise. I could see parties going on in many homes and in shops. The feast is a kind of combination of Christmas, New Year, and the Fourth of July. Firecrackers, sparklers, and simple rockets everywhere, set off in the teeming streets. Kids everywhere. Lights everywhere. People nicely dressed, going to parties everywhere. During the morning, I passed many little groups of women and girls with food presents which they were bringing to someone. Many cars and taxis were decorated with garlands of mango-leaves and yellow flowers. During the course of my evening walk a large firecracker went off right under my feet and a squirt of beetle-nut juice from some window just missed my head. Quite a night for a hike!

Grossman, Salmony, and Kashi

Wednesday, October 27

I find I like Bombay best of anything I've found in India, but I'm glad I saw the other places first, because the typically Hindu motifs are comparatively subdued, and I might have missed them had I come here first. Bombay reminds me a bit of San Francisco: they are about the same size—and you feel the port, the water, in the same way. It is not as handsome—but its crowds make up for that. In the markets and streets are many more types of people—more urban, livelier, more fantastic—than in other Indian cities, and the buildings are stranger, more Oriental: comparatively, every other city I've seen is rural, much less mixed and cosmopolitan. Being out on this peninsula, the city is cut off from the farmers, and you don't have herds of cattle and wandering cows, or peasants. More women, better dressed and better looking women, are visible in the streets: but males still outnumber females about a thousand to one. Bombay, perhaps, represents best the focus of new industrial and Occidental influences in India. The city is full of American movies.

Also, I note, there are more Europeans and Americans here than elsewhere.

In this morning's *The Indian Express* I read what seems to me to be about the ultimate in the anti-American campaign: "The most disturbing phenomenon of our times is the horde of international spies—too often really national spies—operating under the temporary halo of Point Four Aid or the sanctity of the U.N. welfare organization. Even if we brush aside the American attempts to dictate to the U.N. Secretary-General on the treatment of staff, this is not a negligible affair for us."

I went out for a walk and, when I reached the Prince of Wales Museum, entered. Whom do I see, almost immediately? Alfred Salmony, with two gents, one American, one Indian (their bearer).[113] Great greetings, and a museum cruise together. Salmony spoke almost immediately of the anti-American atmosphere. Monday night he gave a lecture, and the Indian who introduced him spent twenty minutes abusing America, the Ford Foundation, Fulbright grantees, etc. Salmony also spoke of the unloading of some ships that had arrived in India with wheat: American ships bringing free wheat, and one Russian ship bringing wheat that India had paid for. The former were unloaded normally, in silence; but for the latter there was a great ceremony with speeches.

I think that the arrogant anti-Americanism is what sticks in my craw the hardest here. The poverty, the people trying to sell something, the beggars, the bad railroads, and the dreary hotels: these I can now swallow; but not the arrogant insults.

I guess it can be said that India is undergoing a sort of psychological enantiodromia of self-rediscovery,[114] and consequently cannot be expected to behave in a civilized manner. Psychological crises always make for a sort of compulsive boorishness.

But I renew my resolve never to speak or write again for India. *About* India, perhaps; but not *for*. I shall return in my work, as rapidly as possible, to my main line of comparative mythology, and then press on to the problem of the present crisis in our *Western* consciousness—a very different consciousness, as I now realize, from that of the East. Or perhaps India's situation is an acute parody of our own, brought on by its forced westernization under the British. As we are seeking contact with our own unconscious, so are they with theirs, and their problem is stranger than our own, because the archetypes in *their* past are not related to the Occidental rational principles that are even now shaping their world. The very machines that they are buying, their psyches reject as alien. They're in a mess—and I shall try now to regard them with more charity. And, incidentally, it is possible to regard the whole contemporary moment as one in which the various peoples of the world are undergoing—each in its own way—an acute psychological crisis. Here is a theme for the conclusion of *Basic Mythologies.*

Spent the afternoon catching up with this diary, and, after dinner, went around to the Taj Mahal Hotel for a chat on the fine second-floor balcony with Alfred Salmony, his friend Jason Grossman (who has a car!), and an English collector of bronzes, a Mr. Dane. Our principal topic was plans for a visit at the end of this week to Elūrā and Ajaṇṭā—in Grossman's car. We drank lime juice, and disbanded about 10:30 P.M..

Thursday, October 28

Met Salmony at the Taj Mahal Hotel at 10 A.M. and went with him to see Father H. Heras, S.J., a wonderful old man with a white beard and white cassock. One of the big experiences of the trip: the meeting of three scholars with a common range of interests: Father Heras, plump, humorous, and very learned knew Salmony's name, and Salmony asked him for contributions to his periodical. Then it began: first, a view of Father Heras' publications (just out: *Studies in Proto-Indo-Mediterranean Culture*—a must), then a view of his college library, one of the best Orientalist libraries in the country, and finally, his collection of bronzes. "Fabulous! Fabulous!" was all Salmony could say. Our visit lasted two hours, and was great.

In the afternoon I went to American Express and found a lovely letter from Jean; also a repentant and chastened letter from my Narasimhan.

> All the clouds in my heart has vanished. With clear mind I am writing that there is not the least of selfishness in my heart. I fully realized my mistake. I request you kindly excuse me taking me as your own child. This is a sort of experience for me to go to a better life....

I tried to catch up with my mail. A quiet afternoon and evening alone.

Friday, October 29

Taj Mahal at 10 A.M. to plan trip to Aurangabad and caves. Nasli's mother and brother at hotel.[115] Salmony told me that Rudy and Nena von Leyden (friends of Mme. Moitessier) would like to see me for dinner.[116] Afternoon packing and writing. Evening at the von Leydens'; a very nice couple. Rudy showed me his collection of Indian playing cards.

Saturday, October 30 ***Aurangabad (Elūrā)***

Off in the dark at 5:45 to meet Salmony and Grossman at Grossman's West End Hotel. Fine drive to Aurangabad. Made two stops on the way to look at country markets, one for lunch. Arrival, about 5 P.M. Tea, dinner, bed.

Sunday, October 31

Elūrā, Caves I-XII (Buddhist) and XIII (Hindu).[117] Great experience. At lunch we ate at Cave XIII, then had a chat with a Swedish scholar named Lamm, with whom Salmony picked an argument. He was the type of European who tries to make surprising yet precisely pertinent observations—this time about Elūrā: but they were not surprising and almost inevitably missed the mark. A bit hard to drop him but we finally got away. Then, toward dusk, a first quick view of Kailāśanātha.[118]

Monday, November 1

Elūrā again, from Cave XIV to the end; skipping Kailāśanātha, then returning to it for the grand finale. Of the Buddhist caves seen yesterday, the most impressive were Caves II, X (Viśvakarman), and XII (Tīn Thal). Of the Hindu: XV (Das Avatāra), which offers a series of magnificent sculptural panels, XVI (Kailāśanātha), XXI (Rāmeśvara), and XXIX (Dhumar Lena), where we discovered an obscene crude engraving scratched on the face of a pillar, perhaps by the workmen. The little Jain cluster of caves at the end was surprisingly charming.

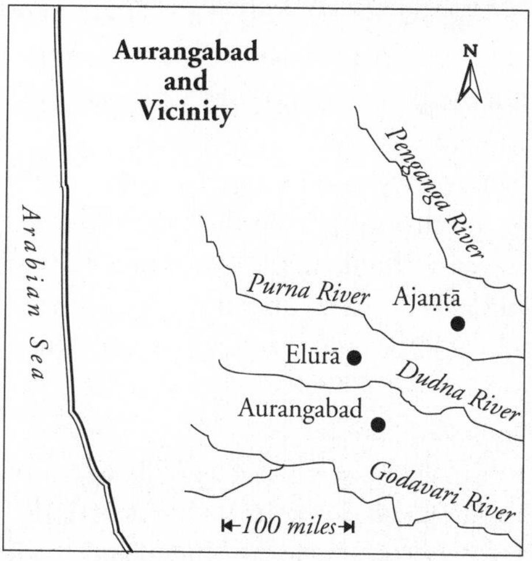

Returning from the caves this afternoon, we paused for a chat with the young director of the Archaeological Survey office and his wife,the Hapars; then we stayed for tea and invited themto the hotel for dinner. They are vegetarians of brahmin family and represent what is beginning to seem to me to be the best type of young person in India: the intelligent, modern yet orthodox, upper-class Hindu.

Tuesday, November 2

To Ajaṇṭā, a rather longer drive. I have been doing all the driving: a Hillman station wagon with four gear shifts forward and one reverse. We spent the morning in the caves with wall paintings, where a light was required; the afternoon in the remainder. A lovely day. Ajaṇṭā is not as great an experience as Elūrā, but it is somehow more charming. The valley is glorious, and the caves, all Buddhist, constitute a wonderful unit.[119]

Wednesday, November 3

This morning we visited a small series of caves in Aurangabad. Cluster I–V was in rather bad shape and seemed to me to be not too exciting, but among the cluster VI to IX there was one, Cave VII, that is certainly a match for much that we have seen. It is a Buddhist cave with elegant *dvārapālas*, then at either side of the entrance to the cella two panels showing female deities and attendants of a glorious, late Gupta elegance. Within the cella itself is a magnificent Buddha; on the left wall there is an extraordinary panel of a female dancer with six musicians, three musicians arranged symmetrically on each side, in a powerfully rhythmical composition; on the right wall is a standing male and female. Query: Does the dancer represent a *devadāsī?* If so, is this not exceptional for the Buddhist cult?

In the afternoon we visited two Muslim monuments: first, the tomb of the wife of Aurangzeb—built by her son, in imitation of the Taj Mahal—smaller, made in cheaper materials, and less magnificently proportioned, a good example of a poor second; then the so-called *pāñcika*—a garden, pond, library, mosque, and tomb, pleasantly arranged in a typically Muslim style. Salmony and Grossman, at this point, seemed to lose their minds, making believe they couldn't imagine why we were looking at these things; but I found the jump from the Gupta-Cāḷukya days to the Muslims rather exciting and illuminating. The power of the Muslim garden to cast a spell is to me amazing—and whether the garden is large or small, in Damascus or Aurangabad, the spell is always the same.

Thursday, November 4

Off to an early start for a good day's drive back to Bombay. This whole visit to Aurangabad and its caves has been delightful. The weather was lovely, the hotel one of the best in India, and the monuments easy to reach. The road quite good, and we arrived in time for a bath and dinner—Grossman this time coming to my hotel, while Salmony returned to the Taj.

Friday, November 5

Ten A.M. meeting with Salmony at the Taj to make plans for our trip to Bādāmi–Aihoḷe–Paṭṭadakal. Visit to the Indian Tourist Bureau for advice, and then with Grossman to the Indian Automobile Association. Letter writing in the afternoon, after which a visit to the American Express to cash some money, when, behold!—Swami and his two ladies. Pleasant greetings, and my promise to look them up. After dinner, a stroll with Grossman through the lively streets in the neighborhood of the hotel.

Saturday, November 6

Morning: to automobile licence bureau to get an Indian driving licence; very polite and pleasant treatment from the officers, but the slowest kind of office work I've ever seen. After two hours and seven rupees, I had my licence.

Afternoon: with the von Leydens and Salmony, in a motor boat to Elephanta. Lovely, lovely, lovely—the top experience of the trip. The great central figure is simply something.[120] "Walk right in, slowly, and let it come," said Rudy: and it did. We spent a long while in the cave, and then went in again to see it in terms of Rudy's idea that the original entrance was the one at the left. Makes very good sense. We visited the caves around at the side of the hill. Then Nena and I went back into Cave I. On the ride back we had a pleasant snack from a picnic basket; later, at the von Leydens', we had a lovely dinner. An excellent day.

Sunday, November 7

Sent off some proofs and corrections to Pantheon[121] at 10 A.M. and joined the von Leydens for a visit to their swimming-pool club whereWesterners and Indians (the latter, mostly Parsees) were sitting around under parasols. At the table next to the one at which we settled there was a company of Hindus, including one young woman who turned out to be the sister of Rama Mehta.[122] When she heard my name she said, "You are a friend of my sister. I am reading your book. It is inscribed, 'To Rama, with love...'!" Apparently Rama and her husband will be coming to Bombay next week.

I had met at the pool some of the people from the von Leydens' two Sundays ago, and the sense of pleasant social fooling around was very soothing. For lunch we had a sort of second breakfast and left at about 3:00 P.M.

I returned by bus to my hotel, and then tried to get to Swami Nikhilananda's talk at the Ramakrishna Mission; but when I reached Malabar Hill, I learned that the Mission is some twelve miles out of town, and so I abandoned the try. Took a pleasant walk in the lofty garden on Malabar Hill then returned for dinner and early bed.

Bombay to Bangalore and Back

Monday, November 8 ***Poona***

Up at 5:30 A.M. to prepare for an early start to Bādāmi. Packed, sent my bags downstairs, and sat down for breakfast at 6:45. Meanwhile, Salmony and Grossman were outside by the car with Kashi (Grossman's charming bearer) and a flock of porters, discovering that the combined bulk of their two vast sets of luggage was too much for the car to hold. It took until eight o'clock or so for the realization to sink in.

A series of discussions, phone calls, and conferences was initiated, involving all kinds of surprising people, including taxi drivers and passersby on the street. Presently we all got into a taxi behind a driver whom Kashi had consulted, and were driven to the office of a man who earlier in the morning had suggested over the phone that a light car like the Hillman would not be able to make the trip at all. Both Salmony and I were by this time ready to drop the whole thing, but Grossman seemed willing to risk anything. The man came out of his office, which opened like a stage (as do all Oriental shops) right onto the street, and, with his wife protesting, stepped into our taxi. He directed our driver to the State Transport Office, where he very kindly conducted us to the desk of a young man, Mr. T. V. S. Iyengar, for a consultation on the problem of getting our luggage and ourselves to Bādāmi.

The roads, Iyengar said, would be all right for the car as far as to Bādāmi; Aihoḷe, also, would probably be all right; Paṭṭadakal, on the other hand, would be out of the question. This agreed with most of the other advice we had received, and so we accepted it as a working hypothesis. Next, as to the luggage: it would be dangerous to ship it without an attendant. A man could be sent, however, to Bādāmi *with* the luggage. He could go by train, leaving tonight, and would be there when we arrived. The cost would be about two hundred rupees (a jolt for me, but the others seemed to think it great). O.K. The young man himself would come to our hotel this afternoon at two, to be introduced to the luggage, and then, at seven, would return with the fellow who would see it through to Bādāmi. We could depart with carefree hearts after the two o'clock look. Splendid!

Return to the hotel. Further sitting around. Three for lunch. Further sitting around. It was 3:30 before we got away—but at last we were off and heading for Poona.

What a lovely countryside inland from Bombay!—and I do like the way the peasant women in this part of India wear their saris—hiked up like pants. The saris are of many colors, in contrast to the monotonous dirty white of the

Gangetic area. And the countryside is wonderfully mountainous, in contrast to that utterly flat land of paddy fields. At one of the higher points of our mountain driving we came to a sort of resort area, with nice-looking city Hindus strolling along the roads—in direct contrast with the peasants who were likewise on the roads, but with loads on their heads. I could not but think of the Woodstock area—the city vacationers and the natives.

Poona, which we pulled into shortly after dusk, proved to be a rather large and pleasant city. The hotel was about on the order of that in Gwalior. Kashi took over and settled us in our rooms. We lay down for a brief rest, and after dinner took a short stroll before retiring.

Tuesday, November 9 ***Bījāpur***

The cooks in the kitchen began clattering dishes and shouting (in India, "talking") to each other at about 4 A.M. and I got the full benefit of it all through my window. We got up at six, had breakfast, and set off for Bījāpur.

Again a lovely drive, along adequate roads. Toward 4 P.M. we approached the city across a great plain and began to notice that the bullock-carts that we were passing were exceptionally colorful. Most of them were crowded with men and women in bright attire—the men with clean turbans of yellow, blue or green, and the women with lots of trinkets. Moreover the horns of the bullocks (beautiful, long-horned zebus) had been freshly painted—green, or red, or, most often, a brilliant magenta. Some of the animals wore gay shoulder capes. And all had jingling bells about their necks. The bullock carts were trotting at a lively clip and were exceptionally numerous: also, the animals were exceptionally difficult for their drivers when our car went past.

We entered Bījāpur and found that the two Dak bungalows were occupied. Jason Grossman and Kashi did most of the talking, and neither seemed to be able to make very fortunate connections. The language here is Kannada, so that Kashi was hardly better off than his boss. We were sent from place to place, looking first for the Dak bungalows, then for the "Collector"—the officer in charge of their occupancy—and finally, with no success of any kind to our credit, back to one of the Dak bungalows, where we picked up a sort of porter in a dirty white turban who scratched himself a bit too much. This chap guided us first to a large area surrounded by buildings, where it was learned, through a brief conversation, that there were no rooms, and then to a crowded street where he told us to stop before a Hindu hotel.

This was going to be good.

Grossman and Kashi went into the hotel where, it appeared, there were a couple of empty rooms; Salmony went across the street to an apothecary shop, where he thought he would probably discover someone who spoke English; and I remained in the car, which almost immediately attracted a multitude of kids and adults, who simply stood around, peering in at me and examining the contents of the car through all the windows. One cute little girl stood in front of the car and I flashed the lights. Her eyes grew wide and she laughed. Then I made them dim, and she was delighted. I made the "left turn" wink and then the "right turn"; flashed the high, the dim, and the parking lights, etc., made the windshield wipers work, and again flashed the lights. It was a great entertainment. Presently Salmony came out of the apothecary shop and joined me at the car, standing outside and playing with the kids, until Kashi came out of the hotel and we all moved in. I drove the car into the small yard of the hotel, and the game was over.

The proprietor was a tall, very nice gentleman, in the usual dhoti and long white shirt, whose desk was at the left of the verandah. Upstairs there was a little balcony, where two Hindu gentlemen were sitting, and a number of small, stone-floored rooms. Kashi supervised the porters and we were soon installed—Salmony and I in a room at the back, which had a little balcony of its own, and Grossman with Kashi in a larger room (no private balcony) at the front. Both rooms had just been washed down for us, under Kashi's supervision, so that the effect was one of sanitation. The smell elsewhere in the hotel, however, was a bit heavy, and we were told that it would be all right for us to urinate on our balcony: there was a drain that would carry the water to the eaves, whence it would fall harmlessly into a back yard.

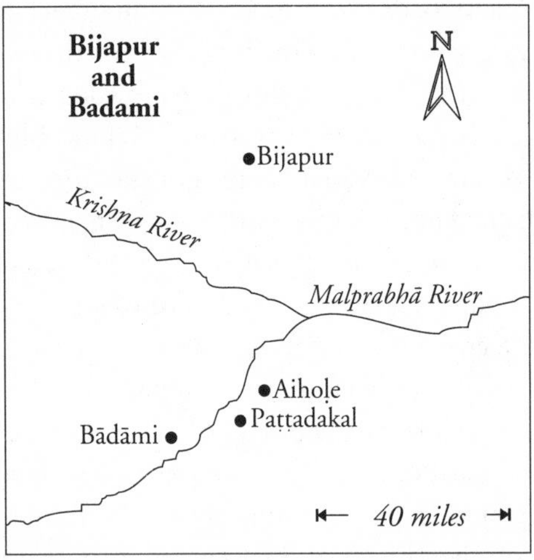

Buckets of water were brought to us and we all bathed on the little back porch; Salmony first, then Grossman and I. And I was later engaged in helping Kashi open our bed-rolls onto the two beds in our room, when Salmony came up to invite me downstairs to meet his friends: the friends being the fruit of his trip to the apothecary—a darling cluster of young men, all interested in art, who, when he had presented his card to the proprietor of the shop, declaring that he was an art historian in quest of a bed, had gradually accumulated around him. They were now downstairs, in the main sort of dining room of our hotel, inviting us to have some tea. Kashi and Grossman joined us. And the youths then invited us to have dinner with them at their home: they were the sons of a large brahmin family—brothers and cousins—and their chief father was a banker, one of the big men of the city. Now, since we had been about to retire on practically empty stomachs, this invitation was a valuable surprise—quickly accepted.

The youths returned for us at nine and we drove to their home, through the crowded streets of Bījāpur in a holiday mood. The festival is a Mohammedan one—the birthday of the Prophet—and Bījāpur is a predominately Mohammedan city. Hindus and Mohammedans, the young men told us, live together peacefully in this area: during the period of the partition there were no incidents. Bījāpur was once a great Mohammedan capital—principally, following the fall of Vijayanagar in 1565: thus the city is the Mohammedan contemporary of Madura. One sees the remains of its ancient glory everywhere, and far out over the flat plain: old Mohammedan tombs by the score; old battlements. The modern city is considerably smaller than that of great sixteenth and seventeenth centuries.

Politely guided, we stopped before a decent house at the end of a short blind street, doffed our shoes at the door, and ascended a stone flight of steps to a moderately large living room, without windows, on the second floor. There was a long white cushion on the floor along one of the walls, and a square rug in the middle of the floor; a row of stiff chairs across the room from the cushion, and perhaps another chair or two: but we all sat on the floor. We also viewed with interest and cordial remarks the pictures hung about the walls, which proved to be the needlework of the young men's aunt. The lady herself appeared, briefly, for congratulations, and we were shown some newspaper articles celebrating her work. Three of the pictures were copies of Mughal paintings, one was the portrait of a horse, others were of birds and flowers. Salmony was particularly unctuous and utterly noncommittal in his polite remarks; for, as an authority, he had to protect his honor while honoring his role as guest. The youths brought out their poems, pictures, and thoughts, and we had a sort of spiritual repast before our trip downstairs to the Hindu meal.

It was an acrobatic, orthodox Hindu affair, in which a company of gentlemen sit on slightly raised wooden platforms placed in mathematical order around the room, and convey rice, dhal, liquids and chopped-up surprises to their mouths with their unaided hands. Jason Grossman studiously tried to do it and dropped only very little on his clothes. Salmony sat sideways, with his legs out to the west, and tried to look happy while eating in a radical position of twist. I simply asked for a spoon. Salmony then got a spoon too. The ladies served, like furtive servants, and when they arrived, severally, with their bowls and serving spoons, they were introduced as Mother, Wife, Auntie, etc. We men presently finished and returned to the upper room for a continuation of our elevated conversation.

The question of Hinduism and caste arose, and when our Hindu hosts looked a little amused at the thought that Westerners should think caste intrinsic to Hinduism, I quoted Śaṅkara to the effect that one was lucky who was born a brahmin and a male, because only he was capable of *mokṣa.* The youths concurred, with accurate quotations, and it appeared that a problem was indeed present. The talk moved to communism in American colleges—and Jason was sounding off, in what I was displeased to recognize as the regular communist direction, when one of the young men signaled me to his room for a talk about how to get into an American college.

It was a typical student's room: bed, desk, a few chairs, and significant pictures on the walls. The pictures, however, were of Krishnamurti (looking much as he looked when I knew him, 1924–29, only with greying hair),[123] Sri Ramana Maharishi,[124] and T. S. Eliot, with a tiny figure of Christ crucified hanging on one of the walls, suspended from the molding—with the cross missing. Written on the wall under each of these icons was a quotation from the savior in question. The typical problem of an earnest modern youth religiously oriented, of coordinating in terms of modern life the wisdoms of the past and present!

We all descended, finally, to the ground floor, where, I believe, we committed our only real faux pas of the evening. For we entered a room in which the ladies were assembled, one of them with a little baby in her arms, and imagining that we had stumbled into the seraglio, we quickly withdrew. I realized later that they must have been assembled there to hear us marvel at the baby.

Before we left, we were treated to the culminating marvel of this actually quite marvelous adventure, namely, an interview with the mighty father of this clan. He sat in his special room, on the floor, clothed in his white dhoti and brahminical thread—greatly paunched, cordial and smiling. Around him, in a convenient semi-circle, was a low book-stand supporting six identical closed volumes, which I thought for a moment might be the *Mahābhārata* but which, more probably, were his account books. Behind him, against the walls, was an array of safes. And he spoke to us in Kannada, with his eldest son serving as interpreter. The great brahmin's thesis: that the philosophy of the West is materialistic, that of India spiritual (an old Indian cliché: shades of Nikhilananda); that the condition (the poverty and squalor) of India is a consequence of its philosophy; and that therefore the philosophy of India is inferior to the philosophy of the West (surprise!).

We thanked our hosts, returned to our Indian hotel, and went to bed.

Wednesday, November 10

On the quiet morning air, the muezzin from a nearby mosque—my first since Constantinople in 1929. A wondrous sound. After a chary breakfast of tea, bread and butter, and bananas, we were taken by one of the young men of last evening to see the sights of the city—these included the ancient fortress, with a great bronze cannon, a large Muslim tomb, and another tomb, the largest (or perhaps second largest) dome in the world. This young man also brought us in touch with the clerk of the Collector, who arranged for us to occupy the Dak bungalow at Bādāmi, but failed to give us a slip as certificate. The Collector himself, a Mohammedan, had been supervising worship the night before and consequently had been inaccessible. We were assured, however, that everything would be O.K., unless some department head appeared in Bādāmi. The protocol now gives top rights to the Government Heads, next rights to tourists, and then come the lesser officials. The Forest Officer of Poona had been scheduled for this bungalow, but we had precedence, and he would simply have to get out.

We invited the young man to have a Hindu lunch with us as our hotel. He was a large, rather sleek young man, and ate like a bear. I took very little. Salmony and Grossman seemed to like the rice. And then we set off, with eager hearts, for Bādāmi, arrived at five, drove to the bungalow and found—guess who—Iyengar himself with Salmony's and Grossman's bags and gear.

Among the objects to have been transported there was a heavy box containing a dozen bottles of Vichy and Evian water; which the officials at the Bombay railroad station had challenged as possibly containing wine or champagne. Bombay has prohibition. The chap who was to have accompanied the luggage took fright at this point and refused to go, lest he be challenged again; so Iyengar took over.

We thanked him profusely. After the Bījāpur adventure, we were now completely overwhelmed by the evidences of the kindness and hospitality of the people of India.

The Dak bungalow, however, contained but one grim bed and the only water was in a large washtub in one of the three washrooms. The groundplan of the sturdy building was about like this:

Unit I contained three rooms and two washrooms; Unit II one room and washroom. The portable toilet was placed in the washroom at the far left; the luggage was in Unit II, and the bed in the sleeping room at the far left. We decided that Iyengar, who had no bed-roll, should sleep on the bed and the rest of us on the hard stone floor, Salmony and I in Room 2, Grossman and Kashi in Room 4. We uncanned a bit of supper: tuna, asparagus, cheese and crackers, sweet limes and Vichy—and using the Vichy as champagne, toasted Salmony, whose 64th birthday was this day. My God, I never knew that any water could taste so good. It was, in fact, the first thing with a really interesting taste that I had had since the treacle tart in Darjeeling. After dinner I took a little, final cup of the water and drank it as a liqueur.

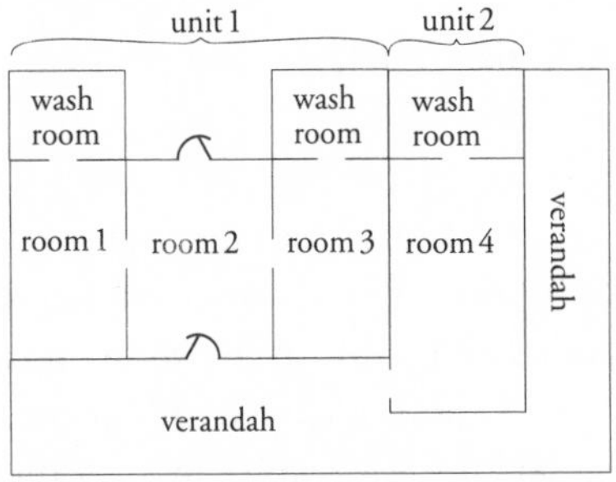

Thursday, November 11 ***Bādāmi–Paṭṭadakal***

In a building behind the Dak bungalow there lives the caretaker with his wife and son—a pitiful wisp of a little man, with a high, thin voice, thin black arms and shanks, a prodigious white turban, from beneath which his gaunt little face looks out like a sort of joke, and a simply horrifying, long, and loosely rattling cough. The wife is like every other poor Indian woman with a short broom. And the son is a polite little, helpful boy of about 12. These poor people and Kashi prepared our hot water, tea, and boiled eggs. After breakfast, we locked all our affairs into Room 4, and drove off to Bādāmi to visit the four caves:[125] Salmony, Grossman, Iyengar, Kashi, and myself. It is a charming town—like a vast pueblo—in a beautiful setting, with high rocks around it crowned by battlements, and with a lovely pond or tank, where the noise of the washers beating clothes filled the quiet air. We spent an excessively long time waiting for Iyengar to give instructions to some old restaurant owner who was to prepare our lunch. We wanted a roast chicken, plain rice, and bit of dhal. The discussion of how to prepare these things went on for about an hour.

Then we set off for the caves. I turned off, alone, to wander a bit through the village—at every turn reminded of the New Mexican pueblos—and I came to the caves long before the others. I had finished my study of Cave I before they arrived. A couple of monkeys added to the fun. I went up to Cave

II,[126] then to Cave III (the great one)[127] and finally to the pretty little Jain cave, Cave IV. Then I sat and looked down at the great pond below, with its thumping washers, watched a kid swimming in the middle of the pond plop the water, and thought of Wolf Lake in Pike County with nostalgia. I climbed next to the fort above, and snapped a few pictures, and then, having lost my friends completely, walked through town to the Malegiṭṭi Shivalaya Temple[128] on its little height, and returned to the car. The group presently arrived, having arranged with a taximan to drive us that afternoon to Paṭṭadakal. We fetched our lunch from the restaurant and returned to the Dak bungalow to eat it: mutton curry, rice with sand, and a spicy dhal. I quit very soon, but the others went on a little longer. And then we lay down to wait for the taximan, who was to call for us at 1:30.

At 2:15 we decided to go and see whether he was still in town and encountered him on the road with his taxi (a Dodge station wagon) full of Hindus. We all returned to the bungalow and learned that all but two of the passengers were policemen, come to look at our passports and papers. They were somewhat illiterate; so Iyengar took over, filled out the forms for them; and at 2:45 we took off for Paṭṭadakal.

The road was no road. The twenty-five yards along the bottom of a broadly flowing stream were the best. At three quarters of a mile from Paṭṭadakal we had to get out and walk. But the visit was great. We visited first the Mallikārjuna Temple (c. A.D. 740), the Virupākṣa (c. A.D. 740), Jambhuliṅga, and finally Pāpanātha, with hasty glimpses of several others.[129] We had pitifully little time. And the village, furthermore, in which this beautiful cluster of temples stood, was worth a long study too. Grossman was audible in his protests against viewing such things in a hurry and thought we should promise to return. Salmony and I, however, hurried on, knowing that it was now or never. Toward dark we started our return, and if the drive out was difficult, the drive back was worse; for at "the hour of cow-dust" one is faced, in India, by homing droves of cattle—flocks of goats and sheep, herds of water buffalo and other kine, not to mention the peasants themselves, bearing hay, baskets, or what-not, on their poised heads.

We arrived at our Dak bungalow after dark, only to find that Unit I—that is to say, three quarters of our establishment—had been padlocked by some servant of the Forest Inspector of Poona, who, coming to prepare the way for his superior, had found the bungalow occupied, scolded the wearer of the turban, and claimed his master's portion. The master, that night, did not arrive; we all slept, however, on the floor of Unit II. Before retiring,

Grossman decided that he would remain in Bādāmi and let Salmony go on to Bangalore alone. He wished to live as an artist—not as an art historian: he would relax into this idyll of rural India—as, formerly, he had relaxed into that of rural Mexico, rural Italy, rural Spain. He is a rather heavy-headed type and I think has become pretty well tired of the dates and periods of ancient Indian art.

Friday, November 12 ***Bādāmi–Aihoḷe–Bādāmi***

Salmony announced this morning that he had been unable to sleep because of the tumult of Jason's snoring. "You are a monumental snorer," he declared. It was all with a laugh; but the atmosphere was not altogether good. The first thing I did was to go out and look at the padlock that had been put on the door. I saw that the staple could be pried open—so I opened it, removed the lock, and flung open the doors of Unit I. We bathed, breakfasted, and prepared for a visit to Aihoḷe.

I drove Iyengar to the station and sat and talked with him for a while. He was returning to Bombay—with my watch, which had stopped two days ago. We would get in touch with each other when I returned. Then I drove Salmony, Grossman, and Kashi to town, where we wired Bījāpur for a confirmation of our occupancy and I pretended, before some local officers, to be very angry because of the impudent padlock. The idea of jungle law being very powerful, apparently, in the circles of Indian officialdom, I decided to be a sort of lion.

Then we set off for the temples of Aihoḷe,[130] with a package lunch, which we ate on the verandah of the lovely Durgā Temple. It was an excellent visit. I was impressed particularly by the figures in the shallow cave temple, which have a brilliancy of form that is quite unique. I realized that the way the women wear their saris, hitched up between the legs, is the fashion of the peasant women around Bombay to this day. We cruised around to the Huchimalligudi, Lāḍ Khān, and numerous other temples—including one small Jain unit, and a Śiva temple with an interior door-frame (to the sanctuary) of obscene, cunnilingus arrangements; the earliest, as far as I know, in the history of Indian art.

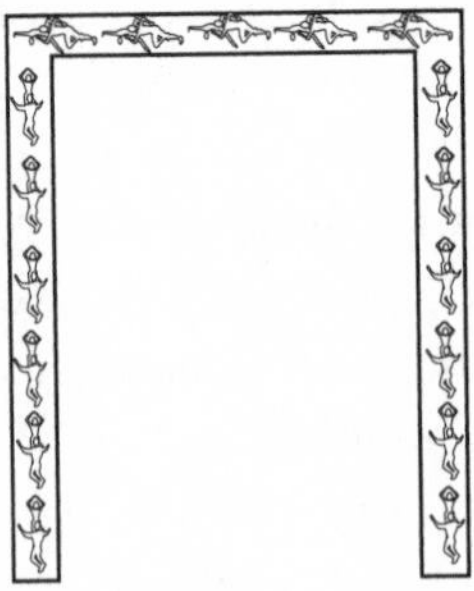

Returning, somewhat fatigued, to Bādāmi, we plodded up the hill to the Malegiṭṭi Temple, which Salmony and Grossman had not yet seen, and then returned to our Dak—holding, in triumph, a telegram from Bījāpur.

The Forest Inspector of Poona, a young man of considerable self-assurance, had complacently installed himself during our absence in the great three room section of our house, and it was pleasant to make him realize that he had to go. It had been our intention to invite him to share the building; but when we saw his style of taking over, we let him have it on the nose. The exit was graceful enough. A tonga came, about 11 P.M., and took him to the home of a friend in town! Nice guy! Nice ad for the Indian Tourist Office!

Saturday, November 13

Salmony, two evenings ago, on learning that he was going to have to go to Bangalore by train, had invited me to accompany him and declared that, in return, he pay my air passage from Bangalore back to Bombay. Both of us wanted to visit Hampi (Vijayanagar) on the way. And we had managed, by psychological pressure, to get Grossman to consent to drive with us to Hampi and let us take the train, then, from there.

Sunday, November 14 ***Bangalore***

Our train pulled into Bangalore 5:50 A.M. We found that the West End Hotel was full, and went to the Central. Nice room. Hot baths, etc. Finis to the Bādāmi adventure: hello again to Bangalore.

It is a charming city and we were in a mood for repose. After baths and a pleasant breakfast we took a short stroll to the museum. Nicely arranged exhibit of paleolithic, neolithic, and later materials. We visited the young curator: another of these enthusiastic young Indian scholars.

Shortly after our return to the hotel we were visited by a distinguished retired officer of the state, Rājamantrapravīṇa (that is his title) A. V. Ramanathan, and his son Subrakhmanya. Salmony chatted with the father and I with the son, who, when he learned that my wife is a dancer, waxed eloquent and enthusiastic about the life of art. He told me, too, that the great dance festival of the year is held at Madras, December 20 to January 20 every year. (A great change of plans for Jean's visit is indicated.) After a cordial visit the two gentlemen left, with an invitation for us to visit them at five tomorrow afternoon.

Shortly after lunch we received the visit of another distinguished citizen, Dharmaprakāśa Rao Bahādur (his title) K. Kuppuswamy! After tea, he offered to introduce us to the city, and so we joined him in his little car.

I could not make out whether he was pleased to be showing us the city or just doing it out of a sense of duty, but he did an excellent job. He showed us the great gardens and the botanical exhibition hall, two interesting temples (where Salmony had his first experience of *pūjā*), and his own home, with its garden (his pet) and family chapel.

The first of the two temples was to the bull Nandi—a big stone animal, like that on the hill at Mysore and those before the temple of Halebīd. Precisely the same form. The interesting point was that here Nandi was not the mere vehicle of the god but the worshipped deity. It is the only Nandi temple in India, we were told.

The second temple was a cave temple—a natural cave, but with a circumambulatory tunnel carved around the central shrine. Particularly interesting were four large stone standards set up in the court before the temple entrance. The first two were, respectively, a trisula and an hour-glass drum—the latter looking very much like a double ax. The second two were identical wheels with crosses—and their total effect was that of the Christian cross with a halo.

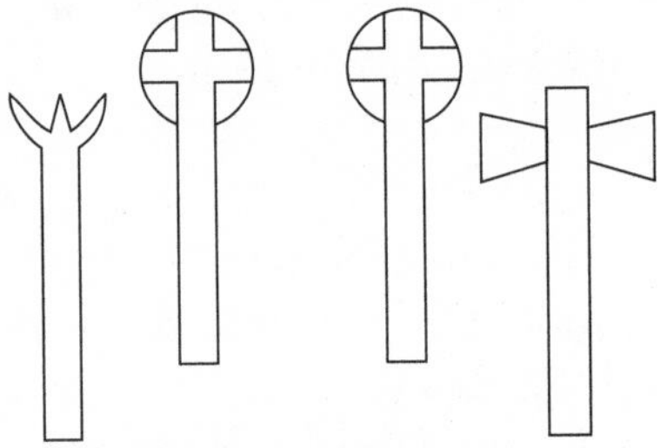

Interesting in the very rich gentleman's own chapel was a large picture just above the main Kṛṣṇa shrine, showing a brahmin talking to an earnestly listening young Kṛṣṇa. Our host told the story—of a poor brahmin who performed some pious act in honor of Kṛṣṇa and immediately found his poor home turned into a palace of wealth. (The wonderful complacency of the rich. Like that of the so-called Boston brahmins!)

Mr. Kuppuswamy invited us in for a cup of hot milk (can you believe it?), introduced us to his nice son and daughter, and then told us that he was making arrangements to "give" his daughter (age 18) to a young man who for the past five years has been working for an engineering degree at the University of California. The girl had never seen the boy, nor the boy the girl. But he was earning considerable money in California, and would probably make an excellent husband. (I could not but wonder what the boy had been learning about American erotic ideals in California...and the girl is lovely.)

We next were driven to the really palatial home of a somewhat chubby Indian tycoon, who had a handsome German Police Dog: the first nicely bred dog I have seen in Indian hands—and whose whole manner and attitude reminded me of my friend Dhar in Calcutta. Whiskey and soda for the

Westerners. A pleasant talk about Belūr and Halebīd, which at Kuppuswamy's invitation we are to visit Tuesday.

Monday, November 15

A quiet day—and welcome. I am enjoying my sojourn with Salmony. He is the scholar for whom Zimmer wrote his first important article: Zimmer would have been precisely his age today: but he is not the spirit that Zimmer was. His learning is much less grandiose, much more restricted and pedantic—and he takes it rather seriously, this being a scholar. It has been amusing to watch how ponderously he lets everyone know of the lectures he is to give in Bangalore, Mysore, Madras—Rome, and Paris. Then one learns that the fee is one hundred rupees and the audience a group of about forty. He has with him a batch of the brief offprints of an article on a Gandhāra Buddha that he published in his *Artibus Asiae,* and he passes these out to people with enormous solemnity—his head thrust a little too far forward. Also, his new book, *Antler and Tongue,* is here. I am reading it today with interest; reading, also, the articles in the new *Artibus Asiae.* After my months among the Swamis the breath of the harvest (even though stuffy) air of scholarship is great joy.

In the morning we set off on a gentle stroll—went to a bank, paused at the library of the U.S. Information Service, visited the Mysore Information office to procure a pamphlet on the monuments of Talkad, stopped again at the Museum (where Alfred presented his offprint to the young Curator), and then went to the Indian Airlines office, where he bought and paid for my ticket to Bombay.

After lunch, we visited a second-hand bookshop on Mahatma Gandhi Road, where we met a bookish Englishman who, with the bookseller, declared he would be present at "Alfred's" lecture tomorrow evening at the Mythic Society. We returned to the hotel to plan our visit to Belūr and Halebīd. And then Subrakhamanya arrived to drive us to his home for tea.

Apparently this family is of an older vintage than that of the newly rich Kuppuswamy. The father, Ramanathan, dresses, like Kuppuswamy, in a business suit, but wears a white turban with bands of red and gold. Kuppuswamy showed us with pride when we visited his house, a gold medal with jewels, given him by the Maharaja for some philanthropic deed, and a copper medal on a broad red ribbon awarded by the English king. No such display of honors in the modest, Victorianly cluttered home of Ramanathan. The "old" gentleman—now sixty-six—had retired at the age of fifty-five. When I told him that I had edited Nikhilananda's *Gospel of Sri Ramakrishna,* he said,

"Then you understand the nature of my present life." Apparently he regarded himself as in the life-stage of *vānaprastha*, retirement from the world for contemplation. The son brought in tea and sweets; and the father was gently solicitous that we should taste of everything—a little awkward in passing the plates—clearly a much older gentleman than Salmony, who was sixty-four!

The son then showed us his works of amateur sculpture and painting (Śivas, Pārvatīs, Venuses, and *apsarases*): remarkably good. And on the way home he talked with touching earnestness and feeling of his art. "When I work in clay," he said, "Mother tells me to be careful: I will catch cold from the wet clay. And when I work in stone, Father tells me to be careful, the dust will get in my lungs and I will catch cold." His hope—his ideal—is to get to France, to experience the world of art. But he is a good *fils de famille* in provincial Bangalore.

After dinner the bookseller of yesterday evening's guest arrived to take us to his shop—and Salmony bought a number of rare books.

Tuesday, November 16 ***Belūr–Halebīd***

6 A.M. departure by taxi (paid by Kuppuswamy) for Hassan, Belūr and Halebīd.[131] It was a delight to see these temples again, in the sunshine. I took a lot of photos. At Belūr we had the guide who had shown me the temple before. I was impressed particularly, this time, by the bracket figures of Belūr, and the gods as well as the epic scenes of Halebīd. Salmony pointed out that the figures at Halebīd were less vital than those of Belūr. He was immensely impressed by both.

On the way home our car ran out of gas two miles from Hassan, and we waited an hour while our two boys walked to town and came back with a can.

Home after dark (about 7:30 P.M.)—a pleasant dinner, and early to bed.

Wednesday, November 17 ***Bangalore***

Two booksellers arrived at 8 A.M. and at 8:30 the secretary and curator of the Mythic Society came to show us the hall in which Salmony is to lecture this evening. During the course of our genteel visit, it gradually dawned on my good friend that he was not going to be paid for this lecture. He took it manfully, and we continued to give fulsome praise to the library that we were being shown.

After we returned to the hotel, I began reading a booklet that Salmony had found on the problems of Indian archaeology, and suddenly the main pattern of the scholarly work before me on this trip, and after my return to New York, fell neatly into form—as outlined on the following page. We spent a quiet afternoon, at a quarter to six went to the society for Alfred's talk (the curator, at the slide machine, got all fouled up), went with Kuppuswamy to his club for a drink, and went early to bed.

Orientation Plan, Bangalore, November 17, 1954

I. Coordination of India Studies with Mythology Studies

Lascaux etc. { A. Paleolithic, Mesolithic, Microlithic

Al Ubaid etc. { B. Neolithic, Chalcolithic, Megalithic

(A and B) → *Tribal Studies*, Africa–Melanesia Link

C. Indus Valley Civilization
D. Aryan Problem
E. Vedic–Upanishadic Age
F. Buddhism and Jainism
G. Early History (Maurya through Gupta)
H. Medieval History (Cāḷukya–Vijayanagar)
I. Late History
  1. Islam and bhakti
  2. Arrival of the Europeans
J. India Today

II. Similar schedules for
  1. Ceylon
  2. Burma
  3. S.E. Asia and Indonesia
  4. Philippines
  5. Japan

III. Eranos–Basic Mythologies coordination

IV. SLC course revision

V. Writing program:
  1. Viking Book—Introduction to Mythology
  2. Bollingen Book—Basic Mythologies
  3. Related articles (for Artibus Asiae)
  4. Related stories (King & Corpse type?)
  5. The New World of Bartolomé de las Casas

Go to work immediately on III, IV, and V.1 (Viking). When III is finished, begin work on V.2 notes (Bollingen). Keep V.1 writing going, watching leads for the commencement and chapters of V.2.

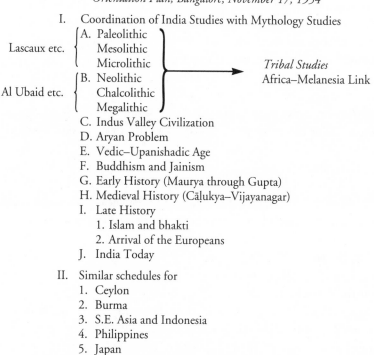

The Space-Platform

Bombay

Thursday, November 18 ***Bombay***

Up at 4:45 A.M. for goodbye and good wishes to Alfred. Plane off at seven, arrival at Bombay Airport at 12:05, then by bus to the Grand Hotel. To the American Express for my mail, then the rest of the day in my room, reading letters and *Time Magazine,* to catch up on the U.S.A.

Jean's affairs and taking handsome shape: a warm review of her Cooper Union demonstration in the *Dance Observer,* by Louis Horst himself;[132] dates settled for concerts in California and Hawaii. Then a concert at Bard and one at Sarah Lawrence in April—and a return in June to Colorado.

Friday, November 19

Letters to Jean and Helen McMaster and an attempt to catch up on my diary. Mild walks through town, bebrooding a few ideas. Saw von Leyden in the hotel after lunch, and gave him the story of our Bādāmi adventure.

Saturday, November 20

I spent the day catching up on my diary, and now (6:15 P.M.) have arrived here. As for the new ideas:

They take off from a "letter to the editor" in the *Times of India* for November 18, in which the author, an Indian, takes precisely the position of brahmin-banker host of Bījāpur, namely, that everything worthy of the name of civilization has come to India from the West—while her own philosophers have been priding themselves on their Sanskrit. With technology, new social ideals, anti-toxins, and money pouring into destitute India from the Occident, how can any Indian dare to vaunt the "spirituality" of his Oriental culture with the dictum "Happiness lies within"?

With this letter in my mind I have been strolling through the squalid bazaars of Bombay—and I find here much the same general mood and style of life that I have just seen in the Indian villages—only with no trees about, and consequently no sense of the idyll. What I see is that these people are amazingly composed and yield an air (in spite of their obvious misery) of well-being.

I think of Boethius' title, *The Consolation of Philosophy,* and recall his saying that if philosophy cannot support us in the time of our misfortune it is little good. India's time of misfortune, apparently, is forever: and India's philosophy in this circumstance, one might say, has stood her in good stead.

The Orient	*The Occident*
Terminus of the Neolithic	Growing point of the New World
Tradition (Guru)	Revolution (Hero)
Faithful obedience	Intelligent striving
The Archetypes	The personal factor
Immutable law	Volition
Caste	Equality
Transformation of Consciousness	Transformation of the world

And now a slightly different train of thought; once again, with a takeoff from *The Times of India*: this time, November 19, editorial page, a review-essay based on Stella Kramrisch's new book on Indian art,[133] by a gent named Adib. He queries the Coomaraswamy idea that Indian art is throughout a religious intuition of reality and identity—and now that I have had my view of India I suddenly see a certain point; to wit: that, from the U.S.A., a student of Vedanta is likely to see India as a function of Vedanta, but from the vantage ground of India itself one sees Vedanta as a function of a certain aspect of India.

A. India, as viewed from the U.S.A.

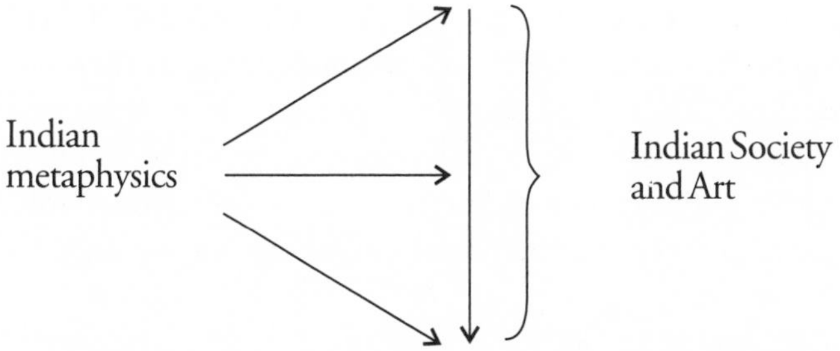

B. India, as viewed from India

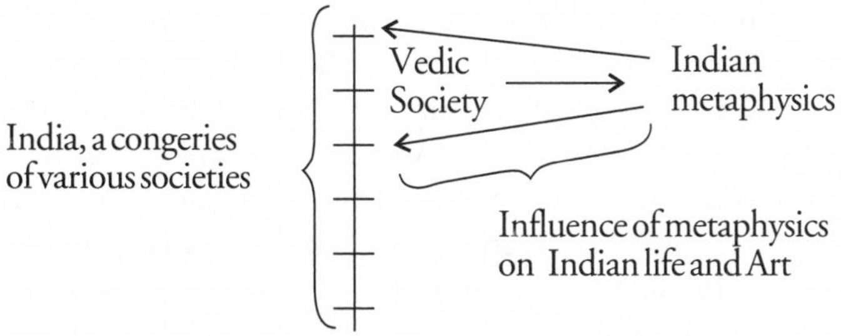

Somehow, this idea means a great deal to me just now. It seems to summarize the whole import of my reaction to this Indian experience during the past three months. Moreover, it is an idea that can be applied to any viewing of any society. The idea has given me a great feeling of release from something—Coomaraswamy, perhaps, and all my other gurus.[134]

In relation to Indian art, for example, one may think of the gent who scratched the obscene engraving on the pillar in the Dhumar Lena cave at Elūrā. Was he unique? Or has something of his inspiring spirit perhaps contributed to the obscenities of Koṇārak and Belūr? May it be that these are not primarily religious intuitions of reality and identity, but more nearly what they seem to be?

Yesterday's *Times of India* contained a second section, of twenty full pages, celebrating the "Formal Opening of Stauvac Bombay Refinery" and describing the progress, projects, contributions to civilization, etc. of Standard Oil. In today's edition we read of the opening ceremonies and learn that this was the "First Industrial Project With Foreign Capital." Suddenly (dope!) a little light goes up for J.C.! Standard Oil deeply involved in India. Standard Oil—the Rockefellers—The Rockefeller Foundation—curious interest of the Rockefeller Foundation in the business-philosophy of India: my various conferences with the fellowship people. Well, well! I seem to be learning something in India after all.

Then I find in the same paper two headlines in one column. At the top: "World-Wide U.S. Aid Programme: Major Spending in Asia." At the bottom: "Chinese Delegation expected from Canton in the first week of December."

Meditation: the U.S.A. sends money and machines, and, consequently, is regarded as materialistic. The Chinese and Russians send cultural delegations, and, consequently are regarded as cultured. We should begin storming the world with our culture—not Hollywood, but our composers, artists, dancers, etc. But this would require the assassination of a number of our senators.

Sunday–Monday, November 21 and 22

Bombay is my first space-platform. I am pausing here for a while, on the outgoing journey, after my first three—so to say, introductory—months in the Orient, to finish off all unfinished business, all of those last tag ends still dragging from New York, and to refurbish my light equipment, straighten out my thoughts, and prepare for the real experience—whatever it is to be.

My first Indian visa expires this week and I am making application for a second three-months touring permission. That one will expire about the time Jean leaves, and I should be ready by then to push off for Japan.[135] So I have ahead of me three more months in India, then two months of travel to reach Japan and perhaps one month (May) of touring in Japan, after which I shall arrive at my second space-platform, that of the return threshold, where I shall pause again, again collect my thoughts, and prepare—for New York. Kyoto, I think will be that platform.

And so, from here to there is the far curve of the adventure, with something—I don't know what—that is to happen as a climax.

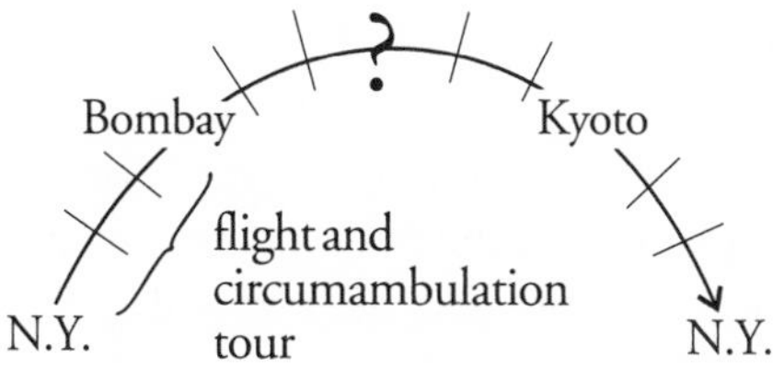

Tuesday, November 23

Continued work on the Sarah Lawrence chapter.[136] Yesterday I began operations to have my three-month visa, which expires November 29, extended for another period of three months; today I paid a visit to a third office. Someone has to guarantee my financial condition, and I think Rudy von Leyden is the one to do it.

While at work this morning I received from Rudy an invitation to a vernissage—of a painter named K. H. Ara, to whom Rudy has been a patron. A large and handsome exhibition room full of people and with a great splash of colorful paintings all around the room. They were imitations of the various masters of the Paris school, but with a cheerful brightness of their own that was frank and charming. A number of the still-lifes and two or three of the stylish nudes were particularly good. A slightly stilted young man of the world, however, opined that the exhibition looked like something collected from the ash-cans of Paris. I broke the question to Rudy about guaranteeing my visa. He consented to help.

From the exhibition I went to the home of Rama Mehta's father and sister—for a delightful dinner and evening's talk. Mr. Mehta's collection of Rajput paintings, bronzes, and other figures, is quite wonderful, and the gentleman himself I fell for right away.

A younger man named Roy Hawkins, from the Oxford Book Shop, was at dinner. Ferenc Berko had told him to watch for me—and had written to me to watch for him. So a number of things are coming together in Bombay. Hawkins drove me home and invited me to drive with him on Sunday to Kanheri. O.K. Very nice indeed.

Wednesday, November 24

Finished the Sarah Lawrence chapter about 4:00 P.M. Feeling great, feeling free: that darned Sarah Lawrence chapter is the last of the great commitments.

I must henceforth watch myself like a policeman to see that I never never never get myself or let myself into one of these wild work-jams again. It is exactly three months since my departure from New York.

Thursday, November 25

Wrote letters, mailed them, then went to the Oxford Book Store to discuss with Roy Hawkins plans for Sunday's trip to Kanheri, then by taxi to the Sarabhai[137] office. It turned out that Gautam and Gira were in town (arrived yesterday—leave tonight).

After lunch I went to von Leyden's office, and obtained his signature on the financial guarantee for my visa; delivered the visa papers to the C.I.D. office, and returned home for tea, nap, reading, bath, etc. At 5:45 P.M. Gautam phoned. I am to have dinner with him.

It was an exceedingly deluxe, New York-style apartment with Oriental effects. Gautam and Gira looked as sweet and fine as ever. We drove then to Gautam's father's apartment, which was equally deluxe, with great views of the panorama of the city. Dinner commenced at 8:00 P.M., and their train would leave at 9:05. Gautam gave me a lot of names to help me arrange for Jean's concert in Bombay. His father asked me about my relationship to Indian philosophy and phoned to make an appointment for me with Sophia Wadia. After dinner, a great dash to the station. A very pleasant atmosphere and event.

Friday, November 26

Mail and shopping tour in the morning. More letters written. Still finishing off the last tag-ends of my Pantheon affairs.[138]

While I was at lunch old Mr. Sarabhai walked into the hotel dining room and joined me for the meal. He had a little trouble getting the vegetarian meal that he wanted; but finally won. Later I went around to the Sarabhai office to meet Mr. Ezekiel, director of the Bombay Theatre Unit. He seemed to be interested in presenting Jean's concert, and I felt sure that the way was beginning to open.

At 8:30 P.M. at the hotel I played host to the von Leydens. Rudy thought the Bombay Theatre Unit was correct for Jean's concert; Nina thought the bigger possibility should be tried by way of Pipsi Wadia, who would be arriving in town next week. Rudy contended, however, that Pipsi's set were interested in the Menuhin type of thing because of highly advertised names, but that the theater set were interested in the modern movement. Nina suggested that I should send for Jean's publicity, etc.: that would help her to judge.

Saturday, November 27

Post Office and American Express route in the morning. Letters, wires, and diary the rest of the day, until 6:00 P.M., when I visited Mr. Mehta again. He took me to the Willingdon Sports Club for fruit juice and a pleasant chat. Good jazz band and a very Honoluluish sort of club atmosphere. People (Indians) actually dancing Sambas. Then—in a vast limousine—Mr. Mehta saw me back to my hotel. It looks very much as though Jean and I should lean a bit on this Bombay group: sweet people, delighted to introduce us to *their* India, and with promising connections all over the map.

I telephoned Mrs. Sophia Wadia: I am to go to a dance concert at her house Tuesday evening. See? It works as quickly as that!

Sunday, November 28

Up at 5:30 A.M. to meet Roy Hawkins at his place and drive in his little Fiat to the Kanheri caves. A lovely morning. There were literally thousands of people—schools and families—walking from the nearest railroad depot the several miles to the caves, and as we passed through them in our tiny car they cheered and laughed. When they arrived at the caves they set up their picnics in the various old monastic cells and were a lively and colorful addition to the delightful height: a volcanic-rock dome into which over a hundred Buddhist caves—a few large, most of them fairly small—were carved during the centuries between 100 B.C. and A.D. 900. Hawkins led me through underbrush and woods over the brow of a hill to a cave that is still occupied—but the sadhu was out. His yellow pennant, on a long bamboo staff, was flying, and his cave was locked with a padlock! (Not *much* of a sadhu, I'm afraid.) He had converted the front part into a nice little verandah, with a high wall of clay, and before him was the bed of a steep mountain stream. I could not but think of Hervey White at Woodstock: precisely his ideal![139] Except that within the cave, behind the locked gate, there was a little shrine.

We next drove, over a lovely wood road and along the shore of a beautiful lake, to a large, model dairy farm, where we stopped to have ice-cream at the farm restaurant—much as at the dairy farm near Bennington, Vermont. Once again, there were crowds of prettily dressed people, lively and full of color: a set of young chaps playing a crazy ball game on the lawn, and many families sitting about.

We got back to Hawkins' rooms at about 1:30 P.M. and were served a pleasant luncheon by his two manservants. Then he drove me home.

The contrast of what I am seeing and hearing these days in Bombay with the world and point of view of Swami and his monks is considerable. My India visit is falling neatly into three divisions: Religion–Archaeology–Dance.

I. My period with the monks—from New Delhi to Madras; devoted to an experience of the contemporary religious situation;
II. My period alone and with Alfred Salmony—in Bombay, Aurangabad, Bādāmi, and Bangalore; devoted to a recovery of my proper, scholarly position and an experience of the great works of the great middle period of Indian religious art;
III. My period, beginning now, with the Mehtas and Sarabhais, which will include the months with Jean; devoted to an experience of the contemporary acculturation through the influence of the West, in the worlds of modern social life and art: the central theme will be the dance.

I am greatly interested in the conversation and point of view of Mr. Mehta, who is no worshipper (his wife has a shrine, he tells me; but *his* point of view is not that of the *bhakta*), and yet is a Hindu. He has thought of the dark side of Indian mythology: the crime of Kṛṣṇa's parents in their swapping of the children at the time of Kṛṣṇa's birth; the crime of Rāma in his dropping of Sītā.... He recognizes the profound psychological interest of the implications: *these crimes represent, as it were, the dark side of the Indian dharma: bringing them out into the open is an act of importance for the modern Indian mind.*

Here is a formula for the literary treatment of the ancient mythological material that would be of considerable psychological and sociological interest.

I find it interesting, also, that the schoolchildren of Bombay are being brought in great number to the ancient sites—in a manner that makes me think of New York's kids at Bear Mountain Park. Here we have a Western influence that is being referred, however, to Indian themes and experiences. The holiday crowd at Kanheri is comparable to the holiday droves leaving New York by car—only here the travel is by train and foot.

Monday, November 29

I took the usual walk to the Post Office and the American Express mail desk; then to Oxford Book Shop to give Hawkins a copy of *Philosophies of India* and finally to the police office for the extension of my residence permit. Pleasant chap in the office gave me my permanent "number" for India: 42931, which will be my number if I ever return. I have also to keep reporting my movements to the police, and I have to get an exit permit to leave. I'm glad I'm not *quite* behind the Iron Curtain.

When I returned to the hotel I found a phone call from Mr. Ezekiel, whom I presently went to see at the Sarabhai office, and learned that his Bombay Theatre Unit will present Jean: first in a concert, then in a lecture demonstration, and finally at a dinner. They will handle all publicity, radio interviews, etc. Simply great. Came home and wrote Jean all about it and sent a wire.

Spent the afternoon and evening reading and taking notes on the strata of Indian archaeology and history.

I. Paleolithic, Mesolithic, Microlithic
II. Neolithic, Chalcolithic, Megalithic
III. Indus Valley
IV. The Aryans
V. Pre-Maurya Period (Vedas—Buddhism and Jainism)
VI. The Great Dynasties
VII. Islamic Period
  1. Conquest (1175–1400)
  2. Early *bhakti* poets (1400–1550)
  3. Mughal Period (1550–1800)
VIII. British Period
IX. Svarāj[140]

It appeared to me—and I think that I have here found something—that the great division that one now feels between the religious and social patterns of India and the West derives from the period of A.D. 1400–1550. Whereas that is the period in Europe of the Italian Renaissance, with its breakthrough into psychological adulthood from the religious formulae of the Middle Ages, India at that time, overwhelmed by Islam, stressed the folk-religion of *bhakti.* This was the period of Rāmānanda, Kabīr, Nānak—the founders of modern Hinduism: anti-Sanskrit, anti-brahmin, in a sense. There was a stress on *the childlike attitude of refuge in a personal God* (kitten-monkey differentiation;[141] yet both remain childlike). Contrast to this the attitude of the *vīra,* rendered in the medieval temples. The stress now is on the Mother and Father images, as found in the approach to Catholicism in its *paśu* formulae.[142] Whereas in the period of the dynasties India's religion was heroic and that of Europe largely childlike, after A.D. 1400–1550 the contrast was reversed.

This explains to me why all the patterns of Indian life and religion now seem to me to be precisely what I left behind when I broke with the Church, whereas the philosophies of India suggested a bold adulthood even surpassing that of the European-American ideal.

Tuesday, November 30

It might be noted that the *dialogue with Islam* was the prelude to both the Indian and the European transformation. India collapsed before Islam and assumed the attitude of the child; Europe overcame Islam and became the master of the world. It is perhaps significant also that Europe's democratic movement immediately followed, as did also the anti-caste inflection of the Indian *bhaktas.* To this day the democracy of Islam is a model unsurpassed.

Rudy thought that the Indian loss of power had commenced already when Islam broke through. The flowering and culmination of the temple architecture in the seventh to thirteenth centuries (compare the parallel in Europe) had been accompanied by a scholastic crystallization of the religion. Formula and reference to the books of the past instead of creative attention to the symbolizations demanded for the present, is a prelude to collapse.[143]

In Europe the conquest of Islam led to a vigorous, humanistic movement, adult, and breaking the shell of scholastic *bhakti*. In India the conquest by Islam led to a loss of nerve and an infantile attitutude of submission.

Another idea here: whether in Europe or in India, the religious attitude has lost its style. Where style is lost, the spirit has withdrawn. Religion, both in India and the West, is fundamentally folk religion today. The condition of the folk dictates the character of the cult: American Methodism, Italian Catholicism, Irish Catholicism, Indian Vaiṣṇavism.

History-making man has passed into a new stage. The date of this passage: 1492.[144]

After dinner I taxied to the Mehtas' to pick up Lila. I found the family at their dessert course: Lila, her father, and her mother—the latter, who has been ill for some time, looking quite haggard and full of self-pity, but gracious—for brief moments—nevertheless. Lila and I departed, then, in the Mehtas' sumptuous limousine, for the palatial (that's the only word for it) residence, "Āryasangha," of Mrs. Sophia Wadia. I met the hostess at the steps, and we entered a large, airy hall with tile flooring, set with chairs, and with a stage area marked out with flowers.

The occasion was a performance of Indian dance in honor of Mr. Novokof, general secretary of the Council for Cultural Freedom, who is on a brief visit to Bombay and New Delhi. The first dance, "Peacock Dance," by a spry young woman in a blue "sleeper" with peacock's tail attached—was simply bad. The second dance, however, by a pretty little girl dressed as a *devadāsī*, was excellent. I was reminded of the young Balinese dancers. After that came the queen of the evening—the wife of a gentleman of some importance who, as secretary or something of the Council for Cultural Freedom in Bombay, was largely responsible for this event: and she was not good. A folk dance in the second part of the program, by eight men with sticks; a brilliant Manipuri drum dance, then, toward the close, a gypsy dance by the pretty little girl, were very good. Finally the queen returned while I was watching the musicians.

I was satisfied, when the evening was over, that I had done the right thing in arranging for Jean to be presented by the Theatre Unit instead of the society crowd. Behind me, at this event, sat the inspiring spirit of Bombay's socially patronized events, Pipsi Wadia—and if she had been dressed in a low-cut evening gown instead of in a sari, she could easily have appeared *chez* Mrs. Murray Crane. I was amused to see a face, furthermore, dimly remembered from somewhere else, which turned out to be that of a self-concerned young poet, Arthur Gregor, from New York; just arrived in Bombay today, en route to Trivandrum, where he will seek his soul under the pilotage of Sri Krishna Menon.

An elegent evening, in the high social atmosphere—and I was driven back to my hotel, again in the sumptuous car, with Lila. Nice finale for my first three months in India.

Wednesday, December 1

In the morning, after my walk to the American Express Office, I left my passport at the Ceylonese Consulate for a visa, and went to the Prince of Wales Museum to meet Dr. Moti Chandra,[145] father of the young man, Pramod, who greeted me in the New Delhi museum. A surprisingly boyish and sweet gentleman, of about my own age: a very pleasant conversation. I left with a lot of museum bulletins in hand and an invitation to lunch on Friday.

At 5:30 P.M. I went around to the Sarabhai office to go with Ezekiel to the workshop of his Theatre Unit. At the office I met his nice little wife, who will be too busy with their child to come to dinner this evening at the home of the inspiring genius of the group, Mr. Alkazi. A long, slow bus-ride to the workshop—a lovely, fresh, well-planned building with the workshop on the roof and studios (sculpture and music) below: a sort of foundation, in memory of an Indian patriot, Desai.[146] The atmosphere was familiar and pleasant—that of a seriously working New Theater group—with the additional touch of being the *only* serious theater unit in the metropolis of a prodigious country. I watched their rehearsal of *Oedipus,* which I enjoyed immensely. I was then taken to the home of Alkazi. It was up five flights, and there was his pregnant young wife—it could have been in Greenwich Village. There was a lovely crowd, and a nice evening of talk, in which I took over on the history of the American Dance: they want me to talk of this to their group next Wednesday evening.

Fortunately, in their workshop library, I put my hand on the *Borzoi Book of the Modern Dance* and opened to the pictures of Jean.

Thursday, December 2

At 11:15 A.M. I went to Mrs. Sophia Wadia's place, and found that the palatial house of two evenings ago is very busy during the day, with a children's class in something or other being conducted on the seaside verandah, and young editors of P.E.N. and Theosophical journals busy in various rooms of the house. A tiny tot conducted me to an editor, who showed me upstairs, where another editor pointed the way to a large sitting room (just above the salon of the dance recital), and as I entered Mrs. Wadia came to meet me. We sat down for an hour's talk on India, my journey, and her works here, the Bollingen Foundation, the Ramakrishna Mission, and Jiddu Krishnamurti. I left with an invitation to a P.E.N. lecture next Tuesday on "The Humanities and Literary Criticism"—to be given by Richard McKean![147]

During the course of our talk I told of my arrival and voyage with Swami Nikhilananda: and Mrs. Wadia told of being on the platform with Swami at the Bombay mission in honor of the Holy Mother. She had not liked Swami's stress on the idea that Ramakrishna and his "wife" had lived without sexual relations—and I agreed. She thought also that the dressing, feeding, and putting to bed of images at the *maṭha* is a pretty shameful business—and again I agreed. The whole pattern of the thinking of the monks is backward-looking, even in spite of their very good social work.

She told of an organization with which she worked that was trying to help Indian wives to solve their problems when they come up against blank walls of suppression and misunderstanding in their marriages. The number of suicides, apparently, is very high. Among many of the orthodox members of the community, though, there is a great resentment of this work. This came out in connection with my discussion of the impression I had of a pretty harsh marriage situation. The organization was founded by an Indian gentleman who remains anonymous: it is called, simply, "Father's House," and is run entirely (necessarily in India) by women. She told me also of the difficulties encountered when she tries to mix boys and girls in classes. They are soon sitting again in segregated groups.

It was a lovely talk, and confirmed me in many of my thoughts about the *archetypal* vs. *personal* principles in Indian life: also about the unpalatability of Swami's "spiritual" fare: his notion that the West has "material" and the Orient "spiritual" goods to offer.

I wonder if it might not be said that *the Orient is essentially archetypal in its thought and life and the West personal*—and that what the Orient has to offer the West is an image of the archetypal, whereas the spiritual contribution of the West to the Orient is an awakening of the personal. The response of each should not be to parody the other, but rather, to bring his own newly activated function into a significant balance with the excessively dominant function in his own personal way.

On the way to take a taxi to the von Leydens' for dinner, I was accosted by a young man who has frequently hailed me in the neighborhood of Ballard Pier. His usual call is "Want any beer, whiskey, gin, rum? Dope? I got anything you want!" This time he hooked on to me and began telling me that he hadn't chosen this kind of business because he liked it. He required food: and when the police brought him to jail he always told them to tell him how to earn a decent living in India and he would quit this line. He was talking at a great clip and I let him delay me some twenty minutes.

"India doesn't need America's money," he told me. "India has lots of money—in the wrong places—in private hands and in the temple coffers. A contractor gets money from America for a job. Where does the money go? Lakhs of rupees into the pockets of the contractor: annas to the workers.[148]

"What about Goa? Goa's a nice city: the people of Goa were perfectly happy as they were. Now Salazar in Lisbon and Nehru in Delhi begin to make things hot for all. India's blockade of food to Goa has raised all prices way above the reach of the people. Looks like they're trying to get a war going. Who will suffer? Not Salazar in Lisbon or Nehru in Delhi.

"The anti-cowslaughter people want to stop the killing of cattle for beef. They tell you, 'Eat vegetables.' They prevent the killing of cows: the price of vegetables goes up: who wins? I don't know: these people are crazy. They got millions of gods and they want more.

"The preachers of religion: they come and they tell you to believe in God. What good is that? Everyone believes in God already: the poor man, the rich man, they all believe in God. I say to them: you don't have to tell me about God, you have to tell me how to lead a decent life in this rotten country. What does it matter if I call God Jesus, Śiva, God or Allah?

"My father was a fool to spend all he had on my education. I graduate and I get two rupees a day. During the war I was in the navy—Indian Navy under the British. After the war I work in the merchant marine. The work and life were hard and the pay no good. I gave it up. I worked for contractors: they paid with annas. Now I sell only monkey business—nothing honest. Dope, liquor: the city's full of it. Black market. Anything. These kids in the street that you see: lots of them are full of dope."

Earlier in the day I had bumped into a young waiter from my hotel who had been serving me at table, but then had been dropped from the staff. He told me that eight had been dropped, because business in the hotel was not good this year. Formerly they had had a Swiss manager and business had been fine. Now the manager was not very good. And prohibition had made things bad. They had dropped him after a month's notice and now he was looking for a job. It was hard to get a job. The state was favoring Hindus (he, I took it, was a Christian).

At von Leydens' I met a Swiss gentleman, here on business for a pharmaceutical firm. I told him of the complaints I had heard from my recent conversationalist, and he generally supported them. Indian businessmen will not invest unless they can foresee a large rake-off for themselves almost immediately—within a year. Long-term investments involving patience and foresight don't interest them. The moneylenders get as high as 80%. When they say 4% they mean 4% a month. So Indian money is not going toward the development of Indian business.

The policy of the government in business, furthermore, is a bit crazy. They want everything all at once. They want to manufacture in India what is already manufactured better abroad instead of developing ideas and products of their own. And their imitated articles are inferior.

I spoke of my impression of a rich land, as I traveled through India: a rich land with poor people. They complain of drought, but they get three or four crops a year. Where in Europe or the United States do you get three or four crops a year? The people, we agreed, had been exploited to the marrow of their bones. And exploited, I should say, since God knows when? Certainly the Mughal "pleasure gardens" that I have seen ("If there is a paradise anywhere, it is here, it is here!"[149]) represent an application of monies to dynastic luxury instead of to the development of the well-being of the state, and the same pattern of absolutely selfish exploitation—though on a scale, comparatively, of peanuts—can be said to underlie the zamindar system.

An additional item to this theme: an article in the *Illustrated Weekly of India* points out that most of the beggars are the agents of a manager who takes a large percentage of their receipts. (I recall the flower-seller of Greenwich Village whom Jean and I saw stepping, with her tray, into an elegant Chrysler.) They are trained and given their props (children to carry in their arms, for example) and then sent out. I noticed, long ago, that the beggars everywhere in India use identical formulae of approach, identical tones of voice, etc.

Perhaps it can now be concluded that, for a number of reasons, the spectacle of dire poverty that India presents to the eye of the visitor is misleading. It is true that the huge majority of the people in India are poor; but it does not follow that *India* is poor. The rich in India tend to be miserly to a criminal degree, and the poor in India do not exert themselves even to clean the dirt out of the alleys of their own neighborhoods. Whereas one day of mildly energetic activity on the part of the people sitting around by the score in any given street would suffice to clean at least the surface filth away, the people add to the filth that day by defecating and urinating in every corner and gutter. Moreover, the beggars are in the employ of hidden managers, so that the spectacle which they are presenting (and which is one of the horrors that the visitor has to learn to assimilate) is partly a fraud. And Swami tells me that many of the people seen sleeping in the streets are not destitute. ("It is the most superficial way to judge India!" he said with proud indignation.)

Friday, December 3

I went at one to the Prince of Wales Museum to meet Dr. Moti Chandra for a very pleasant lunch, then I went at four for tea at the Mehtas' to see Rama.

The conversations at tea, the Club, and dinner, ranged widely, and finally, under a couple of questions put to me by Rama, got to pretty touchy ground. At the Club, Mr. Mehta offered an interesting idea to account for India's failure to advance into the scientific age before the West. In the traditional Indian family, he said, where everyone lives in very close association, closely observed all the time, and in an atmosphere established by the concerns of a group ranging through all ages, from childhood to old age, there is no place or time for privacy, and no period in life when the individual, thrown onto the world, is forced to experiment with life. Moreover, this circumstance accounts also for the erotic idealism of India's poetry and art. The individual has no opportunity for actual adventure and so, in his imagination, compensates with images of delight, and these lead to no disillusionment in reality.

Rama's questions were: "Do you find India very spiritual?" To which I had to answer, "No. No more than other places." "What do you think of East-West relationships?" To which I had to answer that I thought the West was giving India not only machines and money, but also ideas and ideals—and that these would have to be given in great quantity so that a world balance might be established. The influence of the East upon the West, however, was at present only very slight—in the form of an intellectual contribution to the intellectual élite.

I added (perhaps ineptly) that I thought it was still a little early for India to begin seeking to build its tourist trade because, first of all, the hotel and food accomodations were spectacularly inadequate; and the beggar-menace was not only fiercely troublesome to the tourist but also a bad advertisement for India—an impression of squalor, disease (lepers), and of especial agression (since the tourist can readily see that Indians on the street are not being assaulted by the beggars as he is: I have never seen a beggar, vendor, or rickshaw boy hang on to an Indian for six blocks, whereas for me it has been, outside of Bombay, a daily—almost hourly—experience). Worst of all, it is impossible to discover the true art and life of contemporary India: no music or dance performances, unless expertly sought out and found; all social life hidden within the family walls; e.g. no restaurant or theater life. Rama took issue, but Lila supported me, and Mr. Mehta maintained a balance—but I think the whole subject was a little too close to the quick. The conversation has left me feeling a bit shaken.

The conversation of the day, in other phases, touched on the question of India's contemporary teachers and sages:

Krishnamurti emerged as an important figure (as a break with the guru tradition, and the idea of people thinking their problems out for themselves). *Aurobindo's* ashram was described as a nicely organized American institution, but *Dilip Kumar Roy* (the great quack-quack of last winter's New York season), who is Aurobindo's chief disciple, seemed to receive a bit of carefully phrased respect (I had already said something about the unsteady impression he had made on me last year).[150]

Sri Krishna Menon of Trivandrum came off best. A number of instances were cited of people who had found "ineffable peace" in his sphere of influence. He is a *jñāna* yogi, who talks things through.

Mr. Mehta's opinion of the Ramakrishna monks is very high, and he spoke at length of their work in India. I praised the influence of their writings in America, but had to confess that I thought that most of the people who frequent the Centers were psychological cases.

Mr. Mehta has taken on the task of introducing Jean and me to the Indian dance, and so has planned a number of valuable meetings. I am to come to his house tomorrow afternoon to meet a number of artists and Sunday evening shall attend a dance concert by special invitation. I was driven home in the great limousine, with Rama and Lila as companions.

Saturday, December 4

Spent part of the day reading a little book about Vinoba Bhave that I bought on my morning walk, and part writing to Jean and making plans for our month together. She will come via Colombo and will arrive about January 12. I suppose she will have to leave about February 20. The concert is to be about February 3 in Bombay.

Sunday, December 5

With my plans for the next five months fairly well straightened out, I begin to feel that my space-platform days in Bombay are drawing to a close.[151] My business now is to finish off my affairs here and push off. The most pressing affairs, I should say, are those connected with the two talks I am to give next week (one to the Theatre Unit, and one over the Radio), and the matter of a text either about or by Jean for the Theatre Unit Bulletin, set for December 20. The talks are going to require me to settle a few ideas in my unsettled mind, and this, perhaps, might be termed the final task of the platform. Two aspects of this task are to be distinguished:

A) What are my fundamental ideas about my place in the world of scholarship? i.e. What is my central subject, and what is its relationship to the numerous wisps and strays of my wandering interest?

B) What is the status of my present field-trip study of the Orient? What have I learned? What are the outstanding problems? What plans should I make for specific research?

The need for a bit of basic thinking of this kind struck me rather forcefully this morning when I opened the morning paper. For the past day and a half I have been feeling rather badly and uneasy about the dinner conversation Friday night at the Mehtas' where I seemed to be taking an essentially negative, largely frustrated attitude toward my Indian experience. A couple of particularly unpleasant beggars had revived in me, earlier in the day, a number of my earlier attitudes toward India and my growing feeling of pleasure and interest in the country had been momentarily subdued. My negative reply to the question as to whether I found life in India very spiritual was the one that troubled me most; for I realized that it must have been unnecessarily harsh and rude. Had I possessed the wit to elaborate a bit on my negation, the situation would have been greatly improved. But I had found myself unable to develop the point—and this, I now realize, was the consequence of a lack of clarity, in my own mind.

Then, this morning, in the paper, I found a number of challenging items. Firstly, a front page spread, featuring the Opening of the Marian Congress in Bombay. Cardinal Gracias presiding. Swami Radhakrishnan the guest speaker. A great assemblage on the Azad Maidan (I had seen the crowd, on my way last evening to the Mehtas'). Then, a large gobbet from Radhakrishnan's speech: "Mankind Must Be Guided by Spirit of Religion: Vice-President's Call." And next on the inner pages, pictures of Richard McKean, with whom I studied at Columbia, and Professor L. Venturi, whom I met the other evening at von Leyden's, with a couple of good quotations from their firm and self-confident remarks. The contrast with my own, present state of philosophical fluidity hit me hard—and I determined to pull myself together. After my decade of work along the lines of Zimmer, which I have brought to an end right here on my space-platform, it is time for me to begin—right here on the platform—a straightening out of my own basic ideas. And what more appropriate place for such a task than India, which is itself trying to locate its own mind? So then:

What are my fundamental ideas about my place in the world of scholarship?

The name that best suits my field of study is *Comparative Mythology:* it is a study of symbols, in relation, primarily, to the fields of art, literature, philosophy and religion. M. Réné Guénon has distinguished two great categories of symbol. The one he calls *le symbolisme qui sait* and the other *le symbolisme qui cherche.* Guénon's (and Coomaraswamy's) fixed preference was for the former, the symbolism that *knows*; my own, on the other hand, is for the latter, the symbolism that *seeks*—and here, I believe, I am in accord with Zimmer.[152] This interest in the active, questioning attitude toward symbols has led me to give considerable stress, in my studies and writings, to the work of the psychoanalysts, Freud, Jung, Roheim and the rest, since there one can see the process of symbol formation and interpretation from within. Guénon and Coomaraswamy, on the other hand, have given their whole attention to a comparative study of the symbolical vocabularies of the past. I am interested also in modern art and literature, as controlled renditions of the symbolic themes of contemporary significance, and my chief masters in this field have been Joyce and Mann, Klee and Picasso, with Jean and her associates as my immediate guides and examples.

In Sanskrit two words appear, which designate two categories of the inherited Indian tradition, namely *śruti* ("what is heard") and *smṛti* ("what is remembered"). The Vedic hymns belong to the former and the brahminical theological writings to the latter.[153] Essentially, the priestly attitude represented in *smṛti,* preserving the past, looking back and interpreting what has already been found, represents the attitude of *le symbolisme qui sait*—the analysis of "the fixed and the set fast"—whereas the poetical attitude that yielded *śruti,* harkening to the voice of the living God, the Muse, represents *le symbolisme qui cherche*—"striving toward the divine through the becoming and the changing." Compare Goethe's (and Spengler's) *Vernunft* and *Verstand.*[154] I tend, therefore, to associate the work of the creative genius in art, literature, science and mathematics with the living, creative aspect of my subject, and the work of the scholiast, priest, and academician (preserving, judging, and formulating rules on the basis of the created works of the past) with the dead and the anatomical or schematic. As in all fields of the spirit, so here: the footsteps or traces (*mārga*) of the spirit, which may guide us to the spirit, derive from the past, and are to be studied by all candidates for illumination, but the living, immediate presence of the spirit is one step in front of the last footstep—out in the air over the bottomless abyss.[155]

In *The Hero with a Thousand Faces* I distinguished between the spheres of the village compound and the realm of adventure. In the former the "religious" people remain, whose spiritual needs can be satisfied by the fixed patterns of the already found, while into the latter go the heroes who meet and become the vehicles of the living spirit. In *The Basic Mythologies of Mankind* I shall review the history of the symbolisms of the past (the village compound, *le symbolisme qui sait, smṛti),* from the standpoint, however, of the living realizations through which they were brought into being; and the work will conclude with a stance taken in the immediate present.

Briefly, the historical circumstance determining the field of pertinence of any one of the various "village" religions is a function of the economic-political scene. The course of history shows a gradual enlargement of the "compounds," from a village size to tribal, from tribal to regional, from regional to sectarian (the so-called "world religions"), and now to global. The immediate problem is to formulate an effective symbolism for the "global compound," through which, on the one hand, simple people will be held in form, and on the other, creative geniuses will be led to seek their destiny.

What is the status of my present field-trip study of the Orient? What have I learned? What are the outstanding problems? What plans should I make for further research?

The genesis of my interest in the Orient and specifically in India is twofold:

The first is *personal:* the help that I received in solving my adolescent philosophical and religious problems through my meetings with Krishnamurti and his friends (1924–29), the help that I received in resolving my Schopenhauer-Nietzsche dilemma[156] through a reading of Nikhilananda's translation of the *Māṇḍūkya Upaniṣad,* Coomaraswamy's *Dance of Śiva,* and my subsequent study of the Upanishads, with a bit of Ramakrishna (1939–41); and the impact of Zimmer (1940–54).

The second is *scholarly:* the recognition that in the field of folklore and myth India constitues a kind of axial tradition, with a continuity dating from the chalcolithic and surviving, still alive, to this day (this dating from about 1934); a period of heavy concentration on Indian materials following the death of Zimmer (1943–54); and the need now to find a point of view of my own with respect to the relationship of my India studies to the whole field of my science.

My reactions to my experience of India have been somewhat emotional because of the implication of my personal interests in matters that I should have liked to have handled in a purely scholarly way.

So, with reference to my *personal reactions* I have made some important kindergarten discoveries, as follow.

Indian society is not a function of Indian philosophy, but on the contrary, Indian philosophy is a function of *one* section of Indian society. Consequently, Indian society as a whole does not illustrate (as Coomaraswamy suggests it should) the ideals of Indian philosophy.

The *poverty* of India is not a result of English exploitation alone, but also of the Muslim conquest, the caste system, the dishonesty of contemporary Indian officials, and the Indian love for a restful life.

The *squalor* of India is not a result of Indian *poverty* alone, but also of an indifference to dirt, the inefficiency of city officials, and an intentional spectacle of poverty presented by professional beggars: moreover, the assault that the visitor endures from the beggars gives him an exaggerated view of the seedier aspects of the Indian scene. This whole matter of Indian poverty and squalor may be summed up as a function of the *Baksheesh Complex,* which has two major forms of manifestation: that of the beggar, that of the retired pensioner. The formula for both is *Something for Nothing.*

India's pretext of spiritual superiority is another consequence of the Baksheesh Complex and does not accord with the actualities of the modern international scene. India is in fact receiving all of her progressive ideals (spiritual principles) as well as machines (technological principles) from the West. The clue to the Indian psychology of "spiritual superiority" is supplied by Nikhilananda's statement that Vivekananda was a proud man and did not wish to receive something for nothing: he saw that India required the machinery and organizations of the West. He therefore determined to give the West the spiritual goods of India in return. The fact was, however, that the West did not need these "spiritual" goods as badly as the Orient needed the West's "material" goods; also, that the Oriental spiritual gift was not quite as great as Vivekananda had to pretend to himself, to bolster his pride. The pattern has been to pretend that the West is without native spiritual fare, so that the exchange will seem to the Indians themselves to be a fair one.

What India has received from England is its whole character as a modern state. If England asked and took a lot for the teaching of this indispensable modern lesson: such a toll has a precedent in the Indian concept of the rights of the guru. Moreover, India was left with the difficult, yet not impossible task, of finding her own feet—which is good pedagogy. All of my earlier opinions of English imperialism have had to be revised.

The Oriental psyche is structured so differently from that of the West (symptom: the absolute separation of the sexes in public life; consequent limitation of heterosexual experiences to the archetypal realm of marriage and prostitution; no development of intersexual personality influences) that the guidance of an Oriental guru cannot but mislead the Westerner. Each psyche must develop along its own lines (at least for the present) in a world that is receiving all of its creative life and inspiration from the West. We cannot yet speak, therefore, of the Orient having something very important to teach us, which we should learn. What is important for us in the Eastern tradition has already been found and presented to us by Occidental scholars—Jones, Wilson, Muller, Rhys-Davids, Oldenburg, Zimmer, etc., with a couple of Easterners working in the Occidental frame—Coomaraswamy and Suzuki. I am sure that more work remains to be done, but it does not have the importance of a historically necessary task for us. It will be a joy for us and an amplification of what we know of a great and beautiful world age, which is now in its twilight, and the descendants of which will certainly, one day (but hardly in this century), have a creative contribution to make to our global civilization.[157]

The hope, the immediate future, and the teacher of the modern world is the West. The main problems of the modern world are functions of the Western style of life and thought. The most significant approach to the modern problems, therefore, must be via the modern Western psyche—and most emphatically, via the modern American psyche, since America, at the present moment, is the ideal-giver even to Europe. This realization has moved me to dissolve my earlier thoughts of a series of works on Oriental religion and legend—for example, my *Life and Lives of the Buddha, Questions of King Milinda*—and to plan to concentrate on the legendary and mythological themes of the West—for example, *The Life of Judas, The New World of Bartholomé de las Casas,*[158] *The Death of Captain Cook.*[159] I think also of the comparative themes of my *Twelfth Century*[160] idea, as still good, because here a panorama might be presented of the whole global context of our variously inflected world culture without suggesting that one or another had the answer for all. This line of thought has led me to abandon the intention that I brought with me to India to make a big thing of my Hindi and Sanskrit; better now, develop my European languages: French, German, Spanish, and Italian; also, perhaps, a bit of Greek and Latin. Become a Westerner again. And finally, the *Eranos Tagung,*[161] with its Occidental emphasis, now seems to me an excellent field. What my own special *Fach*[162] would be in this vortex, I do not quite see. So much, then, for the personal aspect of the lessons that I am learning on this journey.

What now of the *scholarly?*

Like a damn fool, I left in New York the papers in which I had stated for the Bollingen Foundation the headings and purposes of my India project; however, I believe I can recall the best part of the plan—and perhaps it is just as well that my dear mind should be called upon to formulate the whole thing in the terms that I can conjure up here today.

My primary project was, to study the functioning today of the traditional Indian philosophies of *artha, kāma, dharma,* and *mokṣa,* and I listed under the last named heading, the patterns of the Vedic-Upanishadic tradition, those of Buddhism and Jainism, the Purāṇic and Tantric, Vaiṣṇava and Śaiva, the philosophies of Śaṅkara and Rāmānuja; and then the *alien* philosophies and religions of India; Zoroastrianism, Islam, Christianity, Western Science and Scholarship, Democratic Constitutionalism and Totalitarian Despotism. Also to be considered were the fates of the 19th-century movements: Theosophy, Brahmo-Samaj, Ramakrishna Mission—and of the 20th-century personalities: Tagore, Vivekananda, Ramana Maharishi, Krishnamurti, Gandhi—to which now I should add Vinoba Bhave and Sri Krishna Menon. I believe that I have learned a great deal about all of these things, but I shall postpone my discussion until I have covered first the minor projects of my journey.

My second project was, to visit, if possible, some of the tribal villages of India. This I have not even attempted, nor am I likely to make any attempt. I have had a few glimpses, however, of tribal peoples: those horse people in Kashmir, the Lambanis that we saw in Gadag, and the Santāls on the way to Darjeeling. One thing that is perfectly clear is that they are not Hindus, and that they have hung on hard to their non-Aryan, tribal ways. Actually, now, I don't think it would make much point to go and try to study them for a day or two. It would require weeks to gain more than a surface view of their lives. Better simply to be satisfied with the works of Verrier Elwin.[163]

A third project, which emerged during the course of my spring and summer work on the Zimmer material, was to visit as many as possible of the important monuments of Hindu art—and this I have accomplished pretty well. I can say, I think, that I know the feeling of the cave temples and *vihāras,* the great medieval temples, and the temples of the southern style; also of some of the smaller gems. There remains the experience of the *stūpa,* which I shall get when I visit Sāñcī. There remain also a number of specific monuments that I wish to see, and these I shall try to include in the itinerary of the remaining weeks of my stay in India.

Project number four (three, I believe, in my original statement) was, to acquire experiences that should assist me in the organization of my *Basic Mythologies.* These I have had in abundance: the majority, where they do not coincide precisely with the findings for my primary project, might be said to be those points discussed above as affecting my personal interests and beliefs.

A fifth project has emerged in connection with the planning of Jean's visit to India, namely, the experience of the contemporary state of the arts of dance and music, which in turn is but part of a possible study of the problem of the contemporary Indian artist. It might be said that I have just begun this study (if it can be given such a ponderous name) with my meeting of the Theatre Unit, visit to Ara's exhibition, chat yesterday with Mr. Mehta's artist guests, and proposed continuation of this line of action. In the light of what I have just written about the *smṛti* and *śruti* aspects of my subject,[164] this art project might be said to be a necessary complement of my primary study of the functioning today of Indian philosophy and religion.

And finally, project number six is a comparative study of the religious areas of the Oriental world (this links in with project number four). This plan emerged after my first few weeks in India, to continue the comparative experience that I had already had through pausing in Beirut, Jerusalem, and Damascus. The reduction of my stay in India to six months was a radical transformation of my plan, brought about directly by my disappointment in India, but now justified, I think, by my realization that my main subject is rather comparative than Indian mythology, and my conviction that the sort of deeply driving teaching that would justify a long stay, or even a two-month period of concentrated language study, is no longer demanded in my revised view of the role that India is to play in my scholarly life.

So now to the *review of the present status of my primary project*, the study of the functioning today of the traditional Indian philosophies.

My first realization was that throughout the Orient religion is in a much stronger position than it is in the West. The visit to Jerusalem and then that to Brindavan let me know that Catholicism and Hinduism are not radically different and that in the Orient Catholicism is definitely an Oriental faith. My friend Mr. Cage, the Pentecostalist, was equally at home in this religiously oriented world. My view of Cardinal Gracias in Madras and the talk with Father Heras here in Bombay have reinforced this picture of a fundamental religious continuum in which all faiths operate in the Orient—a continuum, which, in our civilization, was radically shattered *circa* 1492 and has been falling to bits ever since.

In the Orient, then—or at least in as much of it as I have experienced—religion is as strong as it was in Europe in the Middle Ages. A man's religion determines his character, position in society, and everything else. The concept of the Free Thinker is almost totally lacking. A few Westernized gentlemen may claim to be atheists, but their wives will be religious. And those who grow past the elementary patterns of their religious practice still think of themselves as members of the religious community of the birth (or conversion). (This I have from Mr. Mehta.)

My second realization was that the predominant atmosphere of contemporary Hinduism is that of *bhakti*—the *bhakti* of the post-Mohammedan period; that of Rāmānanda, Kabīr, and Nānak, where the reference to a personal God is as good as final. (This, of course, increases the resemblance to Catholicism.) Even the Ramakrishna monks, who are supposed to be the followers of Śaṅkara, not only behave publicly, but also talk, as though a God were the final term. In the *maṭhas* the worship of the Ramakrishna image is quite orthodox Hindu in style. I am told that in the ashrams there is a Vedantic emphasis; but when I said one day, before Swami Nikhilananda, "there is no Vedanta in India, there is only *bhakti*," he said: "We think of the two as the same." One can say that in Catholicism too there is a realization among the clergy that "God is far superior to anything that man can think or say of God"; but the emphasis in both cases is equally on God and his worship through rite and meditation.

My third realization was that a radical division exists between the largely illiterate lower castes and the upper, so that the whole problem of religion in India breaks in two. We have to consider first the religions and religious life of the lower and vastly larger section of the population (perhaps 80%, i.e. about 320,000,000 if the total population is 400,000,000) and then, separately, as a smaller yet more active force, the religions and religious life of the upper fraction (perhaps 20%, i.e. about 80,000,000).

A. Lower Castes:

1. Hindu — about 150,000,000
2. Mohammedan — about 30,000,000
3. Sikh — about 6,000,000
4. Tribal — about 1,700,000
5. Catholic — about 5,000,000
6. Protestant — about 2,500,000
7. Buddhist — about 200,000

B. Upper Castes:

1. Hindu — 150,000,000
2. Mohammedan — 5,500,000
3. Jain — 1,600,000
4. Sikh — 200,000
5. Parsee — 100,000
6. Catholic — 500,000
7. Protestant — 200,000

8. Brahma Samāj
9. Ārya Samāj
10. Theosophist
11. "Atheist"

The "Gurus" (int'l following)
Tagore (Sautiniketan)
Ramana Maharishi
Aurobindo
Krishnamurti
Krishna Menon

The "Leaders"
Gandhi
Nehru
Vinoba Bhave

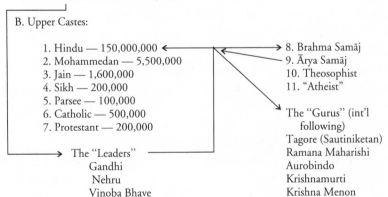

The report of the opening of the Marian Congress on the Azad Maidan states that there were 50,000 Catholics present, "representative of the entire five million Catholic population of India," with seventy archbishops and bishops from all over India as well as from Rangoon, Singapore, Syria and Lebanon. S. Radhakrishnan made the following statement: "The great need of our age is revival of spiritual values.... The need of the world today is human unity, and religions are proving to be great obstacles in its way.... Love of God is not a mere phrase, not an intellectual proposition to which we consent with our minds. It is a transforming experience, a burning conviction. The destiny of man is not natural perfection, but it is life in God. Human nature finds its fulfillment in God. Religion in all its forms declares that the human being should be made into a new man.... He has to reach inner completion through *meta-noia*, which is not adequately translated as repentance.... Religion is the force which can bring about this inward renewal.... The followers of the different religions are partners in one spiritual quest, pursuing alternative approaches to the goal of a spiritual life, the vision of God. It is this view that has been adopted by this country from ancient times...."

Nehru, on the other hand, sent the following words: "I am not concerned with the religious aspect of this Congress, but I am interested in the civic aspect. I understand that this civic aspect will receive much attention at the Congress. I welcome this attention to the cultural and civic aspects of our national life. We want our people to maintain and develop their rich culture in all its variety, at the same time always remembering the essential unity of our nation. Therefore, every community should help in this development of unity in diversity...."

A nice contrast of the spiritual and the patriotic points of view—the two that in Swami Nikhilananda have become inextricably confused. And I am afraid that Swami and the Nehrus have helped to pitch me into a patriotic mood too, so that my view of India is being somewhat distorted by antagonistic reactions. Let me try to forget that I am an American, even though every beggar in the street is reminding me that I *am* one. Let me try to see India as it *is*—not comparatively. Let me try to be the one who asks the questions from now on, rather than the one who answers: this will bring out news instead of mere reactions.

I spent the whole day writing the diary entries for Saturday and Sunday—except for an hour and a half in the late afternoon (6:15 to 7:45) when I went to the meeting room of the United Lodge of Theosophists to hear Mrs. Sophia Wadia deliver a lecture on "This is an Honest Universe." She lectured well, to an audience of about 175, in a large, neatly kept hall-and-library. I spoke to one of the members afterward, and learned that the United Lodge is a sort of fundamentalist Theosophical group, which reacted to the innovations of the Annie Besant faction back in the 1890s and owes allegiance to Blavatsky-Judge, not Blavatsky-Besant-Leadbeater. The Besant group is centered in Adyar, and has more lodges in India than the United; also, Krishnamurti talks largely under their auspices. The United Lodge has its headquarters in New York, and has (as I recall) about seven lodges in India—in Bombay, Bangalore, Baroda, and some four or five other cities. My impression of the attendance was very good: almost completely Indian, intelligent and nice looking people—rather different in tone, I should say, from what I have seen of Theosophy in America. And the talk of *karma* and reincarnation seemed more natural here than it does in the West. Finally, I should say that although the number of Theosophists in India may be small, when one considers the force of the intellectual élite in this country, their importance may be great.

And so, today I have gathered a bit of news on Catholicism and Theosophy in India. I have also been reading, lately, about Vinoba, and here I have run into a number of important bits of information, which I shall bring together later on. With respect to the religious statistics, I must learn what the geographical and economic distributions are of the various groups.

Monday, December 6

An item in this morning's paper places the number of Jains in India at about 20 lakhs, i.e. 2,000,000. A sacred *cādar* has been presented to the spiritual leader of the Jains, Maharaj Atmaram. The *cādar* is from the All-India Vardhaman Asthanik Vasi Jain Shramak Sangh. On receiving it the leader said that love, justice, truth and non-violence are the pillars of peace, and that truth and non-violence are interlinked. Here, certainly, is traditional Jain doctrine—and one sees the link with Gandhi's *satyagrāha.*

Mr. Mehta has spoken to me a bit about the Jains. Largely a wealthy group (bankers), now concentrated in Gujarat and the Bombay areas. Their sadhus are still serious: "no hanky-panky yogis." The laymen do not like to see their own children become monks and nuns, but are glad to support the religious institutions. There is almost no creed in Jainism, but a great deal of emphasis on rules. He regards it as a very curious, unspirited religion.

After lunch a young man named Ralph Mendonça, from one of the newspapers, came for an interview (Ezekiel-Alkazi context),[165] and remained until about 4:30 P.M., and had lots to say about India and the West. He liked Radhakrishnan's talk at the Marian Congress, but thought Nehru's greeting inept. He said that Joyce was no longer read in India, and seemed to accept my suggestion that the Western psychological problem, which Joyce typifies (humanistic personality discovering play of the archetypes in the field of experience), is the opposite to India's (archetypal life awakening to the humanistic values and seeking to incorporate them).

I developed the idea, which has been growing in my mind, of the East West contrast: in the Western unconscious, the forgotten, security-yielding archetypes; in the Oriental, the disregarded personal values. *Every instant of traditional Oriental life is one of* satī, *wherein the claims of the individual personality are immolated.*

That was *one* of my bright remarks. Another had to do with the corresponding focal point of the West: that of the tragic decision. *Every moment of a Western life is one of personal decision, wherein a consciously considered choice is made: the individual takes upon himself the responsibility and does not assign it simply to his dharma.* The result is a psychological tension and complexity of character, which has been wrongly interpreted as a function of the "speed" of Western life. The tragic tension will be found in the country as well as in the city. Moreover the "speed" of our life is much less apparent to one living in America than to one looking at us. Going eighty miles an hour on an American road is more restful than going forty on an Indian road. Life on an American campus is quieter than life in Bombay or Calcutta. It is not speed, but our psychological focus, that supports our tension.

The typical Indian (perhaps Oriental) tension, on the other hand (and now I am developing a point that did not come out in our talk) is that between the archetypal patterns of life and the experience of eternal rest—as symbolized in the Dancing Śiva, repose in action. To the modern Western mind, caught in the vortex of time's dilemmas and decisions, this spectacle and symbol of balance has a great appeal: it is rendered in the whole range of India's great art (from Sāñcī to Koṇārak and Belūr). However, the balance there rendered, between eternity and the great archetypes of the cosmic and collective round-of-existence (*nirvāṇa* and *saṁsāra*), does not quite resolve our problem. Our experience of history and life is not that of the round (*yugas* and rebirth: a changeless society since the millenniums of the neolithic), but that of the destiny-shaping decision, and that of conflict of values implicated in every decision—the rejected continuing to assert their claim, if not in our consciousness, at least in our unconscious.[166]

In Indian life (and here I am back in the conversation of this afternoon), where each caste, each life-way, is insulated from all the rest, the individual has only to enact his *dharma*, immolating his personal resistances indeed, but never doubting the rightness of his "right action." On the other hand, as soon as a modern Occidental child enters school, he finds himself in a room with children whose backgrounds, whose system of inherited ideals, are different from his own. The result is an immediate crisis of decision: and from there on, his spritiual life will be one of decisions made and then experienced as either right or wrong, apt or inept, just or unjust. In this sense, every man is a king on the judgment seat: the jury system is a consequence and symbol of this experience.[167]

For a Westerner, Oriental literature, which is a rendition of archetypes, has the quality of fairy tale. The problem of the modern Indian poet and artist might be said to be that of recognizing and bringing to consciousness the traditional "sins" of his tradition, e.g. that of Rāma *vis-à-vis* Sītā. Contrast the historic decision of Edward VIII in giving up his throne.[168] Edward's decision, from the point of view of the royal *dharma*, was a shameful sin (the old Queen Mother felt that); but from the point of view of the individual Rāma's act (not decision, since he never for a moment doubted the claim of his *dharma*) was a brutal sin.[169] We cannot say that either position is right or wrong absolutely. Each, however, involves a repression of the claims of the other, and these claims live in the unconscious in the form of character-making pressures or insensibilities.

Women, in the Orient, represent archetypes and do not have to depend upon the radiance of their individual personalities. Furthermore, since marriages are arranged, they do not have to pull themselves together to "win" someone. As a result, they seem comparatively secure and uninteresting.

The problem of the Westerner "dropping back" into an Oriental way of "resting on the *guṇas*" is not convincingly solved. We are committed, so to say, to the symbol of the Crucifixion—the Tragedy.

Problem: what about the *Greek* tragedy? Sophocles' *Philoctetes* would seem to be a prelude to the modern experience. *Oedipus,* on the other hand, treats the problem of conflict on the unconscious level: it is a tragedy of "irony." In the mythological sphere there is no sense of irony or of tragedy: the archetypal act takes place in perfect innocence of its own darker implications. A study of this whole problem is indicated.[170]

Orientals tend to dress according to their group commitments. This defends them against personal criticism and explains their acts. The modern Western dress is largely non-committal: the individual is responsible, from moment to moment, for his irrevocable history-making decisions!

During the course of our conversation, Ralph Mendonça told me of a Jain sadhu now in Bombay, whom I may be able to visit. He travels with a great entourage. They all have to walk (no use of machines); they go to the seashore (four miles) to defecate (no use of machines), they carry their manuscript library of thousands of volumes wherever they go. Their hair is pulled out by hand, etc. This sadhu has been publicly revered by Nehru. He cannot eat food cooked for him, but may eat cooked food that has been prepared for others; if, however, the others who have given him of their food then prepare more food for themselves, to supplement the lack, they sin.

He told of a guru (perhaps this one: I didn't get it quite clearly) who had a very devoted devotee, a business man, who kept clinging to his leg. The guru asked for a drink. Cocoa was prepared. He left a little in the cup, spit into the cup, and passed it to his devotee as *prasāda*. It was taken with joy.

The whole pattern of *mokṣa* and guru now appears to me as a perfect counterpart of the Indian experience of the social archetypes. The way is given—not found. Something of the quality and character of Theosophy seemed rather clear to me yesterday as I heard Mrs. Wadia talking of *karma* and honesty: the honesty of the universe and the honesty in life that puts one into tune or accord with the universe. Theosophy takes certain themes from Indian thought and stresses them, giving them an application meanwhile to certain Western problems of ethical life. It is consequently, a rather good bridge—but it tends to misrepresent, meanwhile, both shores.

I dashed home to be picked up by Adi Heeremaneck for dinner at his sister's apartment. Two sisters, one very beautiful and with four equally handsome children and a rather interesting yet ominous, dark husband; the other sister, very nice and warm, with a tight, sort of jockey-boy of a husband. Old Mrs. Heeramaneck was lovely.

They served me drinks—and when there was a knock on the door were a little afraid. In Bombay, the police can enter a home and nab people for drinking. (I think our scheme, horrible as it was, was better than this!) The knock, however, was simply that of the arriving second husband.

This was a family of Parsees.[171] More emancipated I should say, than a Hindu family: yet perfectly Indian. I asked about the Parsee temples. I have seen that they are closed to non-Parsees. They are flanked by Assyrian sphinxes, have the symbol of Assur in his sun ring over the door, and on the verandah have a little box containing neat sticks of kindling. My guess was that the devotees purchase their stick at the door and place it on the fire—correct! The sticks are of sandalwood and cost about a rupee. They are handed to the priest who places them on the fire. "But don't say," said the lesser husband with a laugh, "that we are fire worshippers!" "No," I replied, "I think I know better than that."[172]

One feels, actually, that there is little difference between this and *pūjā*: sticks on a fire, flowers before the god. The general attitude is the same. However, here, fire, the symbol of light (*Agni*, Mazda) visibly consumes the stick (the offering, the body of this death). It is a very vivid and simple event. I must ask, next time, whether hymns are sung, what sort of prayers are recited.

Tuesday, December 7

At the American Express this morning I found a lively letter from Jean and a packet of publicity materials. It begins to feel as though our trip together had actually commenced. I am going to see the theater people tomorrow and get things started.

While on my walk, to and from Flora Fountain, I kept thinking of this new, and I believe very keen idea, about the Orient and its time-eternity archetypes and the West with its tragic-ironic decision tension. Everything seemed to fit into it very neatly. I felt as though I had found, at last, the best answer to one of my most puzzling problems.

At 5:20 P.M. Mendonça called for me and we went to the home of Farouk Mulla, whom I had met last week at von Leyden's, to view a small exhibition of the young modern painters in Bombay. Professor Venturi was present, and after he had carefully studied the offerings he sat down and was closely questioned by the artists and newspaper people present. He spoke of the modern movement in Italy: the comeback of the painters who had been disregarded by the Fascist group, and the present status of their work.

Asked whether he thought Indian art could be presented in Europe, he answered yes—an exhibition should be arranged of 150 to 200 paintings—with *no* examples of the restoration movement, copying Ajaṇṭā, etc. The international movement that began with the post-impressionists in Paris *is* modern art, and to be in the game one must participate in this movement—speak with this vocabulary but say what you will. Indian artists, as evinced by the present showing were making their own statements and would inevitably be "Indian" no matter how consciously so.

Represented in the showing were Ara, Hussein, and Samant, whom I had met Saturday at Mr. Mehta's, both quite interesting, Hussein doing thin two-dimensional compositions and Samant working with a strong and heavy quality of rich paint. Pals Seker was another like Samant. One—or rather I—could not find anything particularly Indian about either of these. They could easily have hung in Betty Parsons' gallery. A painter named Raval, to whom Mulla, our host, was special patron, had a number of canvasses—rather Gauguinish and lyrically charming. To these Venturi paid little attention. Samant and Pals Seker seemed to be his choices. Another painter, Bendre, had done an interesting fresco-like little piece, showing a well fused composition of a ceramic horse, elephant, and bird-like form.

I had to leave while Venturi still was talking, to keep an appointment with Mrs. Puri (also met at Mr. Mehta's party) to see her film of Amarnāth, Kashmir. She was ill however, and so her very gracious husband treated me to a drink and a chat about India. His main point: in India one finds the sublime and the ridiculous side by side—which certainly is true enough. One finds also, I should say, the squalid and the luxurious.

Mr. Ezekiel came to Mulla's and gave me a copy of the new *Theatre Unit Bulletin.* I am to talk to the group tomorrow on "The Development of the Modern American Dance."[173]

Wednesday, December 8

The mail today brings news from Helen McMaster that my chapter MS. has arrived. Great relief. *Strich darunter.*[174] Bill McGuire writes that the title of the Indian book is to be *The Art of Indian Asia.* Sounds fine to me. I am arranging to leave here next Tuesday night—two days before Jean's departure from New York—spend Wednesday in Baroda, and land in Ahmedabad Wednesday night, December 15. This will give me time to attend to everything pertaining to Jean's concert before my departure from Bombay.

A letter from Lisa Coomaraswamy contains the following:

"You can see, now, it is 'we' and our way that is different, the old-world-wide mode of living (before the industrial era) was really one and the same from one end of the world to the other...it took so very little to upset the applecart, but that is so only because it (the cart) was already somewhat tipsy.... I love your description of the two 'cops' being friends, it's like a picture out of Plato! And, of course, the same goes for the women in the *zanāna,* they are so close..."

Thinking over all my great brain waves, I think that three are the best.

1. The sex separation theme.
2. The archetypal *dharma* vs. individual decision theme; *and*
3. That of Indian civilization not being a function of Indian philosophy but Indian philosophy a function of one section of Indian society.

Number 3 above has to be weighed against 1 and 2, which represent a general background for an Oriental and archaic philosophy. The specifically Indian patterns, however, have to be bounded carefully according to history, geography, and social stratum. How much of Indian philosophy belongs to layers 1 and 2 of this formula, and how much to layer 3? Very important.

But the new age—new India and new everything else—belongs definitely to what knocked the applecart over. In the arts, this is represented, as Venturi stated yesterday, to the post-impressionist movement that originated in Paris. All the nationalist, Fascist, and Communist politically and regionally oriented "restorations" are sentimental, romantic exoticisms. Likewise, it can be said that all sectarian religions are out of date. The problem is to find the "grave and constant"[175] in the world tradition and see it rendered in the vocabulary of the International Age of modern art, poetry, music, and prose. It occurred to me today, however, as I was walking along the street, that in contemporary India Western dress actually functions as a caste mark, setting its wearers apart and indicating their spiritual commitment.

This evening, at the Theatre Unit's place, I gave my talk to a gathering of about thirty people, then came home, had dinner, and went early to bed.

Thursday, December 9 ***Karle–Bhājā***

Up at 6 A.M. to catch the 7:15 train from Victoria Station to Lonāvale: arrival about 10:15 (three hours to go 75 miles). Tonga to Karle Caves, arriving about 11:30. Stayed about an hour and a half and then went in the tonga to Bhājā—two wonderful sites. My tonga got me back to Lonāvale just in time to catch the 3:15 for Bombay: arrival at 6 P.M. Walk to hotel. Tea. Bath. Sleep. Dinner. Diary. And so on to bed, dead tired. But now I've seen everything I came to Bombay to see.

A couple of thoughts about Indian philosophy:

Mokṣa: when it means the attainment of the standpoint of eternity (*nirvāṇa*) is one thing; when it means renunciation of the world of time, however (as it does with the monks), that is something very very different indeed.

The step from the normal Indian social situation of sex separation to the state of monkhood is a very small one. The turn from our modern Occidental life context to monkhood is a very different crisis.

Since the chief problem of Indian youth is not whom to marry, but "am I going to pass the exams and get a high-paying job?" it is no wonder that Indian layman's libido is all tied up in money. (In no other country have I ever been asked how much I earn. In India, every gentleman who has conversed with me has asked that question—without exception.)

Since "peace of mind" seems to be the inheritance of everybody in India, from the lepers on up to Radhakrishnan, I suppose it is natural that Indian philosophy should be one yielding "peace of mind," but in India such a boon would seem to be supererogatory.

But now I am taking a vow: henceforth I shall try to seek out and announce, not the disillusionments of my trip, but the positive aspect of what I am finding in India.

Friday, December 10

A word about duties, rights, and spirituality: the neolithic-Oriental stress on duties seems, at first, to be more spiritual than the western-modern stress on rights—and when considered from the point of view of the individual in bondage it may indeed be the less selfish view: however, when considered from the point of view of the individual in the commanding position, it is definitely not so. The whole Afro-Asian movement now for freedom and equal rights finds support not in native ideologies but in the European-American doctrine of rights. And the remarkable (spiritual) fact is, that the claims are being recognized by the West; just as, in the U.S.A., the claims of the Negro slaves were recognized in the 1860s. A theme for my *Bartholomé de las Casas* work. The "new world" is that of recognized and conceded rights.

Try to imagine what the case would be of India today if England's mode of conduct had been that of the Aryans to the subjugated Dravidians—forbidding them, on pain of torture and death, even to read or hear the Vedas[176] (in the case of the English, the works of Burke, Locke, etc., and the doctrine of freedom and rights). Not a single idea now inspiring Asia's fight against the West has been drawn from an Oriental text.

A question to be asked when Orientals speak of "spirituality" (which they love to do), is, "What do you understand by this term?"

And so I find that I have already broken my vow of yesterday evening. In the Orient I am for the West; in the West for the Orient. In Honolulu I am for the "liberals," in New York for big business. In the temple I am for the University, in the University for the temple. The blood, apparently, is Irish.[177]

One more new thought, however: this time, touching the matter of the relationship of religion to philosophy. I have been regarding it as unquestionably good that the two should be kept in close relationship, as they have been in the Orient. However, I now wonder whether it is exactly edifying to see philosophers taking the dust off the feet of monks, and so-called Vedantist monks dressing and undressing the images of Sri Ramakrishna? Does this not place too much weight where weight already resides, namely on the side of superstition, leaving the cooler, cleaner side without its proper champions? May it not be that the Western break with religion and the consequent attempt on the part of the clergy to come over to the obviously winning side without reversing their collars has served to clarify our religious and our whole spiritual atmosphere in a manner that would have been impossible had the Darwins and Nietzsches fallen flat in front of the Cross? An important point to keep in mind.

During the course of my trip to Karle and Bhājā, I considered, though vaguely, the status of my present plans for my studies and work after returning to New York. My former idea of stressing the Orient-Occident interplay, with works on the Buddha etc., is definitely out. I am regarding my present visit to India as a kind of Graduation Tour, not Commencement Tour.

I believe that my next two books, *An Introduction to Mythology*, and *The Basic Mythologies of Mankind,*[178] in that order, coupled with my work on the Eranos Series,[179] the Coomaraswamy volumes,[180] and my Mythology Course at Sarah Lawrence College, should serve to put me back onto my own rails—and my effort should be, while working on these vast, *general* projects, to bring my work to focus on some pertinent, *specific* aspect of the mythology-modern man problem. Perhaps a definition of the transformation of symbolic thinking in the Western sphere. I have thought of some themes that might be helpful, working around *The New World of Bartholomé de Las Casas* (Rights *vs* Duties);[181] *Apollonius of Tyana* (Alexandrian period);[182] and *The Life of Judas* (Orthodox-Heterodox Symbology).

And in my scholarly papers, special studies of the Eastern and Western development of common symbols.[183]

Now let us turn to the possible contribution that India (the Orient) may make to the West. First, in the fields of philosophy and religion:

1. *Ātman-Brahman idea—śunyatā idea.* Stress on the transcendent aspect of the divine (an idea present, but not stressed, in Western religion). This idea tends to be lost, however, in the modern *bhakti* religions of India, where, as far as the eye can see, sectarian gods and the attitude of sheer worship prevail.
2. *Ātman-jīva idea.* Stress on the immanence of the divine (hardly felt at all in the Western cults).
3. *Avidyā-māyā idea.* Instead of "The Fall." No "original sin." Stress on the problem of knowledge, rather than on that of guilt: "righteousness" a matter of wisdom, not simply of ethics.[184]
4. *Boddhi-mokṣa idea.* Instead of "repentance." (The idea is lost, however, when it becomes linked with "*escape* from the world of temporal sorrow.")
5. *Iti iti idea*—the eternal *Now.* Release from Heaven-Hell and after-life thinking. (Lost entirely, however, in the transmigration image when the latter is read concretely.)[185]
6. *Cosmic śakti idea*—The world as power: eternal Creation.
7. *Erotic mysticism*—Anti-Platonic (anti-homosexual) orientation. Body-Spirit polarity undone. Theme of mutual instruction. (Plays no role whatsoever, however, in Indian life. Actually better represented in the Occidental post-Troubador approach to sex.)
8. *Kuṇḍalinī yoga*—to be studied via C. G. Jung.[186]
9. *The harmony of religions*—to be studied via Comparative Mythology. In practical Hinduism the idea does not really operate—except in such fine moments as Radhakrishnan's Marian Congress speech, where it is for world consumption. (The true Indian attitude is that of Nikhilananda: Harmony of Religions, yes; but Hinduism, having recognized this, is the supreme religion.)

Second, in the fields of aesthetics and art:

1. *Theory of the rasas*—a vast amplification of the Aristotelian Tragic and Comic principle.[187]

2. *Stillness in movement, movement in stillness*—Elūrā (Das Avatāra: Tīn Thal), Elephanta, etc.
3. *Art as yoga*—the invocation of inspiration. (Amplification of the Muse-inspiration principle.)
4. *Theory of the rāgas*—static-cumulative (instead of progressive) music: music as the coming into manifestation of permanent strata of accord, consonant with certain spiritual states. I do not know whether any counterpart to this view exists in the West.[188]
5. *Rāga-mālā principle*—harmony of the arts: all the arts as manifestations of the one spirit.

Third, in the sociological field

1. *Society as an icon*—

Bing!

Life has begun to speed up. At 11:15 Alkazi arrived to drive me to the Bhulabhai Institute to see some photographs of Indian temple art; then to a new Bombay building, to see some more, used as wall decorations; then to the offices of *Marg,*[189] to talk about pictures with one of the editors. Next he came to the hotel to have lunch with me. Ezekiel joined us, and we had a conference on Jean's Bombay concert. We drove to the proposed theater, Jai

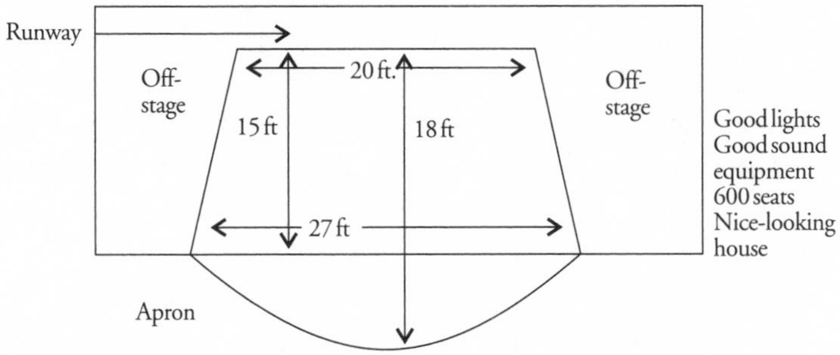

Hind Auditorium, and settled the date. I measured the stage.

Certain writings are required, and I am to furnish them: an article (1250 words) about Jean, for the *Theatre Unit Bulletin* and program notes, including two pages on modern American dance; two pages on Jean; and a page or half a page on each dance.

Alkazi dropped me at the American Express Office and I went in to get my mail: a letter from Jean. She will arrive in New Delhi (not Colombo) January 15 (not January 12). This involves a total shift of plan both for her visit and for my remaining weeks alone. I decided also that unless things develop surprisingly in New Delhi, one concert in India will be about all that can be handled—that is to say, if Jean is also to see any Indian dance.

How are we to do it?

I wrote a letter to Jean—realizing that it will be too late for her to receive it in New York. I must *wire* her the concert-date news. The letter I addressed c/o Watts in San Francisco.[190]

When I returned to the hotel from the American Express, I had to sit for a newspaper photographer in my room. One hour later he phoned to ask if he could shoot me again—there had been no photographic plates in his camera.

As I was preparing to go to bed, the phone rang. Rama Mehta, rebuking me for failing to phone her this week and inviting me to lunch at the Willingdon Sports Club, tomorrow at 1 P.M.

Saturday, December 11 ***Bombay***

According to the morning paper, a Digambar Jain yogi, Śri Nemisāgar (chief disciple of His Holiness, Śri Śānti Sāgar, head of the *digambara* community) has come to town. He is on his way to Girnār in Saurashtra and will spend a month in Bombay, giving religious discourses in a temple at Bhuleśvar. "The 66-year old muni, who does not use any mode of transport, visited Jain temples in Bhuleśvar and Kalbadevi before reaching Hira Bag. He will stay at the Digambar Jain Temple in Bhuleśvar from next week. His Holiness Śri Nemisāgar renounced the world at the age of 33 and since then has been preaching the message of *ahiṁsā*."

Last evening while strolling through my part of town, I passed an open hall all lighted up and filled with people. Two rooms: one of women, one of

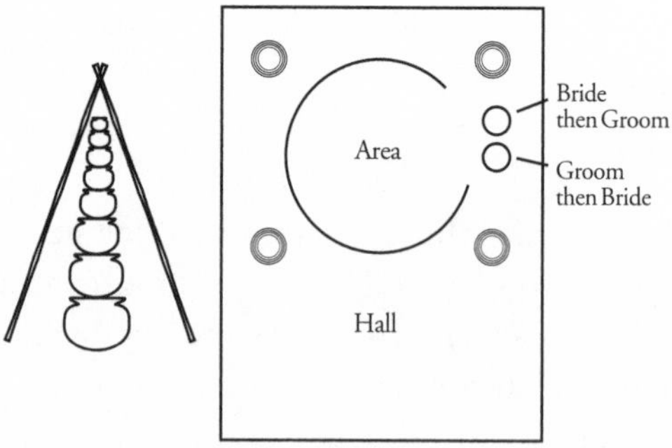

men. When I passed again, a little later, all were in the larger room (formerly the men's) and a wedding was taking place. A nice gentleman came to my side and explained what was happening. The ceremonial area was marked out by four little towers of diminishing-sized pots with bamboo teepee uprights tied above them. The "four legs"—whole—totality—my informer told me.

The two youngsters walked clockwise, bride following groom, with a tied white cloth connecting them, then sat down. Again. Again. Again. Last time sitting with groom at bride's right.

There were lots of kids and stray watchers who finally so blocked my view that I left.

New worry: a dangerous sensation in upper right first molar, which supports a bridge. Today, for some reason, I feel that this whole trip may be falling apart at the seams.

An appropriate word, culled from a London magazine: *Always behave like a duck—keep calm and unruffled on the surface but paddle like the Devil underneath*—Lord Brabagon.

At 1 P.M., I arrived at the Willingdon Sports Club to have lunch with Mrs. Pupul Jayakar and the Mehta girls and Rama's husband.[191] Very pleasant affair. Mrs. Jayakar had a lot of photos of late Gupta sculpture and temples in Rajasthan and invited me to visit a few such monuments with her and her husband in New Delhi.

After the luncheon, which ended about 4 P.M., Mrs. Jayakar drove me to the Bhulabhai Memorial Institute where I watched the Theatre Unit people rehearse their *Oedipus.* The rehearsal went on till 8:30 at which time I was told that in half an hour a music concert would begin downstairs. I decided to skip dinner and let Mrs. Desai take me to the concert.

This Institute's building, I was told, was the home of her father-in-law, Bhulabhai Desai, who was one of the great companions of Gandhi at the time of the national struggle. Gandhi, Nehru, Bhulabhai had all lived and worked here, and if Bhulabhai had not died, it would have been he, not Nehru, who would now be leading the nation. With the passing away, first of Bhulabhai and then of her husband, Mrs. Desai decided to convert this building into an institute of living art; a building that young artists could use. So it is now the home of the Theatre Unit and of a sculpture school, dance school, music school, etc. The Institute is responsible also for the map of Indian Art that one sees all over India.[192]

The concert was not very interesting as music. When the young sitar player got through two hours of tuning up the first part was over. He was accompanied by a strong-looking drummer, whose head movements always indicated when he was doing something particularly good. A large and very nicely mannered audience sat quietly, on the floor mostly, in obvious appreciation. I thought the whole affair comparable to an American jam-session, where jazz and bebop appreciators will sit for hours listening to the ad lib virtuoso stunts of a team of artists. The present team, however, never got really going: I'm quite sure of that.

If the performance was any indication of what Indian live music is like, it can be compared, roughly, to a six day bicycle race, where the riders pedal along uneventfully for long stretches and then suddenly bust into important sprints. The concert was scheduled for 9; got going at 9:45, and at 10:45 or so, the first *rāga* was suddenly terminated.

Then a girl child of about nine came out and performed Bharata Natyam[193] movements for three-quarters of an hour. She was astonishingly firm, clipped, and sophisticated in style, when she was actually dancing, and charmingly simple in her moments of non-performance.

I bade Mrs. Desai good night at 11:30 and drove in a taxi to my hotel. Having no dinner, I asked for tea and sandwiches at the desk, and they ushered me into the hotel's air conditioned "Rainbow Room" for a handout. There I found a band playing Hawaiian tunes with an electric-steel guitar: a jammed dance floor with the usual types; tea and cheese sandwiches for Joe, and at 12:15 to bed.

Sunday, December 12

I spent the first part of the day trying to write the article on Jean for the *Theatre Unit Bulletin.* No luck. At about 10:30 Salmony's friend Lance Dane phoned and drove me out to a lovely residence at Juhu to see Mr. Fielden's bronzes and remain for lunch. Lunch went on till four; Dane drove me home and I got dressed to attend the "initiation" ceremony of the seven-year-old son of a Parsee gentleman, Mr. Farouk Mulla.

What a party! 350 guests for dinner—mostly Parsees; the men in their little hats (once the cores, I have been told, of turbans) and the women in a spectacular display of saris. Lights on the trees in the front yard, and hundreds of chairs, lining the driveways and scattered among the trees. "Es ist wie ein Oper!" said the little Hungarian mother of Mrs. von Leyden.

I arrived at 5:20 and got a second row seat for the ceremony. The little boy was darling, sitting cross-legged in the center of a white rectangle, with two candles burning at either side and the Parsee fire of sandalwood sticks

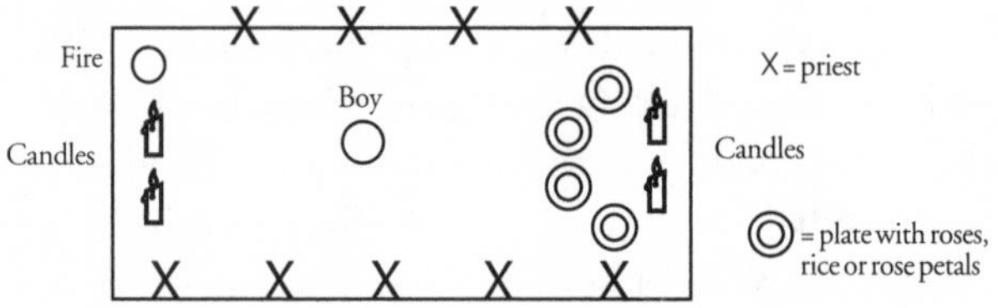

burning at his right, behind him, on a silver salver placed on a large silver urn. Nine priests appeared—looking precisely like surgeons in their white gear and little round white hats. Five sat before the boy, with their backs to the company, and four behind him.

The ceremony began with the priests beginning to mumble in unison. Then the main priest took over and said a prayer in Old Persian, which the little boy repeated. He put a big lei around the little boy's neck, dusted him with rose petals, then rice (if I remember correctly), then handed him a rose. He handed a rose to each of the priests. Next he and the other priests stood around the boy, removed the red shawl that was covering his shoulders and put on a little white shirt. The priest then took the sacred thread, and standing behind the boy (who looked like a little angel) held the thread in front of him, took his hands in his own, looped the thread around the boy's waist and around itself in a special way, while reciting a prayer, which the boy followed in unison. It was extremely gentle and sweet. The high pitch of the priest's voice was something special to hear. The priest then sat down. Mr. Mulla came and placed a pay envelope in each priestly hand and the clergy withdrew. The boy's mother and aunts then came forward, stood before the little chap, kissed him, and dressed him in his new suit—long-trousers, Western style; a cute little white suit. Daddy knotted the red necktie, put a little red cap on the boy, where formerly there had been a white one—and, immediately, the orchestra on the front porch struck up a rhumba! After that, congratulations all round. "How sweet! Wie süss!" and it had actually been darling.

I stayed for dinner—an endless mess of Indian stuff flopped onto banana leaves before you—but, thank god, on a table, and with a fork and spoon close at hand.

Mrs. Jayakar was there and I had dinner with her, talking: about India, etc. At about 9:30 I left for home.

Monday, December 13

Slightly sick last night after all the cockeyed food! No mail at the American Express this morning. On the way home, heard some drumming and singing, with a lot of men standing watching. I approached. A corpse was being prepared for the funeral pyre—covered with a white cloth, on a bier that had been placed in the gutter. The face and feet were visible: a good looking young husband, whose wife and three little boys (I thought of the Zimmers)[194] were standing on the curb, poor people: the wife in a green sari, put on in the Marathi peasant style: she was holding the hem to her eyes and simply standing and weeping. The oldest boy was wiping his tears. The two little fellows were simply standing. They stood on the curb while the priests put flowers all over the white shroud, and then a lot of vermillion. They cracked a coconut and let the family, in turn, splash a handful of its sweet water over the dead father. The band meanwhile, squatting at the foot of the bier, was chanting, clanking symbols and beating a drum. They got up. The bier was lifted and, feet first, carried away behind them while the mother and her three boys remained standing on the curb. The crowd withdrew. They remained about two minutes, weeping and dazed. Then the mother turned and took her three boys into the house.

This afternoon I went to four o'clock tea at the Mehtas: talked of plans. At 6:45 I went to the von Leydens' who took me to a lovely apartment where we saw some movies of Darjeeling, Kashmir, and Orissa. Seeing again in the movies what I had already seen with my own eyes, I had a very pleasant sense of the magnitude of the experience that I have been having this year. In the course of my tour I have been seeing India only piece by piece, little by little. Seeing it all again—as it were all at once—I felt how big this whole thing is. The Orient as a vast natural phenomenon, like a continent of trees, mountains, animals, and peoples.

We had a late dinner at the von Leydens' and I returned home at about midnight.

Today my article on Jean got going, and I began to feel that I might be able to complete it on time.

Tuesday, December 14

A day of getting ready to leave. A nice letter from Jean in this morning's mail. She leaves Thursday (December 16) for San Francisco where she will give a dance concert there December 18. I am to write her now to Honolulu. Did a bit of shopping, got a haircut and tried my hand again at that essay on Jean for the *Bulletin.*

I got a taxi to Central Station to catch the 9:05 P.M. Gujarati Mail. Ezekiel and his little wife came trotting down the platform to see me off about two minutes before the departure of the train.

Ahmedabad and New Delhi

Wednesday, December 15 ***Ahmedabad***

Three of us filled the compartment. Myself, a Hindu gentleman, and a young Mohammedan. The night was rather cold and I was awake a good deal of the time. At about 5:30 A.M. I got up and dressed. Then the Hindu got up, then the Mohammedan, who was in an upper berth. When he was dressed, he returned to his berth, put a scarf over his head in a certain way, and sat absolutely still for about twenty minutes, saying his prayers.

The train pulled into the station about half an hour late. Geeta Sarabhai was there to meet me. She brought me to a large limousine and we drove to the great gate of the estate—and in. After all I had heard about the squalor of Ahmedabad, the city seemed to me less squalid than, say, Calcutta or Benares. It was interesting to see and feel oneself in an Indian industrial town. Compared with what I have seen in England and Pennsylvania, it seemed to me quite O.K. Nor did the Sarabhai estate seem to me to be exorbitantly large. After all—five or six families are dwelling here, and the Sarabhais *are* rich. Moreover, they are doing a great deal to improve the community. Kamalini is running a nursery school on the estate for 150 kids—only eight of whom pay full tuition. Gautam is building museums to help teach the people about such things as town planning, house building, and machine weaving. Mrs. Sarabhai is involved very deeply in the work of the village-rehabilitation groups. Bharati is involved in some kind of little theater group. Gira works with Gautam in the factory. And Geeta has her darling little family of three.

I had breakfast with Geeta on the verandah outside of my suite. (Corbusier is in the suite next door to me.)[195] Then she showed me about the estate. What a collection of bronzes! Second only to the Madras museum, but better displayed. Then Gautam and Kamalini paid me a brief visit and I went off with Geeta and her youngsters to visit some of the sights of the town.

Our first visit was to the Temple of Swami Narāyaṇa—a large Hindu establishment with a temple in which there are many shrines with rather garish, doll-like images and innumerable pictures on the walls which visitors went around touching and worshipping. Men went around close in to the shrines, women remained further out, beyond a high rail fence. I was taken on by a nice old man who grabbed my hand and showed me all the shrines. When he had done so I offered him a tip—which he declined and I apologized with a *namaskāra* gesture to which he responded deeply. He took me by the hand again, and led me to the ashram—part of the temple compound.

Here a lot of saffron-clad monks were sitting around on a vast verandah. I went above and saw some more chapels, then came down and went to the center of the compound where I found Geeta again, who had visited the women's section: a building for widows who have decided to quit the world. No male—even a male child—can enter their building.

From this temple we proceeded to the Jain Nagar Sethis Temple. The atmosphere was distinctly different from that of the other, and yet the *pūjā* seemed about the same. Little ladies were moving rapidly from shrine to shrine, reciting their prayers. The temple compound was trim and clean, and the sculpture on the buildings suggested Mt. Abu. In the main shrine and sanctuary, a number of people were sitting on the floor in quiet worship—a man reading to himself from a prayer book. And one old lady with a large chowry in her hand waved it before the image while doing a dance (cute as could be!). I noticed after that that a number of the women visiting the temple were carrying chowries.[196]

We returned after this to the beautiful Sarabhai compound, and had lunch with Mrs. Sarabhai and Kamalini. On the floor in the corner was an old gentleman—Geeta's drum and music teacher—eating his lunch Indian style. During the afternoon I worked at my attempt to write a paper about Jean for the Theatre Unit. Tea was served to me on the verandah outside my rooms; then at six I was driven to Gira and Gautam's Calico Museum; I visited the offices at the Sarabhai factory—Modern Art Museum style. Very nice indeed. Dinner was at Gautam's "farm house," where I stayed after the others had left, to talk with Gautam and Kamalini. Lots of changes of balance in my orientation to India are already beginning to take place.

Thursday, December 16

I had asked for morning tea at seven. The light was turned on in the living room at that hour and I got up to find the tea in place. After dressing in the wonderful bathroom, I attempted to do something about Jean's article. A table was being set up on the verandah for breakfast. Geeta arrived at nine and about half way through breakfast the nurse arrived with her children. I worked some more on Jean's paper—beginning now to feel a bit of panic, because I can't seem to find any angle from which to begin. At about eleven I went in quest of Gautam, with whom I was to have an early lunch and found him, finally, in his modern little house in the compound. Gautam and Kamalini drove me in their new, zippy roadster to a point where I was transferred into another car and then driven to the home of a learned gentleman, Sarabhai Nawab, who for two hours showed me his illuminated Jain manuscripts, early (pre–12th-century) Jain bronzes, and several of his own learned publications. Big news here. The man knows a lot—and has been plundered somewhat (according to his own account) by W. Norman Brown, who visits him but manages not to mention his name when he publishes. (Stella Kramrisch has resided with this man's family also). Nawab showed me the room in which Brown stayed. He has written to Brown for the names of institutions in America that might be interested in his publications but has received no help. I promised to send him a full list when I got home.

During the afternoon I worked some more on that stubborn paper, and began to feel that I had found a line that I could follow to some sort of end. Gautam wants me to give a talk of some kind in Ahmedabad—and this now creates a double pressure. I hope I can get through this thing!

Gautam and Kamalini took me to the movies at the "Club." Horrible. Betty Hutton in some silly thing about the career of a cabaret singer. I suddenly realized that in thinking about America I tend to be ignorant of what foreigners see, just as Indians, in thinking about India, tend to ignore what I have been seeing. We left at the intermission and I tried my hand again at the article on Jean.

Friday, December 17

This morning I transferred the scene of my writing efforts to the bathroom, where I feel a bit more closed in and in control of the situation. Had a nice breakfast again with Geeta and then was taken next door, to the Khasturbhai's to see a magnificent collection of Mughal, Rajput, Lucknow, and Śāntiniketan-style paintings. Simply wonderful. The paintings were stored in racks and a couple of servants took them out and handed them to me while I sat royally in a chair, for about an hour and a half. One amusing number was of Kṛṣṇa riding on an elephant composed of *gopīs.*

After lunch I retired to the bathroom to work on Jean's paper. The situation is approaching the critical stage. I begin to feel that I am going to produce a mess!

I went down to Papa Sarabhai's where I chatted with him for about an hour, waiting for guests to arrive from Baroda: a young American couple named English, she badly bent in the middle (crippled), he a psychiatrist over here on a Fulbright. They know zero about Indian thought and are a bit touchy on the point, when their psychoanalytic judgments of the phenomena that they observe are challenged.

Saturday, December 18

Mr. English and wife were at breakfast with Geeta and myself on the verandah. While the set table and I were waiting for them to arrive a crow flew to the verandah, hopped onto the table, picked up a napkin and winged away to a neighboring balcony. When I went to the railing to watch, I heard the flutter of another bird and behold! there descended onto one of the high cornices of the building a male peacock. He walked along the cornice and disappeared behind a wall. I felt then that I was living in a Rajput painting—which I believe I am. This whole thing of living here is simply dreamily delightful.

The morning was spent once again in the bathroom at work on Jean's article. It is really going now, and I think it may not be too bad. The only problem is time. The due date is December 20, which is Monday.

Sunday, December 19

I took breakfast on Papa's piazza with Geeta and the Englishes. Then another morning in the bathroom devoted to Jean's article (almost finished), and to preparing a talk that I am to give this afternoon to an invited audience. At 11 A.M. I went with Geeta to the library of the Vidya Sabha, where I was shown a few late Rajput manuscripts and some 13th-century paper. Nice visit.

At five the people began to arrive for the talk. It was an impressive gathering: the vice-chancellor of the University, the head of the psychiatric profession here, head of the nursery school, head of some sort of psychological institute, scholars of various sorts, their wives, etc. I was really on the spot. All settled in one of the large living rooms and I talked from about an hour; then a fine discussion developed, which went on till after seven. After that came dinner and a quiet evening of sitting around while Gautam exhibited the various manners of wearing a dhoti.

My talk had as title *A Comparison of Indian Thought and Psychoanalytic Theory.*[197] I introduced the talk by pointing to the East-West contrast of gods soaring on rapture with gods soaring on wings: the Oriental experience of vision-rapture and the Occidental interest in mechanics. We have turned to the dream world from the sphere of waking consciousness and see dream as a fact for science to consider; the Orient turns to life from the realm of rapture and sees life as a dream. In the whole range of Western science it would seem that the field of psychology approaches the closest to the Orient in its findings.

Part I of the talk was concerned with a brief review of the main themes of psychoanalysis:

A. Conscious - unconscious
   1. Charcot - Breuer (hypnosis)
   2. Freud: Free association
      conscious { resistance
      unconscious { censor →
      "repressions"
   3. Jung: Conscious { personal ←
      Unconscious { collective →
   4. Myths and Deep Dreams ←
      Heavens (expanding consciousness) – Hells (constricting)
   5. "World" a function of psyche.
      yoga/māyā – Image/Analysis

B. Libido
   1. As sex
   2. As *eros - thanatos*
   3. Compare Kāma-Māra in the legend of the Buddha

C. The Two Aims
   1. Curing the patient back to society (Freud) } Rank
   2. Curing the patient beyond society (Jung) } theses

      Lead of unconscious

Part II (very brief) was a review of the *Māṇḍūkya Upaniṣad* formula: Waking Consciousness, Dream Consciousness, Deep Sleep, *turīya.*

And in conclusion I presented my idea that in the Orient the Personal Unconscious is very strong (*satī* of the personality at every moment: conscious acceptance of the Collective patterns), while in the Occident the collective is in the Unconscious. Orient resists individualism, Occident resists the relaxation to the collective—"oceanic" feeling, etc. My finale was the myth of the Churning of the Milky Ocean: *asuras* (Occident) and gods (Orient) combine to produce, first the poison (which our generation must hold in its throat) and then the ambrosia of immortal life.[198]

The discussion commenced immediately with a Mohammedan gentleman holding the floor at length. His best point: *karma* serves to help the individual submit to the collective, to his fate, etc. and blocks the development of an individualistic effort.

A Dr. Maiti then held forth very well indeed on the relationship of Indian thought to psychoanalysis. Main points: Kṛṣṇa in the *Gītā* is like an analyst: Arjuna's confusion healed by a synthesizing formula (cf. Jung-uniting symbol[199]): he is then returned to life, fit to act.

India is more permissive than the West of *psychological deviations.* In the West, heterodox behavior runs into trouble sooner than it does in India: anxiety is increased thereby and neurosis rendered the more likely. It is more difficult to push through to a transcending realization. (Later query in my mind: This applies, I believe, only to the male. In the Orient the deviant female is absolutely blocked.)

Mr. English made the good point that the aim of psychiatry is to set people at ease with themselves and their world—and this involves taking their religion into account when they have a religion: but psychiatry does not teach religion.

The vice-chancellor was asking whether people could be cured without religion. Dr. Maiti cited some cases where they had, others where they hadn't, and still others where, with religion, they had *not* been cured. It was a fine afternoon.

At dinner Papa Sarabhai asked about the problem of Catholics in the West: were they not as strictly held to the archetypes as Orientals?

At dinner, also, Mrs. English challenged the term "Collective Unconscious." and finally decided that what it meant was "Capacities."[200]

And after dinner, in a conversation with Gira I realized that in the Orient individuals are no less individual than they are in the West: the difference is really that in the West the individual is *attached* to his individuality, whereas in the Orient the chief attachment is to some group: family, caste, tribe.

With respect to the problem of women. Some days ago I said that Indians were not much interested in sex, and Geeta said, later, that she was surprised that I had already noticed this. Then she said that she thought the reason was that people marry without love affairs and think immediately of having children. Sex is simply a means to children. It is not experienced in its own right as something pleasurable. Moreover, for many women it is experienced too soon.

Monday, December 20

I finished my piece on Jean before breakfast this morning, had breakfast with Geeta (the Englishes have gone), and then went over to Gira's to talk with her about some of the problems of the Museum that Gautam and she are interested in. I made a few suggestions for possible exhibitions and came home, to begin catching up on my diary. Later we conversed about the problem of taste in India—destroyed, according to Mrs. Sarabhai, by the British. (That tale of the cutting off of the fingers of the weavers is one of the major legends of modern India.)[201] Mrs. Sarabhai also explained to me why it is that the saris in eastern India (Bihar, Bengal, etc.) are not colored. It is the result of a boycott that was instituted against British dyes at one time during the course of the nationalist struggle. Mrs. Sarabhai has a very strong Gandhian inclination. She is busy now arranging for a large meeting of the village workers, which is to take place in a couple of weeks. Last evening at dinner I spoke with her about Vinoba Bhave. His direction, she thinks (as I do), is the proper one for India and she believes that Nehru is coming around to that view too. I glimpsed an article in yesterday's paper that seemed to be saying that neither the West's way nor Russia's way is right for India—and if that reflects the thinking of Nehru, it is a good sign.

After lunch I returned to my diary and at 3:15 P.M. was called for by a gentleman named Dr. Trivedi, who had attended yesterday's event. He drove me to his home, some distance away, to meet and talk with his father, an old gentleman of eighty-one, who is a Vedantist. The old man—a lovely old gentleman—entered the room wearing his black cap and jacket and we sat down. His first question was, did we in America take an interest in spiritualism? (Not much *here* of Vedanta!) Then he asked me if I had seen any spiritualistic phenomena. I replied in the negative and asked if he had. He too replied in the negative and so did the other gentlemen in the room—Dr. Trivedi and a Mr. Shah who had entered with the old man.

There was a shout from outside and an old friend, Mr. Vyasa, about seventy-five years old, came in and joined us—a rather taller man, genial and amusing. We now turned to Vedanta. What did I think of Śaṅkara's Vedanta?[202] I said I preferred the *Bhāgavad Gītā's karma yoga* to the monastic rejection of the world. I said (and this is a nice idea) that the main problem is, what is *mokṣa?* Is it release from the world? or is it release from ignorance? If it is the latter and if *ātman* is *in* the world, release from the world is superfluous and may even represent a wrong notion about the nature of *mokṣa.* Old Mr. Shah said that when acting we always acted with desire for the fruits: there would be no action without desire. Drinking tea (and we were drinking tea) would not take place without desire for the tea. It was getting late and so I let the argument stay at this pleasant point, suggesting, however, that if one had found or even heard about the still point in the center of Śiva's dance, involvement in the fury of the world was different from what it would be without that knowledge.

On the way home, with Dr. Trivedi, I did somewhat better. If one knows of the immanence of *ātman-Brahman* in all things, then what if one responds to desire? I should gladly go crazy with desire, knowing of its divinity—and perhaps this very point is the one illustrated in the sculpture of such temples as Koṇārak. O.K. Bull's-eye.

Returning home at about 4:30 and settling down on my verandah, I started work again at my diary, and have finally brought it, now, to here. So at this point I can begin to relax a bit and discuss some of my new impressions and recent conversations.

Yesterday's talk: I think that here, in the field of psychoanalysis, India can be said to stand ahead, even though they may not have such good psychoanalysts as we have; because the easy transition from psychoanalysis to the doctrine of the *Gītā*, etc., is not only possible but is actually taken for granted by such a man as Maiti. My whole argument was completely supported by him—and apparently as something that he already takes for granted.

The yogi problem is prettily illustrated here in Ahmedabad by the case of a little man who planted himself under a tree three years ago and is still there. Mani told me of him first and showed him to me as we drove home from Vikram's. The tree is not far from the entrance to a factory—so the place selected was far from quiet. The advantage, however, is that people clear away the little man's filth for him, give him water and food, and even a piece of cloth to protect him in the winter—which is now. I have seen him five or six times. At night, he was sitting up asleep, covered by his cloth. Once he was smoking a big cigar. Twice he was lying down beneath his cloth. Once he seemed to be sitting in meditation.

Jung's image of the stage of becoming a tree is well illustrated here.[203] The little man is stuck. In the West he would be taken away, perhaps, to an institution and cured back (shock treatment, etc.) to society. Here, he is permitted to sit it out and perhaps go through to Buddhahood—perhaps, on the other hand, simply to remain stuck, as a living symbol of spiritual effort.

There are no hospitals, there are no asylums. The lepers sit out on the streets and so do the madmen. But some of the madmen can break through, and these breakthroughs are giving India *something that the West really lacks.*

Gira, the other evening, spoke of the dismal impression she had had of the American small towns and small cities. This is something that we all recognize. But we live, as far as possible, in places and with people who are not dismal, and *our* America is the one we like. Similarly in India—what the tourist sees is not what the inhabitant sees.

Here, in the Sarabhai household, I am having an experience of Indian life that is the best and strongest I have had so far. The mansion itself, as I already remarked, is something out of a Rajput painting. And the other homes that I have seen are comparably beautiful. Gautam, of course, has elegant taste; and his influence—in the splendid bronzes that are everywhere for instance—gives a tone of grandeur that may be particular to *this* establishment. But one can see that India, with many people of this kind, would have its own way of being perfectly modern.

The Sarabhais are interested in modernizing Ahmedabad. Other rich men here, they tell me, are interested in patronizing holy men. (The latter, of course, would be more to Nikhilananda's taste.) And so, one feels that both ends of the line are meeting here—as they must be in many Indian cities.

My principal term of comparison for the Sarabhai family is the Eugene and Agnes Meyer family in America.[204] The same pattern of a large family (here eight), great wealth, and an active (exceptionally active) interest in the community.

My new image of India is that of an old mansion full of bats and dust (people sleeping on the pavements, etc.). On first beholding, one sees mostly the dust: afterwards the handsome lines and strong structure of the house begin to be apparent. Then, finally, one doesn't see the dust anymore. Visiting India is like visiting an antique shop: one has to develop an eye. I think that my eye, at last, is developing. I find myself with a new feeling for this whole adventure.

One remarkable thing that I have observed in the course of my visit with the Sarabhais is the absolute freedom of the numerous servants to come and go at all times anywhere, to break in on conversations, and to be generally present all the time. Also, there is a close and gently familiar relationship between master and servant, mistress and servant, that is much more "democratic," it seems to me than anything I have ever observed in the West. A corollary of the ever-present servants is that one is almost completely without privacy. No wonder the yogis retreated to the Himalayas. My own bathroom retreat for the writing of Jean's article was the only possible answer.

Mani called for me, to take me to dinner with a very interesting fellow—Yashoda Mehta—whom the Indians regard as a sort of bad boy. He is a lawyer, and some time ago wrote a book that has been banned under section 292 of the legal code: against obscenity. He is a lively chap, in the middle forties I should say. He and his wife greeted us at the door of their home, and he immediately served the only alcoholic drink permitted in Bombay, a "medicinated" port known as Hall's. This he and I drank while he began a few lively opening gambits to test me out: early dating of the Vedas, etc. I steadied down his wild Indian style of flinging little chunks of information around, and we finally came to some of his chief interests:

India's present negative philosophy, he rejected. For him, the one way to enlightenment is sex. (His wife said nothing to this point.) We agreed that the Ramakrishna attitude of the child was not appropriate to India's present state of freedom, where the attitude of the hero is called for (this point was mine), and that the present puritanism of India was English not Indian (this point was his). Then he told me of an old man, 116 years old, who will be arriving in Ahmedabad Wednesday and whom I must stay to see. He is a holy man with a positive orientation to the world. "Anxiety doesn't eat me," says the old chap, "I eat anxiety." Heavens and hells, past and future, are all figments of the mind. "God is not the creator of man; man is the creator of God." This sounds to me like the type of holy man I came to India to see.

They told me also that there is a holy woman in town whom I should see. Mani will take me to see her.

And then, of course, there is the little old chap under the tree. Yashoda Mehta declared that he has been known to speak, and he says that he is in such rapture sitting there that there is no point in going anywhere else. That is to say, the little man has already gotten over the bump and is a symbol of the joy of the world!

I am beginning to hear about all kinds of holy people wandering about India. Apparently the country is full of them. There are, for instance, the two Jain holy men who are in Bombay right now—one Svetambar and one Digambar. And then there are people like these in Ahmedabad. Also, there are the ash covered yogis that I have seen. Furthermore, there are the well known teachers, such as Aurobindo, Ramana Maharishi, and Sri Krishna Menon. Their influence is actual and perhaps very strong. One must add also, Vinoba, and the Gandhian tradition.

Yashoda Mehta told of two encounters, one at Nasih and one at Haridvār, where he approached holy men in a critical mood and was astounded to have them speak to him his very thoughts.

Tuesday, December 21

At about 10:30 A.M. I began to be worried about a car to take me to my date with Dr. Maiti at the Child Study Institute. I went downstairs and found Kamalini, who was to take me, taking care of one of the little children of her school who had just fallen and cut its face. Presently I got off in a large car and, after driving quite a way, arrived at a large building near the University. Here I was met by the young people working with Dr. Maiti. They told me something about the history of the Institute and then took me in to a room with charts along both walls illustrating their plans and work methods. I was greatly thrilled and impressed: a beautifully planned campaign for the study of the problems of Culture and Personality Development in India today. As

I was looking at the charts, Dr. Maiti came in, and when I had finished studying them, we all sat down in a room—Kamalini had meanwhile arrived—and talked till about 1 P.M. about mythology and culture. I learned many things pertinent to my own interests, of which the most important are perhaps the following:

The young expectant mother goes to her own mother's house to bear her child and returns to the husband only after forty days (I think it's forty). Compare the legend of the Buddha's mother on her way to her own family when she bore the Buddha. Child and mother are taboo and are gradually inducted into society by means of a series of rites—here is the Hero-journey motif. The mother brings her earlier children with her on the journey.

The mild, permissive treatment that I have observed in India in relation to children lasts until about the tenth to twelfth years, when, suddenly, the child is expected to be an adult. Here is the maturity in action that I have noticed among youngsters working in shops, in the fields, etc. This amounts to a traumatic change, leaving childhood behind as a Golden Age. Here, perhaps, *a clue to the religious crises of Ramakrishna and others at the age of twelve or so.* Ecstacy is as a return to childhood, taken care of henceforth by the community, and is fed, etc., as an image is fed. Note the little yogi outside the factory: most often when I pass him he is lying down under his cloth. Note, also, Ramakrishna's statement, to the effect that the one who, instead of going out into the world (and becoming adult) cries for the mother to take him back will surely be taken back by the mother.

There is no tradition of conduct for the successful individual who makes a lot of money and gets ahead: hence the rawness of certain Indian money men. They are out on their own (rugged individuals more blatantly than our American variety of the pre-Depression era).

I was impressed by the exhaustive approach of Dr. Maiti and his people to every scrap of evidence they can gather. At my meeting Sunday, they were taking notes not only of my talk but also of the audience reactions. They were interested, for instance, in the attitude of the vice-chancellor: his anti-science, anti-West pattern. He represents a certain large group of the Indian intelligensia.

Several Indians have remarked, by the way, the contrast at our Sunday talk between the objectivity of the approach of the Westerners (English and myself) and the tendency to vast abstraction and loose terminology of the Indians. This criticism, however, would not apply at all to Dr. Maiti.

This Child Study Institute was set up in plan by Lois and Gardiner Murphy[205] when they were over here two or three years ago. Their first director died, and the Institute remained dormant then until Dr. Maiti arrived. It has been functioning in its present style for less than a year.

I had lunch with Kamalini at Gautam's (he is in Bombay) and we had an excellent talk, from which the following ideas emerged: Gautam, at the Sunday talk, had been a little upset by the use of such terms as *ātman*, which have no meaning: why did I let such terms get into the discussion and what role did they play? Answers: the term *ātman* has a transcendent reference and so cannot be defined; and the fact that India recognizes such a term is important for Indian psychology and psychoanalysis because it enlarges infinitely the field into which the libido is permitted to flow;[206] i.e., *the Hero Adventure into the abyss is facilitated*, since the society itself recognizes by a nondefining term the area in which a total dissolution and restoration is effected. This in turn reduces the likelihood of neurotic developments in the individual who feels himself moving out of the social cadre: *he* is not afraid and neither is the society.

At the Institute, I asked Dr. Maiti whether he agreed that India's permissive attitude applied more to men than to women, since women are compelled by very strict formulae to fit into the patterns designed for them in the matter most important to them, namely sex; and he—reluctantly, it seemed to me—agreed.

America's innocence of the fear that it is creating everywhere in the world is partly the result of America's failure to realize the magnitude of its own strength. Others see it, and feel its impact in every sphere, spiritual as well as material, and are afraid that it will destroy their own heritage, one way or another.

When I remarked that it was unfortunate that the most vulgar aspect of America was what was presented first to the world in such films as the one we saw the other night, Kamalini said that it was precisely the vulgarity that India wanted and, in its own films, imitated. This was a release of much that the Indian norms failed to free.

After leaving Kamalini, I went to give a talk to the faculty of Mani's school. Theme: My Impressions of the Contrast of America and India. It was simply a restatement of my present ideas: India's reception of America's ideas as well as machines, in flat imitation. India's own religious heritage and repose in the archetypes. What will the process of assimilation be?

The questions afterward were good, and brought out one suggestion, namely, that the blatant interest of the Indians in money might be the result, partly at least, of the fact that it was a merchant nation that conquered India. I noticed here as everywhere in India a tendency to blame as much as possible on the British while taking for granted the boons bestowed by the modernization of the country.

When the talk was over we drove to a home that, for the moment, was sheltering a holy woman, Ānanda Mayī.[207] In the car, accompanying us, was a French chap, who is teaching in Mani's school, and he challenged my whole talk on the score that it had misrepresented the West by not mentioning Marx (these tiresome people!). I said that I was not pretending to talk about Poland, Yugoslavia, Estonia, Latvia, Lithuania, Czechoslovakia, and the other communized countries of Europe, but the West—Western Europe and America—which may shelter a number of communists but in the visible aspects of its life is democratic and individualistic. Perhaps communism would help India to find the way to a non-individualistic assimilation of the machine; but India would have to decide whether mass liquidations were quite what she wanted to pay as a price. In my lecture I had favored the way of Vinoba Bhave, but I did not press it at this juncture.

The *darśana* of Ānanda Mayī was *something!* Ramakrishna all over again. Apparently, she experienced her first *samādhi* at the age of twelve, and has been treated as a kind of incarnation ever since. She does not use her hands to eat, but is fed.

We entered a large tent full of people, with a platform in the upstage left corner, where a woman in white was sitting in the crosslegged posture, with a mild smile on her lightly tan features and her hair done up in a bun on top in the manner of a yogi. Music was playing and someone singing a *kīrtana*, but almost as soon as we arrived the music stopped and the session was over. We remained as the crowd cleared. Ānanda Mayī left the tent and we waited. Then it was possible to follow into a room of the host's house, where Ānanda Mayī was to be seen seated (or half-reclining) on a wide bed, with standards at the four corners to which strings of flowers were attached.

People were sitting on the floor, all around the walls, simply watching her, and she too, was simply sitting quietly, with her mild smile, and her eyes only half looking: and yet she was taking everything in. Her nose came down straight from her high forehead, like the classical Greek nose, but there was something of a slightly bent or crumpled look about it. The woman was in her forties, I should say, and pleasant to see. Young girls were numerous in her environment, some of them, with cropped hair and wearing coarse saris, were her nuns, so to say. A few women and girls bowed deeply before her when they entered or left the room.

Mani asked me if I would like to ask any questions. She explained that I was a college teacher and student of comparative religions. I asked whether the four *yogas* of the *Gītā* were of equal value or were to be regarded as representing progressive stages. She looked a bit puzzled for a moment, then turned a quick question to a monk in yellow robe who was standing at the foot of her bed-couch, and he replied, "*karma, bhakti, jñāna, rājā*,"[208] after which Ānanda Mayī replied to me twice. First she said they represented a series, a road, and then she said that each was a way. Mani asked if I would like to ask another question. I asked whether *mokṣa* meant renunciation of the world or release from ignorance *in* the world. She replied that when *mokṣa* is experienced there is no question of renunciation or acceptance. I bowed my appreciation and for another few minutes the room sat in silence.

Presently there came a question from the host: Was the Kṛṣṇa of the *Bhāgavata* historical or merely a legend? Her reply: the Kṛṣṇa of the *Bhāgavata* is the *līlā* of god, and so, a mystery, not to be understood in such human terms. (True enough, as Kamalini whispered to me, but the question is left unanswered: No, I said, that was the proper answer. It centered the mind in the transcendent, from which point of view the historical query is irrelevant, and the function of this *darśana* is to point the mind to the transcendent.)

The host next asked: "Why am I attracted to you?" The attitude in the room was gently humorous yet sincere and there was a pleasant laugh. The reply was that he was attracted to the Spirit which is present in all, and in all things, but in some more apparently than in others. A few more questions were asked, but for the most part the situation was simply that of a lot of people sitting peacefully in a room. There were more people outside, at the windows, and the windows were presently thrown open, so that they should see.

Presently there was a stir at the door, and a young man tried to enter with a harmonium. Something was said to suggest that all should go back into the tent for a *pūjā* session. Out went the young man with the harmonium and finally everybody was back in the tent. The young Frenchman and I, sticking to Mani and Kamalini, realized presently that we were sitting on the female side of the tent. I, of course, was the one who began to feel uncomfortable. I got up and walked over to the back of the tent, on the men's side, and sat down; then he followed. We talked French for a while, about the gentleness and non-Western tone of ease in this fantastic religious affair.

Ānanda Mayī came into the tent and resumed her position on the platform. The harmonium was playing and a young woman with a good voice was singing a *bhajana*. Ānanda Mayī simply sat there, swaying a little, and halfway inward turned. The music changed a couple of times and then Ānanda Mayī herself began to sing in a slightly rusty voice. The whole tent repeated the phrase. There were several sessions of this, then the lights for the *pūjā* were lighted, a garland was placed around Ānanda Mayī's neck and the waving of lights began. This went on for a long time. The crowd now was standing. (They had stood also when Ānanda Mayī entered the tent.) And while she was being worshipped, she sat there in her half abstracted way, gently swaying and with her gentle smile.

I was full of thoughts of Ramakrishna. This certainly was a close reproduction of the scenes at Dakṣineśvara.[209] I thought also of the conversation this morning, and my idea of this kind of ecstasy as a refusal of the adult threshold. The worship of the young girl at Belūr Maṭh and this worship ran together for me, and I could see how image worship and saint worship were all pretty much the same thing. The worship of Ramakrishna's image is a continuation of the worship of Ramakrishna himself. And the rites of image worship—feeding, clothing the image—are all duplicated in the worship of such a figure as Ānanda Mayī. No doubt, also, the rites of defecation require outside assistance. The life is exactly that of an admired baby.

Directly from Ānanda Mayī we drove to the home of a relative of Mani to have dinner with the children and a grand nephew of Tagore. A beautiful tall man in white dhoti and with a coquettish purse to his lips. And that's all there is to say about this beautiful man. His hair was pageboy bobbed at the back in the style that means in India "I am a poet." He had absolutely nothing to say all evening, but simply sat and would be looked upon. Dinner was on the floor and like all Indian dinners of this kind simply an attack on food—no conversation.

We got home about ten and I went directly to bed—after perhaps the fullest day of my visit to India: certainly one of the richest.

Wednesday, December 22—Winter Solstice

At breakfast this morning and yesterday morning with Geeta we discussed Aldous Huxley, Krishnamurti, and Danielou. Geeta matched Huxley's interest in mescaline by telling me that many of the Indian sadhus smoked bhang (perhaps this is what our yogi under the tree was smoking), which produced visions comparable to those of mescaline.[210] The point about Krishnamurti was that though he would not say whether he was an incarnation or not, he would not have allowed such *pūjā* as I saw last evening. About Danielou: he presses his zeal for Indian music too far, pretending that the notes known as the peacock note, elephant note, etc. are called such because of the overtone intervals actually to be heard in the cries of the animals. Geeta said that when she heard Western fifths they always sounded to her a bit flat: Lou Harrison then explained to her the "corrected" scale of the well-tempered clavichord.[211]

We talked about the lack of romance in India. One does not feel any interest whatsoever in the erotic here—and so, why? Geeta's guess: early marriage, and routine of children. No mystery, and somewhat of a surfeit besides. My additions:

Family-planned marriage relieves young women of the necessity to spruce themselves up for competition; the women do not concentrate on sex allure, the men are therefore left without the heightened stimulation, and nobody wins!

The heat burns all the juices out of the body. One way or another, it is certainly true that there is no romance here, no call to romance, and not even a feeling that there ought to be romance. Europe and America represent a totally different erotic climate—and, ironically, think of the Orient as a realm of Romance. But their Orient, I guess, is largely that of the Arabs—*Arabian Nights*—which *may* be different, though I doubt it.

During the morning Kamalini showed me her nursery school: a wonderful affair. The nine-year-olds, today, were preparing the lunch for the school, rolling out chapatis, etc. The kids who didn't want to do that were doing something else: two were sitting up on top of a jungle-gym and one was lying on a window seat reading a little book.

Mani drove me to the chief monuments and mosques of Ahmedabad. We saw, among other things, Shah Alam's Mosque, from *c.* A.D. 1420 has, as Murray's Guide says "inner details are as rich as Hindu art could make them"—i.e. given the Mohammedan restrictions. On this morning's trip I had a very strong sense of India's Mohammedan art as a transformation of the Hindu art. The columns have the same feeling as the Hindu. The stone is wonderfully carved.

We went on to the Rani-No-Hajero: another mosque, closely surrounded by exceptionally interesting shops. Indeed, the market streets of Ahmedabad are thrillingly crowded with everything India has to offer—yogis, camels, donkey caravans, people, people, and people.

I had lunch again with Kamalini and spent the afternoon catching up on my diary. Mani just phoned to say that the 116-year-old holy man whom I was to meet tomorrow will not arrive till Sunday—the day I was hoping to get to Delhi to catch the Theatre Unit crowd. He will remain in Ahmedabad a week or ten days, however, and so I might come back. My feeling is that I had better let this one go.

During the course of our drive through Ahmedabad, Mani, discussing various things told me that there was a great difference in cultural attitude between the Hindus and Mohammedans in Ahmedabad. The Mohammedans are excellent craftsmen. One always prefers Mohammedan-made to Hindu-made objects: they work better. The Mohammedans also have an elegant sense of decorum and grace in their speech. They put Hindus to shame in this matter. Moreover, they have a talent for the enjoyment of life, which the Hindus lack. The remarkable thing is that both the Hindus and the Mohammedans are Indians: add to this the words of my two Mohammedan companions in the train to Gaya: Mohammedans are grateful for U.S. aid, but give to a Hindu and he will insult you at the next turn. Mani spoke of the great loyalty and sense of honor of the Mohammedans (a virtue celebrated in the *Arabian Nights*).

An interesting thing about the streets of Ahmedabad is the arrangement of doors opening onto the street, which are doors not to houses but to little neighborhoods or quarters of dwellings. Mani says that the social unit is the neighborhood, and the neighborhood loyalty very great. The Sarabhai family at weddings, etc. invites the neighborhood from which the family sprang—if they did not, at the time of a funeral there would be no one to lift the coffin.

One of Dr. Maiti's patients brought him a dream today that supports my statement that dreams can reproduce myth sequences. A violent, paranoid, and homosexually-inclined fellow of a height of about 6 ft. 5 in. After a long history of troubles, his dream last week: a lion, swallowing all kinds of dark objects. Association: Śiva Nīlakaṇṭha swallowing the poison—I am that lion—must hold the poison in my throat and not be killed by it. His dream today: a lovely Goddess with a lotus. Associations: the giving—the will to give—the capacity to give: I have that and would like to give myself. Dr. Maiti's remark: a recognition of the feminine aspect of his own nature. The myth: Churning of the Milky Ocean mentioned in my Sunday lecture.

Kamalini's younger girl, Sharma, at the age of two-and-a-half suddenly declared that she would never wear girl's clothes, only boy's. She tries to behave like a boy, and I recall that I thought she was a boy until Kamalini told me she was a girl. Kamalini gives this as an example of Freud's penis envy actually proven. The little girl, as it were, took a vow at the age of two-and-a-half! I noticed this evening that whenever Dr. Maiti thanked the little girl (now about five) for passing the beans, etc. to him, he said, "Thank you madam," or something similar, to remind her that she is a girl.

Thursday, December 23

Thinking some more about this *ātman* concept, I think perhaps that just as the individual feels free to slip into its sphere of emptiness so does the culture—hence the failure to be disturbed by the general formlessness of Indian life today. The whole culture, so to say, is permitting itself the luxury of a period of disintegration. The general attitude of India seems to be one of permitting and even favoring chaos.

A couple of themes: *India without Romance*—based on the talk yesterday morning with Geeta: why this lack of erotic zeal? how much of Indian life reflects it?

Also, the traditional West (Europe's Middle Ages) contrasted with the traditional East: tradition minus *ātman*-concept and plus Romantic Love. Is there a connection? Lack of reincarnation idea perhaps important: *stress in the West on the poignancy of the irrevocable moment* (compare Nietzsche, *The Birth of Tragedy*).[212] No tragedy in India. This may be a very bright idea. (Read de Rougemont's *Love in the Western World.)*

This West-East contrast is adding up to quite a number of points:[213]

West	*East*
God	*ātman*
Image of God	*śakti*
Transcendence	Immanence
Outward Effort	Inward Plunge
Formation	Disintegration
Dogma	*sādhanā-samādhi*
Neurosis	Transformation
Purgatory	Reincarnation
Straight line	Cycle
Unique Moment	No death
Birth of Tragedy	No Tragedy
Love in the Western World	No Romance
(Post Renaissance)	
Value collisions	*dharma*
Choice of mate	Family Marriage / Separation of Sexes
Sex competition	Early marriage: surfeit
Sex mystery and research	No mystery: all out in the open
A room of one's own	No privacy
"The Life Bud"	"The Completely Open Flower"—Petals falling!

A new turn to Nietzsche's warning: "Be careful lest in casting out your Devil you cast out the best that is in you." No Devil in India—all is *Brahman.* Situation of the completely filletted analysand. Spengler's Fellaheen—the neurosis of the Culture Period quite gone.[214] All is out on the surface—"like a fruit on the palm of the hand." Problem: How much of the difference is West-East? How much is Culture-Civilization?[215]

When this was done I piled into a tiny car with Geeta, Mani, Geeta's two children, a chauffeur and a man to watch the kids. Geeta went shopping and Mani took me and the children to a very interesting sort of yogi farm: a temple compound that dispenses free food to all that come. They have a large herd of cattle. I saw the kitchens where dhal, etc. was being prepared by priests and sadhus in immense cauldrons. The images in the outer shrines resemble those at Puri and the foundation supporting this amazing institution is connected somehow with Jagannātha. Mani brought us to one of the verandahs where a very old man, called simply Maharaj, who is regarded as a holy man, sat amid food and cloths. He is the head of this sanctuary, and doles out food, as *prasāda*, all day. We paid our respects and for about four minutes sat in a row along the wall beside him. He gave *prasāda* to the children and prepared a large packet for Mani and me. I noticed that annas and *paisa* had been left with him by devotees, but when I moved to leave something too, he stopped me. Then, with *namaskāras*, we left him, and wandered slowly among the devotees and shrines. All around and out in front of the temple were sadhus, many covered with ash, all looking quite authentic—and their principal preoccupation seemed to be with themselves: combing their hair, praying and touching themselves in the sacred places, sitting, snoozing, or waiting for the food that would be served at twelve. A beggar approached as we left: in a place of free food and lodging, still begging. And near the temple were many poor hovels.

We drove back into town and I watched Geeta bargain for a bit of cloth, and then we drove home. I went next, again with Mani, to the police, to report on my presence in Ahmedabad, and as we drove we saw a sadhu. "They are very dangerous," she said. "Many smoke opium and are homosexuals; they kidnap boys." She told me also that one class of poor people living hereabouts were Chharas—a caste of thieves. Gautam, when he drives to his farmhouse, has a man with a rifle and bullet belts in the back of the car, for protection against these.

Tea this afternoon with the lovely old couple next door, the Sarabhais' aunt and uncle. The old gentleman had heard my talk Sunday and Geeta had given him Zimmer's *Myths and Symbols* to read. When we spoke about the influence of Indian thought on my students and I told him that the renunciation motif did not appeal, he came through with the formula that I have been wanting to hear, namely, that detachment not renunciation is the goal, and that this detachment has its counterpart in aesthetic detachment. He also declared that he thought the chief religious difference between East and West was in the stress on God's immanence in the East and on God's transcendence in the West. However, people of both worlds held both positions so that the difference is not in kind but in emphasis.

At about seven I went down for an hour's chat with Mr. Sarabhai. He spoke of the Maharaj of the yogi farm as a real holy man, now thinking of ceasing to eat. The farm has a couple of elephants and every year there is a great procession in Ahmedabad. He said also that he regarded Ānanda Mayī as genuine; however, some of the people who were devoted to her were scoundrels. "Some people are generally good and kind but have specific mean points: people whom they ill-treat; conversely, some people are ruthless and mean, but have special points of kindness. Perhaps these in Ānanda Mayī's company feel that they are making up for their guilt in this way." He said also that people like Ramakrishna and Ānanda Mayī may be interpreting their experiences falsely. One can admit that the phenomena of their lives are mysterious without conceding the theological interpretation. Smallpox, for example, used to be interpreted as the wrath of God. Ānanda Mayī, it is said, was three days old when her paternal grandfather visited her and she spoke to him in clear words, asking why he had come.

Friday, December 24 ***Mt. Abu, en route to New Delhi***

A single compartment mate: a silent but gracious gentleman with one peg leg. I had lunch in the dining car and arrived at Abu Road about 2:15 P.M., then took a taxi up the wonderful Mt. Abu, and afterwards drove to Dilwārā and the Jain temples. The temples are being repaired by a large team of craftsmen-workmen, and I watched them for some time. They file down the marble with metal files and chip at it with pointed chisels. They make plaster models of the parts to be replaced and then translate the plaster into marble.

The temples are both worse and better than I expected: the overall effect is greatly cluttered, but each little chapel is simply ravishing. The great marvel is the work on the ceilings—they are delicious, delicate and luminous.

Returning to my hotel, I had tea and then was taken afoot by the hotel runner to Sunset Point: a fabulous view from 3800 ft. of a great plain and remote hills. The sunset was witnessed by a multitude of amusing Hindu families. Then I walked back with an Indian gentleman who wants to hike with me tomorrow to Achal Garh—five or six miles each way, and my bus leaves at eleven! Can it be done?

After the sunset the weather became quite chilly, but in an invigorating, dry way. Abu, I find, is an abandoned Hill Station—palaces here of all the maharajas, but since the State of Bombay is now dry, the place has been abandoned. I think it could easily be turned into a good tourist halt. My hotelkeeper declares that the government is promising to build up the tourist trade but will actually do nothing. "It is a paper government," he declared.

On the train, a couple of new thoughts occurred to me with respect to my West-East problem.

I.

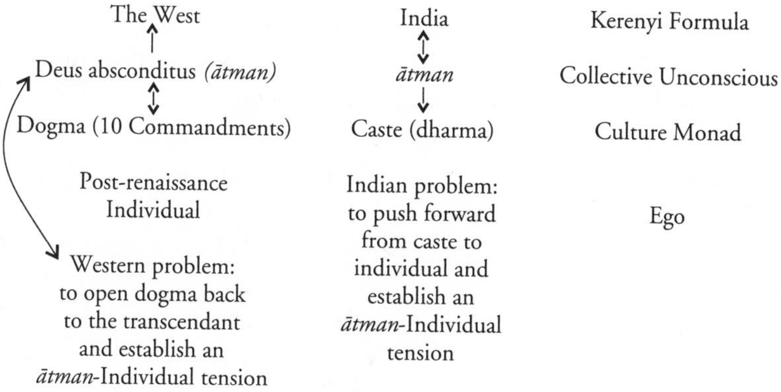

II.

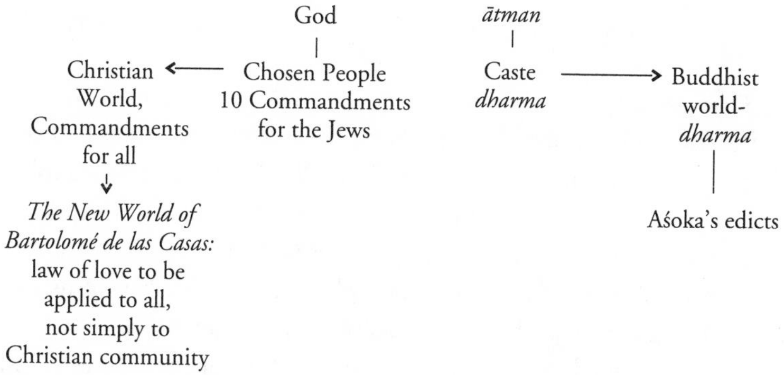

In relation to the above, I have two writing tasks: Biographies, legends, etc. with alchemist-gnosis orientation; *The Life of Judas* could open this series. Second, *Bartolomé de las Casas.* The first is psychological-metaphysical, the second ethical-historical. Perhaps later the two themes could be combined.

A couple of items from my conversations with Geeta: the Indian woman, repressed, looks forward to the day when she is a mother-in-law. The repressed sadistic impulses, when they break out, let loose the horror of the massacres.

Saturday, December 25—Christmas Day

Up at 7:15 to get ready to meet my Indian gentleman at 7:45. Shaved, while shivering, over a mug of warm water. At 7:45 I went out into the sunshine, after two cups of tea, toast, and a banana; but the gentleman had not shown up by 8:00; so I started on a stroll of my own. After yesterday's catastrophe with the film I vowed to steady down and take only good shots very carefully:

too much money pouring out in blank films. Presently, I found myself back on the path to Sunset Point—followed it and admired the view for a while. A world of utter silence—with the bark of a dog somewhere off to the right. Then I walked back and found myself at the celebrated Nail Lake (Nahki Talaō). I walked around it and was amused to see the little cave temples carved into the rocks around it—two or three—the entrances, small squares about three feet high and with the rocks whitewashed around them, as a kind of façade. From within the Hanumān temple I could hear someone chanting his prayers.

I got back to the hotel at 10:15; the table was set for my breakfast. The host and hostess were extremely solicitous for my happiness and Merry Christmas. The porter put my bags on the head of a woman who walked ahead to the bus—about half a mile down hill, then I went with the porter, and for the rest of the day had the usual experiences of Indian travel.

Sunday, December 26 ***New Delhi***

Taxi to the Swiss Hotel, which I had wired for a room because it had advertised Room and Bath for fifteen rupees. When I had inscribed, they told me my room would be thirty-five rupees. I decided to remain for the day and night, bathe, freshen up, and recover my poise, then go back to the Cecil, which is almost next door and very much pleasanter, English-run instead of Indian. I drove to town to buy my Theatre Unit ticket for tonight;[216] the event that I have rushed to catch, so that I may get in touch with some of the folk who might help me settle for a concert.

Took a taxi later to the place of the great event: a brand new auditorium, where the National Drama Festival has just concluded a month or so of highly advertised productions. I wandered around the building to see what it was like and then went in to the auditorium. Presently P. D. Shenoy discovered me—the Theatre Unit's stage manager, and he introduced me to a nice chap named S.A. Krishnan, one of the directors of the National Academy of Art (Lalit Kala Akademi). I made a date with this fellow for tomorrow morning. Then the play took place—*Oedipus Rex*—surprisingly well played and certainly a gripper. I went backstage to congratulate the cast and saw a rather conspicuous blond European.

"Who is that?" I asked Krishnan.

"That is Mr. Fabri, the art critic."

"Fabri?" I said—remembering a lot that I had heard about this man from Salmony. "I want to meet him." So I was introduced.

"Campbell?" said Fabri. "Why, I've just been hearing all about you from Alfred Salmony!"

"Salmony's in town?" I said.

"At the Imperial. My wife's having lunch with him tomorrow."

Fabri asked how long I was going to be in Delhi, and I said, until I have arranged for my wife's concert. There was a blurb for Jean's Bombay concert in the program, so it was easy to be convincing. Fabri then introduced me to the head of the Little Theatre Group, urging him to take Jean on, and even talking as though the whole thing were already taken for granted. I began to feel fine. Next I met Y. C. Rai, who seems to be one of the probably helpful people, and finally, with Alkazi, planned a meeting with him and Krishnan tomorrow.

Fabri joined me in my taxi and we went to his home where I met his Indian wife. The Fabris' cute little four-year old boy—blond as Fabri—was playing with a train on the floor and there were Christmas decorations. So we drank a bit of wine, in honor of Christmas, and they gave me a bit of mince pie. It was all very warm and pleasant, and friendly. I think this thing has gotten off to a good start.

Monday, December 27

At about nine, my laundry was returned, I packed, had breakfast, and removed to the Cecil Hotel. Felt fine on the old premises, my India circuit now quite completed.

When I had settled my things in my pleasant rooms, I took a taxi to the Lalit Kala Akademi, where I was greeted by the chap that I met last evening, S.A. Krishnan. He introduced me to the Secretary of the Academy, Mr. Barada Ukil, who discussed with me the work of the newly founded organization. Its function: to foster the revival of the craftsmen, the work of artists in India, and the arrangement of inter-cultural exhibitions. Krishnan then showed me an exhibition of painting and sculpture, much of which was quite good, and mostly Paris-inspired. The paintings of a young woman, Amrita Sher Gil, who had died circa 1940 were particularly revealing: at first, standard Paris studio student work, which suddenly, in India, crystalized into an interesting style—Cézanne base but Indian feeling, or atmosphere. There was a roomful of revivalist stuff—like fairytale illustrations, with an erotic atmosphere that is altogether out of keeping with the asexual life of modern India. Krishnan agreed that these were of no interest whatsoever as art, but declared that Ukil greatly favored it. Finis. Officials and art: the same stupid story as in the U.S.A.

It was about noon when I left the Academy. I left a note for Salmony at the Imperial Hotel, then went for a long slow stroll along Queens Way and around Connaught Circle, stopping on the way at the American Express to see if there was any mail for me, and to cash the last two $20 Travelers Checks of my original $1500 packet. Four months, average $375 per month.

I went to the restaurant Volga and sat down to wait for Krishnan and Alkazi. Across the room I saw Mrs. Jayakar at table with a gentleman. She greeted me and I went over to say hello, whereupon she invited me to dinner tonight, at the Delhi Gymkhana Club. Krishnan arrived, then Alkazi. We talked of the performance last night and of the newspaper reviews and then of the plans for Jean's concert. All agreed that the Little Theatre Group, under Mr. Inder Das, was the best organization to present the performance. They would handle the theater problems all right, but would have to be watched on their advertising and printing of programs, which they might do badly. Krishnan promised to help me. Then we left (I paid the check) and while Alkazi went to hunt for a hotel room, I proceeded to hunt for Inder Das.

Strolling about New Delhi, on the same streets that I found four months ago, I am amused by the transformation of my level of experience. Whereas then I was coming in touch for the first time with the more prominent surprises and surface phenomena of Indian cities, those are now rather well known to me and I find that I can bump them off and get through to the city itself—which I am finding rather pleasant. I notice that many more Americans are here now and that the police have cleared the streets of the most hideous of the beggars—the lepers; also, they shoo the others away from their victims. It is still, however, something of a trial to walk about: I was approached at least eight or ten times per block, and once or twice rather crudely and forcefully. Finally, I discovered the offices of Inder Das, who will meet with his Theatre Group tomorrow and by Wednesday morning will let me know how things stand.

At about 4:30 P.M. I went to the U.S. Information Office to see Mr. King, and while I was waiting for him to appear, who should come into the office but Salmony. Greetings and cheers. He is planning to go to Kabul, has had a wonderful trip, is chilled to the bone and trying to find an overcoat. Presently King arrived and we had a talk. Then I left Salmony, who will have tea with me tomorrow. I had told Mr. King that I would report to him Wednesday or Thursday on the outcome of the Inder Das conversation.

I arrived at the Gymkhana Club that evening and was conducted by a page to the cottage of Mr. and Mrs. Jayakar, where I found Neogy, whom I had met about seven years ago in New York and who is now director of some branch of the Village Industries organization. We had a wonderful talk and a fine dinner—Neogy turning out to be quite learned and objective, as well as eloquent, in his discussions of Indian history and art. A number of extremely interesting and suggestive ideas emerged.

In general, the materials for a social and philosophical history of India are extremely scanty. The picture that we now have is largely a creation of the imagination of Occidental scholars, augmented by Indians trying to beat them at their own game. As a corollary, it is probable that the main interest of Indian thinkers was not spiritual, as the Europeans and Anglicised Indians suppose, but highly materialistic (this coincides with Zimmer's formula). *The concept of the spiritual that has been applied to Indian thought is not Indian but European.* (O.K.—Bull's-eye.)

In regard to art, there is no word in Sanskrit for "obscene": the Koṇārak sculpture cannot, therefore, have seemed "obscene" to the people of pre-English India. In a conversation with an old man of the village near the temple, Neogy had said that the sculpture was "obscene" and had asked why it was there—to which the old man had replied that anyone who thought that way was unfit to look at a temple: this sculpture was good, and perfectly natural, and exactly what should be on a temple.

The Koṇārak temple has a much stronger architectural interest than those of Khajurāho. One sees first the great overall form; closer, one perceives the main blocks of the secondary elements; still closer the fine lacework and details emerge; and finally, the details of each piece are seen in their formal organization. (I indicated Zimmer's point, however, that at Khajurāho the horizontal bands of the friezes are balanced and absorbed by the verticals of the *śikāra* composition.)[217]

The figures at Khajurāho have a definitely human quality while those at Koṇārak are rather satyrs and nymphs (my point). Neogy mentioned the attempt that was made at Khajurāho to achieve a surface effect of actual skin, whereas at Koṇārak the figures are definitely of stone.

At Koṇārak are six figures of Śiva dancing not on a bull vehicle but on a ship of a kind used not for river but for sea traffic, such as the coastal people manufacture to this day. Just as the bull is the animal form of the god (Nandi) and the god the human form of the bull, so here with the ship. There is an important connection between Koṇārak and the sea trade of the 12th and 13th centuries. The Sun God at Koṇārak shows several interesting forms and traits: riding on a single horse (an archaic form); combined with Śiva elements; and combined with Viṣṇu elements. There are Sun God associations with the west coast forms—sea trade connections again?[218]

The disintegration that I noted at Mt. Abu—where the sense of the whole is lost and the charm is in the intricacy and perfection of the details—is matched in the late periods of Indian literature and music. In literature, the device of the frame story becomes so elaborately developed that one simply cannot follow any main thread whatsoever. And in music the present beginningless and endless run of impromptu passages on a timeless *rāga* becomes the rule—we don't know quite when; but there is evidence that in earlier periods Indian musical compositions had a beginning, middle and end. In music the change may have taken place after the Gupta period or toward its close. In architecture, the change is later; in literature it was perhaps earlier.[219]

Related to this, perhaps, is a remark of this afternoon, that for anyone who has learned about the neat structure of the early idea of the caste system, what is actually found in India today comes as a baffling surprise. Here again we have a congeries of discrete interests and systems, with almost no overall structure to hold them in formal relationship to each other.

The female ideal represented by the sari is in radical contrast to that of the ancient queens, who are represented as clad only in jewels. One should observe that in some works (e.g. at Ajaṇṭā), whereas the queen is almost naked her serving maid may be covered from neck to ankle. There is some relationship, apparently, of the ideal of jewel-clad body to the aristocratic principle.

At this point I can add an idea that occurred to me in Ahmedabad, as I was sitting, looking at the Pārvatī on my verandah. Namely, that the arrangement of the garb at the level of the genitals tends to exaggerate the general theme of the organs in such a way as to suggest a trans-human reference: the female as the cavern from which life pours; the male as an axial, cosmic *liṅga.* This *reduces* the erotic element by converting personal into archetypal references! In daily life, where the cosmic aspect of woman is continually stressed, this reduction is maintained.

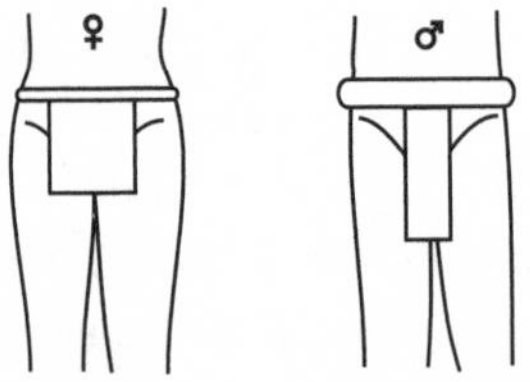

A new aspect of this problem occurs to me now; namely, that where women are beautiful (in the aristocratic élite) the cosmic theme can be suggested by their nudity bejeweled, but where women are simply lumpish (folk, bourgeoisie) the archetype is best suggested by covering in a certain standard way. Hence, the naked ladies of the past and veiled of the present achieve, respectively by positive and by negative means, the same end of archetypalization. The first, however, yields a heroic atmosphere and the second a sentimental.

Well, it was a good evening's talk.

Tuesday, December 28

I am rather amused at my present attitude toward the British atmosphere at the Cecil: after four months of India, with all of my spiritual transformations, I find it thoroughly agreeable. Item from the morning paper, the *Statesman.*

> Dr. Radhakrishnan today called for a "revivalism" in which the religion of caste and dogmas will give place to the religion of unity and oneness.

The challenge today, Dr. Radhakrishnan said, was world unity.

> Religion is an obstacle to achieving this unity. Just as there is rivalry between nation and nation, the religious rivalries stand in the way of international unity.... We want a religion which is of socialist nature: which gives us freedom to think, freedom to act, and which maintains our privacy.... The Socialism that we should acquire should be that which maintains the fundamental dignity of men. It should be built on the basis of deep ethical and moral values: it should not violate the independence and privacy of man....

Truth and love were the basis of all religions, Dr. Radhakrishnan said. This country had made a great contribution to the world in carrying these principles all over...

> If only we can discard hate, jealousy and rivalry, then we need not fear the atom bomb or anything even worse than that.

Perhaps it can be said that whereas the negative task of the West is that of transcending nationalism, that of the Orient is the transcendence of sectarianism; and that the positive task of the West is that of continually advancing in its freeing both of the individual and of each moment of life for free expressivity, while the positive task of India is that of insisting on its primordial experience of *ātman-Brahman* as a dogma-transcending truth. One may well ask: *how can religions be said to favor truth when they insist upon fictions as real?*

I found a pack of mail for me at American Express. Bollingen is still operating on the Zimmer book: they sent proofs to Bachhofer for careful reading and he thought the renderings of OM should be changed. His remark: "I have no idea where these characters come from; they are certainly very unusual; they refer to two different spellings, OM and AUM. There is a possibility that the first character can be identified as OM, though the horizontal bar at the top, so typical of *devanāgarī,* is missing; but the second one, supposed to stand for AUM, looks utterly strange. If you want to be absolutely sure use the characters I gave you. For the others I can take no responsibility..." Lovely. How to sound learned while displaying ignorance! One can learn a lot from some of those old boys.[220]

Later, I had dinner with Salmony at the Imperial. Fabri arrived for a brief chat and listened to Alfred's recital of his plans. Says Salmony: "Everybody says the worst things possible about everybody else. I have heard Stella Kramrisch accused of everything but murder." This is important. I have noted it too. I think perhaps that the social disapproval of overt violence leaves all of the aggressive instincts rankling for expression. They come out in petty malice—and in mass explosions.

About the art of Koṇārak: Salmony says he noticed not only heterosexual, but also homosexual groups, male and female; also human and animal. Coomaraswamy's metaphysical explanation just doesn't apply here, he agrees.

He has learned from his directors of archaeology here and there, that the temples to which childless women came for children from the god kept a crew of lusties on hand who did the work of the god. The women entering the temple would leave their bodices at the door. The lusties would choose bodices, and then take care of the women to whom the bodices belonged: an impersonal, blind date arrangement—and the work indeed of the god Śiva or Viṣṇu.

There are parallels here to the Phoenician, Cyprean, and Armenian temples of Venus. Also, I should now re-examine the legends of the Indian saints.

Wednesday, December 29

Visited Inder Das to learn that Delhi is jammed with plays and concerts for the period of Jean's visit, but that the Little Theatre Group is going to try to help arrange something for Jean between the time of the Bombay concert and the date of her departure two weeks later. At American Express, I picked up a wire from her "No Japan Concert Arriving Delhi January 11. Leaving for Tokyo January 3rd Love Jean."

I am now trying to plan Jean's visit and a possible trip of my own, before her arrival, to Khajurāho, Sāñcī, and Jaipur. Went to the Indian Tourist Bureau this morning to try to make plans for the Khajurāho-Sāñcī trip, and found things about as difficult as ever.

I strolled down to Fabri's in the afternoon and found the master in his bathrobe, shushing me to be quiet because his blond little son had just been put to sleep. He sat down and talked, and I let him beat around the bush for a while, then I said that Inder Das and his group were unwilling to back the concert and so I thought I might go to Madras and try to arrange for something down there. He was immediately very firm in insisting that there *had* to be a concert by Jean in New Delhi. He asked if I would be willing to put up a thousand rupees for the hall and advertising and I answered yes. Then we were off on plans: to get the American Women's Club to sponsor it and help arrange for a hall, and to begin enlisting other interests. I felt when he was through that this thing might be a lot of fun for all concerned. He wanted me to bring Krishnan down to his place after dinner for a chat.

Krishnan arrived at my hotel a bit after eight, full of eagerness to push Jean's concert through, and we talked over plans all evening, beginning with brandy for him and whiskey for me, then through dinner, and finally, up in my room until 11 P.M.

This is a very interesting and lively young man—twenty-eight years old, of a Mysore brahmin family; left his family to be an artist (which they regarded as *infra dig*[221]) and has ended as a newspaper critic—helped (according to Fabri) very much by the advice and instruction of Fabri, of whom he is overtly critical. His pride is in his honesty and critical integrity. When I went out of the room to fetch him a tin of cigarettes, I returned to find him jotting the following observation on the corner of a newspaper:

> This is an age of individualism. I do not mean by individualism an excessive representation of one's eccentricities, but the reaction of a man or woman as an individual in the form of any human activity. This reaction may be different from what we know or what we think we know...

The inspiration for this jotting was our conversation about the modern creative as contrasted with the various traditional dance forms—and the jotting itself represents pretty well, I think, the problem of the modern young Indian, whose culture has no tradition of search and freedom. Alkazi, Ezekiel, and Krishnan are pretty good representatives of the young intellectuals in India—Hussein, Samant, Ara, and the other young painters can be added to the list—and on the wealthier level are the Sarabhais, whose father was already a free spirit.

Krishnan asked me, with some emotion, how long I thought he and Alkazi had known each other. Having noted that they were very close friends, I said well, perhaps, since boyhood. "Two days!" said Krishnan intensely, and with a smile. "When we met, we embraced, and he picked me up in the air!" They had read each other's works and had been in correspondence. "When he left this morning, I know that he would have stayed if I had asked him to, but I knew that he was disturbed and I didn't feel that I had the right." (Alkazi's wife is on the point of having a child.) And so here it is again—the same highly passionate relationship between males that I have already met with in young Narasimhan. "When he left," said Krishnan, "we kissed each other; we just couldn't help it."

Thursday, December 30

To William King's office for the next move. He suggested Mrs. J. Wesley Adams, wife of one of the embassy secretary generals and chairman of the American Women's Club. I paused to make a date for tomorrow with Jack Macy, and proceeded to Mrs. Adams—a nice young mother, very much like a Sarah Lawrence alumna, who showed great interest in the idea, said that she would break it to her club at their meeting on Monday.

Invited to lunch by Salmony, I spent the afternoon with him at the main offices of the Archaeological Survey of India, watching films of Sāñcī, Agra, Khajurāho, and the newly found frescoes of the great temple at Tanjore done *c.* A.D. 980, between Ajaṇṭā and the Gujarat illuminations: a beautiful series.

Our host for this occasion was Ramachandran, one of the two chief directors of the Survey. He was deaf, tall, and impetuous. He bossed his menials around like a petty king, but he gave us a wonderful view of the work that his survey is doing.

Ramachandran talked almost without stopping during the course of our visit and let fall a good many ideas, some good, some no good. One that was no good was that he could place Kālidasa in the Śuṅga or Āndhra period, or perhaps earlier, by showing on the Sāñcī *stūpas* motifs comparable to those in Kālidasa's poems.[222] Two interesting items were the following: the King who built Koṇārak was a leper; and the artisans restoring the inlay arabesques of the Taj Mahal first make a mica tracing, then, from this, a thin sheet-metal stencil which is fixed to the bit of precious stone that is to be cut, and then cut the stone with a metal-wire bowstring and abrasives.

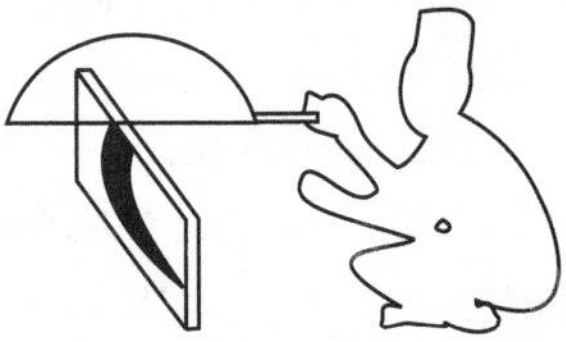

Salmony and I walked from the Survey offices to the Imperial, where we had tea together on the verandah. I bade him goodbye (he is off to Agra, Mathurā, and Gwalior), and returned to the Cecil for dinner and an evening of diary and letters.

Friday, December 31

End of the year 1954, and therewith of the Zimmer project.[223] This morning I found that the hotel situation in Delhi for the months of January and February is quite jammed. Another score for India: When the tourist season finally arrives, they have no room. I made reservations at the Cecil for the following dates: January 1, 5, 8, 15, and February 5, 7, 12, 18.

Spent most of the day writing letters, and then went to meet Jack Macy for lunch. He brought me to his flat, and we talked in lively fashion about India and the U.S.A. Why is America viewed so unfavorably in India?

The American technique of disposing of its money creates an unfavorable impression. The money then *has* to be spent, and the officers in charge of getting rid of it practically shove it down the receiver's throat—not caring much *how* it is spent.

Diplomats are people interested in cocktail parties. The best cocktail parties are in Paris, London, Rome, Copenhagen, etc., and the Orient is therefore a sort of probation area to which diplomats are assigned for a period of two years before they can become eligible for the better life. Result: no interest in the Orient or understanding of the Orient in the Oriental staffs.

American tourists leave a bad impression. The irony of the situation is that it is precisely the people who most love America and are most complacent about themselves as fine citizens who leave the appalling impression behind.

Our cultural exhibits misrepresent our cultural life by stressing the dull, traditionally archaic art works, which can be of no interest to anybody anywhere, and rejecting the avant gardistes, whom the young artists abroad would like to see and who might exert an influence.

The performing artists sent over here have been *very* few. The Americans appearing in India have been: Yehudi Menuhin, at the invitation of the Government of India; Helen Traubel, who was passing through; Isaac Stern, the only one brought over by the U.S.; and (soon to be) Jean Erdman, who was passing through and had to arrange her own concerts. (Her bid for help—after A.N.T.A. had approached her to learn how she had fashioned her tour—was rejected by A.N.T.A.'s dance committee: Martin, Terry, Martha Hill.)[224]

The Voice of America is not heard. It plays for one hour a day on a clouded beam. On the other hand, Hollywood, Tin-pan Alley, and paper-bound detective stories are everywhere: no wonder we are thought of as a vulgar lot. Americans who are not vulgar always hear the remark (which is regarded as a compliment): "But *you* aren't like an American!"

In any case, contemporary India is totally devoid of an aesthetic sense. An exception is in Indian music. The new Punjab capital built by Corbusier is a case in point: it is already falling apart, electric wires dangling, etc. One gentleman hung on his great clean Corbusier wall, a little print of Gandhi in a tawdry frame, hung awry. India's tolerance, however (or, perhaps, consequently), is enormous: the real land of laissez-faire. It is a land where one is forever surprised by things previously unseen.

After a very nice lunch, Macy played me a beautiful record (which he then gave to me), which he had made from a tape recording of a duet played by Ali Akbar Khan (on the sarod) and Ravi Shankar[225] (on the sitar—Uday Shankar's brother). It is based on the Bhairavī *rāga*, which is to be played at 11 P.M. He then took me to the Indian Radio Broadcasting building, to meet Narayan Menon.

I returned home at and wrote letters (still a huge stack to go!). Then I set off for the Jayakar's for New Year's Eve.

There were three stages to the evening. The first was at Mr. Jayakar's where I met some of the guests of the evening: a pleasant little, white moustached Belgian count, who did not like to be called Monsieur le Conte; his haughty daughter, who, I am glad to say, soon departed; and Nehru's younger sister Mrs. Hutheesingh, who greeted me very pleasantly, as though she had met me before (quite in contrast to Mme. Pandit, who always makes believe she has never seen me before).[226] We proceeded, after a brief drink, to Mr. and Mrs. K. V. K. Sunduram's, where there was another count—a tall one this time, and French. A lot of pictures by Amrita Sher Gil were on the wall, and Mrs. Sunduram told me that she was her sister.[227] Mr. Sunduram was a sweet but slightly rigid man in white trousers and black Indian full-dress jacket. All the other gentlemen were in tuxedos—and I was in my usual Dacron blue. On to a lovely dinner, then off to the Gymkhana Club for twelve o'clock.

Behold—a roomful of Indians behaving like Europeans at a New Year's Eve Party: the Sikhs had their paper hats up on top of their turbans. A large ballroom jammed full of dancers, some in costumes, and all but a couple of dozen, Indian. At midnight I was standing and talking when Mrs. Hutheesingh approached and suggested that we should dance—which we did—and I felt that to start off the year dancing with the sister of the Prime Minister of India wasn't too bad.

Sunday, January 2

During the course of the afternoon I read an offprint that Agnes Meyer[228] had sent me some time ago of her article on *Democracy and Clericalism*. Very good. A fine attack on the American counterparts of Nikhilananda who speak disparagingly of "materialism," "scientism," and "secularism," as evils that have thwarted the development of America's "spirituality." Agnes's article first outlines the history of the development of our secular morality and then shows why the claims of the right-wing clergy that morality is *exclusively* grounded on a theological dogma would endanger our nation, secular institutions, and freedoms, both civil and religious, as well as our peaceful relations with the other free nations.

Monday, January 3

An idea that must not be lost: "My sins dropped away from me not at the Ganges, but at Koṇārak."

One more idea: mythology as the second womb—it must be constructed of the stuff of modern life. The tendency of the clergy is to hold to the past and therefore reject, not redeem, the contemporary world.[229] A variant of this is the romantic exoticism of the American devotees of the swamis. In my visit to India I have found myself more interested in the relationship of the West to the East than in the East itself.

A vow for the New Year: Finis to all exoticism—whether into the past, or into the East, or into the occult! Back to Nietzsche.

An interesting item in the morning paper:

> Mr. A. S. Sthalekar, Principal of Children's Academy, Bombay, said that if education was neglected the spirit of democracy would become stale and dead. "A nation which educates her millions only to be wage-earners, has certainly failed in her duties towards arousing the higher abilities of the human spirit. The wages of such neglect will be a highly materialistic society which recognizes no other values but the immediate ones.... Character building is the final test of all education.... The student must find an answer other than a mere utilitarian one to the question: 'Why am I at school.'"

All of this, in combination with Agnes Meyer's observations suggests certain common themes and problems of education for democracy throughout the world.

The fundamental energy of democracy is the illuminated public mind, and the generator of this energy is public education. Modern education must cover the following:

1. Science: physical, biological, anthropological
2. Morality: social science and citizenship
3. Psychology: i.e. self-management (including psychoanalysis)—the task of social reference (training to society); the task of the hero adventure (training to the transcendent)
4. Art: i.e. the generation of vision—the history and principles of art and literature; the crafts of the arts (creative art and writing); the aesthetic experience (static rapture)
5. Illumination—"Redemption"—*mokṣa* (meditation): the *Gītā* religion and Buddhism; the Chinese sages; Sufism; the Christian mystics; miscellaneous examples of the mystical experience; the great poets and philosophers of the modern world
6. Vocation: specialized technical training
7. How to enter a room.

The archaic inheritance (of the various local culture traditions, Oriental as well as Occidental) must be gradually transformed. Reactionary hard cores (e.g. the Roman Catholic Church, the Maha Sabha[230]) have to be carefully held in check. Liberal clergymen can be cautiously favored as transformers of the archaic vocabularies (e.g. the Protestant liberal clergy in America, and the Ramakrishna movement and Vinoba Bhave in India). Artists, poets, creative writers, and philosophers should be helped to function, not as Bohemian outcasts, but as respected agents of the society. Academic councils, foundations, etc. should be assisted, and avant gardistes given space in which to function.

In all of this, India's problem, everywhere except under heading 5, is more acute than ours.

Tuesday, January 4

This morning I woke up with the firm idea that Swami Nikhilananda is a crazyman. His patriotic monasticism is a form of lunacy—and his wild ambition is on the Savonarola side. He is Agnes Meyer's archetypal "cleric."

Yesterday at Fabri's H. Goetz, discussing Stella Kramrisch's new book,[231] rejected her idea (and Coomaraswamy's) about Indian art being religious. I asked him to be specific. I said that most of the Indian art that we knew was religious at least to the extent of being in temples. He replied that there is plenty of evidence that there was also non-religious art in India; moreover, the actual artisans introduced motifs and attitudes that were not religious at all. Much of their work was simply mass-production craft work. The idea of Indian art as religious is simply a projection onto the Orient of the old romantic idea about the Middle Ages. We are going to have to talk about this (Goetz and I) at some later date. Fabri, last evening, also lit into Stella. Her theory that the Aryan altar and the temple were related as cause and effect, he declared, was quite wrong. The altar is a place where sacrifices are burned for the gods above: the temple is a *garbha-gṛha*—womb cell—*within which* the divinity resides (one could object, however, that Agni resides in the altar).

Out of the cogitations of the past few pages the idea may be derived that the great spiritual conflict of today is not merely (as so often phrased) between religion and science, but between religion and the whole context of modern morality, science, and art—i.e., modern life—insofar as the religious mind insists on holding to the archaic moral and scientific contexts through which its basic principles have been transmitted. The basic principles themselves, however, when they are abstracted from their temporal context, do not controvert but readily supplement and vitalize the modern forms—just as they vitalized those of the past.[232] These basic principles are those of the relativity of all knowledge to the knowing subject, the transcendency of the transcendent, and the yogas through which the mind and feelings are brought into accord with these primary conditions of its being. The yogas are as follows: *karma* (work without fear or desire); *bhakti* (devotion to an image-god-thing-person-symbol); *jñāna* (philosophy); *rājā* and *kuṇḍalini* (psychological athletics); and art and poetry (*karma* and *bhakti* and *jñāna* and craft).[233]

The art and poetry of the last is art and poetry in what Goetz calls the Romantic sense. In a sense, however, I think that all art and poetry tends in this direction inasmuch as its effect is to establish a harmony, inspire pleasure (charm-rapture), and represent perfection (perfection, if nowhere else, in the skill of the craftsman who made it).

India's vast problem, in this sphere, would seem to be that of effecting a rapid and total transformation of its science and morality without losing the foundations of its meditation.

Fabri told me the other day that vast numbers of the youth of India believe in nothing: his wife Ratna believes in nothing.

"Well," said I, "I too believe in nothing."

All one has to do to make this a profoundly mystical statement is to stress the word "believe." We have come, thus, very fast to the *śunyatāvāda* of the Mahāyāna.[234]

The main danger of Indian philosophy, as I now see it, is not in its ultimate doctrine of *mokṣa* as *vidyā*, but in the incorrigible tendency of the Indian mind to interpret *mokṣa* in the Jain and Sāṅkhya sense of isolation-integration. The more sophisticated psychological reading of the Mahāyāna is perhaps finally uncongenial to the Indian mind. For I notice that even when Indians state that the meaning of *mokṣa* is release, not from the world but from illusion, they tend to add: and so, from the world. Ānanda Mayī's statement that when *mokṣa* is experienced there is no question anymore of either affirmation or negation is somewhat dampened by the spectacle that she herself presents—sitting in a state of semi-rapturous semi-abstraction, being worshipped like an image and fed like a baby. This certainly suggests an attitude of life-negation. (See above, my discussion of the crises at the age of twelve.)[235]

The great deed of Zarathustra, apparently, was directed *against* the Indian yoga of world-withdrawal. The individual was summoned to act—to increase the field of the good. Zarathustra's ethical dualism (good and evil) was as absolute as the Jain metaphysical (*karma* and *jīva*), but life-oriented instead of death-oriented. Perhaps we can say that in the history of the Western world this oversimplified ethical dualism underwent a development and sophistication (culminating perhaps in Nietzsche), somewhat comparable to the development and sophistication of the metaphysical dualism in India, China, and Japan that I shall have to study when I get to Kyoto.

When *mokṣa* is realized, one is beyond not only affirmation and negation, but also good and evil, and the mythologies associated with *karma*, on the one hand, and judgment, on the other, are transcended.

The Indian penchant for renunciation is manifested in many ways: retirement at fifty-five, to meditate (or loaf); stress on the negative aspect of *mokṣa* (the *jīvan-mukti* idea seems not to have made much of a dent); stress on the negative aspect of *karma* (submission, rather than active creation of good new *karma*—the point usually stressed by Occidental theosophists like Sophia Wadia). *Actually, the fundamental principles of Indian philosophy can be read either way:* it is evident to me now, however, that the principal tendency of the Indians themselves is to give them the negative stress.

Perhaps what seems so odd about Theosophy is the positive active reading (ethical and western) that it gives to all the Indian ideas. Which would suggest that it may be doing violence to Indian thought, after all, to read it that way.

Thursday, January 6

With respect to the character and work of the Communists *within* India, Nehru and Vinoba (whom I take to represent pretty well the thinking of the Indian leaders who are interested fundamentally in *India*) are in essential agreement. I read in Vinoba's words:

> Communism with the Communists is not a living thought. They have turned it into a dogma based on a book. Like the Ārya Samājists[236] they pin their faith in that book and take leave of both the existing conditions in a given place and their intelligence. Actually there should be a proper synthesis between the book, the conditions, and one's own reasoning. But they regard the book as their *Veda.* Had Marx been living today in India, he would have certainly changed his ideas. I tell the Communists that you may be Marxists, but Marx was not a Marxist. He was simply Marx and therefore he could change. The Communists have no knowledge of the ten thousand years of the development of Indian thought. Even assuming that this ancient Indian thought is defective in certain respects, its knowledge would still be necessary if only to know those defects. I therefore find that the Communists have two very serious defects: One, they are book-worshippers, and two, they are ignorant of the development of Indian thought.[237]

And now the words of Nehru, in this morning's *Statesman.*

> The Prime Minister criticized the Communist and Marxist Parties in India and said that without understanding the problems of their own country they were

trying to foster an ideology which was outdated and could not fit in here. They should first understand the problems of their country and try to find out a solution internally.[238]

Vinoba's ideals for society can be said to resemble in many ways those of the Communists: e.g. no private possession of land, no disdain for the laborer, or for the work of the hands, no more money for work than the worker requires for living, etc. etc.—but his fundamental belief that the *mind* must change first is diametrically opposite to theirs that by a vigorous *daṇḍa-śakti* the true *loka-śakti* will be ushered in.

Had a visit this morning from Fabri, inviting me to dinner tonight. He introduced me to a young couple on a Ford Foundation grant, to study "India's Reactions to Federalism"—sounds a little obscure, but I think those are the correct words. "I suppose your husband has been studying India for some time?" I said to the young man's wife, and not without malice. "Well," she said, a little bit off balance, "we have been interested in India."

A happy letter from Jean at the American Express office today and a happier telegram from Tokyo, sent this morning: "Tokyo Lecture Recital, American Embassy, Monday; See you Tuesday; Love—Jean." How nice! How wonderful! That gives her a complete tour: San Francisco, Honolulu, Tokyo, and India (Ahmedabad, Baroda, Bombay lecture demonstration and Recital, New Delhi—and whatever else we may decide to arrange after she arrives). *The First Modern Dance Tour in the Modern Orient.* We've got to find some way to make this thing stick.

I went next to the Old Secretariat (only a few blocks, I find, from the Cecil) to look for Pramod Chandra, but found Y. C. Rai instead. Had tea with him and another gentleman, and talked about the dance. I found, to my pleasure, that Pramod and Krishnan are friends. I think this concert is going to catch the whole young crowd of New Delhi. I keep stressing the point that it will be the first example of a free dance form to be seen in India. Rai thought that we ought to publish and sell Jean's *What is Modern Dance?* I think so too.

A wonderful thing about today! Jean's good break in Tokyo, and mine here: I've actually finished every single task hanging over from New York and today finished (completely) my list of left-over letters to write. I feel, for the first time since I can remember, completely released from dead *karma*—and the luncheon tomorrow with Nehru will sort of celebrate the occasion. I walked around all afternoon on air. India, in fact, seemed quite fine to me. In fact, I notice that when I travel India becomes bad, and when I stay in one place, it's O.K.

Friday, January 7
As I now look back over the ranges of my interest during the four months of my India journey, I find that during the first two months of my stay, I was largely among temples and swamis: the whole *religious* phase of the problem was the principal concern. The second stage of my trip was largely in the company of Salmony, and my chief interests were the *aesthetic and scholarly.* From now until Jean's departure, it will be the young and Westernized intellectuals and artists who will be our chief associates—whom I regard as the effective antipole to the world represented by the temple priests, sadhus, and swamis: what I may call, the *educational* aspect of modern Indian life is the chief focus here. In short, the problem of my concern has been, in these different spheres: *The impact of the modern (i.e. Western) age on the traditional forms of Indian thought and life.*

My original formulation was turned the other way round, namely: the operation of the traditional religious and philosophical forms in modern Indian life. The operation, I should say, in all parts of India is all-pervasive. The pattern, primarily is *bhakti,* which, in its outward form and probable emotional appeal is practically the same, whether the details of the cult are Vaiṣṇava, Saiva, Jain, or even Parsee: one can say even that the Roman Catholic pattern of *bhakti* has here been somewhat Indianized. Islam stands apart: but again, the attitude is *bhakti.* As in the West, so here: the great question is whether the religious mode represented by *all* of these sects can survive (or should be encouraged to survive) the impact of the modern age. In so far as they stand for archaic scientific, moral, or psychological dogmas (supersititions) they will certainly be eradicated—not immediately, but gradually and naturally, as a result of the inevitable swing away from them of the educated. However, as supports of meditation—references out of the sphere of time and space to the "ground" of eternity, and consequently as supports of the individual battered by the waves of time—they deserve to be maintained—at least until in the modern pedagogical context an effective representation of the "Enlightenment-Redemption-*mokṣa*" experience can be rendered. The most important means of developing the modern vehicle of this experience, I believe, is that of creative writing and art: poetry, vision, metaphor, held in relation to the researches of psychology—and perhaps, also, physics.

In a way, when seen in this large context of the modern *vs.* the archaic, the problem is essentially the same as that of the West—except that our institutions of modern education are far in advance, both in their development and in their effect—than those of India. There is a special problem to be met in India, however, since the modern scientific world has not grown, by slow stages (as in the West) from the mother soil of the native religious tradition: it comes from without, as a quite alien graft. However, in compensation for this disadvantage, India has the distinct advantage of a transcendentally-based philosophical system, for which all temporal forms are equally secondary. Within the context of Indian thought itself the transition of the individual from *bhakti* to *jñāna* can be readily achieved, from theistic to non-theistic thinking: I should think it likely, therefore, that without too much of a jolt, the young modern Indian could be assisted from his grandmother's *bhakti* to his grandson's science; holding all the while to the stand in the transcendent. Possible indeed!—but honestly speaking, not likely. What is most probable is that the youth of India are going to have to work this thing out themselves—just about as the youth of the West have done and are doing—without much real help from their teachers.

For the old swamis, I find, hang pretty vigorously to what I am calling an archaic religion: a kind of melange of Victorianism and Hindu *bhakti.* An important attempt is being made to convert the archaic world-renouncing patterns into progressive, socially oriented ones; e.g. in the formulae of Vivekananda and Vinoba. But Ramakrishna and Vivekananda were Victorians, and their Victorianism remains imprinted on the Order for which they are the ideals; while Gandhi and Vinoba are primitivists, and their alienation from the inevitables of modern life makes for a kind of romantic escapism.

Let me take as examples of the young men trying to work things out for themselves, the young man in Bījāpur who had hanging on his walls, the figures of Jesus, T. S. Eliot, Krishnamurti, and Ramana Maharishi; also young Subrakhmanya in Bangalore, trying to carry on his art, with his soul in Paris; then the young people of the Bombay Theatre Unit; the young people I have met here in New Delhi (Pramod Chandra, Rai, Krishnan), and Fabri's wife, Ratna, who "does not believe in anything," and "can't take blows" (whereas, obviously, every peasant can).

What has the West to offer here, and what has India to offer the West?

I think the best lead to an answer to this point will be found in my discussions with Maiti in Ahmedabad: psychology (especially, I should say, of the Jungian school) and *ātman* (as an operative supplement to the hypothesis of the unconscious).

Certainly the social danger of India's orientation, however, is what Thomas Mann has called "the sympathy with death." The appearance of the meditating yogi in India as early as the period of Mohenjo-daro[239] points to a long experience here of the bliss (*ānanda*) of *samādhi*. And this has tended to support a romantical interest in renunciation as well as a lazy (heat-inspired) interest in doing nothing (retirement at the age of 55). The holocaust (one might say) of India's best minds—all in quest of *ānanda*—is something quite unique in the history of the world. In the periods of the great dynasties it was counterbalanced by a forcefully heroic attitude; but in modern India this counterforce does not exist.

Within the Indian philosophic systems there is ground enough for an affirmative attitude. It is questionable, however, whether it will ever actually take over. Zarathustra's reform, pitching the mind in the direction of an ethical as opposed to metaphysical dualism, was perhaps the first sign of the world affirmative penchant of the Occident (which finds its manifestation even in the monastic life of the Catholic Church where a balance is insisted upon between works and meditation). Whether India is going to be able to develop an *ethos of hard work* (which is what Nehru asked for in a speech that he made the other day) without some kind of radical philosophical transformation it is very hard to say. The Ramakrishna monks represent a sort of transitional form—but their *bhakti* is extremely reactionary, it seems to me. Whether anyone is working really intelligently and fundamentally on the problem I do not know: perhaps Radhakrishnan—but he is now in politics.

A series of phone calls this morning settled the matter of Jean's New Delhi recital. She will perform under the auspices of the American Women's Club and the New Delhi Unity Theatre with the Little Theatre Group assisting on the lights and staging. (At least, that's the way it all sounds. One must always remember that India has that other, hidden face.)

A little after noon I took a taxi to the Prime Minister's mansion—but since it appeared that I was arriving fifteen minutes ahead of schedule, I had my taxi driver let me off outside the gate and took a ten minute stroll. At the gate—click, click!—the guard; and a young man sitting at a table got up to approach me. Producing my invitation-card (which had arrived in this morning's mail, I was turned over to a military man in olive drab and a fine turban, who walked with me along the spacious, curving driveway, to the *porte cochère*, and there I was immediately greeted by Mrs. Krishna Hutheesingh, who conducted me up spacious stairways. The whole building is filled with mediocre examples of Indian art—mostly Tibetan bronzes—and large photographs of the chief temples—perhaps by the Bhulabhai Institute people. We arrived in Mrs. Hutheesingh's sitting-room and bedroom and were presently joined by others. Gimlets were served, all round: twice for some.

We then were summoned, and, after gulping the last inch, went below.

The great English lawns and gardens at the back of the prodigious estate were to be our setting. Two tables were set—for fourteen.

The Prime Minister,[240] in his usual costume (white cap, brown jacket about to the knees, and tight trousers) came along the lawn with the Indian members of the party and shook hands graciously with us all, then led us to a cage containing a pair of pet Himalayan pandas, who turned out to be the principal ice-breakers of the occasion. Their cute, long, low hung bodies and long, long-furred tails, were a lovely russet, while their woolly legs and paws were black. They were delightful little animals, and when the Prime Minister, putting on a pair of heavy white gloves to protect his hands from their heavy claws, went into their cage and fed them, first bamboo leaves and then peas, the company was enchanted and the scene was that of the simplicity of the great. Actually, it would have made a sweet little picture.

Leaving the door open, so that the animals might roam at will, the Prime Minister next turned to a set of chairs around which we stood while some sort of fruit juice was brought to us for a cocktail; and then we all sat down. If I do say so myself, I was the only one who was willing to broach a conversation, and so the Prime Minister and I talked about sadhus, Buddhism, and the influence of metaphysics on Indian life, while the others sat, largely mum. I was particularly impressed by the three deaf-mutes representing the Ford Foundation, who, as soon as possible after the meal, shook hands all round and took their departure.

Mrs. Hutheesingh told me later that the Prime Minister had been in a particularly pleasant mood today. To me he seemed pleasant and courteous enough, but without very much life—way over on the weary side—and why not, with such a nondescript set of brushed-together companions.

But for me, it was a kind of great climax to my visit to India. The opportunity to meet and talk with the man whose anti-American attitude has been one of the strong experiences of my visit somewhat softened the sense of sheer animosity; and the opportunity to place on the level of human judgment a figure whose importance in the present world scene is perhaps paramount, gave me a new sense of the forces that operate in a world scene. Besides—it was a delightful afternoon.

I left the great mansion, again on foot, and strolled down one of the avenues to a taxi that I saw standing, and drove off to tell Mr. King that Jean's recital in Delhi now was definitely going to take place. "If it goes well," he said, "perhaps we could arrange a tour for her in India. How much longer would she be staying?"

This one almost did me in. Isadora Bennett had written to the Kings four months ago for a bit of help in building up a recital.

"Well," I said, very graciously; for Mr. King, while doing absolutely nothing, has been a very friendly and gracious man, "she will be leaving India for her job in New York within a couple of days." Then I recited the list of the recitals that I had arranged for her on my own, and he said he thought that that would be a very good showing.

I was to call for Mrs. Hutheesingh to go with her to the recital of Shanta Rao at Sapru House, and at the proper time I taxied to the Prime Minister's house, and after passing the challenge at the gate, drove to the *porte cochère,* feeling like an old friend of the family by now.

The performance of Shanta Rao seemed to me magnificent, and yet without magic. She is a powerful and splendid dancer, and, unlike all of the other Indian performers I have seen, made no attempt whatsoever to pretty up either the stage or herself.[241] The dances, as far as I could see, were not composed as carefully structured units, but were more like strings of beads, which could have gone on forever, had the audience the endurance: Shanta Rao certainly had the endurance; a couple of her dances went on for nearly forty-five minutes. Nor were the dances composed with any sense or need for a floor pattern. The dancer came in from the wings to upstage center, and then slowly worked forward to the edge of the footboard; whereupon that passage (or bead) would end, and in a slow, backward walk of rest, she would return to the commencing position of upstage center for another sequence. Neogy's words about the lack of beginning, middle, and end in Indian music would seem to apply to this dance art too. Moreover, as far as my experience went, neither the movements nor the facial expressions had very much feeling-value. They came and went, somewhat as tap-dance steps: and the principal comment of the Indian audience seemed to be one of sheer marvel at the woman's physical endurance.

The dancer had two costumes, one for the Bharata Natyam of part I of the program, and one for the Mohini Attam of part II. The latter, according to the program notes, is a dance form from Kerala that has become extinct, except for the bit preserved by Shanta Rao, who "happens to be the only pupil to whom this art form is passed on along with its special kind of music.... Mohini Attam means the dance of the Enchantress, and as such this is one of the most lyrical and subtle of the dance forms belonging to Malabar. The form is danced by women alone and is always danced solo." As far as I could see, it was not *very* different from the Bharata Natyam.

I was sorry that Jean could not be here, because it seemed to me that we were seeing something pretty sheer and straight. In the intermission, Pramod Chandra came up to me, where I was standing, in front of my super-duper seat—front row center—and expressed his delight in the performance: "This is *Vijayanagar*," he said; and I felt so too. But my two friends, the critics, Fabri and Krishnan, were of a negative opinion. (What are little critics made of?) They said that Shanta Rao's art lacked beauty and gentleness—was too athletic. Well, as one who had never seen Bharata Natyam decently danced before, I could have no opinion. It is, of course, one of the limitations of an academic art that will not allow much scope to the individual talent that has special qualities of its own; but it is my guess that in the lost days of long ago the *devadāsīs* must have been of the stuff of Shanta Rao.

Sunday, January 9

I have begun to feel a bit heavy-headed and I sat around sort of vaguely, till about five, when I went to the Ramakrishna Mission to hear Swami Ranganathananda give his Sunday talk on the *Gītā.* People from last evening's party arrived, reverently—and I felt that my India trip had now come full circle. The talk was good and clear, and was very well attended—Swami sitting cross-legged upon the platform and the audience cross-legged before him. I have heard all these ideas so often, however, that I now feel that it's surely time for me to be getting on to something else. Following the talk, I exchanged a few words with Swami (Nikhilananda and the ladies are sailing today from Bombay). Full circle indeed, except that now I felt that I was definitely on the *outside* of the monastery. Swami Nikhilananda, undoubtedly, had told them something of the secular turn of my interests during the course of the trip.

Dance Tour with Jean Erdman

New Delhi

Tuesday, January 11

The day of Jean's arrival. I went in the morning to pick up a letter from Mrs. Hutheesingh, requesting the Customs Officers to let Jean through with her dancing gear; had a gimlet with the lady in her room in the Prime Minister's house and returned to the hotel for lunch. Next went to the Chandi Chauk[242] to look for flowers for Jean, but though I wandered about in the markets for over an hour, could find nothing but rather dead garlands. I went home, dressed for Jean's arrival, drove to the Hanumān Temple for flowers (Fabri's suggestion), and met Krishnan at the bus. We drove to the airport where I had arrived months ago: cool now. Jean appeared...customs...bus ride to the Imperial...taxi with Krishnan to Gaylords for a supper...Krishnan delivered at his home...and then home with Jean. A magical, strange and lovely, half-stunned, completely unreal world.

Wednesday, January 12

Fabri arrived in the morning and we went with him to Sapru House to settle the date for Jean's recital. We went with him next to Mr. Inder Das to arrange for the Little Theatre Group to take care of all the stage and lighting problems.

We had the Fabris, Krishnan, and the dancer Indrani Rahman and her husband to dinner with us at the hotel. A very pleasant party, with some rather interesting talk about the problem of composing music to dance and dance to music. Fabri began to sound like a European romantic rather fixed in his ideas.

Thursday, January 13

In the morning we went to the Cottage Industries Emporium, where Jean fell in love with everything she saw and we realized that we had a large operation ahead of us in the choice of objects for our friends back home.

Young Pramod Chandra and his colleague Rai came for lunch with us at the Cecil, and Pramod again was charming and certainly one of the most intelligent young men I have met in India. When they left, we spent an easy afternoon talking and planning before the fire in our room. In the evening we went to a dinner party given by Mrs. Adams, which had been described as an opener for Jean's recital propaganda; however, the majority of the people invited were simply Americans who would hardly have any interest in the matter or be of any use.

The others present at the dinner were Mrs. Hutheesingh, Fabri, Krishnan, and a Miss Sheilu, who will represent the Unity Theatre group in our joint project. I was greatly discouraged by what I heard this evening; for it appeared that Mrs. Adams and Miss Sheilu expected Krishnan, Fabri and myself to carry the whole responsibility of the concert—all that the American Women's Club and Unity Theatre were prepared to do was to supply their names at the head of the billing and accept the profits for their various purposes.

Friday, January 14

During the morning Jean and I drove about in a taxi, searching for the office that would give us tax exemption, only to learn, finally, that no exemption would be granted unless *all* the receipts (i.e. the gross) were devoted to charity.

Saturday, January 15

A letter from Mrs. Adams arrived this morning, suggesting that the Unity Theatre and American Women's Club should take over more of the work on the recital than originally planned by them: their names would appear as sponsors, and they were afraid that Krishnan was not competent to do a good job. Also, they wondered whether Jean would like a reception for the press, before the program. Actually, they had read the copy of the *Theatre Unit Bulletin* from Bombay, where the plans for Jean's Bombay recital are outlined, and they finally got the idea of what it means to be sponsoring a recital. Jean and I went over to see Mrs. Adams and discussed the matter. She presented us with a typed-out plan and everything seemed fine.

We went home for lunch and a rest, then, at four, we continued on to an open-air tea and reception given by Mr. Inder Das for Dame Sybil Thorndike and her husband. A very nice affair, where the fine old couple were presented with a hideous plaque of some kind, and made speeches. Her theme: that actors learn to sympathize with and to understand all sorts of people and that the theater is a dispenser of good will to men of many kinds (the Irish are more alien to the English than the Indians are, and yet the Abbey Theatre had succeeded in communicating to the English!). His theme: that India, before building a national theater, should wait to see what form of theater best suited the national consciousness (the old Shakespearean theater was a folk theater, with spectators on the stage; the Restoration, however, had brought an aristocratic theater, with a proscenium separating the audience from the stage: probably for India a folk theater in the round would be more appropriate than a proscenium).

We picked up Krishnan and drove to the Cecil where Jean, Krishnan,

Fabri and I had a meeting, preparing plans for the recital. Krishnan stayed for dinner with us. We packed in a great hurry and rushed to the train that was to take us to Jaipur, with Krishnan in attendance.

To my great displeasure, there were two gents already installed in the upper berths in the compartment that I thought had been reserved for Jean and me. I made a great noise. The conductor arrived and sold us an air-conditioned–class compartment for thirty more rupees. We transferred at the last minute and were safe for the night.

Sunday, January 16 ***Jaipur***

An amusing day in Jaipur. The conductor rapped on our compartment door at about 5 A.M. and we hurried to dress and disentrain. It was still a bit dark. At the station a thin man held out a card that said Hotel Kaiser-i-Hind, and I let him pile us into a station wagon that took us to a nice little place, where an extremely cordial, burly fellow got up from his sleeping-shroud before the door, and showed us to a suite of rooms, then told us what our day was to be. Did we want to ride on the elephant at Amber, price thirty rupees? No? Well then, in the morning we should go to Amber and in the afternoon see the sights of Jaipur; we should have a guide; we should have the station wagon. Meanwhile, we should go to sleep till about 7:30 and then have morning tea and breakfast. And so it went. We seemed to be the only guests at the hotel, except at meal time, when a single, somewhat melancholy chap sat at another table in silence. Shortly after tea, we paid our bill, took our package dinner into our luggage, and piled again into the station wagon, to board the train for Ahmedabad.

Monday, January 17 ***Ahmedabad***

It was quite a night. Again we had a compartment for four, and I was determined that we should have it alone; so, as soon as we entered, I pulled up the blinds and bolted the doors. We ate our package dinner and retired early; but at intervals during the night there would be a banging at the door. Once I opened, and a conductor asked for the numbers of our tickets, then left us alone. The bangings went on, but I did not open again.

We arrived in Ahmedabad at 11 A.M. and were met at the station by the household manager of the Sarabhais. It was a fine feeling I had, being back again in this lovely place—and Jean was enjoying it too. We were installed in the room next to the one that I had occupied before, and for lunch we went around to Gautam's house where we found Kamalini and the Calders (Alexander Calder, the mobile man, and his wife).[243] A charming lunch out under the trees; after which Kamalini drove us to the Gymkhana Club, where Jean is to perform tomorrow.

My own chief problem now is to get that darned program written for the Bombay recital. Once again, I have had to shut myself into the Ahmedabad bathroom to write. We went out to a neighboring mansion to see a large wedding dance and show held in a great tent: dull dancing of *jeunes filles de famille,* but a colorful company—outshone, however, by the color of Calder's shirt.

Jean Erdman and Alexander Calder.

Tuesday, January 18

The day of Jean's first recital in India. I worked all morning on the Bombay program notes, while Jean had her work-out at the Gymkhana Club, where she is to dance. The recital commenced at six, with Jean giving a lecture on the modern dance that went on till seven; then the recital began:

Upon Enchanted Ground
Ophelia
Creature on a Journey
Passage
The Transformations of Medusa

INTERVAL

Lecture on modern dance, repeating *Creature* as an example; then:

Changing-Woman
Bagatelle

The recital ended at about nine, and we went to Gautam's place for dinner. Finis at about midnight. A lovely day. A warm reception for Jean, and, now, a feeling of relaxation all round.

Wednesday, January 19

In the morning Kamalini drove us and the Calders over to Mrinalini's home for a wonderful day of Bharata Natyam and Kathakali. During the forenoon we watched a rehearsal of Mrinalini's group. I found a good deal more here than I had found in Shanta Rao's performance. Mrinalini has a better sense of stage than Shanta Rao, and so has made her works considerably less stark than those that I saw in the Sapru Hall recital.[244] On the other hand, the vigor of the Bharata Natyam was still here: the choreography and the well-rendered facial expressions made it all seem less harsh than the vigor of Shanta Rao. The first two dances were Bharata Natyam, and then, came the thrill of the day: Chatunni Panniker's Kathakali. He danced in his dhoti and shirt, not in costume; and this gave us an opportunity to experience directly the character of his work as dance. The first piece was a hunter's account of his having seen an elephant seized by a serpent and slain by a lion; the second was a group work, including Mrinalini and her three girls, telling the tale of Nala and Damayantī.[245] As Mrinalini pointed out, in Kathakali the male roles are very strong and the female very gentle, whereas in Bharata Natyam the female dance is almost masculine in its strength.

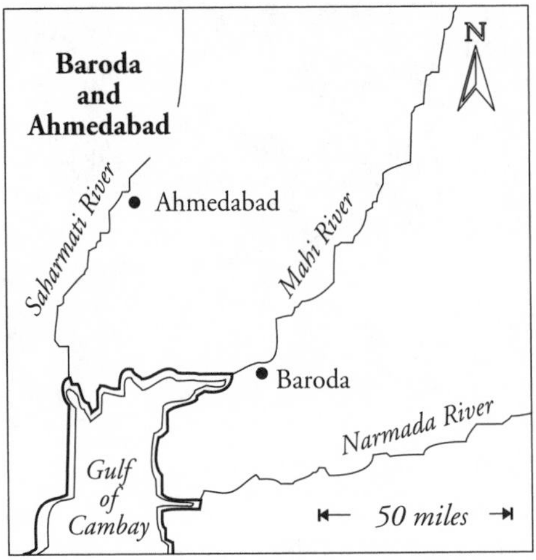

Panniker showed us in detail the posture of the Kathakali—which is danced on the outside edges of the feet, not on the soles, and involves an extraordinary hyperextension of the back. The facial movements are tremendously effective, and the pantomime hits a new level of significant stylization. It is a perfect art for the rendition of myth and fairy tale—and perhaps also for *any* narrative. All that is required, it seems to me, is a creative imagination to carry the style across the modern field of observed experience as it has already been carried across that of the south-Indian peasant world.

A problem that we discussed a little was that of the possible development of the traditional Indian dance in a modern world. It seems to me that as long as the Indian mythology supplies the foundations of an important part of Indian life, this art will be relevant. To be modern, however, an aspect of, or point of view toward, the great motifs will have to be revealed that will be relevant to the problems of the contemporary in his attempts to hold himself in balance between the archetypological stress of the past and the individualistic stress of the present. For example, the attitude of Rāma to Sītā can be rendered questionable through a stress on the personal relationship of the mythological pair. Certainly the Kathakali (which now seems to me to be a much more important and wonderful art than the Bharata Natyam) is well fitted to move in such a direction. To begin with, the mythological costumes could be removed immediately, the personal, human factor would be unshelled.

A more general problem that seemed to me to be greatly illuminated by my experience today of the Kathakali is that of the function and power of *style.* The style itself is the function of a standpoint, and it functions as a "mirror held up to nature," from that particular standpoint or position. Everything that can be brought into its frame is freshly seen from that position—freshly experienced and newly understood. The problem of an artist who is striving to create within the frame of—or rather, on the plane of—a certain given style, is to expand its range without breaking or spoiling the surface. The problem, on the other hand, of the artist creating in the spirit of a completely modern mind, is to find styles that will define new positions: Nietzsche's "perspectivism," in contrast to the single-stance position of an academy or dogmatic canon.

Member of Mrinalini Sarabhai's dance company

Following the rehearsal, we had lunch with Mrinalini and her husband Vikram, then went home for a brief rest, and returning at four, found the company on the roof, in full costume, for pictures.

Following our day at Mrinalini's we were taken to a large wedding reception—for which I donned my white-jacketed tuxedo (dating from my first visit with Jean to Hawaii and carried with me on my present trip to no great purpose). The reception was at the home of a wealthy brahmin family whose daughter is marrying a young man of inferior caste who is a great cricket player. They are both university graduates and they met at college. The crowd was immense, and we stood around for a while meeting people—among whom were a few from my earlier visit to Ahmedabad: and then we watched part of the ceremony from close range.

Jean and I had dinner this evening with Bharati Sarabhai in her rooms. The conversation—which gradually subsided as Jean began to fall asleep—touched, among other matters, that of the problem of the contemporary Indian theater. Bharati is associated with a theater group in Ahmedabad, and holds it against Alkazi's Theatre Unit that all of their plays so far have been European and in English. She finds that though she has been brought up speaking English, the language does not carry the full meaning of her

Member of Mrinalini Sarabhai's dance company on the roof of the Sarabhais' Ahmedabad house.

thoughts and feeling: it is not fully appropriate to Indian life: therefore, a theater in the native language must be developed. She is writing in Gujarati.

And so here we have another aspect of this complex problem of modern Indian art and thought. In the dance it is ancient *vs.* modern; in literature it is also English *vs.* regional languages *vs.* Hindi—a perplex indeed.

Thursday, January 20

I spent the whole day at work on Jean's program notes. In the early evening, a charming party at Kamalini and Gautam's, where a large company of invited guests were shown two films about Calder's work (one with music by John Cage) and then were invited to have fruit juice and snacks in a garden where Calder mobiles were hanging from the trees.

Gira Sarabhai, who seems to be the chief patroness and protagonist of Calder, Bauhaus and *l'art moderne* in Ahmedabad, challenged Jean on the position Jean had taken with respect to the future of the Kathakali style. According to Gira, every attempt to develop the Kathakali into a modern art was only destructive of its proper character. The art survives and can survive only in the villages of the South, where it exists as a popular form. It and its world are completely apart from the modern. Modern man must seek his art in modern art. The only possible relationship of a modern mind to the mythological art of the Kathakali is that of modern man to a museum piece. Gira, apparently, is completely at odds with Mrinalini on this point.

Following the Calder event, we all went back to the wedding party of last evening for the great dinner of the day following the rite of the marriage. The bride and groom, who last evening were seated in a little central pagoda, while everybody else sat in chairs to watch the long rite but actually sat only briefly, to indicate that they had accepted the invitation, now were seated before their dinner on little platforms before the pagoda, and the whole company of about four hundred sat likewise on little platforms all around the walls of the garden. Calder couldn't cross his legs and so devised a position for himself with his dinner tray on the ground before him and his legs at either side. "I feel," he said, "as though I were driving a sulky." We had to eat with our fingers and, for the most part, made out pretty well. The host and hostess were generous to our peculiar plight, and on the whole, the adventure came off pretty well.

A curious day—of traditional India and the modern U.S.A. As far as I was concerned, the Calder films and John's musical accompaniment were something of a bore: a *merely* aesthetic game of effects—like the twinkle of light on a pond, I did not feel that there was much to be said for it, and certainly Calder himself had nothing to say for it except that he enjoyed making mobiles. He has told people, also, that he did not find Elephanta interesting:

but, I dare say, if one were to declare that his mobiles were utterly uninteresting he would feel that his critic was somewhat less than bright. I think it's wonderful to know that Alexander Calder, America's mobile master, did not find Elephanta interesting. In diametric contrast, one can take the position of Alfred Salmony, who found anything created after A.D. 1400 of no interest. Gira, so to say, is in both positions; or rather, represents the negative of both positions: the past is interesting for museums, modern art (including Sandy Calder) for modern life. My impression of the Indian reaction to Calder's part was that it was not enthusiastic. "Our vendors," said one lady, "do similar work."

Friday, January 21

I'm still at work on the notes for Jean's program. Geeta took a copy of the first portion with her to Baroda for Jean's concert there. Jean and I had breakfast together on our own verandah, then set off with Gira, Kamalini, Gautam, and the Calders, to the great Friday morning cattle market. A wonderful sight—and we, a wonderful sight for the shepherds and herders who followed us in droves everywhere we moved.

Gautam then drove us to his factory and Gira took us to the Calico Museum. Later in the afternoon, Jean went shopping with Kamalini and the Calders and I was called for by Dr. Trivedi (of my last visit),[246] to be driven in his disintegrating Citroën to the home of another gentleman. While I drank tea, the gentleman splurged his Sanskrit, asked what I knew about the Vedas, and read to me a speech that he had once given, wherein he bemoaned the crass materialism of the modern West and celebrated the saints and spiritual traditions of India as the coming salvation of a crumbling world. When he stopped, I said, "Well, you have been pretty severe on the modern world!" He laughed, and we had a pleasant conversation. Then he assigned his son to me—an intelligent youth with a little fuzz of beard—to show me his house in the town, "a typical Gujarati home." I admired the cowdung floor of one of the rooms, the fine court, the pots and pans, and a carved wooden table, supported by a carved wooden camel, "all of one piece."

The young man asked me whether I thought the history of the next one hundred years would be determined by the East or by the West—a theme, he said, which had been debated in a Cambridge *vs.* India debating contest. I said I thought the West—since the principal need and determining factor in the world today was the development of the machine, of industry, of dams, irrigation projects, etc., in which development the West is the leader, beyond question. This he conceded, but, he said, the raw materials are largely, in Asia and if Asia wishes.... The car pulled up before the house that we were to visit and the subject was lost.

But I felt again, beneath all of the sincere cordiality and personal friendliness of my host and his son, the profound run of hatred against the West, brought to focus specifically on the United States as the primary representative of the new world that is coming—willy-nilly—to transform the timeless, ageless repose of this otherwise fairly stagnant world. The main themes of reproach are: The atom bomb; divorce; spiritual restlessness (greed for gadgets); materialism (greed for money); support of the European imperialists (who, ironically, are now better loved than we); support of Chiang Kai Shek (a desire for war); a desire to impose our will on the domestic policies of nations (Formosa-China problem again). Not a word of reproach have I heard against Russia throughout the five months of my visit.

Dinner, tonight, was at Gautam's "farm": our final dinner in Ahmedabad. Mr. and Mrs. Sarabhai were present, and on the drive out Mr. Sarabhai asked me what I thought of India's political position; did I think, as *Time Magazine* did, that the Prime Minister was a Communist. "Nehru is not a communist," I said, "but in the International field he supports the Communist position against the Democracies every time." "He believes," said Mr. Sarabhai, "that one nation should not try to impose its ideals of government upon another." "On that point," I answered, "I believe we all would agree." Then I changed the subject.

Mrs. Sarabhai was particularly fond of this older, more Indian house of Gautam's. "This," she said, "is Gautam *before* he went to America." It is a lovely house, full of Indian carved woodwork, and with cowdung floors. We had a handsome dinner, and then returned to Gautam's post-America house (Bauhaus, Museum of Modern Art), where we played some of Jean's records, coaxed Jean to dance her *Portrait of a Lady*, helped her decide what sari to buy for Ramona in Colorado, and finally said good night to all.

Finis Ahmedabad, and I finally got the program notes into the mail.

Saturday, January 22 ***Baroda***

We had breakfast on the verandah before our room. Mani and Gautam arrived to say good-bye; we got into the station wagon and were driven to the station. The train arrived in Baroda at about eleven, where we were met by Geeta at the train and driven to her home: a nice big house with pleasant rooms. Immediately we were taken to see the hall and stage where Jean is to perform at the Maharaja Sayaji Rao University. It's a fantastic little stage with a concrete wall dividing it from its own proper walls.

Jean looked over the situation, and we met Anjali Mehr, dancer, who is

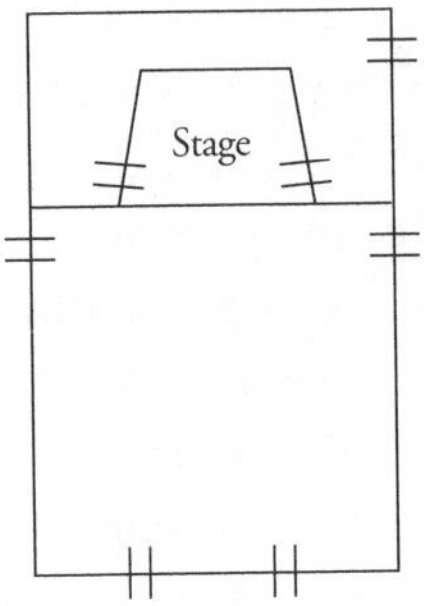

in charge of Jean's event; also the sculptor Shankho Chawdhury, who took us to his home to meet his father and his wife, and then tried to scout out a tape recorder for Jean's music. The town is very busy today with an important cricket match, and so we had to drive around a lot to find people. Everything moving very slowly. Chawdhury was very cordial and helpful. During the afternoon, Jean took a workout in Geeta's living room, and before dinner Geeta and her drummer gave Jean a lesson in the principles of Indian drum-beats.

Sunday, January 23

Breakfast, then Jean's lecture at ten. She did an excellent job. We then worked at the theater, and, before lunch, I fixed her recorder tapes so that there should be no need to swap reels around during the recital. We got to the theater and had to wait till almost too late for the tape recorder to arrive with its operator. Then we had a brief run-through for cues and lights and at 6 P.M. the recital began.

Salutatio
Ophelia
Creature on a Journey
Passage
The Transformation of Medusa

INTERVAL

Changing-Woman

INTERVAL

Upon Enchanted Ground
Pierrot, the Moon
Bagatelle

The recital lasted two hours and five minutes, and Jean was terribly tired after the second interval. We decided that for the next recital she should omit *Upon Enchanted Ground.*

The hall was filled and the response excellent, with lots of autograph-seekers on the stage. The people who had been at last night's party came up and from their remarks it was apparent that Jean's lecture of the morning had helped considerably toward their understanding of what they saw.

We got packed and returned to Geeta's place for dinner—and were interrupted by a gentleman who arrived with his twenty-two or -three year old daughter, the latter wishing to learn from Jean how to fall, and the former coming to tell us about his son who has been in America for seven years. The son's universal religion, we heard, goes beyond Theosophy: it is kind to all things, and not only all beings: one is kind, for example, to furniture. The man was very silly and sweet, and invited us to tea tomorrow. Shortly after his departure, we turned in for the night.

Monday, January 24

We went to the Baroda Museum in the morning. Fine collections: wonderful bronzes (a Ṛṣabhanātha from *c.* A.D. 450 in particular) and a fine series of late Gupta stone pieces from Idar. We stayed for about an hour and a half, then went out and sat under the trees until the car arrived.

After lunch we went to a dwelling in the town to see Anjali Mehr rehearse her program of Bharata Natyam for a recital Wednesday night. She did one of the dances that Shanta Rao performed—less magnificently, but with her own charm. Her *gopī* dances were particularly charming. But I have begun to feel a bit bored with the same old themes returning in the same old way, again and again. Before her dance she saluted the earth and the room, with a quick little ritual gesture. The rhythms of her feet were particularly good, and her facial expressions the best I have seen so far.

Joseph Campbell with a prop from *Pierrot the Moon.*

We next went to tea at Mrs. English's place and met a curious American, a social scientist from Columbia, here on some kind of exchange arrangement; has lectured all over India under the auspices of the U.S.I.S. on American and Indian Education on such subjects as "What is an American?" When I asked him about the first theme, he said that in Indian education there was an almost complete lack of criticism: the students simply accepted what the professors told them and the professors were overly soft on the students.

He next went on to tell of other ideas that he had for the Indians—all implying a criticism of India. He complained, for instance, that in India he was never accepted or befriended as he would like to be, but always in terms of a category of some kind; he never felt that people liked him for himself. Well, actually, he was not a particularly likeable chap: friendly as could be, but his voice was harsh and his speech aggressive. Can the U.S.I.S. not find more attractive Americans to send around in advertisement of the American man?

Jean Erdman Campbell with a prop from her dance *Pierrot the Moon.*

This whole problem of the official picture of America presented to the Orient is one that ought to be carefully reviewed. Business men, politicians, industrialists, and experts (educationalists included), are not always the most agreeable human beings. The U.S.I.S. office in Delhi had stacks of pictures of the U.S.A.—farmers with ears of corn, etc.; factories, and what not. What not?—not anything having to do with American art and music and literature. We tend to export machines and machine men; our U.S.I.S. should present the other side of the picture.

Geeta had another company for dinner: the American-trained Indians this time. All are in the Social Work College: they do not mix well with the English-trained group, and they had not much appreciated Jean's recital. But they were a very nice lot, and we had a pleasant evening. Geeta feels that America is not good for young Indians. They come back with all the superficial wildness, she says; and they are thrown off balance by the wide difference in morals. English ideals are closer than American to the Indians: besides, they are used to England, and in England the donning system keeps them under surveillance—they do not run wild.

Among the guests was an older gentleman, a medical doctor, who caught my ear and talked it off, but let fall a number of good ideas.

Though the final insights of Indian philosophy are not life-negating, the general tenor of Indian moral ideals is negative, and these ideals have tended to keep the main run of Indian thought going in a negative direction. (This idea supplements my observation of the negative disposition of Indian thought, even in spite of its positive possibilities.) The man who seeks release is actually following a desire, and so is not really negating his desires. He is only subordinating his many lesser desires to his one major desire.

Dharma is not really a negation of individual desires either; for *dharma* is an expression of man's desire for social approval. *Artha, dharma, kāmā, mokṣa,* thus, are all manifestations of the human will to life.

The doctrine of the *Gītā* is a positive doctrine; the negative reading is the consequence of a misreading.

Hinduism's affirmation of the divinity of life is what lies behind the obscene images in the temples.

The party ended at about eleven. Our train was to leave for Delhi at 2 A.M. The remainder of the evening, therefore, went into packings and departures.

Tuesday, January 25 ***Baroda to New Delhi***

The Frontier Mail, Baroda to New Delhi, six hours. We had a second-class set-up again (no air-conditioned class available), and there were two gents in the upper berths. But everything was managed decently, and one of the two left the train at 6 A.M. The other was a strange chap with a very high, thin voice, who spent most of his time neatening out his things. He was on his way from Ahmedabad to New Delhi just to see the Republic Day celebrations.

In New Delhi, there was no letter from Mrs. Hutheesingh: no tickets for the Parade Stand and Reception tomorrow. Great disappointment, so we tried to phone Pupul Jayakar, but there was no answer.

Wednesday, January 26—Republic Day ***New Delhi***

There was lots of early-morning noise outside from hundreds of tongas, full of families, trotting to the parade areas. I phone the Prime Minister's house to ask about our tickets: no help. So we went off at 9:00 A.M. to stand on Curzon Road and wait for the parade to come.

Jean was not feeling very well: something about her stomach: result, perhaps, of yesterday's lunch. So the whole parade thing was a bit uncomfortable. The best events were the camel corps and the elephants. Almost all of the bands played Scotch bagpipes. One brass band was on horses. The parade lasted for about an hour. We returned to the hotel and I got in touch with Mrs. Adams.

A little problem has developed in the matter of Jean's recital. While in Ahmedabad I received a letter from Mrs. Adams complaining of Fabri's high-handed assumption of authority: she offered to withdraw. Krishnan has managed to appease her, and at six we went around (Krishnan and I, while Jean continued to sleep) for a meeting. Sheilu (the Unity Theatre woman) was there, and several others. The Adams arrived in full dress from the reception (which Jean and I should have attended too) and we got down to work: straightened everything out, and went off with Sheilu, whom I invited to dine with Jean, Krishnan, and me at the Volga. Pleasant evening at the Volga and in Sheilu's Greenwich-Village–like apartment.

She teaches English literature at Indrarastha College, and has never studied in Europe or America; yet her attitude and style of intelligence is quite Western. In her room hang two pictures in a modern style—and they did not seem more out of place here than their counterparts in a mid-Western or New York apartment. It seemed to me that young college and university people throughout the non-Communist world must be facing just about comparable problems. At dinner she spoke about the problems of literature in India.

As a consequence of the introduction of Hindi, English is deteriorating; Hindi also is deteriorating (since it is being spoken now by multitudes who have just learned it); and the regional languages are deteriorating. India is becoming a nation without a well-formed language.

French, German, Spanish, and other European literatures are studied only in special language classes. American literature, too, is hardly known. There is nothing like our comparative literature courses in India. The link with the West is primarily via England.

Sheilu's own library resembled that of almost any young student of literature in America. We saw lots of Modern Library Giants and similar editions, which used to be cheap here, but now are hard to buy.

Thursday, January 27

Krishnan arrived at breakfast time, and up we went to Fabri's, to settle his side of this recital affair. All went very well. Finally, at four, I managed to get in touch with Mr. Jayakar at his office, only to learn that he had gotten us tickets for tomorrow's folkdance, not tonight's, and that the Prime Minister's house had been trying for two days to get in touch with me and deliver the Parade tickets. Everything, for a moment, seemed a mess. I drove to the National Stadium and bought two tickets for tonight, and when I returned Jean told me that Jayakar had phoned again and we were set for tonight.

We got to the crowded stadium in good time. A rich and beautiful evening of folkdances, after which we went to the Gymkhana club for dinner. The dances gave one a fine sense of the wealth and variety of India's cultural life. The groups were from:

Sikkim—Tibetan-like
Assam—Nāgas: like American Plains Indians
Rajasthan—Dandia Dance
Vindhya Pradesh—Tribal Karma dance
Bombay—Goan Dakni Dance
Travancore-Cochin—a circle dance of girls (Thiruvathirakali)
Bihar—Tribal Oraons of Chhota Nagpur: girls in a row.
North East Frontier Agency
Madhya Bharat
Rajasthan—Drum dance—Large drums—quite wonderful

INTERVAL

Pondicherry—French Indian Ballet (to a Viennese Waltz!)
Punjab—Great cries from the Punjabi gallery
Saurashtra—Pole with strings—wind up, wind back
Madras—Harvest dance: scenes of harvest
Orissa—Jadur, to Barubonga, god of the Bhunrijas
Bombay—Lion Dance; from *Yakṣa Gaṇa* dance drama
Uttar Pradesh—Divali dance of the Ahīrs of Bundelkhand
P.E.P.S.U.—Punjab rainy-season dance
Himachal Pradesh—a Cossack-like group
Madhya Pradesh—Marias with their bison horns
Manipur—folk style
Hyderabad—Sidis (African style)

Bombay

Friday, January 28 ***Bombay***

We are met at airport by Alkazi. Bombay is much hotter than New Delhi. I feel greatly at home, and enjoy bringing Jean to *my* hotel. Back again in the Grand—my space-platform.[247] And again I am to try to bring everything up to date. Jean's concert problems are now largely solved, but I have let my diary and mail and other plan-making lag. I am going to try to bring everything up even again while in Bombay, and press on, if possible, to something new.

No sooner in our room than Ezekiel arrived with a copy of the January 30 edition of the *Times of India Illustrated Weekly*—one full page devoted to Jean: great joy. Jean was really thrilled. Ezekiel went back to work, Jean and I rested, and at 6:00 P.M. Ezekiel returned for tea and a drive to the Bhulabhai Memorial Institute where the Theatre Unit gave their final performance of *Oedipus.*

Monday, January 31

In the morning to American Express, to buy our air tickets for Madras, and then to Laffans, where I ordered a suit made: I had a great sense of being the leopard changing his spots. We shopped a bit in the Cottage Industries Emporium and Jean went off for her work-out. After lunch we returned to Laffans and I ordered a second suit. Tremendous day! Further work on my diary until 5:15, when we had to begin preparing for Jean's first Bombay event, her reception and lecture-demonstration at the Bhulabhai Institute.

A fine crowd of about one hundred and fifty was at the little place on the roof, and Jean's talk was superb. Mr. Mehta was sitting beside me and leaned over to say: "Lucky there aren't many of these talking dancers going around; for we bookmen would be completely discredited. Why, she's wonderful!"

Tuesday, February 1

All morning arranging matters for Jean's recital: recorder, practice time on the stage, slide projector, U.S.I.S. pictures; and, at 1 P.M., back for lunch. The whole U.S.I.S. set-up is really pretty funny: a large building, lots of people, but no clear program for cultural (as distinguished from political) propaganda. In fact, no-one in the office knows very much about American culture. Alkazi is trying to set up a photographic exhibit of the American modern dance in the lobby of Jean's recital, and so he went around to the U.S.I.S. a few days ago to ask if they had any photos. They offered ballet shots, and he had to explain to them that a new dance form has developed in America. He now has found some photos in the *Borzoi Book of American*

Dance, and they are going to reproduce them for him.

After lunch I returned to work on my diary and at 2 P.M. (now) have arrived, at last, at the point of now. Thank god! I feel that I can go ahead now on my future instead of simply trying to catch up with my past. The Bombay space-platform is about to have served its full purpose.

Jean's discoveries about Indian music make clearer than ever the homology in Indian arts. Two prime matters are involved, the *tāla* and the *rāga.* Each is stated, and the work then continues in the manner of a *theme and variations,* the variations consisting of increasingly intricate, layer-over-layer developments of rhythmical and melodic intricacies. Compare the chapels of the temples of Mt. Abu.

We had an engagement to go visit a Manipuri dance school under the direction of the Jhaveri sisters (whom I had seen perform in the Indian National Theatre production in Ahmedabad). But before we left, a note arrived from a gentleman named Dinshah Malegamvala, who had read my *Hero,* had met Gregor[248] in Trivandrum with Sri Krishna Menon, and wanted to meet me. Mr. Malegamvala himself arrived right after the note, and we sat down for a chat.

Promptly at 5:45 the young men arrived who were to take us to the Manipuri *nartanālaya.* The special performance for Jean's benefit was cute and instructive: first the first year class went through its paces, then the second, then the third, then two prize students, then the Jhaveri sisters themselves, and finally the drummers (actually from Manipuri) in a sequence of about five dances, which came to a climax in the drum dance that I had seen these same fellows perform at Mrs. Sophia Wadia's. It was obvious after what we had already seen of the Indian dance, that Bharata Natyam is a *tāṇḍava* and Manipuri a *lāsya* form of the same art. Jean, apparently, has learned something important for the dance from the idea of the *tālas,* which are long enough (as our four-beat units are not) to permit a dance phrase to develop.

Wednesday, February 2

At five Dinshah Malegamvala arrived to continue the conversation of yesterday: he is an engineer, who began his spiritual quest in Sweden: Krishnamurti and Krishna Menon are chief on his guru list. Krishnamurti, he thinks, lacks love; has an intellectual orientation; takes everything away from his disciples, gives them nothing to cling to, and then castigates them for clinging to him and not understanding. The Ramakrishna monks, he feels, did not have a sound guru, have run off the rails, and have no Vedanta in them. I slightly shocked the gentleman by telling him that I did not feel that

I was searching any more, but was quite satisfied with the richness of the materials and life that I had found: that I was not seeking a guru, but that I should look for Krishna Menon when I go to Trivandrum.

At eight to the Mehtas for a very pleasant evening. Much talk of art, Jean's talk, and Indian religion. Rama told of seeing Krishna Menon go into *samādhi* while watching Ram Gopal dance before an image. Rama also said that she thought I should see Krishnamurti: Mr. Mehta distinguished between Krishnamurti's intellectual and Krishna Menon's *samādhi* approach to truth.

We talked of Ānanda Mayī, and Mr. Mehta pointed out that she had given me the essence of India's teaching when she declared that in *mokṣa* there is no question of affirmation or negation (this is the counterpart of *saṁsāra-nirvāṇa* transcendence). Krishna Menon has pointed out, apparently, that peace of mind and *mokṣa* are not the same—that is, in the *guṇas* we do not have *ātman* experience. The calm mirror, however, reflects *ātman* more clearly, or rather, more obviously for the candidate. The problem of affirmation-negation, passion-dispassion, is one of the path, not of the realization.

Jean and I returned home at about eleven.

Thursday, February 3

Great tension these days over Formosa. Even Mr. Mehta, last evening, took the position against the U.S.A. Nehru in London is supporting the Communist claims. India, from top to bottom, seems to be for China in this thing.

Friday, February 4

Jean's Bombay Recital. Alkazi and the girl who was to be Jean's dresser arrived at breakfast time and drove us to the Jai Hind College Auditorium. Everybody preparing gels for the borders; great work all day. There was a lull from eleven to three, however, while various people did various outside jobs. Late start for rehearsal, hence a couple of slips with the lights during the program. Just before the commencement of the show the Pierrot moon fell from its thin strings, adding a fine motif of strain to the whole affair. Full house, fine response. Gautam was present, to our surprise. There were farewells, and dinner in the Rainbow Room.

Saturday, February 5

Our last day in Bombay: busy and full of surprises. At ten Mr. Malegamvala arrived and took us to the studio of an excellent photographer, R. R. Bharadwaj, who had hundreds of beautiful shots of Indian temple art. After visiting Bharadwaj, we dropped in on Ezekiel for a brief good-bye and a cup of tea—

and discussed a bit the position and work of the U.S.I.S. in India. He told of receiving scads of pamphlets full of speeches by Dulles and various senators. He told also of a handicrafts exhibit in November: third-rate items (no match for India's handicrafts) but a luxurious display, suggesting money, money, money. It made a very bad impression. Actually, the best propaganda for America among the intellectuals were the poetry readings of the Theatre Unit itself—first, of Marianne Moore, then of e.e. cummings. I went to the Bhulabhai Institute to pick up Jean's Pierrot moon, then off to the Gateway of India, to take a boat to Elephanta.

I managed to arrange for a fare of 35 rupees, plus a 5-rupee tip, and off we started. Lovely voyage. At the cave I attempted a few photographs and Jean went around looking at the sculpture. The Maheśvara, she said, scared her a little this time: it was like looking at God. I felt the same thing when I really stood and looked at it.

The sea was choppy, and on the trip home the motor conked out and we were left to drift; but, fortunately, a large launch came along and took us in tow. It went around to the other side of Elephanta, where a lot of engineering equipment was at work. The main occupant of the launch asked us to come in; then he got out, a lot more people got in, and I paid our stupid boatman twenty rupees and they acted as though they'd been shot. The launch started, and we were off for Bombay.

There was a vigorous Englishman aboard with a rich tan, who has been in India as soldier and as engineer since 1938. "Glad to be helping to build the new India." India had gotten into his blood. I thought of the many others of his type, unsung in India's official annals, who have been, and still are, teaching the Orientals how to work like modern man. They will never be appreciated.

Madras

Sunday, February 6 ***Madras***

Yesterday the Swedish liner *Kungsholm* docked in Bombay with a load of millionaires and a number of them were at the airport—simple looking, oldish folks, flying today to various parts of India.[249]

At 12:15 we landed in Madras and were met by Mrinalini's sisters-in-law. We took a car to their compound, and found that we had a whole house to ourselves. We lunched, then continued on to a very colorful sort of National Fair, where we visited a number of the exhibits and watched the wonderful crowds. Madras is very different from Bombay and it's pleasant to be here again—darker people, tropical atmosphere, houses with lots of ground around them, palms and huts of thatch.

Mrinalini's brother we met at dinner time; they took us for a drive around town and at the big temple tank we saw the barge of the Goddess, shining with lights, being poled around the central shrine, where a statue of Śiva was placed in state. It was a lovely, crazy event, with a huge crowd to enjoy it. Tonight the barge goes five times around; tomorrow seven; and the next night nine (in honor of the full moon).

Monday, February 7

After breakfast we were off to see if the U.S.I.S. can arrange for Jean to give a recital in Madras. We met a Mr. Paul Sherbert (much like William King) who took a long time to tell us that nothing could be arranged.

At four we drove to the University to see Dr. Raghavan, who wanted me to give a talk; but I suggested that it would be more interesting if Jean should talk; so, immediately, what had been impossible this morning was settled. Tomorrow we shall go to the Kalakshatra School at Adyar and tomorrow evening to Bala Saraswati's school. Wednesday evening we shall see Bala Saraswati perform.[250] Thursday evening Jean will lecture about American creative dance at the Madras Academy of Music. Friday morning we fly to Delhi—the schedule is full.

At 4:30 we arrived at the Institute of Fine Arts, which is the dance school where the old master Chockalingam Pillai teaches. A delightful two hours and I think I have finally caught onto something about Bharata Natyam.

The dances are hymns in gesture and action—wooing the God, as Christian hymns do, but overtly. Each passage is one verse. The dances are those that were danced by the *devadāsīs* on the dance platform of the temples. Bharata Natyam is thus, emphatically, a religious dance—of a piece with the whole Hindu religious tradition. Performance for a public on the stage is comparable to the singing of Bach's hymns, or medieval hymns, on the concert stage—a major shift of values.

The student learning dance is simultaneously studying and practicing her religion. The strong erotic accent, referred however to the deity, amounts to a sublimation, and in marriage this accent is continued: the husband is worshipped as the god who was wooed. Indeed, he is experienced as the agent or earthly manifestation of the god. The whole sexual theme is thus archetypal—not personal. The effectiveness of this dance, when performed even by children, is constant in character.

There were at least four very good little dancers in the school. The secretary spoke English and explained in detail the meanings of the dances. We had a wonderful afternoon.

Late dinner with Mrinalini's brother's family, the Swaminathans—and to bed.

Tuesday, February 8

In the morning, to the Museum, for a look at the Amarāvatī panels and the bronzes: climax, the great Naṭarāja.[251] Then to the University again for a chat with Dr. Raghavan. Three themes: Indian Dance; Sanskrit, Hindi, and English; and traditional *vs.* modern values.

In the dance of India we have an art descending from the period of Mohenjo-daro.[252] Bharata Natyam was performed in the temples (it still is in some places); but was also a court dance, with different themes; the same dancers were masters of both arts, and were masters also of the art of the dance-theater.

In the first decades of the present century there was an anti-dance campaign; but this has been counteracted recently by an anti–anti-dance movement. Indian dance is greatly popular today, and consequently the forms have been debased, as we see in amateur dancers and movie dancers. The Madras Academy of Music represents the traditional standard, and seeks to maintain them, in spite of the contemporary tide, although many of the dance postures employed in the past are not used today: high kicks, etc. (These are considered unladylike: Dr. Raghavan seemed to approve of the omission). Dance is an emanation of the spirit of music: dance, poetry and music are three facets of a single manifold. Jean added later: the sculptured *naṭarājas* that we had seen this morning were also related in beauty to the art of the dance.

Sanskrit poetry and drama are still being written, devoted to religious themes. Sanskrit is the core language of India's religious culture. In South

India, there is resistance to Hindi; nevertheless, Hindi is more closely related than English to the spirit and character of South Indian thought and language. The resistance will probably break down.

English, however, is a vehicle of scientific thought; consequently, of great importance. But learning English as the major language does violence to the Indian thought-style, divorces the individual from his culture, and places him in a perpetually inferior position to the Englishman, who does not admire his English and represents to him a strongly critical factor. (I thought of the Irish and Americans outdoing the English in their own tongue and not caring a damn for the criticism—but held my peace.)

Raghavan's resentment of the West came out in his statement that our scholars, interested only in India's *ancient* philosophy and art, were trying to represent India as of no contemporary moment. He felt that Nehru's turning away from the past was a reaction against this archaization of India. (I did not mention my own feeling that modern India had nothing to teach the West.) Raghavan's resentment came out further in his contrast of the ancient Indian ideal of womanhood with the modern American. The ancient woman was the mistress of sixty-four arts: not only music and dance, but also cooking, household medicine, etc. His aunt was much better than his wife, who had to keep referring to doctors to cure the children. (I did not point out that in recent years the infant mortality in India had greatly decreased.) Maladjustment in marriage was in ancient India exceptional, whereas in America it is the rule. And what, after all, does the modern, educated woman really know?

Rāma and Sītā decided to share equally the suffering of their separation in the name of their *dharma:* this ideal is in radical contrast to that of the contemporary world. I believe that this is a rather sophisticated rereading of the legend. Sītā was publicly spurned and there is no evidence of any such preliminary consideration and mutual decision as Raghavan's statement implies. I was amused to come across the Rāma and Sītā problem again. Apparently it is one that the Indians are having a hard time resolving.

Raghavan then pointed out, however (and here my own thoughts were echoed) that it was the work of the European scholars that awakened the Indians to the dignity of their own tradition. He believed that India's gift to the world would be the Vedantic *advaita* philosophy, which would transcend, yet at the same time support, all religions.[253] He declared, furthermore, that the great majority of Indian intellectuals were *advaitists.* The sectarian Vaiṣṇava pandits, etc., were a minority. He agreed with Coomaraswamy's position essentially to the effect that all Indian art and music and dance is essentially religious: he differed with the professors (Neogy, for example) who reject this view.

I felt again, beneath the wonderful cordiality of Raghavan, the anti-Western resentment. I feel it equally in the household that we are at present inhabiting, where it is curiously out of place; for these are extremely Westernized people. They speak of the very bad impression that the American army made; of the futility of modern medicine (whereas all are at present in the hands of doctors); of the futility of speed and modern methods (in their own bathroom, quaintly enough, in spite of the fairly modern plumbing, one has to bathe from buckets, as though at a village well).

Mrs. Swaminathan spoke with great disfavor of Aubrey Menen's *Life of Rama*, which she had not read, but about which there is, apparently, much talk in these parts. Raghavan's reference to Rāma may have been a reaction to Menen's book. Sacred things, she felt, should not be held up to mockery. No Voltaire for India. Apparently, Menen's book is about the first of its kind.

One can say, perhaps, that the crux of the West-East problem is in the mutual fascination and repugnance of India and America. As Zimmer pointed out, India came to a crossroad in the sixth century B.C. that we in the West are just approaching: that of the step from dualism to *advaita*.[254] But equally (and even more obviously) we in the West passed a crossroad five hundred years ago, that India is now approaching—that of the rationalization of human life, which leads to the machine world of science and the sense of a social conscience.

Raghavan spoke with fervor of the virtues of the great group family, where a sort of social security was supplied to the ne'er-do-well. The great fault of this system, however, was that the social conscience operated only within the horizon of the family. The poor family was left to be poor.

At five we drove to the Music Academy to see Bala Saraswati teach a dance class. We had been told that she was old and fat—actually, we found a woman of about the age and plumpness of the people who had been telling us she was old and fat: in her forties, and moderately sleek; very likely what would have been found dancing in the temples in the older days. The Music Academy, where she teaches, is housed in an old mansion. Some of the officers were present; and before the classes started we heard a good deal about the bad state of the dance in modern India: lots of people who want to learn quickly, no-one willing to take the necessary time.

Bala Saraswati demanded three years of her student for the learning of the fundamentals, seven years were required for the making of a perfect dancer. She taught her little class of four with careful attention—and, immediately, both Jean and I could see that her approach to the task was much more serious than that of the school that we visited yesterday. Attention was directed exclusively to the feet and arms (no neck yet or *abhināya*). Steps were executed in three speeds (six, on one occasion) and on all sides, in various rhythms. When the class was half over a tiny thing appeared for her special, introductory lesson in the movement of the feet. Bala Saraswati drew a little rectangle on the floor in chalk, and the child tried to remain within it. For about ten minutes she followed the counts, in the turned-out *plié* of the Bharata Natyam. Then her lesson was over and she scooted from the room, returned to say thank you to teacher, and scooted again.

Dr. Raghavan's daughter of seven years, who was the best in the class, was a lovely little thing to see. She reminded me perfectly of one of those *apsarases* in photographed frieze of Angkor Thoṁ.

When the dance class was ended we drove to a large tent-covered area where a great male singer was performing, in honor of the thousandth anniversary of Avicenna.[255] The man's voice was considerably better than that of the chap who sang in Bombay, but his chief accompanying instrument was a harmonium—so that, finally, the musical tones were not particularly agreeable. On the way home, Mrs. Swaminathan talked of the music: how the singer had been sent a note requesting more popular, less classical themes, and so, had sung a series of *ghazals* in Urdu: the best language in the world for love poetry; and how, since the restrictions on action are so strong in the Orient, the whole weight of love gets into words.

Wednesday, February 9

We went in the morning to Adyar to the Theosophical Library, to meet Radha (dancer in *The River*) Bournier[256] and Danielou.[257] We had a pleasant talk in the main entrance hall around a little wicker table. Radha was a pupil of Chockalingam Pillai, and declared that he too could teach seriously, like Bala Saraswati; but most of his pupils want to learn in a year, and so he makes concessions.

We spent the afternoon napping and writing letters, then, at about 5:00 P.M., had tea on the lawn with Mrs. Swaminathan's sister, who accompanied us back to the Music Academy for an evening of dance by Bala Saraswati. A supreme event. Bala Saraswati had sent for her best drummer and musicians; her dance class and the members of the Academy were present; Jean was the chief member of the audience and Dr. Raghavan interpreted all of the performances for her. The recital lasted from 6:15 to 9:00. I could have sat for another three hours.

We learned, that, when performing *abhināya*, the dancer improvises verse after verse upon a theme (e.g. "she was beautiful") that is repeated *ad infinitum* by the singer. Another example of the Indian "Variations on a Theme" pattern of composition. Cumulative pantomime.

Thursday, February 10

Spent the morning shopping and writing letters. Jean practiced dancing a bit on the porch of the house we are inhabiting, and, at four, with the dance equipment in a bag, we went out to Adyar again to visit Radha and Bournier. Danielou came as company. They have a perfectly beautiful house on a beach, handsomely furnished. And I felt, for the first time since I've been in India (Ahmedabad, of course, excluded) that I had found a house in which it would be a delight to dwell. We had a very pleasant tea, during the course of which Bournier exhibited a beautiful camera that he had recently purchased, and then he drove Jean and me to the Music Academy where Jean delivered her lecture demonstration before a company—seated on three sides of her—which commenced as a company of a dozen or so and ended with about fifty. Most odd was a bearded gentleman of seventy-two, who tried to tell us, when the talk was over, about some dance that he'd seen, where the dancer stood on a needle with the needle piercing his eyeball—or something of the sort.

Jean had been a bit scared about this lecture all day, feeling that Madras is the conservative center of the classical Indian dance; but she found a warmly sympathetic audience before her—including Bala Saraswati and her mother. She lectured for about an hour and then performed *Creature on a Journey* and *Ophelia.*

Mrs. Swaminathan then drove us to dinner at the home of a gentleman who had been in a Japanese prison camp in Burma during the war, had had one whole side of his face shot away and plastically restored, and now was married to an extremely Protestant lady with white hair. I found that I was in a veritable nest of Protestant zeal. When a queer gent named Alexandrovitch asked me what my subject was and I replied "Mythology, which for me means religion," a hot argument opened—mainly to the effect that Christian theology had nothing to do with mythology. "The creation and fall in the Garden of Eden is mythology," I replied. "But that is not Christianity!" the hostess said. "Theology is based on Aristotle: it is a science," said Mr. Alexandrovitch. Apparently, I had run into something really queer here: some Protestant notion of Christianity minus the motif of Fall-and-Redemption. These people seemed never to have heard of the Christianity of the Middle Ages.

Before going to bed we packed, in preparation for an early departure by plane in the morning.

New Delhi

Friday, February 11 ***New Delhi***

At 2:45 A.M. there was a knock at the door: our bearer and his wife, who thought the time was 5:00 A.M. At 5:00 A.M. they knocked again and we got up. It has been a bit weird living in this house: two watchmen sleep right outside our windows and greet us like spooks every time we move in or out. Our hostesses were present to see us off. Mrs. Swaminathan even drove with us to the airport—all dressed up in her early-morning riding-breeches.

With pauses at Hyderabad and Nagpur, our flight arrived at New Delhi at 3:15. Bus to the Imperial Hotel, tea on the lawn. Letters and a rest. Then to Mrs. Adams, for news of the plans that have been made for the recital. Apparently Fabri and Mrs. Adams have not been able to get along together at all—but the plans have nevertheless developed; as follows: tomorrow a lecture at the University, next day a reception and lecture at Lady Irwin College, and on Tuesday the great recital. Sheilu came to see us at the hotel just before dinner, and Jean—who had just discovered that she had left her black leotard, which is worn in the first dance on her program, somewhere in Madras—made a date with her for tomorrow morning, to hunt for material. The trouble is that in India they have no stretchy jersey: all of their clothes are made to be draped.

Saturday, February 12

We met Sheilu at the store at ten. I left them and went around to the U.S.I.S. office to have a chat with William King. He took me to the Alps for coffee and discussed the problem of the U.S.I.S. and A.N.T.A.[258] Briefly, A.N.T.A. seems to be taking the lead from the Show Biz people in New York and is trying to use the U.S.I.S. as ticket agents for large companies that would be utterly useless in the Orient, for instance the Jubilee Singers or the N.B.C. Symphony Orchestra of ninety pieces—there is no place for them. Much better would be ninety separate artists like Jean. He wants me to send him a report of *our* findings in India. Also, he is interested in knowing more about the Bollingen Series for the U.S.I.S. libraries.

While Jean and I were having lunch in the Imperial Krishnan arrived in a highly emotional state and stayed with us while we packed and drove out to the Cecil. We hurried then to the University, where Jean gave a superb lecture demonstration to a group of about five hundred students at the University of Delhi. One of the lady teachers held a tea party for Jean right after the lecture, and we hurried then to the Kings' for a drink (Krishnan still at hand). The Kings drove us home, dropping Krishnan at Connaught Circle, and soon after dinner we went to bed.

Sunday, February 13

We managed to soothe the greatly ruffled feathers of our difficult friend Fabri when we arrived at his house at ten. Then we all moved on to Lady Irwin College, where Jean gave another superb lecture demonstration on the lawn. Among those present was our exchange student from Sarah Lawrence. "How do you like it?" I asked her. She shook her head. The restrictions are those of a girls' boarding school and the courses about on the high school level. Sarah Lawrence College has made a bad bargain here, I believe.

Tuesday, February 15

The great day of the recital. Jean and I got to the theater at about eleven and Jean had a good morning of dance. The rehearsal was supposed to begin at one but practically no one arrived. By two the man working the recorder wanted to go out for lunch. Jean and I went out with Fay King to have a good meal and Fay helped Jean with her sewing—donating a black zipper to the good work. We returned to the theater at four and I conducted a light and music run-through till 6:15, when we had to let the crowd into the theater. The house has been sold out for two days. About three hundred people were turned away at the door. Great pleas for a second recital were reluctantly ignored (no time). Jean danced greatly and had a good time doing it. Dinner, after the recital, was at the Adams'. Finally we got home, delighted.

Wednesday, February 16

Narayan Menon in *The Times of India* gave Jean an excellent review. Fabri's, in the *Statesman,* was all messed up with a poor attempt to make connections between the Modern Dance and the Ballet. We went around to Fabri's after breakfast and he was all apologies, yet stated clearly the critic's credo: "Some day, Jean," he said, "I will write a good review of you, showing all that's good in your work and all that's wrong, and making suggestions." He complained that there was not enough mugging in *Ophelia* and spoke of various ballets where the facial expressions were as important as in the Indian dance. "My expression," said Jean, "is in my whole body."

Thursday, February 17

"Shall I stay?" said Jean. It was very sad, as though a hole had opened through the floor of our busily programmed life together to show the possibility of another level of relationship.

At nine Krishnan arrived with the bed roll we had left with him at the time of the Republic Day visit. Narasimhan arrived with a friend to present Jean with a carved box and take a photo of us. We had breakfast, finished packing, drove with Krishnan to Fabri's to pick up Ratna, who then spent the morning helping Jean shop. We left Krishnan at Jaipur House and bought tons of beautiful stuff. Then we had to buy a suitcase for Jean to carry it all home. Fabri arrived at the Cecil for lunch and at 2:15, breathless, and we got into our taxi and drove to the B.O.A.C. office, where Krishnan met us, and saw us off on the bus. Long drive to the airport. Long wait in the airport. Plane departure at 5:10.

Jean was in her nice red Honolulu dress and we snapped pictures of each other while we waited. I accompanied her to the stairs to the plane. After she got aboard I could see her through the door until the stewardess closed it. Then the big thing taxied around and down the long track, turned, warmed up, and started. I watched it leave the ground, make a long U turn, and cruised away into the blue, until it became only a flashing dot and disappeared.

I went back to New Delhi in the bus. I went to the Volga for a farewell dinner with Krishnan, who was excessively emotional at the moment of parting. I drove Krishnan to his home and proceeded to the Fabris' for a farewell moment. Then home to pack, and to bed at two. I leave in the morning for Cochin, via Bombay.

Friday, February 18 ***Bombay***

When I woke this morning my chief adjunct was a very heavy head cold. I arrived in Bombay at about two and I went directly to the Airlines office to buy my tickets to Cochin and through to Trivandrum—I am not sure yet to which one I should go first. Later in the afternoon I went to the Bhulabhai Institute for a farewell to the Theatre Unit crowd. They handed me three hundred rupees—Jean's share of the net (their share, 195). Ezekiel told me, also, of an attempt that John Cage is making to get himself, Merce Cunningham, and five others to India on an A.N.T.A. junket: promised support by Virgil Thompson. News for Jean!

A Guru and His Devotees

Cochin and Trivandrum

Saturday, February 19 ***Cochin–Trivandrum***

I caught the plane to Cochin at 6:30 A.M. At Cochin I asked to continue to Trivandrum, where I arrived at about 11:30. I am definitely in the tropics. At first I felt a slight spell of elation at commencing the next stage of my journey. After lunch, however, I took a rickshaw to the Post Office, to mail my letter to Jean, send her a wire, and post some books to New York I got tired waiting to register the books—everyone pushing in ahead of me. I suddenly lost all my euphoria, and felt sort of at the bottom of the well: a fierce din of loudspeakers all over town, Indian music till I thought my head would split.

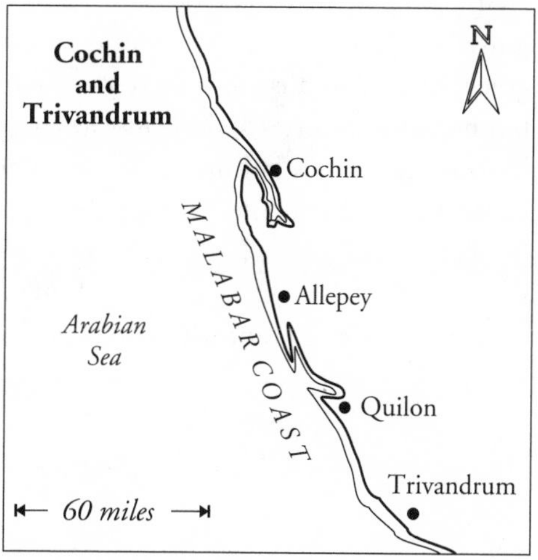

I took a nap and went to work on my diary. Later I took a walk to town to see what was making all the noise, and found an All-India Exposition in progress and several other events besides. I returned at 9:30 to bring my diary up to date, and now, at last, at 10:00 P.M. I am here. Jean right now (11:30 New York time) must be in the Customs at Idlewild Airport. Adventure finis.

Sunday, February 20—Jean's birthday ***Trivandrum***

What I had in mind, coming down here yesterday, was that I should meet Sri Krishna Menon. As soon as I arrived, however, I realized that I did not know where or how to get in touch with him. I realized, also, that if I am going to see Cochin, I should have stopped there on the way down. All of these mistakes gave me the feeling that I had begun to make mistakes—that is to say, had run off the rails. Furthermore, way down here, all of my pleasant Indian connections are broken. I have only the name of Nissim Ezekiel's brother in Cochin and a friend of Jason Grossman here in Trivandrum. I don't know what I expected to find when I set out on his southern spree, but certainly, if I had thought twice I should have proceeded more carefully and written ahead.

However, this morning, in spite of the heavy cold in my head, I feel that it may be possible to make something out of this wrong move, after all. Today I shall simply do the regular tourist act: visit the town and take a drive to Cape Comorin. I have dropped a note to Grossman's friend, who will receive the note tomorrow. And meanwhile, tomorrow morning I can pay a visit to the U.S.I.S. office, to see if they can help me discover the wise man, Sri Krishna Menon.

The hotel in which I am staying takes me back in feeling to the first stages of my India journey—though it is definitely more tropical in atmosphere than anything that I have encountered so far. Yesterday, while flying, after our plane had come down for a brief pause in Belgaum, I had a strong sense of the change in the world below. The predominant tone became green, instead of dust, and there were acres of neatly squared off rice fields—but no villages. Instead, the houses were scattered among the fields—more as in America than as in Europe. Wooden houses, wooden temple compounds, became prominent, and palms, palms, palms, were everywhere.

Over Mangalore, I could see the harbor that St. Thomas is supposed to have entered; the harbor that the Romans must have known: a break in the endless beach at a point where four or five streams converge to enter the sea.

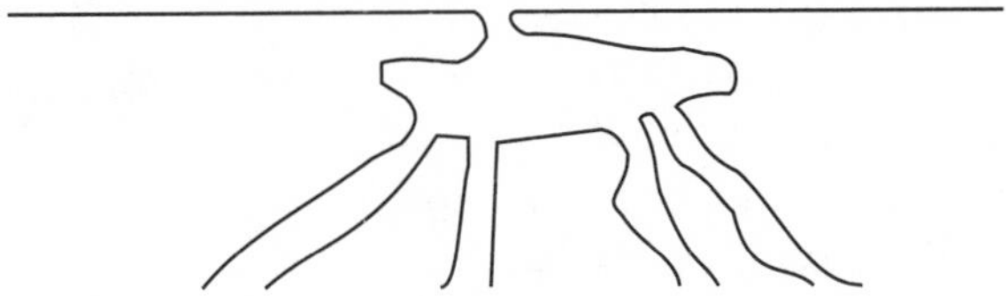

And over Cochin I beheld a most remarkable landscape: thousands of acres of palm gardens, geometrically marked out in rectangles, and flooded, it seemed, with great sheets of water: the closest thing I have seen to the air view above Basra. There the palms were date; here coconut.

Trivandrum is a rather large, pleasantly clean city, and the Mascot a neat, orderly hotel, with its two floors of rooms strung along a long, two-storeyed verandah. The populace of the hotel is of two kinds: one, very silent, solitary business people from Europe, America, and India; the other, very silent, spiritually shocked Americans, here, undoubtedly, to be cured by the sage of Trivandrum. All have elaborate food taboos, which are driving the hotel proprietor to distraction. The male and female at the table facing mine were seen to eat only raw vegetables and fruits, but they feed their tiny, hairless dog red meat. The stunned gentleman whose room is not far from mine on the top balcony, and whom I have seen sitting with his eyes closed, holding a thin book of what look like translated *ślokas*, will eat practically nothing at all. Eggs, apparently, are taboo to him, and so he can't even eat pudding.

After breakfast I went around to the Indian Airlines office to pick up a taxi that had been arranged for yesterday evening: I was to see the town in the morning and drive to Cape Comorin in the afternoon. I found, however, that my driver had no notion of what to take one to see in the town, and so I settled for the zoo and the museum, only a couple of blocks from the hotel.

The zoo was a pretty but pitiful affair, full of sad and solitary bears, tigers, snakes, etc., in excessively smelly cages. One leopard, who had been only five days in captivity, was still full of spirit, however, and snarled and pounced really mightily, when the guard annoyed him. The lion next door would answer commands like a dog. And the largest of the tigers was permitted to go down into a grassy yard and roam as though wild.

The museum had a fine collection of bronzes, undated, including two figures that seemed to me most remarkable: a very tall and thin Śiva Ardhanārīśvara,[259] and a Śiva carrying a dead Satī on his left shoulder. I bought the only pictures the museum had of these pieces, but they are very poor.

At two, I commenced my drive to Cape Comorin, somewhat frightened by the fierceness of my heavy cold, but gradually improving in spirits as the drive proceeded. The land and village world remind me of Hawaii and what I have seen of African photos: typical coconut and palm thatch country. The bullock carts, however, were typically Indian, only filled now, with coconuts and coconut husks. On the left, as we drove southward, were the high mountains, at some distance.

The first, very interesting, stop was at a great palace, in the particular style of this part of the world, called Padmanābhapuram. The supervisor took me all through the long corridors and up the narrow stairs to the various chambers. An architecture of wonderful woodwork (teak and jackfruit), supplemented in certain parts by columns of stone, shaped and carved to resemble the wood. It dated from the fourteenth to seventeenth centuries.

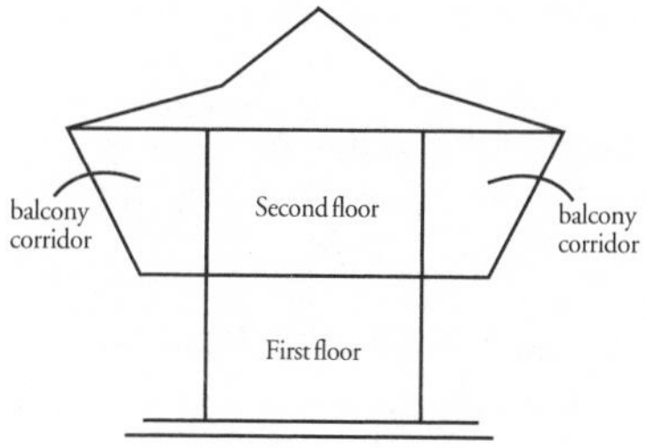

In the audience chamber the king sat with four ministers. And in a series of paintings in one of the corridors, the king was shown, weighing himself against gold (his weight in gold was then distributed to the brahmins), and going to bathe ceremonially in a huge golden jar.

The palace is immense, and part of it, now, is a museum containing some interesting examples of South Indian stone and wooden sculpture. Most unusual: a form of Kālī as the killer of children, biting off the head of a child; also, Nandi with human torso and legs, seated; and a large Kubera, looking very much like the late Javanese *yakṣas.*

My second stop was at the temple of Sucindrum, where one of the several pandas opened a shed to show me the vast, nine-wheeled, elaborately carved wooden car and sold me a fantastic pamphlet, *The Holy Account of Sucindrum, or The Triumph of Chastity,* containing the legend of the origin of this place.

Finally, I arrived at Cape Comorin, "the Land's End of India," had tea in the pleasant rest house, bought a few photos, and strolled down to the shore. The big thing here is the sunset. And as I walked to see it, I was greeted by a Spanish-looking couple named Lopez, he being chief police inspector of Trivandrum. This man was charming and cordial—a Catholic. More than 25% of the population in this area is Catholic.

And now, a nice theme: In the Hindu temple at Cape Comorin is an image of the Goddess Kumārī, with a diamond in her forehead that shines so brightly that it has misled ships onto the rocks. The door is now closed on her at night, for the protection of seamen. On another prominence there is an image of the Virgin Mary—two aspects of the same archetypal figure.

It occurs to me that in discussing deities one must distinguish between the archetypal and the legendary aspects. Archetypally these two Virgins are one; but their legends and historical-cultural context are totally different.

After viewing a lovely sunset from a high mound of blown and rippled sand, I bade good-bye to the Lopezes, returned home in the car, had dinner at the hotel, took two Cosavil pills, and retired.

Monday, February 21

A nice wire from Jean: "Entire trip smooth. Message makes birthday happy. Love." My cold being greatly improved, and knowing that Jean was safely home, I felt much better than yesterday and game to go on.

Last night, when I returned for dinner, I overheard a comical conversation at the next table between a rather sophisticated English homosexual gentleman and the American who will eat no eggs.

"I'm so exhausted," said the American, "from my dreams. You know, it's all there! Life! The whole thing. I wake up so exhausted!"

"Yes?" said the Englishman. "Well, that must keep you from doing all sorts of exhausting things, then, in the day."

During the course of their conversation I heard the Englishman mention the name of Gregor; so when I got up, I introduced myself and asked him to let Gregor know that I am here. Funny funny! Once again, this pattern of Chance developing my journey. Gregor and this whole crowd, I believe, are in the circle of the sage.

There is a large athletic stadium right next to the hotel. Saturday afternoon there was a track meet in progress there; this morning the R.O.T.C. of the University, together with the Police and a patch of young women in white, were having a military review there. The Occident, again, in full force.

At about 11:30 I went around to the U.S.I.S. library to meet the Otwells; only Barbara Otwell was present; and when I spoke to her about Krishna Menon, she drove me to the place where all the devotees dwell: a large mansion, called Vidyuth, in a part of town called Poojahura, with a man named Wolter Kurs in charge. Only one couple was present, however; the rest having gone to the airport to speed a parting devotee. Krishna Menon's series of talks for this season concluded last night.

Returning to the hotel, I lay down to rest. A knock: Mr. K. P. Parameswaran Tampi to see me, to whom I had written Saturday. He will call for me at five this evening and take me for a view of the beach. Will also arrange for me to see some dances.

Again I lay down. Knock. Someone downstairs to see me: Gregor, looking calm and peaceful. I may visit the ashram this evening after dinner, and he will try to arrange for me to have a talk with the sage.

After dinner I went to the hostel Vidyuth, where Sri Krishna Menon's Occidental devotees—the males dressed in Indian attire—were seated at dinner. I met them all, a group of about eight, and spent a pleasant evening chatting. My appointment with the Master is set for Thursday, 5 P.M.

The football match between Trivandrum and Russia was immensely attended. One of the spectators said to Mrs. Otwell: "Why doesn't America send a football team to India?" "Well," she said, "we play a different kind of football." "Anyhow," said the man, "You know, the game wouldn't be half as well attended as the Russian."

At the All-India Exhibition, which I visited Sunday evening, there was a large theatrical event in progress. The curtain had, on one side, a large picture of Nehru talking with Gandhi, and, on the other, one of Stalin talking with Lenin. (This, I think, is the strongest line-up so far.)

Tuesday, February 22

After breakfast, I took a taxi to Mr. Tampi's and then, with him as guide, went on a considerable tour of the town. First, with his brother in the car, we drove to the art gallery, where I was given the VIP treatment and saw a large, nicely hung collection of the usual book-illustration styles. Tampi and I drove next to the beach, while I paused, here and there, to take photographs—particularly among the fishermen, who were hauling in their nets.

Fishermen near Trivandrum.

Finally, Mr. Tampi brought me to a school and orphanage, where I watched the youngsters working at hand looms, doing their lessons, and finally eating U.N. food. I was handed literature about the institution and departed at one for lunch. Everywhere, this expectation of money from the U.S.A.: would the Rockefellers be interested? And meanwhile, this love affair with China and Russia. I continue to find it repulsive. (I have been told that at the Republic Day reception, Nehru confined his attentions to the Chinese: no one else, not even the Russians, could come near him.)

After lunch I napped—and was awakened by a rap at the door: some man who wants me to give money to some sort of young men's association. I spent the better part of the afternoon on my verandah writing letters, and at about five was approached by the gentleman who eats raw vegetables, offering to loan me a little book, *Atma-darshan,* by Sri Krishna Menon. The gentleman's name is Woodland Kahler, and he is an officer in the World Vegetarian Association, visiting India, to organize a branch here. He and his wife, who is a Russian, took up vegetarianism eight years ago, and learned to eschew New York, alcohol, cigarettes, and night clubs. I recalled having heard about this couple in Bombay, from Rama Mehta.

After dinner, I was again sitting on the verandah, when the other vegetarian gentleman approached and invited me to go with him to Vidyuth for a party they were having. I spent most of the evening there talking with Arthur Gregor, who has been greatly stirred and inspired by the Indian philosophy that he has learned from Krishna Menon.

Wednesday, February 23

After lunch I slept and wrote letters. Had a lovely, absolutely lazy afternoon. The weather is hot, hot, and hot. Immediately after dinner I went to bed.

Thursday, February 24

Morning tea, breakfast, and an expedition to the Post Office, and then letters and naps until 12:30, when I went to Vidyuth for lunch.

I have been reading the second booklet of Sri Krishna Menon, *Atma-Nirvriti (Freedom and Felicity in the Self)* and I find in it, besides a good, clear statement of the Vedantic idea of the world as pure consciousness, the following well-stated formulae:

> In between thoughts and in the deep-sleep state shines that principle to which the word "I" points.... When the mind is directed to it, it changes into that, losing the characteristics of mind. This is called *samādhi.*
>
> I am pure happiness. All the activities of the sense-organs and the mind aim at happiness. Thus all their activities are *pūjā* done to Me.
>
> Since feelings rise and set in peace, their *svarūpa* is peace. Since thoughts rise and set in knowledge, their *svarūpa* is knowledge. Deep peace and pure knowledge are one and the same thing. Different names are given to it because it is looked at from different angles.
>
> A sage knows well that consciousness is self-luminous and that it is consciousness that illumines the entire world. He knows also that his real nature is consciousness and experience and cannot as such be known or experienced. Hence he does not desire or make any attempt to know or experience it. The sage knows from the deepest conviction that he is consciousness and that he has attained what has to be attained.[260]

Considering my own position, I think that this last paragraph just about states it; with the addition, however, that since what appears to the waking consciousness to be thought and action is actually nothing but consciousness and experience, I am willing to become as though lost in thought and action, knowing all the time that therein is consciousness and experience: *saṁsāra* and *nirvāṇa* being one and the same.

My visit to the sage of Trivandrum is to be linked in the context of this diary, with the conversations that I had with Dr. Maiti in Ahmedabad: for I am here in contact with the actual meaning and content of the *ātman-Brahman* concept.[261]

And I have chosen to meet this sage, rather than another, because he *seems,* at any rate, to represent a life pattern rather closer to that of the married sages of the Upanishads than to that of the life-and-flesh despising monks whom I have known.

Looking forward to the meeting, I have no idea, either what to expect, or what to say; but I dare say the meeting itself will disclose its proper logic.

I went to Vidyuth for lunch, and spent the first part of the afternoon chatting with Arthur Gregor and his friends beneath a tree; then, got into a taxi with Arthur and arrived at the dwelling of Sri Krishna Menon. Two old gentlemen—one, with his full beard and white dhoti, looking much like an ancient *ṛṣi*—stood on the porch and wagged their heads in welcome, signifying that we were to proceed immediately upstairs. I went up first, and the guru, in his white dhoti and with a cloth over his right shoulder, moved back from the stair-rail to receive us. Arthur introduced me and disappeared; the guru signalled to three chairs facing his own and I chose the middle one. We sat in a large and airy room and I said that I had come to him to learn whether I was right in thinking that the monastic revulsion from life was not altogether consonant with the sense of the Upanishads, where it appeared that all is *Brahman*, and where the way of the householder was not despised.

He replied that for some the way of *sannyāsī* was correct and for others that of the *gṛhasthī*—and that if the way of the *gṛhasthī* could be incorrect that of the *sannyāsī* could also be incorrect. As for my view of the Upanishadic teaching, it was perfectly correct. The true meaning of renunciation, he declared, was that one must renounce all thoughts and things in the contemplation of *ātman*: that is the meaning of one-pointed contemplation.

He went on to speak of the three states of waking, dream, and deep sleep—the latter not one of ignorance but of pure consciousness. In that state one "knows nothing" except "peace." The term "knows nothing" does not here mean ignorance, as some aver; it means, rather, that all else has fallen away save only that state of pure consciousness, which is peace.[262]

We are in our true state (*ātman*) every night in sleep, but also during the period of waking consciousness every time we are "between two thoughts."

At this point I made the sign of *namaskāra*. Twenty minutes had elapsed.

The *ātman* is never bound, the *ātman* is never released, he said; it is always free.

The way of self-identification with this *ātman* he called the "direct approach," in contrast to the "cosmic approach," which is the way of seeking *Brahman* in the world.

The way of discovering *ātman* while remaining in the world, he declared, was the way of the *Gītā.*

I asked whether there were many in India today teaching this heroic way, and he answered that there were only one or two, and named a couple of names which I did not catch.

Then I thanked him for his teaching and went down the stairs to find gathered outside the company many of those who were about to go in to him for their group meeting. Arthur helped me into my shoes and walked me a way up the road; then suggested that I might join them all at the India Coffee House, and returned to his group.

I started slowly walking home, but a bit of rain came, so I took a rickshaw the rest of the way; took a bath and settled to these notes.

Sri Krishna Menon was a very gentle and eloquent teacher, of about seventy, not stingy at all with his words, and directly telling, it seemed to me, in everything that he said. It was a memorable half hour—and great luck for me, I hear, that I came to Trivandrum when I did. For his doctor has ordered him to rest, now, until June. As Mr. Kahler said to me this morning, I "got in just under the wire."

I feel (I think properly) that my India journey has been perfectly fulfilled.

During the talk in the garden, at Vidyuth, in the earlier part of the afternoon, I told of my feeling on coming to India that my own work now should be from the standpoint of the West, and we discussed, also, something of the anti-American feeling in India. In 1947, they said, America was greatly in favor. The anti-Americanism was pre-Pakistan-aid, however; pre-Korea also; probably commenced with the Chinese Communist victory in China and the debarring of Communist China from the U.N. The atom bombs on Japan also had something to do with it.

After a hot bath and a nap, I started down town, but was met at the hotel gate by Tampi, who had come to say goodbye. He brought me a couple of booklets and we had a brief talk. Then I continued down to the India Coffee Shop, where I met Arthur Gregor and a couple of the disciples of the guru, including a Jewish couple from the Argentine named Gutman—he a tall thin man with a large rudder of a nose, she a handsome, dark young woman. I thought at first that they were from New York.

The company told me that Krishna Menon had been "very happy" after his conversation with me—had said that if I were not leaving he would teach me for five days, even in spite of his doctor's orders—that I was very close to full understanding. This made me feel very good: I immediately decided, however, not to stay: it was a quick decision and I do not know whether it was a wise one, but I did not feel that I wished to press the guru beyond his doctor's orders. I think that what he gave me today will be enough for me.

After coffee, we returned to Vidyuth for dinner and then sat out on the lawn again. Presently, the gentlemen whom I had heard talking about Gregor in the hotel dining room Sunday evening arrived—John Levy—and the conversation became simply ghastly. Levy is a perfect Virgil Thompson type of pontificating gas bag—except that he knows a good deal less and consequently is even more abusive of everything and everyone but himself and his two or three ideas. His chatter, combined with Gutman's remarks, almost sufficed to ruin the day. As I left, Arthur Gregor said: "The followers! Aren't they awful?"

I returned to my hotel at about 12:30 and went directly to bed, saving my packing till tomorrow.

Friday, February 25 ***Cochin***

Six months anniversary of my departure from New York. I am debating in my mind whether to return from Cochin to Trivandrum if Krishna Menon is *really* willing to talk to me five more times. After packing I was invited down the verandah to chat with the man who is having so much trouble with his dreams, Benjamin Jerome. His foster father is a medium and he had two hours full of stories to run out to me before I finally told him I had to finish packing. Climax: a watch that he had made for him in Zürich with three extra scales indicating his biological rhythms: good and bad periods a) physically, b) emotionally, c) mentally—rhythms of 28 and 23 days. Someone for Mr. Belk, I should say![263] His principal series of experiences appears to have taken place during his visit to Brazil, where, on one occasion, Presidents Monroe and Lincoln stood at his side and dictated a speech to him.

I left my friend to finish my packing and step over to the Airlines office. Presently one of the young people from Vidyuth arrived, Wolter Kurs, a tall, thin Dutchman, who has been very sweet to me—read my *Hero* some time ago and has treated me as an honored guest. He took a snapshot and boarded the bus with me to the airport. There we found Arthur Gregor and a nice little French lady. While we sat waiting, Kurs put a garland around my neck. I was given a charming send off—and some forty minutes later came down in Cochin, to be greeted by Nissim Ezekiel's handsome, dark brother, Joseph.

Cochin is really delightful. The resort-like Malar Hotel is on Willingdon

Island, around which the whole port is folded, and boats, sail boats, cargo-skiffs, steamers, and naval vessels are passing to and fro all the time. Joseph, at the airport, told me that he would call for me about six; so I rode to the hotel in the bus, had lunch, admired the place, and took a nap in my large room, with its windows opening onto the port. Cargo skiffs going past all the time. Shortly after teatime, Joseph arrived, and we chatted a while about Cochin.

He and his brother Nissim, are of the ben Israel Jews, who are supposed to have landed on the coast near Bombay (shipwrecked on the way to Cochin?) about 2,000 years ago. The Jews of Cochin, too, have been in India some 2,000 years. They constitute a small, inbred, diminishing group: many of the girls have to look forward to no marriage. The Cochin Jews have held to the typical Jewish life pattern of the merchant; the Jews of the north became, first, oil-pressers then agriculturalists, and when the British came many entered military service. Nissim could easily pass for a New York Jew: Joseph, however, is too dark for that. Otherwise, he is un-Indian in appearance: Jewish wavy hair, for example.

Joseph talked about Cochin: a number of Chinese traits appear in this neighborhood which do not occur in other parts of India. Chinese sun hats on the boatmen (I have already seen a number), Chinese-type fishing nets, Chinese peppers, Chinese-style roofs. There seems to be some relationship, also, between the Jews of Cochin and those of China.

After watching the sun set like a red ball behind the roofs of the area (Cochin Fort and the Jewish quarter) just across the channel, we walked to a boatlanding and took a rowboat to that part of the city (now quite dark), to visit the home of one of the leading Jews of Cochin, Sotta Koder.

A large, spacious house near the water, with a great deal of dark woodwork. One entered, and immediately faced a large staircase going up to the living rooms, a plaster swan at either side of the stairs: on the right with the neck down and stretched forward, on the left with it arched. Upstairs, we were greeted by a fat, middle-aged, absolutely Jewish woman with a Christian Indian guest (Syrian Christian). The host, Mr. Koder, entered: also fat, with a particular, relaxed and casual, Jewish charm. Everything distinctly and absolutely Jewish—we could have been in Brooklyn. We stayed for dinner—Friday night's orthodox meal: Grace was read in Hebrew (in a relaxed and mumbling, but learned style); Jewish foods and wine (grape juice because of the prohibition here) were served, with salt on chunks of bread. Finally, grace after eating, read again (at great length) from the book. Mr. Koder and Joseph put on Jewish skull-caps for the meal: here, however, not black—because black and white here mean mourning—but amusingly colorful. After the meal, Joseph sang, in sweet-tenor, from a little notebook in which Mrs. Koder had written the words of many songs: *La Paloma, Santa Lucia, Blue Danube,* etc. etc. She seemed to love to have singing going on, and kept insisting that I should add my frog's croak to the symphony. Joseph and I returned to Willingdon Island in the Koder's car, via the bridge, at about 11:30 P.M.

My conversation with Joseph included an account of my visit with Krishna Menon, whom, I learned, he regards as his guru. Again, at the Koder's, this theme came up, and Mr. Koder asked me what I thought of the man. (Koder knows John Levy very well).[264] It seems there is a lot of unfavorable, as well as favorable, talk in India about Krishna Menon. He has a gold watch. He smokes English cigarettes (sent to him by John Levy). My guess is that the traditional Indian idea that a holy man has to be a *sannyāsī* is responsible for this talk; whereas the whole point of Krishna Menon's teaching is that the household can be enlightened even while living the householder's life. He pointed out to me, in our brief talk, that in the Upanishads we read of yogis and *sannyāsīs* going to Kings to learn the truth.[265] The way of the ascetic, in fact, can be a false way, since it may stress negation, denial, world-splitting, not as a way, merely, but as a final term.

This noon at the airport, Arthur and Wolter told me some more of what Krishna Menon had said about his talk with me. He had said that he would be glad to talk with me if I came again, but that as far as my own realization was concerned it would not matter: I was already very close and would get there, presently, on my own.

When I boarded the plane I had the idea that I would return and then go to Ceylon via Madura, etc., by train; but on arriving in Cochin I found that it would be impossible to clear my papers here. I shall have to go to Madras. That cuts out Trivandrum. I shall have to pack off to Madras on Sunday, by plane, if I am to get to Ceylon within the time stipulated on my visa.

And so that half hour with Krishna Menon, yesterday, is to be the extent of my meeting with him. Somehow, it seems to me appropriate that that should be so. This whole visit has been a kind of touch-and-go affair—with each touch sufficing to fix for me a great context of ideas. The chief value of my conversation with Krishna Menon is that it assures me that my own reading of the teaching coincides with the authority of at least one Indian sage, and that, simultaneously, that sage pointed out to me a simple and basic formula of contemplation (*turīya* in deep sleep: "one's own glory" between two thoughts)[266] through which a stand in the Self might be readily attained and established. I know, furthermore, that the conversation and image of the teacher in his room of teaching will remain very clearly in my mind. I was pretty well concentrated during the entire talk.[267]

Saturday, February 26

Joseph had told me last evening that he would come to the hotel at 9:00; at 10:30 he phoned to say that he had been detained at the office and would arrive at about 11:00. (India again!) Thus I lost the morning. I made arrangements to fly tomorrow to Madras and took a few pictures of passing craft.

In the course of the conversation at Vidyuth, two nights ago, when John Levy and a Mr. Gutmann were throwing their weight around—or rather were using their guru as a club with which to batter Suzuki, and everybody else—Gutmann challenged me to name any figure in the West who might be compared to the Indian sage. I named C. G. Jung.

"But Jung does not claim," he replied, "to show you the Truth."

I have thought of this a bit, and believe that, essentially, the idea of integration amounts to one of illumination about the Self: it has to do with a realization of truth. Our Western word Truth, however, tends to refer to some sort of Object; hence it cannot be used properly in this context—and indeed it translates the Indian terms inaccurately. It is, so to say, only a figure of speech when the Indian sage speaks of revealing Truth. Even the formula, *satyam eva jayati,* is figurative; cannot be literally true if by *satya* the transcendent (the ineffable) is connoted.

Joseph arrived at about 11:00 and took me, by rowboat, across the channel to Jewtown, where we visited the old Synagogue and one of the Jewish families. On the wall of the synagogue was a list of dates:

Copper plate grant to Joseph Rabban, A.D. 379.
Jews of Cranganore in touch with China, A.D. 900.
First Synagogue A.D. 1345
Moors *vs.* Cranganore Jews A.D. 1565
Cranganore Jews flee to Jewtown, Cochin, A.D. 1567.
Build Synagogue A.D. 1568.
Synagogue decorated with Chinese tiles and the clock tower is built A.D. 1760.

At the time of the sixteenth-century Portuguese persecutions, the Maharaja of Cochin gave the Jews the land on which the Synagogue now stands—right next to his palace, and with a high wall, to protect them. The community has existed in orthodox style ever since.

The community consists of two groups: the "Black Jews" and the "White Jews." The White despise the Black, do not permit intermarriage, and assign to them only special places in the Synagogue.

As Joseph and I approached the Jewtown street (which is composed of houses in a Dutch 17th- and 18th-century style), we were met by a Black Jew, Mr. Salem, who invited us up to meet his father. We entered one of the houses: large upstairs rooms, walls about two and a half feet thick, European style furnishings of old and dark wood. There I met an old, dark Jew, Mr. Salem's father, who had been to Israel the year before to plead for the admission of some 4,000 Black Jews from Cochin (a very few White Jews went with them). They had sold all of their properties—synagogue properties included—to pay the fare; and great misery would be brought to them if they were refused.

The Synagogue at Cochin.

The old man, after a few preliminary words with me, moved into position and launched his attack on the United States.

Why were we supporting both the Arabs and the Jews? The right to Palestine lay clearly with the Jews: God had given it to them four thousand years ago, as documented in the Bible. Did we not still read the Bible in America?

The source of all wealth is the land. America has more land per person than any nation in the world. America therefore has more money than any nation in the world—also, more science, and more traffic of bullock carts. Having a lot of money, America has to get rid of a lot of money: that is why America is spilling so much money all over the world.

Why does America not give more of its money to Israel? True, the American Jews are giving a lot of money; but why not the American Christians also? Were they not reading the Bible any more? Did they not realize that the right to Palestine belonged to the Jews?

I must confess, when the old man started, I thought him rather cute, but when he continued and I could see, not only that he was dreadfully serious, but also that he represented a point of view held by millions of his like, I began to feel a bit sick at the stomach, and I was glad when it was time to go.

We descended the stairs and were met by a White Jew, in a pink cap, who opened the Synagogue and let us in. Joseph told me later that his daughter was married to the son of the Black Jew, Mr. Salem—the youngsters had had to elope to Bombay. The synagogue looked rather Dutch (Spinoza was in my mind)[268] and cute. Lots of brass; lots of lamps; a place above and behind a grill for the women; benches around the walls (Mr. Salem, being a Black Jew, may sit on only one or two, specially allowed). I tried to take a couple of photographs. Then out we went, and after a walk up and down the one street, we returned to Mr. Salem's house for a cool drink and a chat with his wife and a shy little girl (White Jew) named Hazel. I noticed that the women wore either Western dress or saris, as they pleased. As we walked on the street we passed several clusters sitting on the thresholds of their homes (it being Saturday, the shops were closed). Many were as fair as Westerners.

The community, I was told, is fast diminishing: hardly more than a hundred now remain.[269]

At four I boarded the hotel launch for a two-hour cruise of the "backwaters": the most fascinating two hours, I think, of the entire trip. I was alone on the launch with a crew of four, who were eager to help me to good photos. Unfortunately, most of the shoreline was into the sun—and *most* unfortunately, when I reloaded I put in a cartridge made for artificial light! I could shoot myself! Anyhow, the trip was great: a world of Polynesian style fishing villages on numerous islands: lovely kids waving and screaming from the shore: a world of coconuts, rice, and fish. In many places people pounding coconut husks for copra; in others, great fish traps, and places for the spreading out and drying of prawns. In the monsoon season rice is raised in these same fish-trap areas. At the end of the first hour of the trip, the boat turned left into a lovely, palm hung canal, and stopped at a large and beautifully kept village where I disembarked, and with one of the crew, took a lovely walk. A number of charming houses with very nicely painted facades: also, a couple of new, large mansions, built by wealthy citizens. At one corner I turned into a well crowded street where baksheesh was being distributed (every Saturday) to the poor. In these villages many of the older women wear no clothing over the upper body: one has the feeling that one has come really into an earlier world. All of the village lanes are perfectly swept and clean.

In the main square (surprise) is a large, white, Spanish-Portuguese style, Catholic church. Toward the close of my walk I was followed by a cute band of six little boys, whom I photographed a couple of times, to their great pride (with the dud film). Then I was brought back to the launch and returned, in the light of the declining sun, to the hotel.

Joseph walked home with me, and declared that he would see me off tomorrow on the plane to Madras.

Sunday, February 27

A very lazy morning, breakfast, strolling about the hotel lawn, and packing. On the stroll I fell into conversation with a businessman from Bombay who—touched with the usual Indian tendency to talk—gave a long monologue on God, ethics, and his departure from Burma after the commencement of the war. An amusing story was that of his family's valuables: stored in a safe, and the safe buried in the ground. But there was a deep hollow beneath, washed out by underground water; and when the Japanese bombs dropped, the safe dropped into this and disappeared forever.

God, he told me, is our servant—just as Nehru is; and if we are good he will give us what we need, but if we are bad he will hang us. Comparably, as long as God is good, and a good servant, he can stay in office; but if he fails in his duty, we can throw him out. All said, of course, in a rather amusing, half-sophisticated manner.

Joseph arrived a bit before lunch; chatted for a while on the verandah, took his meal with me, and bade me good-bye at the bus. The stewardess on the plane was the one who had come two days ago, from Trivandrum. The flight was (and she told me, always is) rather bumpy.

Madras

Monday, February 28 *Madras*

This *may* be my last day in India: if I can get my permission to leave from the Commissioner of Police—and *can't* have the validity date on my Ceylonese visa extended beyond tomorrow. If I *can* do the latter, I may remain a day or two longer and visit Madura.

As I think of leaving and look back over what has happened, I feel that I have had a wonderful six months and that I am now very much at home here, though not reluctant to depart. I wish I had seen Śāntiniketan, Khajurāho, Sāñcī, Māndū, and Hampi, and should like to see Madura and Tanjore; wish that Jean and I had seen a bit of Kathakali; and regret the fumble in New Delhi that lost us our places at the Parade and the Reception on Republic Day: but otherwise, everything has been accomplished that I came to accomplish—and a bit more besides. Moreover, I have met a lot of charming people, many of whom I should like to think of as permanent friends.

The climax of the visit was my talk with Sri Krishna Menon, which settled for me a number of fundamental matters. One is my thought about the relationship of the swamis and *sannyāsīs* to Indian life and religion. I should say that one of the great needs of India is more men like Krishna Menon, who will demonstrate the dignity of secular life. I feel that the monks have the notion that their *way* is the *goal* of religion—forgetting that the goal is illumination, which few of them have achieved. Another was my problem about the real sense of the positive teaching of the *Gītā*, which the monks turn into a negative teaching. And a third was my judgment of the validity of the feeling I have had for some time that I am pretty close to understanding what the Indian scriptures are teaching.

The main difference between this teaching and the Jungian goal of integration—as I now see it—is that in the Jungian, psychological literature, one is not invited to identify the Self with the Universal: this identification is what gives to the Indian teaching its religious tone, which is precisely the tone that Jung rejects in his commentary to the *Golden Flower*.[270] I think that I may find that, whereas in Vedanta the stress of the identity experience is on the transcendent, in Zen the idea is to keep the eyes open: "There are streams and there are mountains."[271] This, certainly, does not conflict with Krishna Menon's teaching. I told him that I felt that one should know that in turmoil, loss, unhappiness, and passion there is *Brahman*, no less than in peace, victory, happiness, and repose—and he indicated assent. *Brahman* is to be found not in one term only of a dichotomy, but beyond and within both! Clear enough! Why not hold on to it?

(Not to be forgotten is the contrast of Mr. Salem's Bible-grounded talk with the Hinduism of Krishna Menon: historical, race-centered, aggressive, generally nasty. But here too, of course, is *Brahman.*)

I suppose my second most important Indian climax was the meeting with Nehru—and here something of the contemporary historical situation came to focus. If I put together Nehru, Mrs. Pandit, and Mrs. Hutheesingh, I think I see an elegantly cosmopolitan family undergoing in various degrees, and Asianization (enantiodromia). The most critical experiences in this crisis are that of China as Asia, and that of Hindi as Asia. The first is dissociating India from the ideology and historical context of Democracy, and the second is soon going to reinforce this tendency by reducing the means of communication with the West. The principal motivation of the Hindi movement, I feel, is pride. "The British," said Mrs. Hutheesingh, "never thought our English good: they always ridiculed it." So India is going to become, more and more, an Asian, instead of modern, cosmopolitan nation—and I think they are going to be surprised at how far behind this leaves them pretty soon. The tables in my room wobble. The new hotel is ill-designed. The lighting in the room is quite bad. Copying (translation) is never as good as action out of the creative center; and no Asian language is *ever* going to move into the creative center of the industrial age.

The newspaper—*The Hindu*—this morning is full of editorials and reports of speeches attacking the United States—for its atom bombs, for its SEATO program,[272] for its "horror comics," for its materialism. (The same paper, meanwhile, runs a Tarzan comic.) My reaction is not very different from what it was when I first came to India and read these things. I am not sure of what I shall or should say about India when I return to the United States and am asked questions. One thing I know is that I do not want to engage in any attack upon India; but another thing I know is that I will not attempt either to mask or to defend what appears to me to be the Indian position. I suppose the best approach would be to retain a carefully and tentatively descriptive attitude. And I am going to be very, very chary of lending a hand to Indian causes.

India, fundamentally, has to be considered under two great categories: that of the huge majority, leading their lives in greater or lesser ignorance of the non-Indian world, and that of the leading minority, occidentalized and in an ambivalent emotional relationship to the West.

Both groups, as far as their approach to the Occidental foreigner is concerned, can be divided in two: those whose welcoming smile is sincere, innocent, and expressive of an almost boundless hospitality, sympathy, gentleness, and warm humanity, and those whose smile is the prelude to a touch for aid.

I am sure that, actually, the great majority in both of the fundamental categories is of the first (welcoming) type; but certainly the great majority in the actual experience of the alien visitor is of the second type. Certainly the representatives of this second type run all the way from the beggar in the street and bearer in the hotel, through the merchants with their "just to look" and the journalists and professors who hope that you will be able to get things published for them in the U.S.A., to the high politicians, who, while feeling greatly superior in their spirituality to the materialism of the West, and while insulting the West in every utterance, are nevertheless hoping and asking for aid—that the Rockefellers should restore their temples, fertilize their soil, finance their visits to the U.S.A., repair their idols, send books to their libraries—and what not. It is this that makes India, veritably, *the land of waving palms* (Joseph Ezekiel's term).

I have spent the morning trying to get out of India.

1. To the Police Commissioner's Office, Foreign Registration Department at 10:00. The officer arrived at 11:30 and asked thirteen rupees for a telegram to Bombay to get me cleared.
2. To the B-O-A-C office to get my ticket to Ceylon. Asked if I had my income tax clearance, I answered No. The clerk accompanied me to the income tax office.
3. Told that since I shall have been in India 184 days (182 days would have let me out) I have to pay *an income tax on the money I brought into India.* $1421+750=$2171. Tax of 519 rupees (over a hundred dollars). "I'm going to see the U.S. Consul," I said. "I regard this as a criminal act."
4. The taximan drove me back to the hotel for lunch and charged me twenty rupees for the morning.

Hail to the land of waving palms. My love for India may or may not survive this visit.

After lunch I went to see the U.S.I.S. director, Paul Sherbert, to talk about A.N.T.A. and the Orient: first, however, I told him of this highway robbery. He could hardly believe it, and got in touch with a chap named Edward C. Ingraham, Jr., American vice-Consul, who said he would see me.

When I left him, I went around to Ingraham—who was surprised at the tax, but verified it and could give me no help. I returned to the B-O-A-C office and told them that I would certainly not be able to go tomorrow (since Ingraham refused to give me a letter guaranteeing my character, which would have permitted me to leave before the arrival of the clearing telegram from Bombay). I returned, next, to the income tax office and filled out my tax return: 10,313 rupees; tax 519 rupees. Then I went back to the hotel and wrote the following letter.

Madras
February 28, 1955

Minister of Finance
Government of India
New Delhi

Dear Sir:
You will perhaps be interested in learning what good will is gained by taxing a tourist on the funds that he brings into this country. I am an American professor; have published four books on Indian religion, art, and philosophy; have lectured on the spiritual culture of India for twenty years; have looked forward eagerly to a visit to India, and have given up a good deal to make this trip. I arrived in New Delhi, August 30, 1954; lectured, gratis, at a number of Indian colleges and institutions; spent as much as I could afford on Indian textiles; gave as generously as I could to your temples and beggars; overlooked the anti-American propaganda in the newspapers; learned to admire and love the Indian people, as I had long admired and loved their culture—and when it came time for me to buy my ticket to depart (that is to say, today), my way was blocked by your income tax officials, to whom I am compelled to pay 519 rupees—not on any moneys earned in India (for I have not received one rupee here) but out of the funds that I brought into India and spent here. After this final experience of the baksheesh motif—played *fortissimo,* now, by the government itself—I am afraid that I am going to find it harder than it used to be, to speak and write about the Indian character with the respect it deserves.

Hoping that you may some day be able to collect taxes from your own citizens as efficiently as you have exacted this toll from one who came as a friend, I assure you that it is going to be very difficult for me to forget you when I remember India.

Very Sincerely, etc.

I find that I am not going to be able to remain in this hotel, because it is full up after tomorrow. The desk phoned to the Victoria, where I shall go tomorrow morning. Also, I am going to have to get another Ceylonese visa. It's all simply great.

While sitting in the lounge, waiting for the desk to find a room for me, I met a nice American Negro couple, Dr. and Mrs. Cecil Marquez of New York. We talked for a while about India. He remarked, among other matters, the bare feet: "there is a relationship between the wearing of shoes and health," he said. The character and depth of the poverty in India had shocked them, as it had me.

Feeling—really—like hell, I ate a late dinner and went early to bed.

Tuesday, March 1

I find myself, this morning, actually hating India and wanting to get away. The motif that struck me early, when the fortune teller caught me in New

Delhi when I first arrived—"something for nothing": baksheesh, baksheesh—has drowned out everything else just now. I feel exactly as I would about a house in which I had been rolled. The reaction is perhaps a bit strong. But then, so is a $110 toll.

I woke up at 5:30, sat brooding for an hour and a half, had morning tea, dressed, and ate breakfast; returned to my room, packed and brooded for a while, and then paid my bill and taxied to the Victoria: a fairly crummy hotel of the upper Hindu order. I spent the rest of the morning strolling around the Mount Road area, and visited Sherbert, who invited me for lunch tomorrow and expressed helpless amazement at my plight ("I've always said," he said, "that if you can reconcile yourself to being stabbed in the back at least once by everybody who's nice to you in India, you can have a lovely time here.... They just haven't got the idea of service.") Then I left my passport at the Ceylonese High Commission, with, of course, ten rupees, and walking home through a typical Madras residential district (slum, with the kids shitting in the gutter), I entered my hotel for a lousy meal.

After lunch and a brief rest, I went around to the Police Commissioner's office and was handed my permit to leave India; went next to the Ceylon office and received my new visa; walked to the airlines office, and was told that I could pick up my ticket tomorrow for a March 3 departure; and went, finally to the U.S. Consul's office, to see if I could cash my American Express checks there for the payment of my income tax.

As I entered the building—surprise!—I was greeted by Kashi, Jason Grossman's bearer. Jason was upstairs. I found him talking to the young man who had informed me that I could not get out of the payment of this tax. Greetings—and a long talk about the tax problem.

Then I drove with Jason to a little house that someone has loaned him, for a drink. He introduced me to his hosts, and for two and a half hours, these nice people projected Jason's color photos onto the wall. I thought some of them quite fine—but began to fear for my own. I'm afraid I have not been using a wide enough aperture: 5.6 with an exposure of 1/50 or 1/25 has been Jason's norm. Mine has been more like 8 with 1/60 or 1/40.[273]

After the films finished at 9:30 P.M., Jason and I drove down Mount Road to a *Chinese* restaurant, for the best restaurant meal either of us had had in India. He wants me to join him and drive up the coast to Amarāvatī, Orissa, and Calcutta—but I feel very strongly that I am fed up with India. The Chinese meal seemed to me the promise of the future. I think it will be quite a while before I shall feel the lure of India again.

Just before dropping me at the hotel, Jason announced that he was going to have his new cholera shots tomorrow. This reminded me that my own six-month certificate is now outdated, so I shall join him tomorrow, leave my miserable hotel, and move, then, to Mr. Sherbert for my last Indian night.

Wednesday, March 2

Up at 6 A.M., shaving and packing. At 8:45 Jason called for me, and the day began.

Yesterday, in the U.S. Consul's office, studying the Indian tax manual, I noted that Kashmir was a non-taxable territory and recalled that I had been in Kashmir during the first days of my visit. I mentioned this fact to the young man in the office who was helping me, and he said he would look into the matter. When I came downstairs this morning, I was told that there had been a phone call for me last evening from the U.S. Consul's office. Our first act today, therefore, was to drive to the Consul's. We were told that the man we wanted was out and would return in about an hour. We met him, however, when we were going out the door, and he said that he had found that my days in Kashmir might be subtracted from the period of my stay. There remained a problem though; for I had absolutely no evidence of my trip.

Jason, Kashi, and I drove first to a young Australian doctor for our cholera shots, and then to the Health Office for a certification of his certification of our inoculations. Next we drove to the Income Tax bureau, and the battle began. I had two points: that I had been in Kashmir, and that uncashed Travelers Checks are not currency. The second point, finally, was disallowed, and the first was rejected because Kashmir had recently been brought into the taxable domain. Jason asked if it had been taxable when I had been there, and at 12:15 they found that it had not, and that if I would write out a statement, sworn to before the U.S. Consul, to the effect that I had been in Kashmir for four or five days, I would still have one or two days in which to get out of India.

We drove to see Mr. and Mrs. Sherbert for lunch. I had been invited to spend the night there, and so we brought my luggage in the car and left it—with the exception of my Indian bed roll, which I gave to Kashi as my farewell gift. After lunch, Sherbert returned me to the Consul's office, where I wrote out my statement—hoping that it was true (five days in Kashmir, counting the day of the drive over the mountains from Pathankot). Jason drove me back to the Tax Office and at 4:15 P.M. I received my release: I have to leave India, however, by the 4th, or I shall be back under the blanket. The last problem that came up was that of $750 that had been sent to me from my New York bank in December. This was still taxable if it was a direct earning, but not if it was a remittance. I swore that it was a remittance from my savings—and was clear.

The next problem, however, was that Jason had asked for a statement from the tax people, clearly showing him when *he* would become taxable in India. The rule is fantastically complicated; for the Indian fiscal year ends on March 31, and the 182-day period must fall within any *one* fiscal year, to trap you. Jason arrived in October. March 31 he will not yet have been here 182 days. Therefore, he may remain for 182 days after March 31.

It was 4:45 when Jason received his letter, and we had then to dash like mad to reach the B-O-A-C office in time for me to buy my airplane ticket to Colombo. We hit the office at 4:58. I paid with a twenty-dollar traveler's check, and came out with my ticket and thirteen rupees to my name.

We drove to Jason's for a drink, then to the Chinese restaurant of last night, where I, this time, treated him. He dropped me at the Sherberts' for the night, and we bade each other good-bye and good times.

About the tax event, there is something still to be said; namely, that the group of young men, who finally managed to help me through, reminded me, not a little, of some young naval officers I met earlier in Cochin: youngsters, working India through its awkward period of transition—highly intelligent, and proud of the responsibilities. It is a fantastic situation; young law graduates holding the jobs that in any other country would be in the hands of seasoned professionals. It gives a kind of freshness and quality of impromptu to this whole affair.

I think my final image for India is going to be that of the group of boy beggars outside the Chinese restaurant. Their chief figure was an absolutely naked little kid of about seven—cute and charming, with a mop of tangled hair—who would walk alongside or in front of us saying, "No fatha, no matha, no seesta, no bratha...etc.," with a winning smile, and then, in the classical Indian beggar style, clap his stomach, look up at you with half-open mouth. The first night, I gave him one anna. Tonight he appeared again, as an old friend, and when I put him off, said, "Tomorrow?" I said, "Tomorrow." Another, this evening, put out his hand, and said, "Baksheesh!" I put out mine to him and said, "Baksheesh!" He looked surprised at first, and indicated that he had nothing. Then he smiled and said, "Wait," ran away and came back with two annas. When I came out of the restaurant, he appeared again. "You're the boy who gave me baksheesh?" I said. He answered yes, and I gave him two annas.

The other image that I will remember, I think, is that of the truckmen of this city, working like animals at their trucks, two in front, and one pushing with his head from behind. They are practically naked, and represent the most emphatic image of sheer physical work that I've ever seen.

And finally, the slums of this city: thousands of dirty, miserable women sitting around in the filth, playing with their babies or searching each others' heads for lice.

Thursday, March 3

The little room on the roof of the Sherbert place was delightful. After breakfast, Mr. Sherbert and I sat talking while we waited for the U.S.I.S. car to call and he told me a few things about the Maharani of Travancore, who is still "quite a gal," at about sixty.

The first wife of the Maharaja, it seems, produced only girls, so he married this one, who produced two boys and a girl. The second boy, however, is generally regarded as the son, not of the Maharaja, but of Mr. C. P. Ramaswamy Aiyar, one of the most charming and ruthless crooks in the world, is today a trustee of the Asian Institute in San Francisco, and a candidate for a position in the U.S. Foreign Service as advisor on Indian affairs.

After the Maharani had born her sons, the first wife of the Maharaja bore a son also, and a series of attempts to poison the sons of the Maharani then was initiated, which she, personally, frustrated.

With the death of the Maharaja, C. P. Ramaswamy Aiyar's influence in Travancore became enormous, and his iron suppression of the working classes is one of the major causes of the Communist tendency in that region. He and the Maharani soon began to suspect that they might have to take refuge somewhere, someday, and so they employed two men to bring up from underground a certain temple treasure, which had never been evaluated, stored it in various safe deposit vaults in Europe and America, and killed the two men who had brought it up. No one knows what the treasure was worth.

Aiyar has been writing faithfully to the U.S.I.S. directors in Washington. Senator Wiley has been taken in entirely, and it looks as if he might get a job.

We talked a bit about Sri Krishna Menon: I have talked about him also with Jason. It seems the gossip against him brings in the problem of his son, who is, apparently, a fairly unsuccessful movie director with worldly habits.

The U.S.I.S. car arrived about 8:30 and we piled in. When everyone had been delivered, I and my luggage (minus, thank God, that bed roll) were dropped at the TWA Air Ceylon office just across the street from the U.S.I.S.

"Sir! Sir! Baksheesh!"

It was my little naked friend of the past two evenings. Just as the bus was about to leave I gave him my last piece of Indian change: a half anna—and he gave me Godspeed in his own charming style.

APPENDIX A

This essay, "Hinduism," was first printed in 1959 in Basic Beliefs: A Simple Presentation of the Religious Philosophies of Mankind, *edited by Johnson E. Fairchild.*

I imagine that when one thinks of Indian philosophy the first thought is of yoga. The great classical text of yoga is that of the sage Patanjali: the *Yoga Sūtras,* "Thread or Guiding Thread to Yoga." At the opening of this amazing work, we find the following definition—and I want to start with this, because it is a very important point: "Yoga is the intentional stopping of the spontaneous activity of the mind stuff."

Now it was the idea in ancient Oriental psychology that within the gross matter of the brain, within the grey matter, there is a very subtle substance, which is in continuous activity, taking the shapes of whatever we behold. This subtle matter is in a state of continuous activity, like the rippling of waves on a stirred pool. And when you shut your eyes, the mind stuff continues to operate that way. If you should try to make it stop, you would find the process very difficult.

Just try this some time. Take into your mind an image—somebody that you care for, some image that you would care to contemplate—and try to hold this image still in your mind. You will find that you are immediately thinking of other images, associated with the first; for the mind continues spontaneously to move. Yoga is the intentional stopping of this spontaneous activity of the mind stuff. It is an intentional bringing to rest of this continuous action.

But why should one wish to do this?

A favorite simile used in Indian discussions of this subject is that of the surface of a pond with its waves in action—a wind blowing over the pond and the waves moving. If you look at the surface of a pond moving in this way you will see the many reflections—many broken forms; nothing will be perfect, nothing complete; you will have only broken images before you. But if the wind dies down and the waters become perfectly still and clear, suddenly the whole perspective shifts and you are not seeing a lot of broken images, reflecting things round about. You are looking down through the clear water to the lovely sandy bottom, and perhaps you will see fish in the water. The whole perspective changes and you behold, not a multitude of broken images, but a single, still, unmoving image.

This is the idea of yoga. The notion is that what we see when we look around, like this, are the broken images of a perfect form. And what is that form? It is the form of a divine reality, which appears to us only in broken images when our mind stuff is in action. Or, to state the case another way: we are all, as we sit here and stand here, the broken images, the broken reflections, of a single divine perfection; but all that we ever see when we look around with our mind stuff in its usual state of spontaneous activity, is the broken rainbow-reflection of this perfect image of divine light.

Let us now open our eyes, let the waters stir again, let the waves come into action—and we shall know that these flashing sights before us are reflections, broken images, of that one divine radiance, which we have experienced. And it will now be delightful to see them moving in this way; for we are no longer at a loss to know what they are. We shall have seen the source; we shall know that the source is within all of these broken reflections—including ourselves; and there will come a wonderful experience of a harmonious system: all things inflecting in various ways this one perfection. This is the realization that underlies the whole thought and sociology and action of traditional India.

Now since we are all broken reflections of that image, that image is present within us. However, it is impossible to describe it in terms of its broken reflections. How would you possibly describe its form to someone who had not seen the complete image itself? It cannot be described in terms of its fragments. The first principle of Indian thought, therefore, is that the ultimate reality is beyond description. It is something that can be experienced only by bringing the mind to a stop; and once experienced, it cannot be described to anyone in terms of the forms of this world. The truth, the ultimate truth, that is to say, is transcendent. It goes past, transcends, all speech all images, anything that can possibly be said. But, as we have just seen, it is not only transcendent, it is also immanent, within all things. Everything in the world, therefore, is to be regarded as its manifestation.

There is an important difference here between the Indian and the Western ideas. In the Biblical tradition, God creates man, but man cannot say that he is divine in the same sense that the Creator is, whereas in Hinduism all things are incarnations of that power. There has been no "Fall." Man is not cut off from the divine. He requires only to bring the spontaneous activity of his mind stuff to a state of stillness and he will experience that divine principle within him which is the very essence of his existence. And this essence within is identical in all of us. We are, as it were, sparks from a single fire; and we are all fire. There is therefore an eternal revelation of the truth all around us, all the time, and we require only the proper focus of the eyes to experience this.

Now let me give you a couple of basic terms: the divine principle within each of us is called *ātman. Ātman* simply means "the self." And this "true self" is the same in all. However, each conceives of himself as being a special independent person, and this concept of oneself as an independent entity is called "ego," *aham;* also, *aham-kara,* "making the noise 'I'." "Making the noise 'I'" is what we do when we set ourselves against each other.

The name given to *ātman* when it is experienced, not only within, but also in the world, is *Brahman;* and *Brahman* simply means "divine power." *Brahman,* the divinity immanent in the world, and ātman, the divinity immanent in yourself, are the same divinity; and so the great experience in Indian thought—indeed, the fundamental illuminating principle throughout the Orient—is this realization that all of these beings that seem so various are one.

Now this realization that though we are many we are also one, is a magical realization. And what is the magic that transforms the one into the many? It is called *māyā. Māyā* means the force that builds forth form. And this *māyā* has three effects. The first one is to cut off our vision of the perfect unity of the immanent world power. This is called the "obscuring effect" of *māyā.* The second is, to project all of these broken reflection that we see around us; and this is called the "projecting effect" of *māyā.* But *māyā* holds the possibility of a third effect also; for by contemplating all of these forms with the feeling that they are one, and by going around with the thought in your mind that you are in essence one with all these beings, you may come to realize that this is true. *Māyā* thus can reveal, through the manifold, the one; and this is called the "revealing effect" of *māyā.*

I have said that it is impossible to talk about *Brahman-ātman.* The goal of Indian religion, the goal of Indian philosophy, is to point people's minds toward the realization of this truth and then to let them suddenly have the experience in their own minds. The images of Indian mythology and religion that we see on the beautiful Indian temples are called, in our language, "gods." But they are not gods in the same way that the god of the Old Testament is a god. The god of the Old Testament is conceived to be the ultimate truth. There is said to be nothing beyond this god. But the Indian gods are only pointing toward truth; because it is impossible, according to the Indian view, to speak about truth or to picture truth, to personify truth. The personifications, the images, the forms, are only clues, merely guides.

And now, to give you a notion of how some of these deities are pictured:

There are three very important deities in Indian worship, and they are Vishnu, Shiva, and Kālī. Vishnu is pictured as the divine dreamer of the world dream. Vishnu sleeps on a great serpent, whose name is Ananta, which means "Endless." The serpent floats on the universal ocean, called the Milky Ocean. But this Milky Ocean and the Serpent and the sleeping God: these are all the same thing. They are three inflections of the same thing, and that thing can be thought of also as the subtle substance that the wind of the mind stirs into action when the universe of all these shifting forms is brought into being. Vishnu, the God, sleeps, and the activity of his mind stuff creates dreams, and we are all his dream: the world is Vishnu's dream. And just as, in your dreams, all the images that you behold and all the people who appear are really manifestations of your own dreaming power, so are we all manifestations of Vishnu's dreaming power. We are no more independent entities than the dream figures in our own dreams. Hence, we are all one in Vishnu: manifestations, inflections, of this dreaming power of Vishnu; broken images of himself rippling on the spontaneously active surface of his subtle mind stuff. Moreover, this sleeping god's divine dream of the universe is pictured in Indian art as a great lotus plant growing from his navel. The idea is that the dream unfolds like a glorious flower, and that this flower is the energy—or, as the Indians say, the shakti or goddess—of the god.

I hope that some of you are recalling the counterparts of some of these images in the Biblical tradition. The waters that are stirred into action when creation takes place are comparable to those of the first verse of the Bible, where it is said that the wind or breath of god blew, or brooded, over the waters. This metaphor represents the miracle of creation, bringing the world into being as a multiplicity out of the stillness of an unstirred sleep. And the bride of the divine being, coming forth in the Indian myth from the navel of a dreaming god, is drawn in the Biblical myth from the rib of a dreaming man. What was originally one has become two. And how delightful it is to see such an image-reflection of an aspect of one's own being—which was not present to consciousness before, and yet was there, nevertheless! So it is with Vishnu's dream. The god becomes aware of his own power and is delighted by the charms of his own power, as represented in the presence derived from him: the presence of his own dream, which is the universe. Thus, the universe is the dream-bride, or dream-goddess, of God.

Another image that appears frequently in Indian art is that of the god Shiva dancing. Shiva has four arms in this manifestation, and he is dancing on a prostrate dwarf. His first right hand holds a drum; and this drum beats; and that beat is the beat of time, which sends a ripple of movement over the face of eternity. The tick of time, then, is the creating principle, and this first right hand , therefore, is the hand of creation. It is bringing forth the world-dance just by beating the drum. But on the other side of the god, one of his two left hands holds a flame: the flame of illumination, which destroys the illusion of the world. This, then, is the hand of destruction. But destruction so conceived is rather paradoxical; because what we all want, surely, is to know the truth, even though full knowledge may come only with the dissolution—or stilling—of the activity of the world. And so, whereas we have a deluding creation in the one hand, we have an illuminating destruction in this other, and between the two, flows the enigma of the universe.

Śiva Naṭarāja

The second right hand of the god Shiva is held palm outward in a posture known as *abhāya,* which means, "don't be afraid." Nothing terrible is happening. Forms are breaking, your own form is breaking, death comes; yet nothing is happening. The eternal principle, which never was born, never will die: it is in all things: it is in you now. You are a wave on the surface of the ocean. When the wave is gone, is the water gone? Has anything happened? Nothing has happened. It is a play, a game, a dance.

The second left hand of the god Shiva is held out before him in what is called the elephant posture. It is a posture suggesting the forehead and trunk of an elephant, and this is the teaching hand. For the elephant is likened to the teacher: where the elephant has walked, all animals can follow. It is a huge animal and where it has gone ahead, breaking down the forest, the other beasts can easily follow. This elephant or teaching hand points to the left foot, which is lifted; and that lift signifies release. Meanwhile, however, the right foot is driving down into the back of the dwarf, whose name is "Ignorance." This foot is driving souls into ignorance—that is to say, into the world, into creation, into this life that we are leading. But the other foot is lifted, yielding release.

And so here is the god Shiva's image: one foot driving souls into life and the other releasing them, in a cycle of birth-into-ignorance and return-to-truth: birth and illumination. One hand controls creation, another destruction, while a third is saying, "Don't be afraid; nothing is happening!" and a fourth, "Look at the cycle down there, and realize that your ego (*aham*) is but a wave rippling on the ocean of eternity, while your true self (*ātman*), what you really are, is the water, which endures."

A third figure commonly seen in Indian religious art is the goddess Kālī. For if you wish to personify divinity (according to Indian thought), it is no less proper to picture a mother than to picture a father. Why, indeed, should one attribute sex to a divine being who is transcendent; that is to say, beyond all attributes? If beyond description, why attribute sex? So it is optional: you may decide for yourself whether you prefer to think of the divine principle as a mother or as a father, as a dreamer, or as a dancer. Any image will do, so long as it will help you to collect the main principles of this realization and hold them in your mind.

God as the mother is pictured in a very strange way. She gives birth to beings but then eats them; and so, she is a terrifying, frightening mother, represented with a great tongue hanging out to lick up the blood of her slaughtered victims. She is a horrendous thing. And this may give you a notion of the realistic seriousness of Indian imagery. Life is not all goodness, it is also frightful. So that, if we are going to assign to the creator only the qualities of benevolence, how shall we account for these other aspects of existence? Indian thought does not trouble itself as greatly as Western with the problem of evil; because there is no evil, really. Forms come into being, forms go out of being. Of course they do; for time passes! And how do the forms go out? Some comfortably, some uncomfortably; but they all go. It is this passage and fluency of time that is the great thing: and if you realize that it is all divine, whether going or coming, there is then nothing to fear. The goddess, therefore, is depicted as a frightful consumer of all beings as well as the mother of beings. She is the sow that eats her farrow, consuming her own children. Her upper right hand is in the posture of *abhāya,* "do not fear!"; the lower is outstretched in a boon-bestowing posture; the upper left hand holds a sword and the lower left a head, which the goddess has just cut off. She is the deliverer of both life and death. Horrendous yet fascinating, she is the very image of the dual nature of life.

These deities, these supreme beings, are held before the mind as objects of contemplation because they suggest the mysteries of this created world. It hurts the dwarf to be tread upon; and the dancer himself hurts his feet, dancing. But anyone with the power of creativity, the power to live, is not afraid of life's hurt. Therefore, if our consciousness is saying *aham* all the time, saying, "I, I, I am hurt, I and my friends are hurt, I and the principles I care for are being hurt, we're not getting on, the world's going to pot!"...if we begin thinking that way, we are out of touch with the creative principle and dynamics of the world, and we are already, from the standpoint of Indian thought, dead things.

The notion of the universe, then (for I want to move on, now, from the god, down to the universe itself); the notion of the universe in Indian thought is that it is a great organism, manifesting this divine dance, or this divine dream, in a harmonious, magnificent display. And every one of us is a part of that organism. Every one of us has a role to play in it. In their sacred books the Indians commonly represent this cosmic organism as a Great Man, with each class of humanity compared to a part.

Now, in the old agrarian societies—societies of the sort fundamental to Oriental culture—there were primarily four classes of human beings: four social strata. The most important of these in India was the brahmin or priestly class, whose function it was to know the divine revelation, to know the truth and how to teach the truth, how to instruct the community and its governors in the way of truth. The Brahmins are compared to the head of the Great Being; and the second class—that of the rulers, or Kshatriya—to the arms and chest. It is the function of the ruling class to administer the truth that the Brahmins teach, maintaining the society in the way of the cosmic order. And then we come to the merchant and land-owning class, who represent the middle of the Great Man: his trunk and viscera. These, the Vaishya, constitute, so to say, the backbone and guts of the social order. They are the community that we call the Middle Class. And finally, the members of the fourth class, the Shudra, the workers and craftsmen, are compared to the feet of the composite being.

The notion is that everybody has a fixed and proper function, just as the different organs of the body have, and that by performing his functions, each keeps the divine society in harmonious health. Suppose the moon were to say one morning, "I'd like to be the sun." Or suppose the sun one day were to think, "I'd like to get up a little later this morning," The whole universe would go out of gear. The Indian idea of the social order is that all of us are just as tightly fixed to our ways and laws of life as the sun and moon.

Furthermore, when one reads the old law books, the *Book of Manu,* for example, one sees how, in ancient India, the life rules became more and more demanding as one proceeded up the social scale. The rules for the Brahmin are minute to a degree that can hardly be imagined; but the restrictions become less and less demanding as one goes down the scale to the Shudra level. For the notion is that there is a particular morality, or virtue, appropriate to each class, in accordance with its functions in the organism of the Great Man. For example, the morality proper to the worker, The Shudra, was simply to do as told. By doing as he was told he lost his sense of ego, and so was introduced to the great religious principle and experience of egolessness. He learned this on the simplest, crudest level. And then, it was thought, after this experience of egolessness had been assimilated on the obvious level of physical service, he would have gained a spiritual character rendering him eligible to be promoted, in his next life, to the merchant or land-owning, Vaishya class. For here the duties were more severe; but, also, the honors considerably greater, so that there was a greater temptation to egoism. It is harder to be egoless, harder to learn how to be selfless, on this level of wealth and comfort than on the lower levels of obedient toil. And since, for India, the goal of life is to learn selflessness, it is important that people should be graded properly according to their capacity.

But the ruling, aristocratic, or warrior class, of course, has more temptations than even the merchant to become egocentric. The members of this class have the power to do as they will, and so here the disciplines were extremely severe. And then, finally, for the Brahmin, who was worshipped as a god, the temptation to ego was prodigious, and the rules of life were almost incredibly constraining,

Now everything that is described here implies the idea of reincarnation, and this idea is fundamental to all Indian thought. It is believed that through our experiences of life, we are gradually clarified in our vision, so that we become less and less the victims of ego and its systems of hope and fear. We learn more and more how to become egoless. In our Occidental, democratic society, we do not believe that people are born into precisely the social class for which their souls are ready. We believe in a loose social structure, with equal opportunities for all. The Indian view, on the other hand, has always been that people are born into the class for which they are ready, and so the system is designed to hold them there. It is important for us to realize, however, that the Indian system of caste is not associated primarily with wealth. People even of the very lowest caste may become wealthy; and a Brahmin priest in a little rural temple will almost certainly be very poor indeed. It is only on the level of the third, the Vaishya caste, that life is devoted primarily to the ideology of wealth. Hence the caste organization itself is not to be understood as an organization based on money. It is based on what is regarded in India as a spiritual principle: the idea that one must learn the lesson of life first on its lowest levels, and then return in later incarnations for more and more difficult lessons, until achieving complete release from this school of rebirth.

Let me tell you a story, to indicate something about the nature of this Indian idea of the spiritual value of the performance of duty. It is taken from a very interesting Buddhist text, the *Milindapanha,* which dates back to perhaps the second century A.D., and it tells of the great Buddhist emperor Ashoka, who lived in the third century B.C., in the city of Pataliputra (which is now called Patna). The river Ganges flows past this city, and the river, according to this tale, was rising at that time with such force that it was threatening the city with a flood. The Emperor was greatly troubled, and everybody in the town was greatly troubled, and so all—the Emperor included—assembled on the bank of the river to watch the waters rise.

There is an Indian notion that if you have fulfilled your life duty to perfection, you may perform what is known as an Act of Truth. You can say (and this is magic now): "If I have performed my duty without any trace of ego, but, like the sun rising and the sun setting, have done just what I should have done, every hour of my life, then let such and such happen!" And such and such will happen. This is called an Act of Truth. For, since you are part of the organism of the universe, and perfectly so, you partake of the power of the universe. You have become a conduit of universal energy and can perform miracles.

And so now, this story tells us, when all the city had gathered along the bank of the river Ganges, the emperor Ashoka, perceiving the danger, asked: "Can no one make an Act of Truth and cause the waters of the Ganges to flow back upstream?" Apparently the Emperor himself could not do so; nor could any of the members of his court: they stood around and looked embarrassed. The Brahmins hung their heads, the nobles hung their heads, and the merchants hung their heads. But way down the way there was an old prostitute, and her name was Bindumatī, and she belonged to what was regarded as the abyss of the social structure. She was the lowest of the low. And yet she said to those around her, "I have an Act of Truth."

The old woman shut her eyes and presently the Emperor noticed that the waters of the vast river were slowing down, backing up: there was a roar, and the waters of the Ganges began to flow upstream.

You may imagine the action of the people. "Who," asked the Emperor, "performed this Act of Truth?" But no one around him knew. He looked about, and no one within range of his eye gave any sign of either being or of knowing the person whose virtue had saved the city. In a little while, however, the rumor reached him, and the Emperor proceeded to Bindumatī in amazement. "You!" he exclaimed. "Wicked old sinner! Disgrace of the community! Do you mean to say that you have an Act of Truth?" "Your Majesty," she answered, "I possess an Act of Truth by means of which, if I so desired, I could turn the world of men and the worlds of the gods upside down." The Emperor requested to be told this Act of Truth, and the old prostitute replied: "Whosoever gives me money, your Majesty, whether he be a Brahmin, Kshatriya, Vaishya, or Shudra, I treat him as any other. I make no distinction in his favor if he is Kshatriya; and if a Shudra, I do not despise him. Free both from fawning and from contempt, I serve the owner of the money. And this your Majesty, is the Act of Truth by which I caused the mighty Ganges to flow back upstream."

The obvious part of this remarkable tale is that any way of life whatsoever is a way to God, if followed faithfully, selflessly, in perfect humility. This woman had power as no one else in the community, because she had performed to perfection the duties of her coarse and humble role. But the second lesson of the story is that she did not rise in the social scale for having saved the city: she remained Bindumatī, serving the owner of the money.

Which indicates an important thing about Oriental thought—namely, its distinction between moral and spiritual judgment and its ultimate dedication to the latter. This is something a little difficult for us to understand, since practically all of our own religious emphasis is moral. The religious interest of the Orient, on the other hand, though moral in large measure, is finally metaphysical; and its main idea is this: that by some act, some experience, some realization, some knowledge, we should achieve an effective relationship to our essential being, which is identical with the being that creates, supports, and annihilates the world.

When one reads the *Bhagavad Gītā,* which is the most important single text of Hinduism, one comes across a very strange statement. The God there declares that he is the essence of all things: of the lion, he is the power and the fury; of thieves, the thievery; and of cheats and the cheating. "I am the victory of those who conquer," he declares, "and of those who die, the death." In other words, since divinity is the essence of every being, we must not let our moral judgments obscure from us the fact that God is shining through all things, even those of which we cannot approve; yet this should not disturb us in the performance of our own duties, according to the terms of our own system of ethics. There is a very nice paradoxical principle involved here, which, though it may be difficult for us to appreciate, is fundamental to the Indian point of view.

Moreover, there are many means, or ways, by which we may learn to shift our perspective from that of the multiplicity of this world to that of the unity of all things; and all these ways are called yogas. A number of apparently contradictory teachings have therefore been developed in the great domain of Hinduism. Yoga, in the broadest sense of the word, is any technique serving to link consciousness to the ultimate truth. One type of yoga I have already mentioned: that of stopping the spontaneous activity of the mind stuff. This type of mental discipline is called Raja Yoga, the Kingly, or Great Yoga. But there is another called Bhakti Yoga, Devotional Yoga; and this is the yoga generally recommended for those who have duties in the world, tasks to perform, and who cannot, therefore, turn away to the practice of that other, very much sterner mode of psychological training. This much simpler, much more popular, yoga of worship consists in being selflessly devoted to the divine principle made manifest in some beloved form. One may dedicate oneself, for example, to the service of some god or goddess—one of those that I have just described—or any other, for that matter. Bhakti Yoga will then consist in having one's mind continually turned toward, or linked to, that chosen deity through all of one's daily tasks. But since divinity is present in *all* things, one may devote oneself equally to some living person as an incarnation or manifestation of the divine—or even to some animal or plant. In the Hindu marriage the woman is to be thus devoted to her husband. He is god for her, just as the deity of his caste or craft-guild, the deity of his particular system of duty, is God for him.

There is an illuminating story told of the deity Krishna, who, in the form of a human child, was raised among a little company or tribe of herdsmen. One day he said to them, when he saw them preparing to worship one of the great Gods of the Brahminical pantheon: "But why do you worship a deity in the sky? The support of your life is here, in your cattle. Worship these!" Whereupon, they hung garlands around the necks of their cattle and paid them worship.

This wonderful art of recognizing the divine presence in all things, as a ubiquitous presence, is one of the most striking features of Oriental life, and is particularly prominent in Hinduism. I have seen very simple people out in the country, climbing a hill, who, when they became tired and paused to rest and eat, set up a stone, poured red paint around it, and then reverently placed flowers before it. The pouring of the red paint set that stone apart. The idea was simply that those people were now going to regard it, not as a stone, but as a manifestation of the divine principle that is immanent in all things. The pouring of the red paint and placing of the flowers were typical acts of Bhakti, Devotional Yoga: simple devices, readily available to anyone, to shift the focus of the mind from the phenomenal aspect of the object as a mere stone to its mystery of a miracle of being. And this popular form of yoga, no less than the very much sterner and more difficult discipline of Patanjali's *Yoga Sūtras,* to which I first alluded, is a technique to link consciousness to the ultimate truth: the mystery of being. The sense of the whole universe as a manifestation of the radiance of God and of yourself as likewise of that radiance, and the assurance that this is so, no matter what things may look like, round about, is the key to the wisdom of India and the Orient.

And now there is one more little story that I should like to tell, to conclude all of this with an image to remember. It is the fable of a tigress, who was pregnant and hungry, prowling about in great distress, until she came at last upon a herd of goats, whereupon she pounced. But as she sprang she gave birth to her little tiger, and this incident so injured her that she died.

The goats, of course, had scattered. But when all was still, they returned to graze and found the tiny tiger, warm and alive, beside the dead body of its mother. Being generous hearted, gentle creatures, the mother goats took the little animal to themselves and brought it up as one of their own. Learning to eat grass, which is poor fare for tigers, the foundling grew up to be a scrawny, very mild example of his species, and the members of the herd got on very well with him. None paid attention to the obvious difference in complexion, and the little tiger himself had no realization that he was the least bit different from the rest.

But then, one day, a big male tiger discovered the herd and pounced. The goats scattered, but the little tiger, now an adolescent, stood where he was. He felt no fear; he just stood there. The big one blinked and looked again. "What is this?" he roared. "What are you doing here among goats?" The little fellow, not knowing that he was not a goat, was unable to grasp the sense of the question. Embarrassed, he bleated and the other, shocked, gave him a clout on the head. Confused, the little thing began to nibble grass. "Eating grass!" the big one roared again, and the scrawny cub only bleated.

Having studied the pitiful youngster for a while, the big male took him by the nape of the neck and carried him to a pond with a quiet surface, where he sat him down. "Now look into that pond," he said. The little tiger looked, and the big one, sitting beside him, also looked into the pond. "Look at your face, mirrored there in the water," he said, "and now look at mine: this one is mine. You have the pot-face of a tiger; have you not? You are not a goat." The cub became very quiet and thoughtful, absorbing the image of himself as a tiger. Then, when the master felt he was ready, he took him again by the neck and carried him to his lair, where there were the remains of a gazelle recently killed. Forcing a large piece of this raw flesh down the gagging throat of the revolted, frightened little tiger, the one compelled him to swallow—and gave him more, until, presently, he began to feel the tingle of the warm blood going into his veins. This was a new feeling altogether, and yet one congenial to his awakening true nature. Stretching for the first time in his life in the manner of a great cat, he suddenly heard his own throat emit, to his amazement, a great tiger roar. Then said the old fellow: "Aha! Now let us hunt together in the jungle."

And the lesson of this fable? The moral?

The lesson is that we are all tigers—living among goats.

APPENDIX B

CHRONOLOGICAL CHART

PERIODS OF INDIAN ART

Mesopotamian Cities and Empires *(ante c.* 5500–*c.* 1000	B.C. *c.* 3000–1500	DRAVIDIAN PERIOD Ruins of the Indus Valley Civilization	Mohenjo-daro, Harappā, Chanhu-daro
Aryans enter Near East	*c.* 1750–1000	ĀRYAN SETTLEMENT OF NORTH INDIA	
Assyrian, Hittite, and Medean Empires (*c.* 1500–*c.* 550)	*c.* 1500–450	VEDIC PERIOD V*edas, Brāhmaṇas, Upaniṣads*	
Achaemenid Persian Empire (550–330)	*c.* 500 B.C.–550 A.D.	BUDDHISM AND THE RISE OF BUDDHIST ART EARLY HINDU AND JAINA ART Mahāvīra, 24th Tīrthaṅkara, d. *c.* 526 Gautama, the Buddha, *c.* 563–483	
	325: ALEXANDER THE GREAT ENTERS N.W. INDIA		
Seleucid Persian Empire (305–64)	*c.* 321-184	Maurya Dynasty Aśoka, *c.* 272–231	Aśoka Pillars; early stūpas
Arsacid Persian Empire (250 B.C.–226 A.D.)	*c.* 185–*c.* 73	Śuṅga and Kāṇva Dynasties	Sāñcī: Stūpa No. 2; Bhārhut reliefs; Bhājā; Bodhgayā railing
	c. 73 B.C.–II cent. A.D.	Satavahana Dynasty	Sāñcī: Stūpa No. 1; rockcut sanctuaries; Amarāvatī
	SCYTHIAN (ŚAKA INVASIONS) YUEH-CHI (KUṢĀṆA) INVASION	1 cent. B.C.– 1 cent. A.D.	
Sassanian Persian Empire (226–41)	A.D. I–VII cent. *c.* 320–650	Kuṣāṇa Dynasty and successors Gupta and Vākāṭaka Dynasties and successors	Mathurā,Gandhāra Sārnāth, Ajaṇṭā
	WHITE HUN INVASIONS, *c.* 480–525		
Rise of Islam (Mohammed, d. 632) Muslim conquest of India (*c.* 750–1565)	*c.* 525–1565	MEDIEVAL INDIAN ART	
	c. 525–600	Early Kalacuri Dynasty	Elephanta, Elūrā
	c. 600–850	Pallava Dynasty	Māmallapuram
	c. 550–750	Cāḷukya Dynasty	Bādamī, Aihoḷe, Paṭṭadakal
	c. 750–975	Rāṣṭrakūṭa Dynasty	Elūrā
	c. 750–1250	Pāla and Sena Dynasties	Nālandā
	c. 950–1200	Candella Dynasty	Khajurāho
	c. 1076–1586	Gaṅgā Dynasty	Koṇārak, Bhuvaneśvara
	c. 850–1250	Coḷa Dynasty	Tanjore
	c. 1006–1346	Hoyśala Dynasty	Halebid, Belūr
	c. 1100–1350	Pāṇḍya Dynasty	Tiruvannāmalai
	c. 1350–1565	Rāya Dynasty	Vijayanagar
Portuguese, French, and British in India (*post* 1500)	XVI–XIX cent.	LATE STYLES	
	post 1565	Nāyak Dynasty	Madura
	XVI–XIX cent.	Rājput Dynasties	Miniatures
	1526–1857	Moghul period (Muslim)	

Note: This chart has been updated with the kind assistance of Dr. Walter Spink of the University of Michigan, who helped Campbell compile the original for The Art of Indian Asia *in 1954.*

GLOSSARY

abhināya – Dramatic portrayal, in dance.

advaita – "without a second". In Śaṅkara's Vedantic philosophy, the standpoint from which the world is regarded as being beyond pairs-of-opposites (i.e. space-time, subject-object).

ahiṁsā – "non-injury, non-killing". The injunction not to harm any living thing, a basic law of Jainism and Buddhism.

ānanda – "bliss". In Vedanta, one of the three predications of Absolute Being that is the very essense of reality, experienced in yogic *samādhi* as the rapturous root of the world of phenomenality, transcending even suffering.

apsarases – "[H]eavenly damsels [which] constitute a kind of celestial *corps de ballet* are the mistresses of those who in reward for pious and meretorious deeds during their earthly lives have been reborn among the gods." —*Art of Indian Asia*

artha – "Thing, object, substance". The first of the four aims of Indian life (see also *kāma, dharma,* and *mokṣa*) that consists in the acquisition of material possessions.

asuras – Demons, titans, anti-gods, rivals of the gods.

ātman – "self". Absolute Reality, i.e. the transcendent-yet-immanent mystery that is embodied in the microcosm of the individual as the ultimate source of his consciousness. Sometimes mistranslated as "soul". See also below under "*Brahman*".

baksheesh – Alms. The pervasive begging that Campbell encountered led him to see India as caught up in a "Baksheesh Complex" that dominated its social and political life.

bhairavas – deities attending on the goddess Mahā-Kālī during the night of Kāla-Rātrī. The horrific aspect of Śiva.

bhajana – Devotional song.

bhakti – "devotion." Also, *bhakti yoga,* the yoga of devotion to an object, god, person, thing, or animal, that consists in the annihilation of one's personal will in the service to that object. See note 208.

bhūmi-sparśa-mudrā – A mudrā (q.v.), "one of the most common in figures of the seated Buddha. The left hand rests on the lap, with upturned open palm, while the right hangs downward, the middle finger touching the earth in the so-called 'position of touching the earth'."—*Art of Indian Asia*

brahmacarya (the stage of life), *brahmacārin* (the person)– "going in Brahman". A student of sacred knowledge; refers to the first stage of life), spent in celibate study, before marriage. (See also *gṛhastha, vānaprastha,* and *sannyāsa.*)

Brahman – Absolute Reality in its macrocosmic inflection as a counter-concept to *ātman,* the "self" or microcosmic inflection; the ground of being, or ultimate mystery of which all forms are a manifestation, including the gods. (The formula that Campbell often repeats, *ātman* = *Brahman,* refers to the goal of transcending these apparently opposite aspects of reality.)

brahmin *(brāhmaṇa)*– Priest or teacher, first of the four Indian castes. See also *kṣatriya, vaiśya,* and *śūdra.*

burqa' – Tent-like covering, worn by Muslim women.

cādar – Sheet or large shawl worn as a veil by women.

cakra – One of a series of nerve centers in yogic physiology, rising from the base of the spine to the crown of the head. The second is known as *svādiṣṭhāna,* and is the cakra of the genital area. For an explanation of the *cakra* system, see *The Mythic Image,* pp. 330–381.

caste – The social and religious divisions of people in Hindu society. They are the brahmin, or priest-teacher; *kṣatriya,* king or soldier or political or military leader; *vaiśya,* merchant, and *śūdra,* laborer.

citraśāla – Painting gallery.

copra – Dried sections of the meat of the coconut, used for coconut oil and many other products. A major export of South India, Sri Lanka, Indonesia, and the Philippines.

daṇḍa-śakti (see also *loka-śakti*) – Vinoba Bhave political idea, meaning "power of the stick, ruling by force."

darśana – "seeing". The experience of seeing an image in a temple, a spiritually enlightened person, etc. Also, generically, philosophy.

devadāsī – "slave girls of the god". Dancing and singing girls of temple ritual.

Devī Mahātmya – Part of the Mārkāṇḍeya Purāṇa, "Praise Song to the Goddess." Essential text of the cult of Durgā, it includes the story of the slaying of the Buffalo Demon, a demon often depicted in sculpture.

dharma – "duty". The third of the four aims of Indian life (see also *artha, kāma,* and *mokṣa*), consisting in the performance of the various duties, rights, privileges ascribed to each of the four castes. In Mahāyāna Buddhism, *dharma,* taken in the impersonal sense of "the way things are" or "the structure of things", means "Way" or "Path."

digambara – "clothed in space" i.e., "naked", referring to Jain ascetics. In ancient times, most of the monks went around naked, and so Alexander found them when he invaded India, calling them "gymnosophists." They are to be distinguished from the *svetambara* ("clothed in white") sect, who already in the time of the Buddha had begun to wear white garments as a concession to modesty.

dvarāpālas – Door guardians in architecture.

gandharva – Heavenly musician. They are the consorts of the *apsarases* (q.v.).

garbhagṛha – "womb-room". Sanctuary, inner room of a temple.
ghazal – An Urdu, Persian, and Arabic poetical form.
gopīs – "cow girls". The companions of Kṛṣṇa.
gopuras – Porch towers of the later architecture of southern India.
gṛhastha (the stage of life), *gārhasthya* (the person) – Householder; refers to the second of the four stages of Indian life, spent in marriage and raising a family. (See also *brahmacarya, vānaprastha,* and *sannyāsa).*
guṇas – "strands". In *Sāṅkhya* (the metaphysical foundations of classical yoga), the three *guṇas* are the objective attributes of *prakṛti* (nature, or matter): *tamas* is black inertia, i.e. mass; *rajas,* its opposite, is fiery, red activity, i.e. energy; while *sattva* is pure white crystalline consciousness. All matter is characterized in varying proportions by these three strands. Radhakrishnan has it thus: "*Prakṛti* is, as it were, a string of three strands: *Sattva* is potential consciousness; *rajas* is the source of activity, and *tamas* is the source of that which resists activity. They produce pleasure, pain, and indifference, respectively. All things, as products of *prakṛti,* consist of the three *guṇas* in different proportions." Radhakrishnan, *A Sourcebook in Indian Philosophy,* p. 424.
gymkhana – A Hobson-Jobson word, meaning "sports-club," based on the Urdu or Hindi *geṇḍ-khāna,* "ball-house," with *geṇḍ* replaced by the English "gym". Every British-influenced city in India had a Gymkhana Club.
iṣṭadevatā – The particular god one worships. The aspect of a god one personally worships.
Iti iti – "this, this". The Upanishadic phrase is *neti neti* ("not this, not this"), used to describe *Brahman.*
jīva –The individual life monad which transmigrates from life to life and is unaffected by the *guṇas.*
jīvan-mukti – "liberated in life". Enlightenment.
jñāna – "Knowledge". *Jñāna yoga* is the yoga of mental discrimination between the subject of knowledge and its object. See note 208.
kāma – "Eros, desire". The second of the four aims of Indian life (see also *artha, dharma,* and *mokṣa*) that consists in finding sensual gratification, pleasure, and love.
kīrtana – Devotional song or chant.
kṣatriya – King or soldier or political or military leader, second of the four Indian castes. See also brahmin, *vaiśya,* and *śūdra.*
kumārī pūjā – Worship of a little girl, during the Durgā Pūjā festival.
kuṇḍalinī yoga – Form of yoga which involves the activation of *śakti* ("energy," here manifested as a white serpent) in such a way that it ascends through the seven *cakras,* or centers of consciousness. Each *cakra,* when activated

by the serpent, transforms the practitioner's consciousness to the aims appropriate to that particular *cakra.*

lāsya – Dance in which the emotions of love are represented in gestures.

līlā – "Play". The play of forms in the pouring forth of *śakti*, through the projecting power of *māyā*, into the world as a delightful presentation of separate forms. See Zimmer, *Artistic Form and Yoga*, pp. 24, 76, 86.

liṅga – Phallus. Symbol of male creative and sexual energy, counterpart to *yoni* (q.v.)

loka-śakti – See also *danda-śakti.* Vinoba Bhave political idea, meaning "worldly power"or "people power."

Mādhyamika – "Middle Way". A school of Mahāyāna Buddhism associated with Nāgārjuna (2nd century A.D.), wherein ultimate reality is conceived of as emptiness (*śūnyatā*) to which no thoughts, concepts, or dualisms can be predicated. All of reality, the world, its names, dreams and forms, including the Buddha, are illusory, like a mirage. Also known as Śūnyatāvāda.

mahānavamī – "Great Ninth". Ninth day of the Durgā Pūjā.

mahāṣṭamī – "Great Eighth". Eighth day of the Durgā Pūjā.

Mahāyāna – "Greater Vehicle". A later form of Buddhism upon which most contemporary forms of Buddhism are based. Hīnayāna, "Lesser Vehicle", is an earlier form of Buddhism. In Hīnayāna the ideal is the *arhat*, or saint, who achieves *nirvāṇa* and frees himself from bondage to *karma* and renounces the world. In Mahāyāna, the ideal is the *boddhisattva*, who upon achieving release from *karma* remains in the world and dedicates himself to achieving the same release for all other sentient beings.

maithuna – Image of a couple in sexual embrace.

maṇḍapa – Temple porch.

mārga – Path, way, trace, guidepost.

maṭha – Monastery.

māyā – "Illusion". Generally, the phenomenal world; the superimposition of plurality (space, time, matter) upon *Brahman*, or Absolute Reality.

mleccha – Foreigner.

mokṣa – "Release". The last of the four aims of Indian life (see also *artha, kāma,* and *dharma*), different from the first three, which are concerned with the relation of the individual to the world and society. *Mokṣa*, the supreme aim, is release from the world, society and the other aims altogether.

mudrā – Symbolically significant positions or poses of the hands and fingers in dance and iconography.

namaskāra – A gesture, bowing with both hands clasped together, both as homage and meaning "hello."

Nandi – Śiva's bull.

naṭarāja – An incarnation of Śiva as Lord of the Dance.

nirvāṇa – "blown out". In Buddhism, the still point of release from suffering that is found at the center of one's consciousness; it can be defined as either release from the world and its illusions (Hīnayāna Buddhism), or as release from ignorance (Mahāyāna Buddhism).

paisa – Indian monetary unit of small value.

paṇḍal – "shed". A temporary shrine put up, for instance, during a festival.

paśu – Creature, animal.

pisācas – Demons, as for instance those attending the goddess Mahā-Kālī during the night of Kāla-Rātrī at the Divālī festival.

prasāda – "grace". Food offered to a deity and then distributed to worshippers in its new, sacralized state.

pūjā – The basic form of modern Hindu worship, consisting of worship of a holy sanctuary, image, or person by tossing or pouring on it flowers, rice, water, oil or milk.

Purāṇa – A class of sacred Hindu literature, it consists of volumes of poetry, fables, and myths. See note 153.

purdah – Custom of veiling women in Hindu and Muslim India.

rāga – The melodic structure of Indian classical music, or of a given piece of music, e.g. *Rāga bhairava.* See note 188.

rājā – "the yoga of kings". *Rājā yoga* involves the "intentional stopping of the spontaneous activity of the mind-stuff." See note 208.

rasa –An emotive essense of drama or poetry. There are variously nine or more types. See note 187.

ṛṣi – One of the seers who composed the Vedas.

sādhanā – Method, technique, way of operating, spiritual practice.

sadhu – "good man". An ascetic.

sahaja – "easy, spontaneous". A Tantric coinage. "In sahaja, the adoration of young and beautiful girls was made the path of spiritual evolution and ultimate emancipation. By this adoration we must understand not merely ritual worship (the Kumārī Pūjā [q.v.]), but also 'romantic love'."— "Sahaja" in Coomaraswamy, *The Dance of Śiva.*

śakti – "energy". The energy that moves through all things, seeking to manifest itself in different forms.

samādhi – "concentration, contemplation, trance". Spiritual illumination, the absorption of individual consciousness by *Brahman.*

sāman – A verse or text of the Sāma Veda, or the Sāma Veda itself.

saṁsāra – The endless wheel of birth-death-rebirth, self-propelled by the kinetic impulses of *karma.*

sandhi – Marriage, juncture.

sannyāsa (the stage), *sannyāsī* (the person) – Wandering ascetic; the last of the four stages of Indian life (see also *brahmacarya, gṛhastha,* and *vānaprastha*).

saptamī pūjā – Ceremony during the seventh day of the Durgā Pūjā.

satī (suttee) — The custom, outlawed today but still sporadically practiced, of a wife immolating herself on her husband's funeral pyre.

satya – "Truth".

satyagrāha – "Holding the truth." Mahatma Gandhi's system of non-violent civil disobedience.

satyam eva jayati –"Truth indeed wins out". Upanishadic aphorism.

siddha – "Perfected one". A yoga adept.

śikāra – Dome or spire of Northern Indian temples of the Gupta and later periods.

śloka – "Meter, verse". *Śloka* meter is the epic meter.

smṛti – "What is remembered". One of the classes of sacred Hindu literature, taken as explication or furtherance of the *śruti* works. Included in it are the *Mahābhārata* (which includes the *Bhagavad-gītā),* and the *Dharmaśāstras,* treatises on ethical and social philosophy. See note 153.

śruti – "What is heard". The oldest class of sacred Hindu literature, inclduing the Vedas and the Upanishads, taken as direct revelation. See note 153.

stūpa – Mound, memorializing Buddha. "In its earliest known examples, at Bhārhut and Sāñcī, the form was that of a moundlike central structure surrounded by a railing with sumptuously carved gates. In the course of the subsequent centuries the *stūpa* developed variously, particularly following the spread of Buddhism throughout Asia." —*Art of Indian Asia.*

śūdra – Laborer, last of the four Indian castes. See also brahmin, *kṣatriya,* and *vaiśya.*

śunyatā – "Emptiness". See note 234.

suṣupti – "Fully asleep."

svapna – Dream.

tāla – Rhythm.

tāṇḍava – Dance of Śiva.

tanka – Tibetan Buddhist temple banner.

Tantra – "Thread". (Thread through the palm-leaf manuscript). One of the classes of sacred Hindu literature. See note 153.

toraṇa – One of the monumental gates of a *stūpa.*

trimūrti – "Three-faced, three-imaged".

turīya – "Fourth". Cosmic rapture. See note 262.

uṣṇiṣa – "The true Buddha head is bare...[the forehead] surmounted by a peculiar swelling, the *uṣṇiṣa,* which is one of the thirty-two traditional 'great marks' of the Buddhist superman-savior."—*Art of Indian Asia.*

vāhana – "Vehicle, mount". Animals and other beings that appear beneath the feet of deities in Indian art.
vaiśya – Merchant, third of the four Indian castes. See also brahmin, *kṣatriya*, and *śūdra.*
vānaprastha (the stage), *vanaprasthī* (the person) – Forest-dweller; the third of the four stages of Indian life spent in solitary contemplation. (See also *brahmacarya, gṛhasthya,* and *sannyāsa*).
Vedanta – "End of the Vedas". The system of monistic philosophy based on the Upanishads, which come at the end of the Vedas. Śaṅkara, the 8th-century Hindu philosopher, was it most famous exponent. See *advaita.*
vidyā – Knowledge of any kind.
vihāra – Monastery.
vīnā – A stringed instrument related to the sitar.
vīra – "Hero".
yakṣa – Pre-Vedic fertility gods who serve as attendants of Śiva and Kubera (the "Goblin King").
yonī – Symbol of female creative and sexual energy, counterpart to *liṅga* (q.v.).
yuga – A great world age, four of which—Krita, Tretā, Dvāpara, and Kali—form a world cycle (Mahāyuga), and correspond to the four ages—Gold, Silver, Brass, and Iron—of the Greco-Roman tradition. At the end of a Mahāyuga there is a great world flood which reabsorbs creation back into the Absolute that it may begin again.
zamindar – Large landowner.
zanāna – Women's quarter in a Muslim household.

BIBLIOGRAPHY

Agehananda Bharati. *The Ochre Robe.* London: George Allen and Unwin, 1961.

Agehananda Bharati. *The Tantric Tradition.* London: Rider, 1965.

Arnold, Edwin. *The Light of Asia: Or, the Great Renunciation.* London: Routledge & Kegan Paul, 1964. First published 1879.

Bhave, Vinoba. *Bhoodan Yajna.* Ahmedabad: Navajivan Publishing House, 1953.

Boethius, *The Theological Tractates and The Consolation of Philosophy.* Ed. H. F. Stewart and E. K. Rand. Loeb Classical Library. Cambridge, Mass.: Harvard University Press, 1918.

Campbell, Joseph. "Heinrich Zimmer (1890–1943)." *Partisan Review*, 20 (July 1943): 415–416.

————, and Henry Morton Robinson. *A Skeleton Key to Finnegans Wake.* New York: Harcourt, Brace and Co., 1944. New York: Penguin Books, 1977.

————. *The Hero with a Thousand Faces.* Bollingen 27. New York: Pantheon Books, 1949. 2nd ed. rev. Princeton: Princeton University Press, 1968.

————. *Flight of the Wild Gander: Explorations in the Mythological Dimension.* New York: Viking Press, 1951. 2nd rev. ed. New York: Harper and Row, 1990.

————, ed. *The Portable Arabian Nights.* New York: Viking Press, 1952.

————. "Hinduism." In *Basic Beliefs: The Religious Philosophies of Mankind.* Ed. Johnson E. Fairchild, 54–72. New York: Sheridan House, 1959. Subsequent ed., 39–58. New York: Hart Publishing Co., n.d.

————. "Renewal Myths and Rites of the Primitive Hunters and Gatherers." *Eranos-Jahrbücher* 28. Zürich: Rhein-Verlag,1959. Reprint. Dallas: Spring Publications, 1989.

————. *The Masks of God.* 4 vols. New York: Viking Press, 1959–1968. Vol.1, *Primitive Mythology,* 1959. Vol. 2, *Oriental Mythology,* 1962. Vol. 3, *Occidental Mythology,* 1964. Vol. 4, *Creative Mythology,* 1968. Pb. ed. Arkana, 1991.

————. "Oriental Philosophy and Occidental Psychoanalysis." In *Proceedings of the IXth International Congress for the History of Religions, Tokyo and Kyoto, August 27–September 9, 1958*, 492–496. Tokyo: Maruzen, 1960.

————. *Myths to Live By.* New York, Viking Press, 1972. New York: Bantam Books, 1973.

————. "On the Mythic Shape of Things to Come—Circular and Linear." *Horizon* 16 (Summer 1974): 35–37.

————. *The Mythic Image.* Bollingen 100. Princeton: Princeton University Press, 1974. Pb. ed. Princeton: Princeton Unversity Press, 1983.

————. "The Occult in Myth and Literature." In *Literature and the Occult: Essays in Comparative Literature.* Ed. Luanne Frank, 3–18. Arlington, TX: UTA Publications in Literature, 1977.

————. "The Interpretation of Symbolic Forms." In *The Binding of Proteus.* Ed. Marjorie W. McCune, Tucker Orbison and Philip M. Withim. Lewisburg, Pennsylvania: Bucknell University Press, 1980.

————. "Indian Reflections in the Castle of the Grail." In *The Celtic Consciousness.* Ed. Robert O'Driscoll. New York: George Braziller, 1982.

————. *Inner Reaches of Outer Space: Metaphor as Myth and as Religion.* New York: Alfred van der Marck Editions, 1986. New York: HarperCollins, HarperPerennial, 1988.

————. *Hero's Journey: The World of Joseph Campbell: Joseph Campbell on His Life and Work.* Ed. Phil Cousineau. San Francisco: Harper and Row, 1990.

————. *Freud, Jung, and Kundalini Yoga.* Big Sur Tapes, Big Sur, California.

————. *Historical Atlas of World Mythology.*

Vol. 1, *The Way of the Animal Powers.* New York: Alfred van der Marck Editions, 1983. Reprint in 2 pts. Part 1, *Mythologies of the Primitive Hunters and Gatherers.* New York: Alfred van der Marck Editions, 1988. Reprint of Part 1. New York: Harper and Row Perennial Library, 1988. Part 2, *Mythologies of the Great Hunt.* New York: Alfred van der Marck Editions, 1988. Reprint of Part 2. New York: Harper and Row Perennial Library, 1988.

Vol. 2, *The Way of the Seeded Earth.* 3 pts. Part 1, *The Sacrifice.* New York: Alfred van der Marck Editions, 1988. Reprint. Harper and Row Perennial Library, 1988. Part 2, *Mythologies of the Primitive Planters: The Northern Americas.* New York: Harper and Row Perennial Library, 1989. Part 3, *Mythologies of the Primitive Planters: The Middle and Southern Americas.* New York: Harper and Row Perennial Library, 1989.

————. *The Power of Myth.* With Bill Moyers. Ed. Betty Sue Flowers. New York: Doubleday, 1988. New York: Anchor Books, 1991.

————. *Reflections on the Art of Living: A Joseph Campbell Companion.* Ed. Diane K. Osbon. New York: HarperCollins, 1991.

————. *Mythic Worlds, Modern Words: On the Art of James Joyce.* Ed. Edmund L. Epstein. New York: HarperCollins, 1993.

Coomaraswamy, Ananda K. *History of Indian and Indonesian Art.* Leipzig:

Karl W. Hiersemann. Reprint. New York: Dover Books, 1985.
———., and Sister Nivedita (Margaret E. Noble), *Myths of the Hindus and Buddhists.* George G. Harrap and Company, 1913. Reprint. New York: Dover Publications, 1967.
———. *Dance of Śiva.* London: Simpkin, Marshall, Hamilton, Kent and Co., 1924. Reprint. New York: Dover Publications, 1985.
———. *Time and Eternity.* Ascona, Switzerland: Artibus Asiae, 1947. 2nd ed. rev. Bangalore, India: Select Books, 1989.
———. *Coomaraswamy 2: Selected Papers, Metaphysics.* Roger Lipsey, editor. Bollingen 89. Reprint. Princeton: Princeton University Press, 1977.
Danielou, Alain. *Introduction to the Study of Musical Scales.* London: Indra Society, 1943.
———. *Yoga: The Method of Reintegration.* London: C. Johnson, 1949.
———. *Bharata Natyam; danse classique de l'Inde.* Berlin: Institut International d'Études Comparatives de la Musique, 1970.
———. *Shiva and Dionysus.* New York: Inner Traditions International, 1984.
———. *The Way to the Labyrinth: Memories of East and West.* Translated by Marie-Claire Cournand. New York: New Directions, 1987.
de Rougemont, Denis. *Love in the Western World.* New York: Pantheon Books, 1940. 2nd ed. revised and augmented, 1956.
Dilip Kumar Roy. *Pilgrims of the Stars.* New York: Macmillan, 1973.
Eels, Charles P. *Life and Times of Apollonius of Tyana.* University Series: Language and Literature, Vol. II.1. Palo Alto, CA: Stanford University Publications, 1923.
Erikson, Erik. *Gandhi's Truth.* New York: W.W. Norton, 1969.
Frazer, Sir James. *Myths of the Origin of Fire.* London: Macmillan, 1930.
Frobenius, Leo. *Das Unbekannte Afrika: Aufhellung der Schicksale eines Erdteils.* München: Beck, 1923.
———. *Paideuma, Umrisse einer Kultur- und Seelenlehre.* München: Beck, 1923.
———. *Schicksalskunde im Sinne des Kulturwerdens.* Leipzig: R. Voigtlander, 1932.
———. *Kulturgeschichte Afrikans: Prolegomena zu einer historischen Gestaltlehre.* Zürich: Phaidon-Verlag, 1933.
Guénon, René. *Introduction to the Study of the Hindu Doctrines.* London: Luzac and Co., 1945.
Heras, Henry. *Studies in Proto-Indo-Mediterranean Culture.* Bombay, 1933. Bombay: Indian Historical Research Institute, 1953.

Hixon, Lex. *Great Swan: Meetings with Ramakrishna.* Boston: Shambhala, 1992.

Huxley, Aldous. *The Doors of Perception.* New York: Harper, 1954.

Jayakar, Pupul. *Krishnamurti: A Biography.* New York: Harper and Row, 1988.

Jung, C. G. *Archetypes and the Collective Unconscious.* Collected Works 9. Bollingen 20. Pantheon Books, 1959. 2nd ed. Princeton: Princeton University Press, 1969.

————. *Alchemical Studies,* Collected Works 13. Bollingen 20. Princeton: Princeton University Press, 1967.

————. *Mysterium Coniunctionis,* Collected Works 14. Bollingen 20. 2nd ed. Princeton: Princeton University Press, 1970.

Kramrisch, Stella. *Indian Sculpture.* Calcutta, 1933. Delhi: Motilal Banarsidass, 1981.

————. *The Art of India through the Ages.* London and New York: Phaidon, 1954.

Krishnamurti, Jiddu. *You are the World.* New York: Harper and Row, 1972.

————. *The First and Last Freedom.* New York: Harper and Row, 1972.

Menen, Aubrey. *The Ramayana.* New York: Scribners, 1954.

Krishna Menon, called Atmananda Guru. *Atma-darshan: At the Ultimate.* Tiruvannamalai: Sri Vidya Samiti, 1946.

————. *Atma-nirvriti: Freedom and Felicity in the Self.* Trivandrum: Vedanta Publishers, 1952.

McGuire, William, *Bollingen: An Adventure in Collecting the Past.* Princeton: Princeton University Press, 1982.

McMahon, Robert J. *The Cold War on the Periphery.* New York: Columbia University Press, 1994.

Nietzsche, Friedrich. *The Birth of Tragedy out of the Spirit of Music.* In *Basic Writings of Nietzsche.* Edited and translated by Walter Kaufmann. New York: Modern Library, 1968.

Nikhilananda, *The Upanishads.* 4 vols. New York: Harper, 1949.

Nivedita, Sister [Margaret E. Noble]. *Notes on Some Wanderings with the Swami Vivekananda by Sister Nivedita of Ramakrishna-Vivekenanda.* Calcutta: Udbodhan Office, 1922.

Ostor, Akos. *Puja in Society.* Lucknow, 1982.

Radhakrishnan, Sarvepalli, and Charles A. Moore. *A Sourcebook in Indian Philosophy.* Princeton: Princeton University Press, 1957.

Ramakrishna. *The Gospel of Sri Ramakrishna.* Trans., introduction by Swami Nikhilananda. New York: Ramakrishna-Vivekenanda Center, 1942.

Salmony, Alfred. *Carved Jade of Ancient China.* Berkeley: Gillick Press, 1938.

————. *Archaic Chinese Jades.* Chicago: Art Institute of Chicago, 1952.

————. *Antler and Tongue: An Essay on Ancient Chinese Symbolism and its Implications.* Ascona, Switzerland: Artibus Asiae Publications, 1954.

Schopenhauer, Arthur. "Transcendent Speculation upon an Apparent Intention in the Fate of the Individual." *Parerga and Paralipomena,* v. 1.

Singh, Karan. *The Glory of Amarnath.* Place and date of publication unknown.

Spengler, Oswald. *Decline of the West.* 2 vols. Translated by Charles Frances Atkinson. New York: Alfred A. Knopf, 1926–1928. One-volume edition, 1939.

Taylor, Harold. *Essays in Teaching.* New York: Harper, 1950.

————. *On Education and Freedom.* New York: Abelard Schumann, 1954.

Wilhelm, Richard, editor and translator. *The Secret of the Golden Flower: A Chinese Book of Life.* Foreword and Commentary by C. G. Jung. Translated from the German by Cary F. Baynes. Revised ed. New York: Harcourt Brace Jovanovich, 1962.

Zimmer, Heinrich. *Der Weg zum Selbst; Lehre und Leben des indischen Heiligen Shri Ramana Maharsi au Tiruvannamalai.* Ed. C. G. Jung. Zürich: Rascher-Verlag, 1944.

————. *Myths and Symbols in Indian Art and Civilization.* Ed. Joseph Campbell. Bollingen 6. New York: Pantheon Books, 1946. Princeton: Princeton University Press, 1972. Pb. ed., 1992.

————. *The King and the Corpse: Tales of the Soul's Conquest of Evil.* Ed. Joseph Campbell. Bollingen 11. New York: Pantheon Books, 1948. 2nd ed., 1956.

————. *Philosophies of India.* Ed. Joseph Campbell, Bollingen 26. Princeton: Princeton University Press, 1951.

————. *The Art of Indian Asia: Its Mythology and Transformations,* completed and edited by Joseph Campbell. Bollingen 39. Princeton: Princeton University Press, 1955. 2nd. ed., 1960. 2nd. ed., 3rd printing, with revisions, 1968. Pb. ed., 1983.

————. "On the Significance of the Indian Tantric Yoga." In *Spiritual Disciplines.* Vol. 4 of *Papers from the Eranos Yearbooks.* Ed. Joseph Campbell. Bollingen 30. Princeton: Princeton University Press, 1960.

————. *Artistic Form and Yoga in the Sacred Images of India.* Translated by Gerard Chapple and James B. Lawson. Princeton: Princeton University Press, 1984.

ENDNOTES

Note: References to books are given in their short form for ease of reading. Full references may be found in the Bibliography.

[1]Swami Nikhilananda (1895–1973) was a follower of Mahatma Gandhi and a sometime agitator for India's independence. In 1924 he gave up a career as a political journalist to join the Ramakrishna Math, the monastic order founded in 1899 by Vivekananda in commemoration of Ramakrishan, and to serve India's educational, social, and medical needs. He was appointed to the Vedanta Society in New York to replace an older swami who did not get along with his congregation.

Sought out by Heinrich Zimmer (see note 12) in 1941, Nikhilananda soon introduced him to Campbell, with enduring consequences for both men. When Nikhilananda was editing his English edition of *The Gospel of Sri Ramakrishna* and his translation of *The Upanishads* he sought and received Campbell's assistance. "Swami...seduced me into editing his books for him—always keeping me, in a subtle way, pitched forward toward a vacuum, where, finally, I would discover that I had been used."

[2]Campbell wrote the introduction to the *Portable Arabian Nights.*

[3]Elizabeth Stieglitz Davidson (1897–1956), niece of photographer Alfred Stieglitz, married Donald Douglas Davidson, long-time member of the Vedanta Society in New York. They were among the founders of the Ramakrishna-Vivekenanda Center in New York and were lifetime directors. Campell met Nikhilananda through the Davidsons, whose daughter Peggy was Campbell's student at Sarah Lawrence College. The Davidsons' other daughter, Sue Davidson Geiger Lowe, followed her sister to Sarah Lawrence and later became Campbell's assistant. Elizabeth Davidson travelled twice to India with Nikhilananda.
See *A Fire in the Mind,* pp. 284–285.

[4]Countess Mabel Colloredo-Mansfeld, (1906–1965), née Bradley, the widow of Count Colloredo-Mansfeld of Austria, entered the "inner circle" of the Ramakrishna-Vivekenanda Center in New York in the late 1940s.

[5]In other words, Mrs. Davidson and "The Countess."

[6]"In India, the saffron robes the monks wear are the color of the garment put on a corpse. These men are dead. Are you ready to put on the garment of a corpse?" *Joseph Campbell Companion,* p. 201.

[7]In reference to the Ramakrishna Center on East 94th Street in New York.

[8]Built by the Mughal emperor Shah Jahan (fl. 1628–1658) after moving the capital from Agra to Delhi.

[9]Campbell would often later quote this line, comparing it to the saying of Jesus in the Gnostic Gospel of Thomas: "The Kingdom of God the Father is spread upon the Earth and men do not see it." See *Occidental Mythology,* p. 368.

[10]William McGuire was then Campbell's editor for *The Hero With a Thousand Faces.* He was also editor of various other Bollingen Series volumes, all of which were then being published and distributed by Pantheon Books. See William McGuire, *Bollingen: An Adventure in Collecting the Past.*

[11]Humayun, Mughal emperor, reigned 1530–1556.

[12]Heinrich Zimmer (1890–1943) was one of the scholars who most influenced Campbell's life and work. A friend of Thomas Mann, of Carl Gustav Jung, married to Hugo von Hofmannsthal's daughter, a great raconteur and a man of immense erudition, Campbell found in Zimmer a challenging fellow-spirit. Although they knew each other for only two years, from Zimmer's arrival in New York until Zimmer's untimely death from pneumonia in 1943, Campbell became a friend, and after his death spent twelve years editing and completing Zimmer's work. These works included *Myths and Symbols in Indian Art and Civilization*

(1946), *The King and the Corpse* (1948), *The Philosophies of India* (1951), and *The Art of Indian Asia* (1955), whose subject was the very temples that Campbell was now visiting, and to which Campbell was giving the final polish during his Indian trip (see pp. 39, 52, 111, 191). Zimmer himself never visited India. For Campbell's remembrance of Zimmer, see "Heinrich Zimmer (1890–1943)" in the *Partisan Review*, v. 20 (July 1943) pp. 415–416.
[13]In 1953, the United States and Pakistan entered into a military aid agreement, exacerbating the Cold War in South Asia. See Robert J. McMahon, *The Cold War on the Periphery* (New York: Columbia University Press, 1994). See also p. 254 and note 272.
[14]"Forty Sadhus and One Thief," or literally, "Forty Fathers and One Thief." The title is a play on *Ali Baba and the Forty Thieves.*
[15]Pramod Chandra later went on to the University of Chicago and is now at Harvard. See p. 145. Ananda K. Coomaraswamy (1877–1947), one of Campbell's more important sources for Indian art and scholarship. See p. 120.
[16]Vijaya Lakshmi Pandit, Prime Minister Nehru's sister. See note 226.
[17]*Cakra:* one of a series of nerve centers in yogic physiology, rising from the base of the spine to the crown of the head. The second is known as *svādiṣṭhāna*, and is the *cakra* of the genital area. For an explanation of the *cakra* system, see *The Mythic Image*, pp. 330–381.
[18]*The Statesman.* The leading English-language daily in India, published in Calcutta.
[19]The leftward-turning swastika is an ancient Indian graphical symbol suggesting well-being and conveying auspiciousness. In Mahāyāna Buddhism, it is associated with the involution of consciousness backwards from the waking state into *nirvāṇa* through the practice of meditation. See "The Symbol without Meaning" in *Flight of the Wild Gander*, Figs. 11–12, pp. 172–173.
[20]*Brahman*, "universal soul" or "Absolute Reality," to be distinguished from "brahmin" (*brahmana*), the priestly caste. For a discussion of *Brahman*, see Campbell's essay "Hinduism" included here as Appendix A. For further discussion of India's devotional piety, see p. 64.
[21]In Wagner's *Ring* cycle Fafnir is the greedy brother of the giant Fasolt; in *Das Rheingold* he murders Fasolt for possession of the ring, which corrupts him and transforms him into a dragon. In *Siegfried* Fafnir is slain by Siegfried, who takes his gold from him. Campbell's reference seems rather to recall Wagner's version.
[22]See *Inner Reaches of Outer Space*, pp. 126–129 and Figs. 16–17.
[23]Avanti Varman of Kashmir founded the Utpala Dynasty c. A.D. 855 after overthrowing the Karkata Dynasty. He was especially known for his irrigation works.
[24]Mokuleia: the Erdman family estate on Oahu, Hawaii.
[25]Viet Minh: Ho Chi Minh's army in Vietnam against the French.
[26]Fellaheen: Webster's defines the word as "a peasant or agricultural laborer in Egypt, Syria, and other Arabic-speaking countries." Campbell is here using Spengler's special sense of the word to designate the population "fall-out" that results from the aftermath of a collapsed and burnt-out civilization. Such peoples are no longer culturally productive but have fallen back into the sterile culture-forms of their religion: "At this level all civilizations enter a stage, which lasts for centuries.... The whole pyramid of cultural man vanishes. It crumbles from the summit, first the world-cities, then the provincial forms and finally the land itself, whose best blood has incontinently poured into the towns: merely to bolster them up awhile. At the last only primitive blood remains, alive, but robbed of its strongest and most promising elements. This residue is the *Fellah type.*" (*Decline of the West*, vol. 1, p. 107). See also p. 65 for more of Campbell's view of history.
[27]Zimmer wrote, and Campbell edited, both of these books, *Myths and Symbols in Indian Art and Civilization*, and *Philosophies of India.* See Bibliography.
[28]Yuvaraj Karan Singh, *The Glory of Amarnāth*, p. 8. Campbell later said, "The whole idea of pilgrimage is translating into a literal, physical act the pilgrimage of moving into the center of your own heart. It's good to make a pilgrimage if, while doing so, you meditate on what you

are doing and know that it's into your inward life that you are moving." *Transformations of Myth through Time,* p. 98.

[29]*Glory of Amarnāth,* p. 21.

[30]*Glory of Amarnāth,* pp. 20–21.

[31]Tenzing Norgay, who with Sir Edmund Hillary scaled the summit of Mt. Everest on May 29, 1953.

[32]"The chief aim of Indian thought is to unveil and integrate into consciousness what has been thus resisted and hidden by the forces of life—not to explore and describe the visible world. The supreme and characteristic achievement of the Brahman mind...was its discovery of the self (*atmān*) as an independent, imperishable entity, underlying the conscious personality and bodily frame.... [T]he primary concern—in striking contrast to the interests of the modern philosphers of the West—has always been, not information, but transformation." *Philosophies of India,* pp. 3–4.

[33]Campbell attended preparatory school from 1918–1921 at the Catholic Canterbury School in New Milford, Ct.

[34]"The symbolism which knows"; "the symbolism which searches"; and "the symbolism which thinks that it knows." This dichotomy (the third term being Campbell's resolution of the two) is adapted from from the writings of scholar Réné Guénon. See also p. 142.

[35]This distinction is central to Campbell's understanding of mythology. "Jung's idea of the archetypes is one of the leading theories, today, in the field of our subject. It is a development of the earlier theory of Adolf Bastian (1826–1906) who recognized in the course of his extensive travels the uniformity of what he termed 'elementary ideas' (*Elementargedanke*) of mankind. Remarking also, however, that in the various provinces of human culture these ideas are differently articulated and elaborated, he coined the term 'ethnic ideas' (*Völkergedanke)* for the actual local manifestation of the universal forms. Nowhere, he noted, are the 'elementary ideas' to be found in a pure state, abstracted from the locally conditioned 'ethnic ideas' through which they are substantialized; but rather, like the image of man himself, they are to be known only by way of the rich variety of their extremely interesting, frequently startling, yet always finally recognizable inflections in the panorama of human life." *Primitive Mythology,* p. 32. See also *Transformations of Myth through Time,* pp. 93–94; *The Inner Reaches of Outer Space,* pp. 99–100.

[36]Sarvepalli Radhakrishnan, *Indian Philosophy.*

[37]That is to say, the man looked to Campbell as he imagined his friend, the composer John Cage, might look at sixty.

[38]See Zimmer, *Philosophies of India,* Plate IX.

[39]In the myth, Kṛṣṇa alone can destroy the great serpent, Kāliya.

[40]Campbell has made a mistake here: Aurangzeb's father was Shah Jahan, who was not blinded, although he was imprisoned by Aurangzeb in 1658. Akbar, 1542–1605, was an earlier Mughal emperor. Aurangzeb also had a son named Akbar; he led a rebellion against his father.

[41]Mast Hope: a small station-town in Pike County, PA, where the Campbell family used to spend summers.

[42]Warren Hastings (1732–1818), British colonial administrator and first Governor General of Bengal. He was tried (a seven-year trial) and acquitted by the British Parliament for misdeeds in India, Edmund Burke being his main accuser. Hastings cut off the fingers and hands of the Daccan weavers as a disciplinary measure.

[43]See also p. 46 for another example of an "undying banyan."

[44]See *Creative Mythology,* p. 575

[45]Campbell became associated with Eranos, the annual European conference on myth and symbol, from editing the posthuma of Heinrich Zimmer for the Bollingen Foundation. He later edited six volumes of the collected papers from the Eranos conferences and contributed two papers himself. "The Symbol without Meaning" was included in *Flight of the Wild Gander,*

while "Myths and Rites of the Primitive Hunters and Gatherers" is available as a broadside.
[46]See p. 22 for an earlier examination of this theme.
[47]Surendra Nath Das Gupta wrote *A History of Indian Philosophy*, Cambridge University Press, 1922-1949.
[48]The late Agehananda Bharati was author of *The Ochre Robe*, written about his years as a monk, and *The Tantric Tradition*, among other books. He later became a professor of anthropology at Syracuse University.
[49]For the diffusion and practice of the Neolithic pig-sacrifice and its attendant myths and rites, see *The Mythic Image* pp. 450–481. For the Polynesian context see "Renewal Myths and Rites of the Primitive Planters"; also *Primitive Mythology*, pp. 170–215; and *The Sacrifice* (*Atlas* II.1). See *Creative Mythology* pp. 123–128 for its diffusion into Celtic Europe. See also below, p. 60 and note 70 for the Durgā buffalo sacrifice.
[50]Jean Erdman was teaching at this time at Bard College in Annandale-on-Hudson, New York.
[51]"In other words, the goal of the 'Way of Devotion' (*bhakti-maya*) has to be transcended by the student of Vedanta. The loving union of the heart with its highest personal divinity is not enough. The sublime experience of the devotee beholding the inner vision of his God in concentrated absorption is only a prelude to the final ineffable crisis of complete illumination, beyond the spheres even of the divine form." Zimmer, *Philosophies of India*, p. 418.
[52]"The essential idea in Jainism is that the soul, what is called *jīva*, the living monad, is infected with action, which is called *karma*, which blackens and renders heavy the luminous *jīva*.... The goal of their yoga is to clean out the black, clean out action. How do they do it?... The first step, of course, is to become vegetarians. This is saying 'No' to the way life is.... The Buddha [in contrast] said no, no, no, this is reading the whole thing physically. What you must die to is, psychologically, your desires and your fears." *Transformations of Myth through Time*, p. 109. See also Zimmer, *Philosophies of India*, pp. 413–414.
[53]See p. 36.
[54]Nālandā was a celebrated Buddhist university traditionally dated from the 4th to 5th century B.C. Nāgārjuna, the famous Mādhyamika philospher, began his studies there.
[55]Ronald von Holt: one of Campbell's ranching in-laws from Hawaii.
[56]See Zimmer, *Art of Indian Asia*, Plates 31-36.
[57]Aurangzeb (1618–1707), the last great Mughal Emperor, was a fierce promoter of Islam whose military successes were followed by political failures. See note 40.
[58]See *Atlas* II.1, pp. 38–39, Figs. 71–72.
[59]Irma Brandeis was a friend of the Campbells' who taught first at Sarah Lawrence and then at Bard College. Campbell had arranged the connection between her and the Bollingen Foundation, which gave her a grant.
[60]The Forest Lake Club in Pike County, Pennsylvania, where Campbell's family owned property and spent the summers.
[61]Arjuna, the aristocratic protagonist of the *Bhāgavad Gītā.*
[62]Campbell visited Central America with his family as a teenager. See *Fire in the Mind*, pp. 34–35.
[63]The ideas "lifted" are from *Philosophies of India*, pp. 169–172. See also Appendix A, pp. 269–270 for an example of an "Act of Truth."
[64]See *Oriental Mythology*, p. 211 for a fuller interpretation of the sacrifice.
[65]See *Oriental Mythology*, pp. 5–6.
[66]Paddy: freshly cut rice, including the stalk and husk.
[67]See *Primitive Mythology*, pp. 183–190.
[68]Durgā Pūjā lasts nine days, not three, and is often referred to as Nara Ratrī: "nine nights." Campbell seems to have been present for the last three days. The numbers *saptamī, ashtamī, navamī* refer to the seventh, eight, and ninth days of the waxing lunar cycle. Durgā Pūjā begins

on the first day (the new moon), but according to Akos Oster, *Puja in Society,* pp. 25–26, "The major days of the Durgā festival fall on the sixth (Sasthi), seventh (Saptami), eighth (Astami), ninth (Navami), and tenth (Dasami). The Debi worship proper begins on the seventh (the sixth is the Night of Invocation). This being the major puja of the year the *tithis* [lunar calendar days] are called *maha,* or the great, so Mahasaptami, Mahastami and so on." This explains why Campbell calls the seventh day the first: it is the first day that the goddess is established and worshipped. After the ninth night the images (desacralized) are immersed in the river.

[69]The time of the monsoon is archetypically the time of spiritual renewal. The Festival of Anthesteria, a festival of flowers, was held in the spring at Athens. There the wine of the last vintage was tasted, the theater contests were held, and the taints of the past year were purged.

[70]"The supreme orthodox religious duty of man with respect to the gods and ancestors has always been to offer sacrifice. The inhabitant of the body, presiding over the works of the individual, is the one who enacts the sacred office, as well as all the other deeds of the creatures, whether present, past, or future.... Moreover, it [the Self] is not only the perpetrator of sacrifice, fundamentally it is inherent in all the utensils of the holy rite, as well as in...the 'beast of sacrifice'—the victim roped to the sacrificial post and about to be slaughtered. That one being is the offerer, the offering, and the implements of the offering.... Regarded thus as the mere garbs of the one anonymity, the sacrificer and his victim, the feeder and his food, the victor and his conquest, were the same: simultaneous roles or masks of the one cosmic actor." Zimmer, *Philosophies of India,* p. 411. See also Campbell, *The Sacrifice,* pp. 75–76: "In every sacrifice of this kind, the vicitim is understood to be an incarnation of the god."

[71]"Theodosius II summoned a council in the year 431 at Ephesus, which happened to be the city in Asia Minor that, for millenia before the Christian era, had been the chief temple site of the great Asian goddess Artemis, mother of the world and of the ever-dying resurrected God. We can reasonably assume that her lingering influence, no less than that of the virginal matriarchs of the palace, worked upon the counsels of the bishops there assembled. For it was there that the Virgin Mother was declared to be *theotokos,* the Mother of God." *Occidental Mythology,* p. 410.

[72]For a comparison between Catholic liturgy and Indian temple rites, see *Creative Mythology,* pp. 167–169.

[73]"[A] once powerful cult, derived from Iran, of the Mysteries of Mithra, which came to flower in the Near East during the Hellenistic age as a kind of Zoroastrian heresy, and in the Roman period was the most formidable rival of Christianity both in Asia and in Europe." *Occidental Mythology,* p. 255; see pp. 256-271 for discussion, and see Fig. 23 for a portrayal of Mithra Tauroctonus (Mithra killing the Bull).

[74]See *Occidental Mythology,* Figs. 12, 16, 18, 27, and 28.

[75]Pallava Dynasty, A.D. 600–850 in Māmallapuram. Campbell is probably referring to the image reproduced in *Art of Indian Asia,* v. 2, Plate 284.

[76]Leo Frobenius (1873–1938), a German ethnologist and explorer, originator of the cultural-historical approach to ethnology. His works were of central importance for Campbell's writings on primitive cultures and for his view of history: "I studied ecstatically some fifteen volumes of Frobenius' writings...and emerged with a view of history very much more relaxed and continuous than the view emphasized in [Spengler's] *Decline of the West.*" *A Fire in the Mind,* p. 225.

[77]See *Creative Mythology,* Figs. 28, 58.

[78]For an overview of the goddess and the bull, see *Occidental Mythology,* chapter 2, "The Consort of the Bull."

[79]Henry Morton Robinson: Campbell's friend and collaborator on *A Skeleton Key to Finnegans Wake.*

[80]Here again Campbell sounds a main theme; see also p. 10, where Campbell complains that he hears nothing of *Brahman.*

[81]See p. 17 and esp. note 26 for a fuller explanation.

[82]"This next phase I call the *Second Religiousness.* It appears in all Civilizations as soon as they have fully formed themselves as such and are beginning to pass, slowly and imperceptibly, into the non-historical state in which time periods cease to mean anything (so far as the Western Civilization is concerned, therefore, we are still many generations short of that point).... The second religiousness consists in a deep piety that fills the waking-consciousness—the piety that impressed Herodotus in the (late) Egyptians and impresses West-Europeans in China, India, and Islam.... It starts with Rationalism's fading out in helplessness, then the forms of the Springtime become visible, and finally the whole world of the primitive religion, which had receded before the grand forms of the early faith, returns to the foreground, powerful, in the guise of the popular syncretism that is to be found in every culture at this phase...." Spengler, *Decline of the West,* vol. II, pp. 310–311. Also, "In the end Second Religiousness issues in the *fellah-religions." Decline of the West,* p. 314. For "*fellah-religions*" see pp. 17, 182 and note 26.
[83]René Guénon was the author of *Introduction to the Study of the Hindu Doctrines;* Alain Danielou was the author of numerous books on Asian music, culture, and religion. (See note 257). Ananda K. Coomaraswamy, Sinhalese scholar of Indian art, was the author of *History of Indian and Indonesian Art* and numerous other books. Campbell often consulted Coomaraswamy while editing Heinrich Zimmer's posthuma (see note 15).
[84]See p. 25.
[85]Eliot Elisofon, award-winning *Life* photographer, had done extensive photographing of Indian temple sculpture and art objects from European museum collections. Many of his photos fill Zimmer's *The Art of Indian Asia,* published the following year by the Bollingen Foundation.
[86]"In India they are called, respectively, 'the way of the monkey' and 'the way of the kitten'; for when a kitten is in trouble it calls 'meow!' and its mother carries it to safety, but the little monkey, when carried by its mother, has to ride clinging with its own strength to her body. The type of the 'monkey' way in India is the way of the yogi; in Buddhism it is the way of Zen. Among the types in India of the 'way of the kitten carried by its savior,' the best known today and most popular is of Vishnu in his incarnation as Krishna...; while in Buddhism, the Savior most widely celebrated and revered is the inexhaustibly compassionate Buddha Amitabha (Amida in Japan)." *Atlas* II.1, p. 33. See also p. 133.
[87]Twenty-five years earlier, at college, Campbell was a champion half-miler.
[88]See Spengler, *Decline of the West,* vol. 1, p. 183, for the concept of cultural entelechies, or monads, or as he calls them, *Ursymbols,* which act as a sort of cultural DNA that shapes and structures a culture from within and determines what its outlook upon the world will be.
[89]See pp. 127, 182, for a further summaries of Campbell's evolving distinctions between Orient and Occident.
[90]For another view on this dichotomy, and Campbell's tentative resolution, see p. 22. See also p. 142 for a discussion of these ideas in terms of Campbell's vocation.
[91]Māmallapuram: modern Mahabalipuram.
[92]Conjeevaram: modern Kāncipuram.
[93]See *Art of Indian Asia,* v. 2, Plates 266–271.
[94]See *Art of Indian Asia,* v. 2, Plates 272–278a.
[95]See *Art of Indian Asia,* v. 2, Plates 294–298.
[96]See *Art of Indian Asia,* v. 2, Plates 286–287 .
[97]See *Art of Indian Asia,* v. 2, Plates 284–285, 288.
[98]See *Art of Indian Asia,* v. 2, Plates 279–283.
[99]See *Art of Indian Asia,* v. 1, pp. 275, 277 note.
[100]In some reckonings, this is one of the five "element-*liṅgas*" brought by Śaṅkara from the Himalayas. See *Art of Indian Asia,* v. 1, p. 280, 281note.
[101]Rāmānuja: A Vedantist teacher of the 11th century, of a stature comparable to that of Śaṅkara. He modulated Śaṅkara's non-dualism into a more theistic theology, *Viśiṣtha-advaita*

(monism with differentiation, or distinction). See *Philosophies of India,* pp. 458-460.
[102]Vinoba Bhave: Indian ascetic and founder of Bhūdān Yajña, the land-gift movement. He ws an associate of Mohandas Gandhi.
[103]"The relationship [i.e., 'Thou Art That'] is expressed by the simile of lovers, so closely embraced that there is no longer any consciousness of 'a within or without,' and by the corresponding Vaiṣṇava equation, 'each is both.'" *Coomaraswamy 2: Selected Papers, Metaphysics,* p. 22.
[104]See *Art of Indian Asia,* v. 2, Plates 114–115, 118–121; also v. 2, Plate 224, Plate 213.
[105]See *Art of Indian Asia,* Plate 315; also v. 2, Plate 361.
[106]See *Creative Mythology,* p. 595 for a discussion of the Gothic Black Mass; see also *Creative Mythology* pp. 165–166 for a comparison of erotic Indian temple art with the Black Mass.
[107]*Basic Mythologies,* or *Basic Mythologies of Mankind,* which Campbell is here planning, would later become, in part, the four-volume *Masks of God.* "The Bollingen Foundation, having enabled Campbell to travel in the Orient, carried his fellowship well into the 1960's. With [Jack] Barrett he had followed a program that would culminate in a massive, three-volume work, *The Basic Mythologies of Mankind,* devoted to the differences between the various mythologies, whereas *Hero with a Thousand Faces* was devoted to the similarities.... [T]he *Basic Mythologies* bifurcated. Four volumes under the title *Masks of God,* presenting the mythological and religious heritage of man in a style directed to the general reader, were published by The Viking Press over the years 1959–1968." William McGuire, *Bollingen: An Adventure in Collecting the Past,* pp. 178–179. See also below, pp. 125, 143, 145, etc.
[108]Sri Aurobindo (1872–1950): Seer, poet and Indian nationalist, educated at Cambridge, later imprisoned for political activities. The founder of a new theory of gnosis in which cosmic salvation is linked to human spiritual evolution. He was founder also of an international spiritual community in Pondicherry.
[109]The *yugas* are the four world ages through which we endlessly cycle, going from best to worst. They are represented by Śaṅkara as a cow standing first on four legs, then three, then two, then one. This last is called the Kālī Yuga, the current one, full of strife and evil, lasting 432,000 years. At its end a "holy" age, the Kṛta Yuga, will return. See Zimmer, *Myths and Symbols in Indian Art and Civilization,* pp. 11–19; also Campbell, "On Mythic Shapes of Things to Come—Circular and Linear" in *Horizon,* No. 16, Summer 1974, pp. 35–37.
[110]"When faced with this problem of grasping the ideas of the East, the usual mistake of Western man is like that of the student in *Faust.* Misled by the Devil, he contemptuously turns his back on science, and, carried away by Eastern occultism, takes over yoga practices quite literally and becomes a pitiable imitator. (Theosophy is our best example of this mistake.) And so he abandons the one safe foundation of the Western mind and loses himself in a mist of words and ideas which never would have originated in European brains, and which never can be profitably grafted upon them.... It is not a question of our imitating, or worse still, becoming missionaries for what is organically foreign but rather a question of building up our own Western culture, which sickens with a thousand ills. This has to be done on the spot, and by the real European as he is in his Western commonplaces, with this marriage problems, his neuroses, his social and political decisions, and his whole philosophical orientation." C. G. Jung, in "Commentary on 'The Secret of the Golden Flower'." See also p. 82, and note 88, for a discussions of the dangers going in the other direction, i.e. for Indians taking from the West. See also the diagram on p. 127 for Campbell's contrast of the respective aims of the two cultures.
[111]See Sir James Frazer, *Myths of the Origin of Fire.*
[112]Gymkhana: athletic clubs established throughout India in 1861 by a Major John Trotter for British officers; later converted to various uses.
[113]Alfred Salmony (1891–1958), art historian and critic, Professor of the History of Asiatic Art at the Institute for Fine Arts at New York University. An authority on Chinese jade, he was the author of two monumental works: *Carved Jade of Ancient China* and *Archaic Chinese*

Jades. His book *Antler and Tongue,* which stresses the relationship between the art of Europe and Asia in antiquity, came out in 1954. Salmony was educated at the universities of Bonn and Vienna, and became Curator of the Cologne City Museum of Asiatic Art in 1920. Salmony came to New York in 1933, fleeing the Nazis. He taught at Mills College and Vassar College before coming to NYU, and was editor of the quarterly journal *Artibus Asiae.*

[114]Enantiodromia: A word coined from the Greek by Jung to mean a situation which turns into its opposite.

[115]Nasli Heeramanek, a Parsee art dealer with whom the Campbells had become friendly in New York.

[116]Mme. Moitessier, wife of Gunvor Moitessier, who took many of the photos for *The Art of Indian Asia.*

[117]See *Art of Indian Asia,* Plates 187–247.

[118]Kailāśanātha Temple, or Cave XVI. "This overpowering monument marks the victory of Brahmanism over Buddhism." *Art of Indian Asia,* v.1, p. 291. See also v. 2, Plates 204–226.

[119]See *Art of Indian Asia,* v. 1, pp. 185–190, v. 2, Plates 142- 186. "[Ajaṇṭā is] the main site safeguarding from the ravages of time fragments of an art scarcely matched in the world." *Art of Indian Asia,* p. 185.

[120]Elephanta is an island in the harbor of Bombay, of roughly the same period as the Kailāśanātha of Elūrā (later 8th century A.D.). The central figure is a threefold image of Śiva, 23 ft. high by 19fi ft. across. See *Art of Indian Asia,* v. 1, pp. 297–298; v. 2., Plates 253–255.

[121]For *The Art of Indian Asia,* which was due to come out shortly.

[122]Rama Mehta, an aristocratic patron of the arts from New Delhi, known to the Nikhilananda circle.

[123]Campbell met Jiddu Krishnamurti, the messiah-elect of the world Theosophical movement, on a transatlantic voyage (see Editors' Foreword p. ii). One of the women traveling with Krishnamurti gave Campbell Edwin Arnold's book about the life of the Buddha, *The Light of Asia.* Their friendship continued intermittently for several years. See *A Fire in the Mind,* esp. pp. 41–44 and Index notations.

[124]In 1938 Jung had made the trip to India, visiting many of the same sites as Campbell. When given the opportunity in Madras, however, to visit with Ramana Maharishi, he declined, to the disappointment of Heinrich Zimmer, who had never been to India. When Zimmer died in 1943, Jung took upon himself the task of editing Zimmer's German posthuma, which consisted primarily of a single volume on Sri Ramana Maharishi, entitled *Der Weg zum Selbst: Lehre und Leben des Sri Ramana Maharishi* (1944). Jung wrote a foreword, "The Holy Men of India," in which he wrote of his visit to India and explained his refusal to visit Ramana Maharishi by saying that Maharishi was omnipresent, since Jung had actually seen him everywhere, the "true Son of Man of the land of India."

[125]Four caves from the early Cāḷukya Period, c. A.D. 550–750. Cave III, the earliest, is dated at A.D. 578. See *Art of Indian Asia,* v.1, pp. 85–86, 290; v. 2, Plates 124–141.

[126]Cave II "shelters a magnificent rendition of Viṣṇu as the Cosmic Boar." See *Art of Indian Asia,* v. 1., p. 290, v.2, Plate 138.

[127]Cave III has pillars "ornamented with magnificent human figures in the full bloom of Gupta abundance." See Coomaraswamy, *History of Indian and Indonesian Art,* p. 96.

[128]"The Malegitti Sivalaya Temple...built *c.* A.D. 625, is one of the oldest structural shrines of the Dravidian type, 'the only structural temple in the style of the Māmallapuram rathas now surviving'...." See *Art of Indian Asia,* v. 1, p. 278; v. 2, Plate 141.

[129]The temples at Paṭṭadakal are examples of the Cāḷukya Period, c. A.D. 550–750. See *Art of Indian Asia,* v. 2, Plates 299–208.

[130]The temples at Aihoḷe are predominantly of the Cāḷukya Period, c. A.D. 550–750. See *Art of Indian Asia,* v. 2, Plates 113, 116–123. For the Durgā temple, see v. 1, p. 84; v. 2, Plates 116–120; for the shallow cave temple see v. 2, Plate 123; for the Huchimalliguḍi, see v. 2, Plate

113. The Lāḍ Khān Temple is of the Gupta Period, c. A.D. 450: see v. 2, Plates 114–115.
[131]Belūr (a temple-city) and Haḷebiḍ (a royal residence, left unfinished, interrupted by a Muslim invasion) date from the Hoysaḷa Period, c. A.D. 1100–1310. For Belūr see *Art of Indian Asia,* v. 2, Plates 434–436. For Haḷebiḍ see v. 1, p. 264; v. 2, Plates 428–433.
[132]Louis Horst (1884–1964), pianist, composer and choreographer; musical director of the Denishaun Dancers (1915–1925), and the Martha Graham Dance Company (1926–1945). He was an early mentor and friend of Jean Erdman.
[133]Stella Kramrisch, *The Art of India through the Ages.*
[134]Other "gurus" would include, in this context, Heinrich Zimmer (see note 12).
[135]See the forthcoming *Journey to the Sun's Door: Japan Journal 1955,* to be published by HarperCollins.
[136]Probably the chapter for Sarah Lawrence President Harold Taylor's book on Sarah Lawrence College, *On Education and Freedom,* for which Campbell agreed to do a chapter.
[137]The Sarabhais were a very wealthy textile family of Ahmedabad, already known to the Campbells. They were patrons also of Le Corbusier, and were associated with Gandhi. See Erik Erikson, *Gandhi's Truth.*
[138]See notes 10 and 12.
[139]Hervey White (d. 1944), founder of the Maverick Colony in Woodstock, New York, a more egalitarian offshoot of the utopian artists' colony, Byrdcliffe, which was founded by Ralph Radcliffe Whitehead in the early part of this century. Campbell was a friend and frequent guest at Hervey White's colony. See *A Fire in the Mind,* pp. 138–139, 219–220, 282, 314, 592.
[140]Svarāj, "self-rule," coined by Gandhi during his journey by boat to South Africa.
[141]See p. 81 and note 86.
[142]From a Tantric psychological typology: *vīra* = hero; *paśu* = herd animal.
[143]See *Oriental Mythology,* pp. 342–343.
[144]"Frobenius called this new age, now upon us, the period of World Culture. Its technical determinants are to be the scientific method of research and the power-driven machine, as were agriculture and stock-breeding (*c.* 7500 B.C.) and the arts of unifying and coercive government (*c.* 3500 B.C.) of the Monumental. And the distinguishing feature of its new mankind...[is] of individuals, self-moved to ends proper to themselves, directed not by the constraint and noise of others, but each by his own inner voice." *Creative Mythology,* p. 575. See also *Creative Mythology,* chapter 9, esp. pp. 611–621, on the seven revolutions in man's consciousness of cosmology, from myth to science, beginning with 1492 and ending with 1900.
[145]Dr. Moti Chandra: well-known art historian, originally from Benares. For his son, see note 15.
[146]Bhulabhai Desai was a barrister who defended, along with Nehru, people accused of trying to subvert the British government in India. He later became India's ambassador to Switzerland. There is a road named after him in Bombay.
[147]Richard McKean: a University of Chicago professor with whom Campbell studied at Columbia in the 1920s.
[148]One lakh = 100,000 rupees; one anna = 1/16 rupee.
[149]See p. 6 and note 9.
[150]Dilip Kumar Roy first became known throughout India as a composer and singer, later as a writer and poet. In 1953 he and dancer Indira Devi undertook a world tour sponsored by the Indian government. See Dilip Kumar Roy, *Pilgrims of the Stars.*
[151]See p. 128.
[152]See "The Dillettante among Symbols" in *The King and the Corpse.*
[153]"The orthodox sacred books (*sāstras*) of India are classed in four categories: 1. *Śruti* ('what is heard'), the Vedas and certain Upaniṣads, which are regarded as direct revelation; 2. *Smṛti* ('what is remembered'), the teachings of the ancient saints and sages, also law books

(*dharmasūtras*) and works dealing with household ceremonies and minor sacrifices (*gṛhyasūtras*); 3. *Purāṇa* ('ancient; ancient lore') compendious anthologies, comparable in character to the Bible, containing cosmogonic myths, ancient legends, theological, astronomical, and nature lore; 4. *Tantra* ('loom, warp, system, ritual, doctrine) a body of comparatively recent texts, regarded as directly revealed by Śiva to be the specific scripture of the Kālī Yuga, the fourth or present age of the world. The Tantras are called 'The Fifth Veda,' and their rituals and concepts have actually supplanted the now quite archaic Vedic system of sacrifice as the supporting warp of Indian life."—Editor's note from *Philosophies of India,* p. 61.

For a different perspective, see Radhakrishnan's *A Sourcebook in Indian Philosophy,* pp. xvii–xxii, which divides the Indian texts into four eras: the Vedic Period (the early dating is obscure, but approximately from 2500 B.C. to 600 B.C.), during which the *śruti* texts were composed, showing primarily a demiurgic, creative spirit; the Epic Period (600 B.C. to A.D. 200), the time of the *smṛti* texts, showing a poetic spirit mixed with a great deal of philosophical and semiphilosophical material; the *Sūtra* Period (dated from the beginning of the Christian era), a time of systematic philosophical treatises; and the Scholastic Period (from the end of *Sūtra* Period until approximately the 17th century and the incursion of foreign powers), which is marked by many mediocre commentaries on the *Sūtras* but also by some of India's greatest philosophers, including Śaṅkara.

154 The reference here is to one of Campbell's favorite quotes from Goethe. "The Godhead is effective in the living and not in the dead, in the becoming and the changing, not in the become and the set-fast; and therefore, accordingly, reason (*Vernunft*) is concerned only to strive toward the divine through the becoming and the living, and the understanding (*Verstand*) only to make use of the become and set-fast." *Creative Mythology,* p. 383. Taken originally from Johann Peter Eckermann, *Gespräche mit Goethe in den letzten Jahres seines Lebens, 1823–1832* (Berlin: Deutsches Verlaghaus Bong & Co., 1916), Vol. I, p. 251. Translated by Charles Francis Atkinson in Spengler's *Decline of the West,* Vol. I, p. 49, note 1. The original German is: *Die Gottheit is wirksam im Lebendigen, aber nicht im Toten; sie is im Werdenden und sich Verwandelnden, aber nicht in Gewordnen und Erstarrten. Deshalb hat auch die Vernunft in ihrer Tendenz zum Göttlichen es nur mit dem Werdenden, Lebendigen zu tun, der Verstand mit dem Gewordenen, Erstarrten, das er es nutze.*

155 "The goal in India, whether in Hinduism, Buddhism, or Jainism, is to purge away individuality through insistence first upon the absolute laws of caste (*dharma*), and then upon long-known, marked-out stages of the way (*mārga*) toward indifference to the winds of time (*nirvāṇa*)." *Creative Mythology,* p. 33.

156 This "dilemma" and its solution lie at the core of Campbell's philosophical stance with regard to his material. For a full discussion see *Creative Mythology,* "Identity and Relationship" pp. 333–348, 585. The dilemma revolves around the *Vernunft-Verstand* polarity (see above, p. 142, and note 154) which appears as a motif, in various forms and in different vocabularies, throughout this journal: as the sadhu as against the folk (p. 20); as *le symbolisme qui cherche* as against *le symbolisme qui sait* (pp. 22, 142); the individual as against the collective (p. 151 ff.); as the way of the monkey as against the way of the kitten (pp. 81, 133); as the pedant-scholar in contradistinction to the creative scholar (p. 123); as clinging to the past instead of creativity in the present (p. 134), and especially as *smṛti* ("what is remembered") as against *śruti* ("what is heard," i.e. the creative muse, pp. 142, 147). The table of oppositions reads thus:

Vernunft	*Verstand*
sadhu	folk
le symbolisme qui cherche	*le symbolisme qui sait*
innovation	tradition
forest	village

monkey	kitten
present	past
śruti	*smṛti*
yoga	*bhakti*
nir-guna Brahman	*sa-guna Brahman*
individual	authority
experience	meaning
changing	set-fast
becoming	become
West	India

For other, related tables, based on East-West oppositions, see pp. 127, 182.

157"We westerners have our own heritage and are caught in its mold...as much as the Hindu are in their own.... We cannot readily dress in Indian wisdom without becoming monkeys or dilletante actors. But, in viewing India's basic attitudes and spiritual propensities, we might gain insight of two things: of the subtle and inextricable web in whose meshes the Hindu spider abides and is caught...and, thus, we might realize to a fuller extent in what self-timbered framework of ideas we abide and are caught in ourselves." Zimmer, *Artistic Form and Yoga,* p. xxiii. See also Zimmer, "On the Significance of the Indian Tantric Yoga" in *Spiritual Disciplines: Papers from the Eranos Yearbooks*, vol. 4 (Bollingen XXX), pp. 19–20.

158Some of Campbell's thoughts on Las Casas can be found in the *Atlas* II.3, pp. 310, 314, and the captions to Figs. 420–421.

159This and most other of Campbell's work on the Pacific Islands were eventually to have been included in a later volume of the *Atlas* but remain unpublished.

160In general, these titles reflect themes elaborated on by Campbell in *Creative Mythology.*

161The *Eranos Tagung* were a series of annual meetings held in Ascona, Switzerland, presided over by Frau Olga Froebe Kapteyn. They were attended by Jung, Zimmer, D. T. Suzuki, Mircea Eliade and many others. The attempt was to understand culture through myth and psyche. Campbell attended in 1953, but did not lecture; he later gave two lectures, in 1957 ("The Symbol without Meaning") and 1959 ("Renewal Myths and Rites of the Primitive Hunters and Gatherers"). He eventually edited English translations of some of the papers presented there under the series title *Papers from the Eranos Yearbooks*, published by Princeton University Press. See also William McGuire, *Bollingen.*

162*Fach:* Lit. "shelf" in German, and by extension, specialty, or area of study.

163Verrier Elwin (1902–1964), scholar of Indian tribespeople and their religion, customs, songs, and literature.

164See p. 142.

165i.e., the Bombay Theatre Unit.

166See *Oriental Mythology*, pp. 136–137.

167See *Oriental Mythology*, pp. 13–23, "The Two Views of Ego."

168Edward VIII of England abdicated his throne in order to marry a divorced (and hence, in the eyes of the Church of England, ineligible) woman, Wallice Simpson.

169Rāma, after recapturing his kidnapped bride Sītā after many trials, refuses to take her back into his household because she has been stained by too-long contact with his enemies. See Coomaraswamy, *Myths of the Hindus and Buddhists,* pp. 28–99.

170"...there is nothing of the fairy tale about the atmosphere of a Greek tragedy, no sense of the play of *māyā* to disengage the reality of the characters from their histories. There is no subliminal ground of repose in *Brahman* over which the passions, limitations, and catastrophes of the action play, like the fragments of a dream. The release in Greek tragedy comes, rather, at the end of a piece, in the minds of the audience, as a transformation of perspective." *Inner Reaches of Outer Space,* p. 140.

[171]Parsees constitute an economic and intellectual élite in the Bombay area. Indian Parsees trace the origins of their religion directly to Persian Zoroastrian roots.
[172]In Zoroastrianism, Ahura Mazda, the Lord of Light and Truth, is locked in a world struggle with Angra Mainyu, who corrupted the realm of matter by pouring darkness into the world of pure light created by Ahura Mazda. "The myth tells that there came into the world a savior to teach the way to accent the good.... As a result of the action of this savior, there is now taking place a restoration. There will come a time when the crisis will occur, when all darkness will be wiped out. There will be a second coming of the savior...and darkness will be permanently eliminated, the Lord of Darkness himself eliminated. There will be nothing but light again." *Transformations of Myth through Time*, pp. 107–108. See also *Occidental Mythology*, pp. 192–212.
[173]There is no evidence that this talk was ever published.
[174]*Strich darunter:* "under the wire," i.e. just in time.
[175]"Pity is the feeling which arrests the mind in the presence of whatsoever is grave and constant in human sufferings and unites it with the human sufferer.... Terror is the feeling which arrests the mind in the presence of whatsoever is grave and constant in human sufferings and unites it with the secret cause." James Joyce, *A Portrait of the Artist as a Young Man.* London: Jonathan Cape, 1916, pp. 232–233. See also *Creative Mythology*, pp. 94, 653–654 for this theme applied to contemporary artistic creation.
[176]"It was because of superior wisdom that the Aryan invaders of India were able to defeat the native pre-Aryan populations, maintain themselves in the land, and ultimately spread their dominion over the sub-continent. The conquered races then were classifed as the fourth, non-Aryan caste of the Śūdra, excluded ruthlessly from the rights and power-giving wisdom of the society of the conquerors, and forbidden to acquire even an inkling of the techniques of the Vedic religion.... We read in the early *Dharmaśāstras* that if a Śūdra chances to overhear the recitation of a Vedic hymn, he is to be punished by having his ears filled with molten lead." Zimmer, *Philosophies of India*, p. 59.
[177]"Remember that old Irish question: 'Is this a private fight or can anybody get into it'?" *Hero's Journey*, p. 20.
[178]See McGuire, *Bollingen*, pp. 178–179. See also above, pp. 101, 125, 143, 145.
[179]See McGuire, *Bollingen*, pp. 140–141.
[180]Nothing came of Campbell's involvement with Coomaraswamy's papers. See the brief note in McGuire, *Bollingen*, p. 141. The comprehensive edition of Coomaraswamy was ultimately completed by Roger Lipsey.
[181]Bartholomé de las Casas is treated in the *Atlas*, II.3, pp. 310, 314, and the caption to Figs. 420–421. See *Occidental Mythology* pp. 324–325 for parallels between the Alexandrine period and our own.
[182]Appolonius of Tyana was a Neo-Pythagorean religious reformer who lived from about 4 B.C. to A.D. 80 or 90. In a third-century biography by Philostratus the Elder, he is portayed as a god-like miracle worker who travelled the ancient world from India to Spain absorbing knowledge and effecting miracle cures, with many parallels to the life of Christ. See Charles Eells, *Life and Times of Apollonius of Tyana.*
[183]See "The Interpretation of Symbolic Forms" in *The Binding of Proteus*, pp. 35–59, also "Indian Reflections in the Castle of the Grail" in *The Celtic Consciousness*, pp. 3–30.
[184]"Are *ignorance* and *sin*, finally, two words for the same condition? Are *enlightenment* and *redemption* two ways of pointing to the same psychological crisis?... But are not this darkened understanding, weakened will, and inclination to evil (i.e., original sin) exactly what the Buddhists mean by ignorance, fear, and desire; namely, *māyā?*" "Intepretation of Symbolic Forms," in The *Binding of Proteus*, pp. 42–43. See also *Occidental Mythology*, pp. 207–208, 466–467; *Mythic Worlds, Modern Words*, p. 277; *The Joseph Campbell Companion*, pp. 143–145.
[185]"Heaven and Hell are psychological definitions." *The Joseph Campbell Companion*, p. 159. "Purgatory and reincarnation are thus homologous." *Oriental Mythology*, pp. 308–309. Or, in

one of Campbell's favorite quotes: "The Kingdom of the Father is spread upon the earth and men do not see it." *Gospel According to Thomas,* Logion 113:114. See note 9.

[186]See *Freud, Jung, and Kundalini Yoga,* a lecture delivered at Esalen Institute.

[187]The *rasas* are the nine aesthetic flavors proper to the various modes of dramatic enjoyments. According to the Gupta treatise *Daśarupa* by Dhanamjaya, the nine *rasas,* classified according to the five states of dramatic enjoyment, are: 1. Cheerfulness (the erotic and the comic); 2. Exaltation (the heroic and the marvelous); 3. Agitation (the odious and the terrible); 4. Perturbation of the Mind (the furious and the pathetic); and 5. Happiness in Tranquility (the peaceful). Number 4 corresponds to Aristotle's idea of the tragic mode. See *Inner Reaches of Outer Space,* pp. 138–142.

[188]"When one listens to Indian music, it never has a beginning or an end. You know that the music is going on all the time, and the consciousness of the musician just dips down into the music, picks it up with the instrument, and reads it again." *Mythic Worlds, Modern Words,* p. 194. Or, again: "Music, however, has a role apart; for it deals not with forms in space, but with time, sheer time. It is not like the other arts, a rendition of what Plato calls 'ideas,' but of the will itself, the world will, of which the ideas are but inflections. 'One could call the world "embodied music" as well as "embodied Will,"' Schopenhauer wrote, confirming thus the ancient theme of the music of the spheres." *Creative Mythology,* p. 83.

[189]*Marg:* a Bombay journal devoted to Indian culture and the arts.

[190]Jean Erdman was moving in a westerly direction on her dance tour, stopping with the writer on Asian philosophy, Alan Watts, in California.

[191]Pupul Jayakar, Minister of Culture and organizer of the Festivals of India in various countries during the 1980s; biographer of Jiddu Krishnamurti and Indira Gandhi.

[192]Madhuri Desai was an art collector greatly interested in Indian culture, music, dance and fine arts. She donated her property and founded the Bhulabhai Desai Institute in Bombay.

[193]Bharata Natyam, the classical dance of southern India. See Danielou, *Bharata Natyam.*

[194]Heinrich Zimmer had died suddenly in 1943 leaving a widow and three boys. See note 12.

[195]Le Corbusier (Charles-Édouard Jeanneret, 1887–1965), distinguished architect, built the Sarabhai villa in Ahmedabad (1951–1956); the Punjab state government building at Chandigarh (1951–1958); the Cultural Center at Ahmedabad (1951–1958); and the Villashadan, Ahmedabad (1951–1956).

[196]A chowry is a whisk used in ritual devotions; often visible in temple sculpture.

[197]There is no further reference in Campbell's work to a talk of this title, but a very similarly titled talk was given three years later in Japan and published as "Oriental Philosophy and Occidental Psychoanalysis."

[198]See "The Impact of Science on Myths" in *Myths to Live By,* p. 20

[199]In Jung's system, the uniting symbol (i.e. a mandala, yantra, or hermaphrodite) is produced by the unconscious as an attempt at healing a pysche split by antithetical conflicts, such as thinking *vs.* feeling, conscious *vs.* unconscious, anima/animus *vs.* ego, etc. The symbols thus produced—through dreams, painting, writing, or some other form of active imagination—take up the incompatible value systems of the various functions and unite them harmoniously. See C. G. Jung, *Psychological Types,* definition under "symbol."

[200]For Campbell's view on a collective unconscious, see *Mythic Worlds, Modern Words,* p. 193. Jung says, in *Pyschological Types,* p. 485, that "[w]e can distinguish a *personal unconscious* comprising all the acquisitions of personal life, everything forgotten, repressed, subliminally perceived, thought, felt. But, in addition to these personal unconscious contents, there are other contents which do not originate in the personal acquisitions but in the inherited possibility of psychic functioning in general, i.e. in the inherited structure of the brain. These are the mythological associations, the motifs and images that can spring up anew anytime anywhere, independently of historical traditional or migration. I call these contents the *collective unconscious.*"

[201]See note 42.

[202]Śaṅkara (c. A.D. 788–850), Vedāntist philosopher who expounded the doctrine of *māyā,* the illusory nature of existence. See *Philosophies of India,* pp. 17–19, 373, 375, 626–627.
[203]See Jung, *Archetypes and the Collective Unconscious,* pp. 317, 370. Also "The Philosophical Tree" in *Alchemical Studies,* p. 253.
[204]Agnes Meyer sat in on Campbell's classes at Sarah Lawrence in 1939, and later introduced him to Thomas Mann.
[205]Gardiner Murphy (1895–1979). American psychologist who founded the "bio-social" approach to psychology that was influential in the 1950s. He married Lois Barclay, known for her work in child psychology. Gardiner Murphy taught at Columbia and City College of New York, and was President of the American Psychological Association. The Murphys worked together on the Indian School Project.
[206]See Zimmer, "On the Significance of the Indian Tantric Yoga" in *Spiritual Disciplines,* pp. 17–18.
[207]Ānanda Mayī Mā was one of the better known and revered mystics in India from the 1950s to the 1980s. She had been a school teacher in Bengal for many years when she experienced a spiritual call. She left her husband and children and lived the life of a *sannyasin,* wandering the roads of India. She founded an ashram on Ānanda Mayī Ghat in Benares and died there in 1982. Her name means "Mother Full of Bliss," and her mere presence was said to bestow beatitude or even *samādhi,* or spiritual illumination.
[208]These are the four yogas in the *Bhāgavad Gītā.* See "Confrontation of East and West" in *Myths to Live By,* pp. 97–101. 1. *Rājā yoga* is a discipline of meditation yoga that involves the "intentional stopping of the spontaneous activity of the mind stuff" (See Campbell's essay "Hinduism" in *Basic Beliefs*). 2. *Jñāna yoga* is the yoga of mental discrimination (*viveka*) between the subject of knowledge and the object of knowledge (see Campbell's essay "The Occult in Myth and Literature" in *Literature and the Occult*). 3. *Bhakti yoga* is the yoga of devotion to an object, god, person, thing, or animal, that consists in the annihilation of one's personal will in the service to that object. 4. *Karma yoga* is the yoga of action that anyone can perform; the formula is to act without desire or fear for the fruits of one's actions.
[209]For a poignant evocation of those scenes, see Lex Hixon's *Great Swan: Meetings with Ramakrishna.*
[210]For Campbell's interest in Huxley, see *The Flight of the Wild Gander,* p. 185; for Huxley's experiments with mescaline see Aldous Huxley, *The Doors of Perception* and Albert Hofman, *LSD: My Problem Child* (New York: McGraw-Hill, 1980).
[211]Lou Harrison, a New York composer and choreographer, friend of the Campbells.
[212]"Nietzsche's designation of music, the dance, and lyric poetry as the arts specific to the Dionysian mode...and on the other side, the side of the claims of the unique, ephemeral, induplicable moment, sentiment, or individual—the side of the principle of individuation (*principium individuationis*), Nietzsche assigned to Apollo as the lord of light and the arts of sculpure and epic poetry." *Creative Mythology,* pp. 333–334.
[213]For earlier, related tables of oppositions, see p. 127 and note 156.
[214]For a discussion of "Fellaheen" and Spengler, see p. 17 and note 26.
[215]"Looked at in this way, the 'Decline of the West' comprises nothing less than the problem of *Civilization.* We have before us one of the fundamental questions of all higher history. What is Civilization, understood as the organic-logical sequel, fulfillment and finale of culture?

"For every Culture has *its own* Civilization. In this work, for the first time, the two words, hitherto used to express an indefinite, more or less ethical, distinction, are used in a *periodic* sense, to express a strict and necessary *organic succession.* The Civilization is the inevitable *destiny* of the Culture, and in this principle we obtain the viewpoint from which the deepest and gravest problems of historical morphology become capable of solution. Civilizations are the most external and artificial states of which a species of developed community is capable. They are a conclusion,the thing-become succeeding the thing-becoming, death following life, rigid-

ity following expansion, intellectual age and stone-built petrifying world-city following mother earth and the spiritual childhood of Doric and Gothic. They are an end, irrevocable, yet by inward necessity reached again and again." Spengler, *Decline of the West,* Vol. I, p. 31.
[216]Although known as the Bombay Theatre Unit, the group appears to have mounted productions in other venues as well.
[217]For Khajurāho, see *Art of Indian Asia,* v. 1, pp. 134, 273–274; v. 2, Plates 309–318. For Koṇārak, see v. 1, pp. 10, 258, 274, 358, 362; v. 2, Plates 348–375.
[218]See *Oriental Mythology,* pp. 309–318.
[219]For the flowering of Indian architecture during the Gupta period see *Oriental Mythology,* pp. 326–337; for the subsequent disintegration of India see pp. 342–343.
[220]The reference here is to *Art of Indian Asia.* See v. 1, p. 123 for the symbols in question.
[221]Meaning "beneath dignity."
[222]Kālidāsa, Hindu dramatist, usually dated to the 5th century at the court of Candra Gupta II of Ujjain.
[223]Campbell is speaking specifically of *The Art of Indian Asia,* but finishing this book also marked the end of Campbell's 11-year involvement with Zimmer's papers, which resulted ultimately in the publication of *The Philosophies of India, Myths and Symbols in Indian Art and Civilization,* as well as *The Art of Indian Asia.*
[224]A.N.T.A.: American National Theater and Academy (now defunct). John Martin was a dance critic for *The New York Times,* Walter Terry for *The Herald Tribune.* Martha Hill ran the summer dance program at Bennington, and taught dance in various schools and colleges. Jean Erdman had approached this committee of dance critics and had been turned down. With Campbell's help, nonetheless, Jean Erdman became the first modern dancer to tour India. Martha Graham followed several years later.
[225]Ravi Shankar, son of a high-ranking Bengali, later went on to great fame in the U.S.; his older brother Uday was a noted dancer and choreographer who met the dancer Pavlova in Paris and became friendly with her. Ali Akbar Khan often accompanied Ravi Shankar but became known as a musician in his own right in the 1960s.
[226]Jawaharlal Nehru had two sisters. One married a Bombay industrialist, Huthee Singh. This sister was known to be gracious and friendly. The other sister Vijaya Lakhsmi (Madam) Pandit was more political and was frequently at odds with her brother. During the most critical phase of the Indian independence movement, Mme. Pandit escaped British surveillance and addressed the U.N. General Assembly.
[227]See p. 187.
[228]See note 204.
[229]"Society, as a fostering organ, is thus a kind of exterior 'second womb' wherein the postnatal stages of man's long gestation...are supported and defended." "Bios and Mythos" in *Flight of the Wild Gander,* p. 53 and pp. 53–60. See also the 1964 essay "The Importance of Rites," collected in *Myths to Live By,* esp. pp. 45–47.
[230]Nationalist Hindu organization.
[231]Stella Kramrisch, *The Art of India through the Ages.*
[232]"...the myth has to deal with the cosmology of today and it's no good when it's based on a cosmology that's out of date. And that's one of our problems. I don't see any conflict between science and religion. Religion has to accept the science of today and penetrate it—to the *mystery.* The conflict is between the science of 2000 B.C. and the science of 2000 A.D." *Hero's Journey,* p. 164. See also "The Confrontation of East and West in Religion" in *Myths to Live By,* pp. 88–89.
[233]See Campbell's question to Ānanda Mayī, pp. 177–178; and a discussion of the yogas as found in the *Bhāgavad Gītā,* note 208.
[234]The *śunyatāvāda* school of Mahāyāna Buddhism (also known as *mādhyamika*): a form of Buddhism based on the doctrine of the void (*śunyatā*), a positive principle from which all

phenomenal existence arises. Hence it is a subtle philosophical stance to believe in "nothing." Zimmer, *Philosophies of India,* pp. 521–522.
235See p. 175.
236Ārya Samāj, a Hindu religious and social reform group founded by Swami Saraswati in 1875 that sought to recoup for Hinduism converts to other religions by going "back to the Vedas": condemning such practices polytheism, caste restrictions, and child marriage.
237*Bhoodan Yajna,* p. 128.
238*Statesman,* January 6, 1955, p. 1.
239Mohenjo-Daro, city on the Indus River in Sind in present-day Pakistan, which flourished circa 3000–1500 B.C. For the "meditating yogi" see *Myths and Symbols,* Fig. 42. See also *Oriental Mythology,* p. 155, and Figs. 18–19.
240Jawaharlal Nehru (1889–1964) was the first Prime Minister of independent India (1947–1964). First coming to prominence through association with Gandhi's Congress Party, he committed himself to Indian independence and became head of the party in 1929. During his incumbency Nehru sought to bring a unified India into the modern era. Internationally he espoused a policy of non-alignment.
241Shanta Rao was originally a Bharata Natyam dancer discovered and mentored, as was Bala Saraswati (see p. 231 and note 250), by Alice Boner, a Swiss woman whom Uday Shankar (see note 225) had met in Europe, and who founded Kerala Kalamandalam, the famous school of Kathakali in Chiruthuruthi. See Danielou, *The Way to the Labyrinth,* pp. 90–91.
242A main street in Old Delhi, near the Red Fort.
243Alexander Calder (1898–1976), originally a Scottish stonecutter, did monumental sculpture before turning to the mobiles (Marcel Duchamp's term for moving sculptures) and stabiles (Jean Arp's term, which Calder continued to use) for which he is known.
244Mrinalini Sarabhai, dancer and teacher of traditional dance, was a cousin of Gautam and Gira Sarabhai who had traveled widely in the United States. She was a founder of the Darpana Association of Ahmedabad, which gave instruction in dance, theater arts and puppetry. Her daughter Malika, a little girl when the Campbells visited, later appeared in Peter Brook's film *The Mahabharata.*
245The *Nala upākhyana* is a subplot of the *Mahābhārata* that may represent a pre-existing epic. It tells the story of Nala and Damayantī's courtship and travails, and is a common theme in miniature painting and dance.
246See p. 171.
247See p. 128.
248Campbell knew Arthur Gregor from New York and had met him earlier in Bombay. See p. 135.
249Campbell and his father had traveled aboard the *Kungsholm,* possibly in an earlier incarnation, in 1929. See *A Fire in the Mind,* pp. 121–126.
250Bala Saraswati, the most important Indian dancer of modern times, brought the Bharata Natyam to the stage and to modern audiences. Jean Erdman later remembered being profoundly impressed by her mastery of Bharata Natyam, and her excellent ability to communicate to her students. Saraswati later came to New York on a tour sponsored by the Indian government.
251A famous 12th or 13th-century bronze of Śiva dancing, wreathed in celestial flames. See Appendix A, p. 265. Also *Myths and Symbols,* Fig. 38, and *Art of Indian Asia,* vol. 2, Plates 411–414.
252See *Myths and Symbols,* Figure 41 and pp. 168–169 for a discussion of this prototype of Śiva Naṭarāja.
253See note 202 on Śaṅkara.
254See *Philosophies of India,* p. 1.
255Avicenna (A.D. 980–1036) was a peripatetic Islamic scholar, philosopher, and doctor.
256Radha Bournier was the daughter of the Vice President of the Theosophical Society in

Adyar, and was a student of Bharata Natyam. When Campbell met her she was a frequent companion of Danielou, and had married his lifelong friend Raymond Bournier.

[257]Alain Danielou (1909–1993) was a versatile French-born artist, scholar, and author who had lived in India for twenty-five years. About a year before meeting Campbell, Danielou had moved from a long-term residence in a Benares palace to Adyar to assume the directorship of the Adyar Library. Danielou associated with many artistic and literary figures of world stature: Nehru, Tagore, and the Shankars in India, and in the West with Gide, Cocteau, Stravinsky and many others. See also p. 179, and note 83.

[258]The U.S.I.S., the U.S. Information Service, a branch of the State Department dedicated to international relations.

[259]Śiva Ardhanārīśvara, an androgynous Śiva or Śiva-Śakti/Pārvatī in one figure.

[260]*Atma-Nirvriti,* pp. 18, 22, 11, 6–7, respectively.

[261]See pp. 69–71, 158, 171, 176, 181–182, 191, 203, 226.

[262]Campbell in later years made much of this doctrine, taken from the *Māṇḍūkya Upaniṣad.* "A" = waking consciousness (*jāgrat*); "U" = dream state (*svapna*); "M" = deep sleep (*suṣupti*) but also cosmic rapture (*turīya*). Hence "A-U-M" (or "OM") refers to all possible states of consciousness. See also pp. 143, 168–169, 191–192, and esp. below, note 266.

[263]Mr. Henry Belk, a scion of the Belk family that owned a chain of department stores in the South, turned his interest to parapsychology in his later years. The concept of "biorhythms" received some credibility in the Soviet Union, Europe, Japan, and in the U.S.A.

[264]See p. 246.

[265]*Bṛhadāraṇyaka Upaniṣad.* See *Oriental Mythology,* pp. 198–200.

[266]"We are in our true state (*ātman*) every night in sleep, but also during the period of waking consciousness every time we are 'between two thoughts.'" *Joseph Campbell Companion,* p. 15.

"When I was in India I met and conversed briefly with the saintly sage [Sri Krishna Menon]; and the question he gave me to consider was this: *Where are you between two thoughts?* In the *Kena Upaniṣad* we are told: 'There the eye goes not, nor the mind.... Other it is than the known. And moreover above the unknown.' For on coming back from between two thoughts, one would find that all words—which, of course, can be only of thoughts and things, names and forms—only mislead. As again declared in the Upanishad: 'We know not, we understand not, how It should be taught.'" In "Zen" in *Myths to Live By,* p. 129.

"Then he gave me a little meditation, 'Where are you between two thoughts?' That is to say, you are thinking all the time, and you have an image of yourself. Well, where are you between two thoughts? Do you ever have a glimpse beyond your thinking of that which transcends anything you can think about yourself. *That's* the source field out of which all of your energies are coming." *Joseph Campbell Companion,* pp. 187–189.

[267]For a general discussion of Campbell's meeting with Krishna Menon, see *Joseph Campbell Companion,* pp. 187–189; also *Power of Myth,* Pt. II, "The Message of the Myth."

[268]Benedict Spinoza (1632–1677), Dutch philosopher of Portuguese Jewish extraction.

[269]Today there are only a handful of families left. They have no rabbi to read the Torah.

[270]"Commentary on 'The Secret of the Golden Flower'" (1929), in C. G. Jung, *Alchemical Studies.*

[271]See the essay "Zen" in *Myths to Live By.*

[272]SEATO, Southeast Asia Treaty Organization. An organization created in Manila in 1954 by France, Australia, New Zealand, Pakistan, the Philippines, Thailand, the U.K. and the U.S.A. Its explicit goal was to counteract Communist expansion in Southeast Asia.

[273]Campbell's photographic ability the reader may judge from the photographs in this volume, all Campbell's own. Several entire rolls, however, were lost during this trip due to mishaps.

INDEX

– D –

– N –

– T –